University Research
for Innovation

Published by Economica Ltd,
9 Wimpole Street
London W1M 8LB

© *Economica Ltd, 2010*

First published 2010

Printed in France

Luc E. Weber and James J. Duderstadt (eds)
University Research for Innovation
ISBN 978-2-7178-5797-9

University Research for Innovation

Edited by

Luc E. Weber

James J. Duderstadt

⊕ ECONOMICA

Glion Colloquium Series N°6

London • Paris • Genève

Titles in the Series

Governance in Higher Education: The University in a State of Flux
Werner Z. Hirsch and Luc E. Weber, eds, (2001)

As the Walls of Academia are Tumbling Down
Werner Z. Hirsch and Luc E. Weber, eds, (2002)

Reinventing the Research University
Luc E. Weber and James J. Duderstadt, eds, (2004)

Universities and Business: Partnering for the Knowledge Economy
Luc E. Weber and James J. Duderstadt, eds, (2006)

The Globalization of Higher Education
Luc E. Weber and James J. Duderstadt, eds, (2008)

University Research for Innovation
Luc E. Weber and James J. Duderstadt, eds, (2010)

Other publications of the Glion Colloquium

The Glion Declaration I: The University at the Millennium
The Glion Colloquium, (1998)

The Glion Declaration II: Universities and the Innovative Spirit
The Glion Colloquium, (2009)

Challenges Facing Higher Education at the Millennium
Werner Z. Hirsch and Luc E. Weber, eds, American Council on Education/Oryx Press, Phoenix and IAU Press/Pergamon, Paris and Oxford, (1999)

This book is dedicated

*to Michel Bénard and Wayne Johnson,
two Hewlett-Packard leaders dedicated to the
promotion of good and constructive relations
between industry and university, and to the
development of open research,
for their long-standing and unfailing interest in
the Glion Colloquium,
for their active and stimulating participation at
the last four colloquia,
and for their successful efforts to secure the
generous financial support of Hewlett Packard
for the organization of these four colloquia.
Their endeavours provided great encouragement
to the editors of this book.*

CONTENTS

PREFACE

I n June 2009, university and industry leaders from around the world gathered in Glion-above-Montreux, Switzerland, at the VII Glion Colloquium to consider the role of research universities in an innovation-driven, global society. Launched in 1998 by Professors Luc Weber (University of Geneva) and Werner Hirsch (University of California), the Glion Colloquium brings together university leaders to discuss the future of higher education, frequently joined by leaders from business, foundations and government. Topics have included the rapidly changing nature of research universities, university governance, the interaction between universities and society, collaboration between universities and business, and the globalization of higher education. The papers presented and associated discussions at each colloquium are subsequently compiled in a book available through publishers or downloadable in full-text format on the Glion Colloquium website at http://www.glion.org.

The context for the VII Glion Colloquium is an era in which educated people, the knowledge they produce and the innovation and entrepreneurial skills they possess have become the keys to economic prosperity, public health, national security and social well-being. In particular, leadership in innovation — the transformation of knowledge into products, processes and services — has become critical to economic competitiveness, long-term productivity growth, the generation of wealth and global sustainability. Of course, innovation is more than simply new technology. It also includes economic innovation in integrating and managing business processes, products and services, and social innovation in formulating effective public policies and actions that broadly benefit society.

Whether in the "old world" of Europe and North America or in rapidly developing economies in Asia, Latin America and the Middle East, the message is clear: innovation has become the key to prosperity and social well-being in a hypercompetitive, global, knowledge-driven economy. The core competency of a business, a region or a nation in the early 21st century has become its capacity to innovate. While characteristics such as population diversity, democratic values, free-market practices and a rational and predictable legal system provide a fertile environment for innovation, history has shown that significant public and private investment is necessary to produce the key ingredients of innovation: new knowledge (research), world-class human capital (education), infrastructure (institutions, facilities, networks) and supportive policies (tax, investment, intellectual property).

Today's intensely competitive global economy requires not only leadership in innovation, but also educated citizens capable of applying technology, talent and capital in new ways, with deep analytical skills and the ability to manage ambiguity. Institutions of higher learning must collaborate with industry and government to create a climate and culture that enable innovation to thrive. Here, part of the challenge is the changing nature of innovation itself. It is far more open; it spans virtually all disciplines; and it is increasingly global. And it arises not only in the laboratory and the classroom, but also in the marketplace, the workplace and the community. It requires the development of new academic disciplines, increasingly interdisciplinary research and instruction across the traditional disciplines, and continual learning opportunities to keep abreast of the fast-changing, dynamic nature of work.

Not only is this a challenge to our universities to provide the new knowledge and broadly educate the graduates necessary for innovation, but it also demands that higher education develop and demonstrate the capacity for continuous innovation and quality improvement at both the institutional and enterprise level. Clearly, sustaining a nation's leadership in innovation will require institutions of higher learning capable of embracing innovation in pedagogy, scholarship and organization as key, both to their quality and capacity to serve the changing needs of our society. In fact, innovation in all its forms (technological, organizational, social, financial) will also be of great importance to the university itself as an institution and higher education as a system to respond effectively to the needs of a rapidly changing world.

The VII Glion Colloquium brought university leaders and colleagues from business and industry together with experts on innovation to consider ways that universities can best contribute to an innovation-driven, global economy. This book contains the proceedings from the colloquium, along with summaries of the discussions occurring in each session.

The first session laid the foundation for the colloquium by introducing the importance of innovation in several guises — technological, economic, political and social. The current economic crisis demonstrates that the dynamic nature of innovation-driven economies raises serious challenges to sustainability of growth as the explosion of new knowledge and innovation not only creates new wealth, but also disrupts existing social structures — communities, companies and governments (Weber). New forms of economic and social organizations and practices are evolving that tap human talent on a global scale, so-called "open innovation", and merge competition and cooperation in shaping institutional relationships (Vest). As knowledge becomes more complex, it not only evolves beyond traditional economic disciplines such as science, technology, finance and management, but also encompasses humanities, the arts and social sciences as it extends benefits beyond individuals to social communities (Hazelkorn).

This broader perspective was illustrated in the second session concerned with the various agents of innovation. Chameau provided examples of how individuals of great intellectual span and creativity were frequently the source of new economic activity such as spinoff companies and even entirely new economic sectors. Organizations have also evolved to reflect both the breadth and depth of the knowledge base required for innovation, from the large corporate R&D laboratories of the 1950s such as Bell Labs to today's organizations tapping the triple helix of industry, government and research universities (Johnson). Van Vught reviewed the diverse roles and approaches of governments and local authorities, whether at the national or regional level, to promote or drive innovation, suggesting the importance of information feedback to reshape a policy learning and adaptation process.

The third session brought together university leaders from both long-established (Winckler, Eichler, Munroe-Blum) and newly emerging institutions (Andersson, Ulaby, Al Hammadi and de la Fuente) to compare and contrast how regional and institutional characteristics shape innovation strategies. Although international efforts, such as the Lisbon Agenda in Europe, can facilitate collaboration and standardization, it was stressed that innovation strategies are best addressed at the national and institutional level. The Canadian experience illustrated the need for nations characterized by high quality educational systems to build the infrastructure, such as national research foundations, necessary to stimulate and sustain innovation and entrepreneurial activities. Singapore, Saudi Arabia and Abu Dhabi provided examples of how rapidly nations capable of focusing sufficient resources were attempting to build world-class universities, not only as sources of innovation, but also as change agents in their own societies. Yet, de la Fuente noted that nations characterized by rapidly growing populations, high social diversity and income inequality such as those in Latin America would, of necessity, take a more balanced approach to the dual challenges of expanding educational opportunity while achieving the high quality research programs necessary to drive innovation.

The emerging role of innovation in achieving economic prosperity, national security and social well-being in stimulating new approaches at both the national and institution level was the topic of the fourth session. Crow described the effort to transform one of the United States' youngest universities, Arizona State, into "a new American university", based upon a highly entrepreneurial approach to social responsiveness, global engagement and use-inspired research. Huber reviewed Germany's effort to focus substantial resources to elevate a limited number of its universities to world-class research status as key to economic innovation. Duderstadt discussed a similar national approach in the United States to create a number of translational research centres to address the nation's energy challenges — so-called "energy innovation hubs" — capable of linking fundamental scientific discovery with the applied research and development necessary for technological innovation and economic impact. Such institutional and national strategies were of particular importance as high-tech industry increasingly shifted to open innovation strategies, developing partnerships with both universities and other companies on a global scale to address particular technology challenges rather than investing primarily in internal R&D ventures (Bénard). Salmi concluded the session with a broad discussion of the challenges of creating world-class universities, including the provocative subject of just how one knows when it has been achieved, beyond simply using league tables, a subject stimulating a particularly vigorous discussion!

The last session addressed the deeper intellectual character of innovation and its relationship to the academic mission of the university. Nam Suh proposed a thermodynamic model of innovation in which the key to regional competitiveness was the balance between the formation of nucleation sites for innovation and the rate of knowledge diffusion. Lenzen returned to the early ideas of Humboldt in creating the 19th century research university, in which scholarship was not only conducted for knowledge's sake but also to benefit humanity, to suggest a broader, more diverse and flexible academic framework capable of stimulating creativity. Deshpande demonstrated how innovative organizations could be created both in technology-intensive environments such as MIT and in entrepreneurial ecosystems such as India. Brown suggested that the power of emerging information and communication technologies, coupled with the new forms of social networking and learning of the young, was driving an epistemological shift that integrated tacit and explicit knowledge, from "learning to do" to "learning to be" to "learning to become".

Frank Rhodes contributed the "alpha and the omega" for the colloquium: he first provided the introductory presentation to review the past decade spanned by the Glion Colloquia. Then, very much in the spirit of the Glion Declaration drafted in 1998 following the first colloquium, he led the effort to draft a new Glion Declaration addressing the role of the university in meeting the challenge of global sustainability, drawing on discussions at the VII Glion Colloquium. This declaration, endorsed by the colloquium participants, has been included in the final chapter of this book and will be distributed more broadly as a separate document.

The VII Glion Colloquium was arranged under the auspices of the University of Geneva and the Graduate Institute of International Studies and Development in Geneva and made possible by the generous support of the Hewlett Packard Corporation in California, the King Abdullah University of Science and Technology in Saudi Arabia, the Khalifa University of Science, Technology, and Research of Abu Dhabi, and the Swiss Secretariat for Education and Research. To all of these organizations, we express our deep gratitude for their support for the VII Glion Colloquium, both the event and the publication of this book. Without their assistance, it would not have been possible for us to share so many insights of value to the university and the wider world, and then to present these insights to an international audience through the means of this publication.

We are also grateful for the efforts of those who contributed to the production of this book, including Mary O' Mahony, of Geneva, and Natacha Durand and Anne-Sophie Bentz from the Graduate Institute of International Studies and Development, as well as Edmund Doogue, also of Geneva, who rigorously copy-edited the texts.

Luc E. Weber   James J. Duderstadt
University of Geneva   *University of Michigan*

CONTRIBUTORS
AND
PARTICIPANTS

ANDERSSON, Bertil*

Provost of Nanyang Technological University, Professor Bertil Andersson is a plant biochemist of international reputation and the author of over 300 papers in photosynthesis research, biological membranes, protein and membrane purification and light stress in plants. He was educated at Umeå and Lund Universities in Sweden. He started his research career at Umeå after which he became a Professor of Biochemistry and later Dean of the Faculty of Chemical Sciences at the University of Stockholm. In 1999 he became Rector (President) of Linköping University, Sweden, a post he held until the end of 2003. In 2004 he joined the European Science Foundation in Strasbourg as its Chief Executive. He was appointed Provost of Nanyang Technological University in April 2007.

From 1989 to 1997, he was a member of the Nobel Committee for Chemistry (Chair 1997) and, later, a member of the Nobel Foundation (2000-2006). He is a member of the Board of Trustees of the Nobel Foundation and holds academic appointments at Linköping University and Umeå University. He is a visiting Professor and Fellow of Imperial College London.

---

* Names marked with a * were participants at the Colloquium; the others are co-authors of the chapters.

Bertil Andersson is a member of the Royal Swedish Academy of Sciences, the Australian Academy of Sciences and Academia Europaea, and holds honorary doctorates from several universities.

He is a research advisor to the Swedish government and was the Vice President of the European Research Advisory Board of the European Commission.

AL HAMMADI, Arif S.*

Interim President of Khalifa University of Science, Technology and Research (KUSTAR), Arif Al Hammadi received a Bachelor in Engineering from the Etisalat University College and a Ph.D. in Telecommunications from Queen Mary College of the University of London

He served as Assistant Professor, Associate Professor and then Deputy Head of the Computer Engineering Department before being promoted to Deputy Manager and then Manager of Etisalat University College (currently known as Khalifa University — Sharjah Campus).

He was then appointed Interim President of the Khalifa University of Science, Technology and Research (KUSTAR). He is also a board member of the U.A.E. Information and Communication Technology Fund, and is currently leading U.A.E. universities' efforts in the establishment of the Emirates Advanced Network for Research and Education. Founder of the U.A.E. National Mobile Application Contest and the U.A.E. ICT Research Forum, he served as the Chair of the U.A.E. IEEE Computer Society Chapter in 2003-08.

AL-MUALLA, Mohammed*

Mohammed Al-Mualla received a B.Eng. (Hons) degree in Telecommunication Engineering from Khalifa University of Science, Technology and Research (KUSTAR) — Sharjah Campus (formerly Etisalat College of Engineering), U.A.E., in 1995. He received an M.Sc. in Communication Systems and Signal Processing and a Ph.D. in Electrical and Electronics Engineering from the University of Bristol, U.K., in 1997 and 2000 respectively.

Since 2000, Dr Al-Mualla has been with KUSTAR where he is currently Manager of the Abu Dhabi Campus, providing leadership and strategic direction for the development and management of the campus, and ensuring that the campus and its programs are in line with the overall strategic direction of KUSTAR. In addition, Dr Al-Mualla is leading all research and graduate studies activities at KUSTAR.

His current research interests are in the area of multimedia coding, transmission and digital rights management. He has published widely in internationally refereed conferences and journals, and is the first author of the book *Video Coding for Mobile Communication: Efficiency, Complexity, and Resilience*, Academic Press, 2002.

Dr Al-Mualla is very active in professional societies and services. He is a Chartered Engineer (C.Eng.), Member of the IET, and a Senior Member of the IEEE. He is the Vice-Chair of the Executive Committee of the IEEE U.A.E. Section and the Founding Chair of the IEEE U.A.E. Signal Processing & Communication Chapter. He is a member of the steering, organizing and technical program committees of many international conferences, and has served on many editorial and reviewing boards of international journals and conferences.

BENARD, Michel*

Michel Bénard is Director, Strategic Research Collaborations, in the HP Open Innovation Office. He graduated and received his Ph.D. in Digital Image Processing from the Ecole Nationale Supérieure des Telecommunications in Paris in 1983. He then had R&D positions at IBM and at the Swiss Federal Institute of Technology before joining the sales force of Apollo Computer in 1987.

Dr Bénard joined HP from Apollo Computer in 1989. He was HP Major Account Manager for High-Energy-Physics in Europe from 1990 to 1996. He then joined the External Research Program of HP Laboratories in 1997 where he worked on several programs in Computer Systems, High-speed Networking and Digital Photography. Since 2002 he has been working for HP University Relations, which became the HP Open Innovation Office in 2008.

BROWN, John Seely*

John Seely Brown is a visiting scholar and advisor to the Provost at University of Southern California (USC) and the Independent Co-Chairman of the Deloitte Center for the Edge. Prior to that, he was the Chief Scientist of Xerox Corporation and director of its Palo Alto Research Center (PARC) — a position he held for nearly two decades. While head of PARC, Brown expanded the role of corporate research to include such topics as organizational learning, knowledge management, complex adaptive systems, and nano/mems technologies. He was a cofounder of the Institute for Research on Learning (IRL). His personal research interests include the management of radical innovation, digital youth culture, digital media and new forms of communication and learning. Brown, or, as he is often called, JSB, is a member of the American Academy of Arts and Sciences, the National Academy of Education, a Fellow of the American Association for Artificial Intelligence, the AAAS and a Trustee of the MacArthur Foundation.

CARMICHAEL, Carol S.

Dr Carmichael is a faculty associate in the Division of Engineering and Applied Science and senior counselor for external relations at the California

Institute of Technology. She advises administrators, faculty and staff on the development of sustainability programs and educational issues. She also focuses on the role of the university campus in education for sustainability, both within the campus and in the community at large. She chairs the City of Pasadena's Environmental Advisory Commission (EAC), whose mandate is to advise the Mayor and City Council on the implementation of the City's commitment to the United Nation's Green Cities Declaration. Prior to coming to Caltech, Dr Carmichael was director of the Institute for Sustainable Technology and Development at the Georgia Institute of Technology. She has over 20 years of experience in technology and science policy, with a particular emphasis on sustainability policy and the need to help students learn about the societal context of science and engineering. At Georgia Tech, she was also director and senior research scientist for an interdisciplinary research program in environmentally conscious design and manufacturing. She has developed and implemented corporate research and educational programs that engaged over 100 firms nationally. Dr Carmichael has degrees in higher education, technology and science policy and chemistry.

CHAMEAU, Jean-Lou*

As eighth president of the California Institute of Technology, Jean-Lou Chameau leads one of the world's preeminent centers of instruction and research in engineering and science. Caltech is recognized for its outstanding alumni, faculty, including several Nobel laureates, students and such renowned off-campus facilities as the Jet Propulsion Laboratory, the W. M. Keck Observatory and the Palomar Observatory. Before he assumed the presidency on 1 September 2006, Chameau was at Georgia Tech where he held the positions of dean of engineering and then provost. He also held positions at Purdue University and Golder Associates, Inc. While he is a native of France, he received his graduate education in civil engineering at Stanford University. He was elected to the National Academy of Engineering in 2009.

CROW, Michael*

Michael Crow became the 16th president of Arizona State University on 1 July 2002. He is guiding the transformation of ASU into one of the nation's leading, public metropolitan research universities, an institution that combines the highest levels of academic excellence, inclusiveness to a broad demographic and maximum societal impact — a model he terms the "New American University". During his tenure, ASU has established major interdisciplinary research initiatives such as the Biodesign Institute, the Global Institute of Sustainability (GIOS) and more than a dozen new interdisciplinary schools, and witnessed an unprecedented research infrastructure expansion and doubling of research expenditures.

He was previously executive vice provost of Columbia University, where he oversaw Columbia's research enterprise and technology transfer operations. A fellow of the National Academy of Public Administration and member of the Council on Foreign Relations, he is the author of books and articles relating to the analysis of science and technology policy and the design of knowledge enterprises. Crow received his Ph.D. in Public Administration (Science and Technology Policy) from the Maxwell School of Citizenship and Public Affairs, Syracuse University, in 1985.

DESHPANDE, Gururaj*

Gururaj "Desh" Deshpande is an entrepreneur and has built several successful companies. Currently he is the founding investor and Chairman of Sycamore Networks, Tejas Networks, Airvana, A123 Systems, Sandstone Capital and HiveFire.
Prior to co-founding Sycamore Networks, Dr Deshpande was founder and chairman of Cascade Communications Corp.
Dr Deshpande serves as a member of the MIT Corporation, and his generous donations have made possible MIT's Deshpande Center for Technological Innovation. He holds a B.Tech. in Electrical Engineering from the Indian Institute of Technology — Madras, an M.E. in Electrical Engineering from the University of New Brunswick in Canada, and Ph.D. in Data Communications from Queens University in Canada.

DILL, David D.

David D. Dill is Professor Emeritus of Public Policy at the University of North Carolina at Chapel Hill. From 1984-94 he served as Assistant to the Chancellor for Planning at UNC-CH. He has been a Visiting Research Fellow at the University of Manchester Business School, a Visiting Fellow at Wolfson College, Cambridge University, and a Visiting Professor at the Center for Higher Education Policy Studies (CHEPS) at the University of Twente in the Netherlands, as well as the European University Institute in Florence, Italy. He received his Ph. D. in higher education from the University of Michigan. He has conducted research in academic and industrial settings, has consulted with academic and government organizations and agencies in the U.S., Europe and Asia, and has written numerous articles, chapters and books. His research interests include public policy analysis, the regulation of academic quality, and research policy. He is Director of the Research Program on Public Policy for Academic Quality (www.unc.edu/ppaq), a cross-national study of quality assurance policies in higher education supported by the Ford Foundation.

DUDERSTADT, James Jim*

Dr James J. Duderstadt is President *Emeritus* and University Professor of Science and Engineering at the University of Michigan. A graduate of Yale and Caltech, Dr Duderstadt's teaching, research and publishing activities include nuclear science and engineering, applied physics, computer simulation, science policy and higher education. He has served on or chaired numerous boards and study commissions, including the National Science Board, the Intelligence Science Board, the Executive Boards of the National Academy of Engineering and American Association for the Advancement of Science, the National Commission on the Future of Higher Education, the DOE Nuclear Energy Research Committee and the NSF Advisory Committee on Cyberinstrastructure. He has received numerous awards, including the E. O. Lawrence Award for excellence in nuclear research, the Arthur Holly Compton Prize for outstanding teaching, the Reginald Wilson Award for national leadership in achieving diversity and the National Medal of Technology for exemplary service to the nation. At the University of Michigan he currently chairs the program in Science, Technology and Public Policy in the Gerald R. Ford School of Public Policy, and directs the Millennium Project, a research center exploring the impact of over-the-horizon technologies on society.

EICHLER, Ralph*

Ralph Eichler was born in 1947 and grew up in Guildford, Münster, Marburg and Basel.
He studied Physics at ETH Zurich and completed his Ph.D. thesis at what was then the Swiss Institute for Nuclear Research (SIN). Following research positions in the U.S. and Germany, he was elected as an associate professor at ETH Zurich in 1989. Since 1993 he has been a full professor for Experimental Physics at the Institute for Particle Physics. At the same time, between 1995 and 1997 Ralph Eichler was also chairman of an international group of 400 people collaborating on the German Electron Synchrotron (DESY). In 1998, he became Deputy Director at the Paul Scherrer Institute (PSI) in Villigen and, in 2002, its Director. Ralph Eichler has been President of ETH Zurich since 1 September 2007.

FELDMAN, Stuart*

As Vice President Engineering, Google, Stuart Feldman is responsible for engineering activities at Google's offices in the eastern part of the Americas, with projects affecting most of the company's focus areas.
Before joining Google, he worked at IBM for eleven years. Most recently, he was Vice President for Computer Science in IBM Research, where he drove the long-term and exploratory worldwide science strategy in computer science

and related fields, led programs for open collaborative research with universities and influenced national and global computer science policy.

Prior to that, he served as Vice President for Internet Technology and was responsible for IBM strategies, standards and policies relating to the future of the Internet, and managed a department that created experimental Internet-based applications. Earlier, he was the founding Director of IBM's Institute for Advanced Commerce, which was dedicated to creating intellectual leadership in e-commerce.

Before joining IBM in mid-1995, Dr Feldman was a computer science researcher at Bell Labs and a research manager at Bellcore. In addition, he was the creator of Make, as well as the architect for a large new line of software products at Bellcore. He did his academic work in astrophysics and mathematics and earned his AB at Princeton and his Ph.D. at MIT. He is Past President of ACM (Association for Computing Machinery) and received the 2003 ACM Software System Award.

He is also a Fellow of the IEEE, a Fellow of the ACM, a Fellow of the AAAS, and a member of the Board of Directors of the AACSB (Association to Advance Collegiate Schools of Business, international). He serves on a number of government advisory committees.

De la FUENTE, Juan Ramon*

Prof. de la Fuente earned his M.D. at Universidad Nacional Autónoma de México (UNAM) and trained in psychiatry at the Mayo Clinic in Rochester, Minn. He joined the Faculty of UNAM where he was appointed Dean of the Medical School (1991-94) and Rector (1999-07). He served as Minister of Health of México (1994-99) and as President of the Mexican Academy of Sciences and the National Academy of Medicine.

He has published extensively on health and educational issues, and has been awarded honorary degrees at the Universities of Montreal, Colombia, San Marcos (Peru), Córdoba (Argentina), Alcalá (Spain), Moscow, Santo Domingo, La Havana and San Carlos (Guatemala). He is currently Simon Bolívar Professor and Chair of the Institute for Latin American Studies at the University of Alcalá, Board Member of the United Nations University and President of the International Association of Universities.

HAZELKORN, Ellen*

Professor Ellen Hazelkorn is Director [Vice President] of Research and Enterprise, and Dean of the Graduate Research School, Dublin Institute of Technology, Ireland; she also leads the Higher Education Policy Research Unit. She is a Consultant to the OECD Programme on Institutional Management of Higher Education (IMHE), and is also associated with the International Association of Universities (IAU). She was awarded a B.A. and Ph.D. from the University of Wisconsin, Madison, and the University of Kent, Canterbury, respectively.

Professor Hazelkorn is Rapporteur for the E.U. Expert Group on Assessment of University-based Research, and a member of National Digital Research Centre (NDRC) Management Board, the Arts, Humanities and Social Sciences Foresight Working Group [Ireland], and the International Advisory Council of the Irish Research Council for the Humanities and Social Sciences. She is also a member of the International Rankings Expert Group (IREG), the Executive Committee of the Dean and European Academic Network (DEAN), and of the Editorial Boards of *Higher Education Management and Policy* (OECD) and *Higher Education Policy* (IAU). She has worked with universities and university associations around the world.

Ellen has authored/co-authored over 50 articles, policy briefs, books and book chapters on Irish politics and society; digital technologies, gender, work practices and the cultural industries; relations between the media and the state; and higher education policy. *Developing Research in New Institutions* was published by OECD (September, 2005), and *Rankings and the Reshaping of Higher Education: The Battle for World-Class Excellence* will be published by Palgrave in 2010.

HUBER, Berndt*

Professor Dr Bernd Huber, born in 1960 in Wuppertal/Germany, is Professor for Public Finance, and, since 2002, President of Ludwig-Maximilians-Universität (LMU) München. He holds a degree in economics from the University Gießen (1984), and received his Ph.D. (Dr. rer. pol.) in 1988 at the University of Würzburg, with a thesis on "Government Debt and Allocative Efficiency". He completed his post-doctoral thesis (Habilitation) on "Optimal Fiscal Policy and Time Inconsistency" in 1994. In the same year, he accepted the Chair in Public Finance at LMU München, and was acting dean of the faculty before he was elected president. His research focuses on Public Finance, Government Debt, European Fiscal and Monetary Integration, International Taxation and Labour Markets. Among his numerous functions, he is also a member of the Scientific Council to the German Ministry of Finance and of the Scientific Technical Council to the Bavarian State Government. Since 2008, Professor Huber has been chairman of LERU, the League of European Research Universities.

JOHNSON, Wayne*

Wayne C. Johnson is currently an educational consultant working with the National Science Foundation (NSF) as the management integrator for their Corporate Alliance. In addition, he is representing the Kauffman Foundation as their lead Board member for the iBridge Network strategic partnership in Washington D. C.

Previously, he was Vice President of University Relations Worldwide for Hewlett Packard (HP). Widely recognized as a thought leader and global influencer, Johnson was a delegate to the Clinton Global Initiative in September 2007. He has also been quoted in the press as a subject matter expert on the topic of engineering education and global capacity building. Johnson was one of five members of an expert panel which provided Congressional Testimony to the United States House of Representatives (Subcommittee on Technology and Innovation, Committee on Science and Technology on July 17, 2007) regarding "Bayh-Dole — the Next 25 Years", significant legislation which seeks to address issues of Intellectual Property (IP). Johnson joined HP in 2001 from Microsoft's University Relations. From 1967-2000, he held a variety of positions at the Raytheon Company in Waltham. He serves on the Board of Trustees of Wentworth Institute, the Thurgood Marshall College Fund, and is the Chair of Franklin W. Olin College of Engineering's President's Council. He is also a member of the National Academy of Engineering (NAE) Government University Industry Research Roundtable (GUIRR) and a Board member of Alliance for Science & Technology Research in America (ASTRA).

Johnson's work was also acknowledged in 2005 through a Harvard Business School Case Study — HP Nanotech: Partnership with California NanoSystems Institute (CNSI), which illustrates the challenges of managing industrial-university collaborations and examines issues of US national competitiveness. Johnson received his B.A. from Colgate University, Hamilton, NY, and his M.B.A. from Boston College Carroll School of Management, Boston, MA. He was an Adjunct Professor of Management at Boston University from 1977 to 1999.

JONES, Russel

Russel Jones is senior Advisor at the Khalifa University of Science, Technology and Research. A new institution in Abu Dhabi, U.A.E. KUSTAR offers undergraduate and graduate programs in engineering and science. Until recently he served as Founding President of the Masdar Institute of Science and Technology in Abu Dhabi, U.A.E. — a new university dedicated to graduate education and research, focused on alternative energy. He also serves as President of World Expertise LLC, a consulting company offering services to a select clientele. His primary interests are international higher education and human capacity building through engineering education.

Dr Jones received his education at Carnegie Institute of Technology, earning degrees in civil engineering and materials science. He has spent most of his career as an educator, starting with engineering education and broadening to higher education as a whole. After completing his doctoral degree in 1963, he taught for eight years on the faculty of the Massachusetts Institute of Technology. He then served in a succession of administrative posts in higher education, for several years each: Chairman of Civil Engineering at Ohio State University, Dean of Engineering at the University of Massachusetts, Academic Vice President at Boston University, and President and University Research Professor at the University of Delaware. Prior to forming World Expertise L.L.C. as president, he served as Executive Director of the National Society of Professional Engineers.

LENZEN, Dieter*

Professor Dr Dieter Lenzen has been President of Freie Universität Berlin since 2003 and Vice President of the German Rectors' Conference since 2007. He was appointed Professor for Educational Studies at Westfälische Wilhelms-Universität Münster in 1975 and has been Full Professor for Philosophy of Education at Freie Universität Berlin since 1977. He served as Visiting Professor at Columbia University New York City, Stanford University, and at the universities of Tokyo, Nagoya and Hiroshima. Professor Lenzen's numerous memberships and official functions include: President of "Deutsche Gesellschaft für Erziehungswissenschaft" (DGfE, 1994-98), Chair of "Aktionsrat Bildung" of Vereinigung der Bayerischen Wirtschaft, Member of the Board of Fulbright Commission, Deputy of the Board of Trustees of Roland Berger Foundation.
Professor Lenzen has published more than 800 texts on topics of education and communication.

MAYER, Tony (Anthony Edwin Settle)

Tony Mayer is the Europe Representative of the Nanyang Technological University (NTU), Singapore, based in the U.K., having previously been the NTU Senior Science Officer and Associate Registrar since 2007.
Born in Wales of Austrian and British parentage, he is a geologist educated at the University of Manchester. He was involved in research into alkaline volcanic rocks of East Africa at the University of Leicester and, later, at University College London, he worked on gabbroic igneous intrusions in the West of Scotland and in Sierra Leone.
He then joined the U.K. Natural Environment Research Council (NERC), working in the Earth Sciences and the Atmospheric, Aquatic and Oceanographic science sections. He was the first non-American seconded to the JOIDES Planning Office of the Ocean Drilling Program at the Graduate School of Oceanography, University of Rhode Island.
On his return to the U.K. and NERC, he headed the Council's International Section, including polar programmes. He was also responsible for the Inter-Council Global Environment Research Office. In 1996 he joined the Euro-

pean Science Foundation (ESF) in Strasbourg France, responsible for strategic policy development. In 2003, he became the first Director of COST and established the COST Office in Brussels. In 2005, he returned to Strasbourg as the ESF senior science policy adviser. He was also Scientific Secretary of EURAB.

He is a Fellow of the Geological Society (London) and a founder member of Euroscience, and has served as a Board member and Treasurer.

MUNROE-BLUM, Heather*

Heather Munroe-Blum, Principal and Vice-Chancellor of McGill University and Professor in Medicine, is a distinguished psychiatric epidemiologist. She has dedicated her career to the advancement of higher education, science and innovation, in Canada and internationally, advising governments and other organizations on the role that universities and research play in advancing international competitiveness and enriching societies.

She is President of the Conférence des recteurs et des principaux des universités du Québec (CREPUQ) and she serves on the Boards of the Association of Universities and Colleges of Canada (AUCC) and the Association of American Universities (AAU), as well as on the executive committee of the AAU, and is a member of the Board of Governors of the Council of Canadian Academies. She is a member of the Canada Foundation for Innovation, of the Trilateral Commission and of the Canadian Science, Technology and Innovation Council (STIC), and was a lead contributor in the development of its State of the Nation Report.

Prof. Munroe-Blum holds a Ph.D. with distinction in epidemiology from the University of North Carolina at Chapel Hill, in addition to M.S.W. (Wilfrid Laurier University) and B.A. and B.S.W. degrees (McMaster University). Named an Officer of the Order of Canada for her outstanding record of achievements in science, innovation and higher education policy, she holds numerous honorary degrees from Canadian and international universities. Prof. Munroe-Blum is a Specially Elected Fellow of the Royal Society of Canada and a Senior Fellow of Massey College. She was named a Grande Montréalaise, Montréal's highest honour, in 2008, and received the National Order of Quebec in 2009.

NADISON, Jeffrey

Jeffrey Nadison is a Managing Partner of Sylphium LLC, a life sciences consulting firm specializing in biotechnology, nutrition, food and agriculture. A 1980 graduate of the University of Massachusetts, Amherst, in Food Science and Nutrition, with an MBA from UCLA in International and Comparative Management and Marketing, he has built a diverse international career commercializing R&D and innovation for Fortune 100 MNCs, as well as university spin-outs globally.

Prior to establishing his own life science consultancy, Nadison was Vice President, Marketing and Planning, for a division of Deere & Company. Previously, he served as member of the Executive Committee of Aventis SA's Bio-Science Group. He earlier held various senior management positions with E.I. Du Pont de Nemours and Company, Dalgety Plc, Unilever N.V. and Procter & Gamble Co. (The Clorox Company).

He has served on the supervisory boards of technology start-up life-science companies in Germany, France and the United Kingdom and on the Investment Committees of life-science and "cleantech" venture capital groups in the U.S. and Switzerland. Nadison has also served on the supervisory boards of British-Dutch and British-French joint venture companies involved in the development and commercialization of plant biotechnologies.

Nadison has extensive mergers and acquisitions and new business development experience, having consummated over 30 acquisitions, divestments, joint ventures, licensing agreements, alliances and research collaborations with a total transactional value exceeding US$750 Million. He has overseen the successful launching of 14 profitable, proprietary products.

O' MAHONY, Mary*

Mary O' Mahony was born in Ireland and holds qualifications from the National University of Ireland and the Université Libre de Bruxelles. In the late 1980s/early 1990s, she worked for five years in Brussels, administering European Union student mobility programmes at the ERASMUS Bureau and TEMPUS Office. She then spent seven years at the Association of European Universities (CRE) in Geneva, an organization committed to improving university cooperation that facilitated meetings between rectors of European universities. She left the post of Deputy Secretary General in 2000.

Mary O' Mahony joined the Rolex watch company in 2002 and worked until 2008 as team leader for the Rolex Mentor and Protégé Arts Initiative, an international philanthropic programme that promotes artistic excellence across generations and cultures through one-to-one mentoring relationships. Since 2008, she has headed the Rolex Awards for Enterprise Young Laureates Programme, which aims to foster innovation in the next generation by enabling visionary young men and women to tackle the most pressing issues facing our world. The programme rewards creativity in five areas: science and health, applied technology, exploration, the environment and cultural preservation.

RHODES, Frank*

Frank Rhodes is president emeritus of Cornell University, having previously served as vice president for academic affairs at the University of Michigan. A geologist by training, Rhodes has published widely in the fields of geology, paleontology, evolution, the history of science and education.

He is the former chairman of the American Council on Education, the National Science Board, the Association of American Universities, the Carnegie Foundation and Atlantic Philanthropies. He also served as a member of the board of General Electric and is currently a member of the board of trustees of King Abdullah University of Science and Technology.

He is the recipient of the Bigsby Medal of the Geological Society and the Ian Campbell Medal of the American Geological Institute.

SALMI, Jamil*

Jamil Salmi, a Moroccan education economist, is the World Bank's tertiary education coordinator. He is the principal author of the Bank's Tertiary Education Strategy entitled "Constructing Knowledge Societies: New Challenges for Tertiary Education". In the past 16 years, Jamil Salmi has provided policy and technical advice on tertiary education reform to the governments of more than 40 countries in Europe, Asia, Africa and South America. He is a member of the Governing Board of the International Institute for Educational Planning, the International Rankings Expert Group, OECD's expert group on Assessing Higher Education Learning Outcomes, the International Advisory Network of the U.K. Leadership Foundation for Higher Education, and the Editorial Committee of OECD's *Journal of Higher Education Management and Policy*. His latest book, published in February 2009, addresses the "Challenge of Establishing World-Class Universities".

SUH, Nam Pyo*

Nam Pyo Suh is the President of the Korea Advanced Institute of Science and Technology (KAIST). Previously, he had been at MIT since 1970, where he was the Ralph E. & Eloise F. Cross Professor, Director of the Park Center for Complex Systems and the Head of the Department of Mechanical Engineering from 1991 to 2001. From 1984 to 1988, Professor Suh accepted a Presidential Appointment to serve as the AD for Engineering at the National Science Foundation. Dr Suh has received many awards and honours, including seven honorary doctoral degrees from universities in four continents, as well as the 2009 ASME Medal, NSF Distinguished Service Award, Ho-Am Prize, the Mensforth Medal of IEE and the Hills Millennium Award of IED of the United Kingdom, the General Pierre Nicolau Award of CIRP, the Pony Chung Award of the Chung Foundation and the Inchon Award of the Inchon Memorial Foundation. He is the author of over 300 papers and seven books, holds more than 60 patents and has edited several books.

THOMAS, Douglas

Douglas Thomas is Associate Professor at the Annenberg School for Communication and Director of the Network Culture Project at the University of Southern California. He is the founding editor of *Games & Culture: A Journal of Interactive Media*, a quarterly international journal that aims to publish innovative theoretical and empirical research about games and culture within the context of interactive media. His current research, supported by the MacArthur Foundation, the Lounsbery Foundation and the Annenberg Center at USC, focuses on the uses of virtual worlds for education and global civic engagement.

ULABY, Fawwaz*

After serving as Vice President for Research at the University of Michigan, Prof. Ulaby was appointed Founding Provost of King Abdullah University of Science and Technology (KAUST), which he has since concluded as of April 2009. Prof. Ulaby is a member of the National Academy of Engineering and Fellow of IEEE and AAAS; he has authored 13 books, published some 600 scientific papers and supervised 115 graduate students. He is the founding Director of the NASA Center for Space Terahertz Technology at Michigan, and was chair of the team responsible for the radar guidance system of the Phoenix spacecraft that landed on Mars in 2008. He is the recipient of the IEEE Millennium Medal (2000), the 2002 William Pecora Award — a joint recognition by NASA and the Department of the Interior, and the 2006 Thomas Edison Medal, "the oldest and most coveted medal in electrical engineering in the United States".

VAN VUGHT, Frans*

Frans van Vught is a member of the Group of Policy Advisors of the President of the European Commission. In addition, he is president of the European Center for Strategic Management of Universities (Esmu) and president of the Netherlands House for Education and Research (Nether), both in Brussels. He was president and Rector of the University of Twente, the Netherlands (1997-2005), and has been a higher education researcher for most of his life. Internationally he is a member of the University Grants Committee of Hong Kong and of the supervisory board of the L.H. Martin Institute for Higher Education Management in Melbourne, Australia. Until recently he was a member of the board of the European University Association (EUA) (2005-2009) and of the German 'Akkreditierungsrat' (2005-2009). Van Vught currently leads the European project on the development of a multidimensional higher education classification and also coordinates the design of a global multidimensional higher education ranking system, supported by the European Commission. He is honorary professor at the University of Twente and holds several honorary doctorates.

VEST, Charles M.*

Charles M. Vest is president of the U.S. National Academy of Engineering and president emeritus of the Massachusetts Institute of Technology. A professor of mechanical engineering at MIT and formerly at the University of Michigan, he served on the U.S. President's Council of Advisors on Science and Technology from 1994-2008, and chaired the President's Committee on the Redesign of the Space Station and the Secretary of Energy's Task force on the Future of Science at DOE. He was a member of the Commission on the Intelligence Capabilities of the United States Regarding Weapons of Mass Destruction and the Secretary of Education's Commission on the Future of Higher Education. He was vice chair of the U.S. Council on Competitiveness for seven years. He holds 12 honorary doctorates and received the 2006 National Medal of Technology.

WEBER, Luc E.*

Luc Weber studied both economics and political science, gaining a Ph.D. in economics and business at the University of Lausanne. He was a full professor of public economics at the University of Geneva from 1975 to 2008. From 1977 to 1980, he was a member of the Swiss Council of Economic Advisers. From 1982 onwards, Luc Weber spent more than 10 years in university administration and higher education and research policy. He was Vice-Rector (Vice-President), than Rector (President) of the University of Geneva, as well as President of the Swiss Universities Rectors' Conference. Since the end of this double mandate, Luc Weber has served multiple governmental organizations and international associations active in the field of higher education and research. He was notably a founding member of the European University Association (EUA). He also served for eight years on the Bureau of the Steering Committee for Higher Education and Research (CDESR) of the Council of Europe, the last two years as chair. He was Vice-President and Treasurer of the International Association of Universities (IAU). Professor Weber was a member of the Strategy Committee of the German Science Council in charge of selecting elite universities in the framework of the German excellence initiative. He also carries out missions for the World Bank. In 1998, he co-founded — and has since been a leader of — the Glion colloquia. For his dedication to higher education and research, he was awarded a Doctorate *honoris causa* by the Catholic University of Louvain-la-Neuve in 2006.

WINCKLER, Georg*

Georg Winckler studied economics at Princeton University and at the University of Vienna, Ph.D. 1968. Since 1978 he has been (Full) Professor of Economics and since 1999 Rector of the University of Vienna (reelected 2003 and 2007). From 2000 to 2005 he was President of the Austrian Rectors' Conference. From 2004 to 2007, he was a member of EURAB (European Union Research Advisory Board). Prof. Winckler was Vice President of the EUA (European University Association) from 2001-2005 and President of the EUA from 2005-2009. Since April 2008, he has been a member of ERAB (European Research Area Board) and, since February 2009, Member of the PEOPLE Advisory Group, European Commission, Brussels.

The First Decade of
the New Millennium:
Glion Colloquia
in Perspective

INTRODUCTION

Respice, Prospice
Higher Education:
A Decennial Review

Frank H.T. Rhodes [1]

RESPICE

Glion I

If "[a] week", as the late British Prime Minister Harold Wilson once point-edly remarked, "is a long time in politics", so also, a decade is a long time in higher education. It represents the graduation of two or three genera-tions of students. It reflects the subtle influence of changing scholarly and research priorities and, for all the treasured independence of the academic world, it demonstrates the impact of government policies, social changes, eco-nomic conditions and market forces upon universities.

It is now a decade since *The Glion Declaration* (1998) was published. This Declaration, subscribed by a group of senior scholars, foundation executives and educational leaders from Asia, Europe and the United States, stressed the critical role of knowledge in the dawning new millennium, and emphasized the unique role that the world's leading research universities play, not only in the conservation and transmission of existing knowledge, but also in the dis-covery of new knowledge and in its testing, verification and benevolent appli-cation to human needs.

---

1 I am most grateful to Ms. Rachel Parks, who has provided great help in obtaining the data on which the tables are based and in preparing the manuscript.

The Declaration emphasized the implicit social compact between the universities and their various publics, by which, in exchange for the benefits to society provided by universities — the creation of new knowledge, the development and nurture of informed citizens and leaders in every field, the provision of expert professional skills and the training and certification of professional practitioners — society grants them varying degrees of financial support and recognizes their continuing need for a high degree of institutional autonomy and scholarly freedom. In light of that compact, the Declaration called for universities to recognize their unique responsibilities toward the well-being of their societies by reaffirming their commitment to, and exemplifying in their practice, teaching as a moral obligation and scholarship as a public trust. It urged the creation of new alliances within the university and new partnerships outside it, better to address pressing social needs. It called for harnessing the power of information technology (IT); the creation of imaginative, new career tracks and new approaches so as to extend the universities' contribution to public service; and the development of new patterns of institutional governance, leadership and management within the universities. It also stressed the continuing obligation for accountability. In all this, the Declaration argued that both scholarship and society would be best served by recognition of the university as the custodian of the ancient values on which the growth of knowledge depends and by the university community's reaffirmation of the integrity, excellence, civility, openness and responsibility that have provided the sturdy foundation for their various contributions to society over the last 900 years.

The Glion Declaration formed an appendix to a 1999 volume of papers from the first Glion Colloquium, *Challenges Facing Higher Education at the Millennium* (Hirsch & Weber, 1999). In this volume, the article most frequently quoted by the 17 contributing authors was by Peter Drucker, who concluded that "30 years from now the big university campuses will be relics. Universities won't survive" (Drucker, 1997). No symposium speaker thought that likely, but virtually all expected that existing trends and looming challenges would require universities to undergo major adaptation and that significant changes would inevitably come with this adaptation. The writers predicted these challenges arising from such external trends as:

- Growing globalization and partnerships (Hirsch & Weber, 1999, p. 5).
- Growing need for and use of information technology (*ibid*, p. 5).
- Competition from "new vendors" (*ibid*, p. 60).
- Growing need for life-long learning (*ibid*, p. 136).
- Growing financial pressures and constraints (*ibid*, p. 31), including decreasing state support and increasing internal costs (*ibid*, p. 16).
- Social, economic, political, ideological, religious and cultural pressures (*ibid*, p. 19).

- Changing public views of, and changing government attitudes toward, higher education (*ibid*, p. 22).
- Global challenges, including balkanization of countries and societies, increasing disparities in wealth, continuing growth in world population and migration, environmental degradation and shrinking per capita food production (*ibid*, p. 20).

What changes within the academy did these same Glion authors envision in the new millennium? Again, there was no unanimity, but there was broad expectation of changes involving:

- Increasing costs (*ibid*, p. 12).
- Improved patterns of governance (*ibid*, pp. 13-15).
- Restructuring, including possibly unbundling of functions, growing commercialization, mergers and new providers (*ibid*, pp. 43-47, 59).
- Growing patterns of collaboration (*ibid*, p. 58).
- A reluctant attempt to address "structural inefficiencies" (*ibid*, p. 23).
- Some expected these changes to be revolutionary and transformative, involving a "paradigm shift" (*ibid*, pp. 56, 63), while others saw them as likely to be more gradual and incremental (*ibid*, p. 50, 158, 168).

Glion 2009: A Decade of Change

Our world has undergone profound changes in the 10 years since the Glion Declaration, and most of those changes have made it less secure. In addition to the inevitable toll of natural disasters, the economic collapse has brought great hardship to many in every country, the Aids epidemic has ravaged the populations of many parts of Africa and elsewhere, terrorism has become a global issue, and the war on terror continues to exact a terrible toll in death and suffering. Food shortages have increased in some areas, with famine in the Horn of Africa and growing numbers of undernourished children in several regions. Meanwhile, the sharp spike in energy prices has contributed to increasing concerns over the impact of climate change and growing interest in alternative energy sources.

In 2009, the mood is bleak. Moody's sees the universities, especially private colleges, facing "stiff challenges" from increasing pressure on tuition and financial aid arising from a decline in household income, investment and home equity; loss in endowments; pressure on liquidity; and volatility in variable rate debt markets. (Carlson, 2009)

This view represents the first negative outlook by Moody's for all sectors of higher education since the credit-rating agency started publishing outlooks for higher education in the mid-1990s. In the present situation, the author of the Moody's report concluded, "management and governance [are] extremely critical for how colleges weather this cycle."

How, then, have the universities performed over the last decade? How have they responded to the societal and economic changes that have marked the new millennium?

It is not possible to give global answers, though I hope our discussion will produce details of individual countries and regions. Let me, instead, seek to provide responses from the two regions that I know best and for which reasonably comprehensive data are available: the United States and the OECD.

For these regions, virtually all the changes predicted at the first Glion Colloquium have come to pass, although changes within universities have been limited. I propose to describe changes in six broad areas: finance, institutions, students, faculty, partnerships and governance.

Financial changes

Rising costs in higher education in the U.S. over the last decade are now attracting increased attention, having far exceeded those in housing, transportation and even health care. The cost of tuition, room and board at a four-year public college, even after taking into account financial aid, was equivalent to 55% of the household income of the poorest 10% of American families in 2007, compared with "only" 39% in 2000 (Blumenstyk, 2008). But, in spite of these harsh realities, 18 million students still attend colleges where tuition and fees average less than $2,400 a year, and most colleges are increasing their contribution to financial aid. Private colleges increased financial aid from their own resources by 173% in inflation-adjusted dollars from 1996-2006.

But at public universities, the loss of state funding has increased the overall share of the cost borne by students and their families, from 35% in 1996 to 47% in 2006. "Will Higher Education Be the Next Bubble to Burst?" ask Cronin and Horton (2009). Consumers "are now asking whether it is worth spending $1,000 a week to send their kids to college. There is a growing sense among the public that higher education might be overpriced and under-delivering."

Several recent studies suggest that these rising college costs have done little to improve graduation rates or reduce educational inequities. One such comprehensive study, the *Delta Project on Postsecondary Education Costs, Productivity and Accountability*, published in 2009, concludes that over a five-year period, the major increases in "private" financial support have failed to reduce the growth of tuition, except at private research universities, and that, although tuition is now covering a greater share of the costs of attending college, the proportion spent on classroom instruction is declining. Jane Wellman, executive director of the Delta Project, has commented that in many cases "people are paying more and arguably getting less" (Blumenstyk, 2009).

Over the period 2002-2006, each type of institution covered by the study (public and private research universities, public and private master's degree universities, private bachelor's degree colleges and public community colleges) increased tuition by an average of at least 12%, while at public master's degree and public research universities the average was about 30%. All categories except private research universities engaged in "cost shifting" from teaching to research, administrative and service functions. At public research universities, 92% of the tuition increases were attributable to cost shifting. One single example will illustrate the issue. The University of Kansas is a flagship state university that greatly increased its expenditure over the past decade (Schweber, 2009), tripling its spending and raising tuition and fees by a factor of five since 1988 in order "to compete with the best private universities". Similar increases are reflected in the overall increase in tuition and fees of 439% over the last 25 years, in contrast to median household income, which increased by 147%.

Such studies provide no conclusion as to whether such cost shifting is improper or inappropriate. What they do provide is information which allows university leaders to raise these questions. And they should. It is time now to reconsider expenditure patterns.

In contrast to U.S. universities, universities in some other countries, especially those of Western Europe, still offer low, or often what amounts to free, tuition, with costs covered by government financing. Attempts to impose even modest tuition charges of some 500 Euros led to organized student protests. In these countries, universities do not generally provide the expansive range of collegiate facilities and services (residential, athletic, counselling, health services and other amenities) that American students enjoy, class sizes are generally larger, and teaching loads are substantially higher. Full professors in German universities, for example, are expected to teach for nine hours a week: the equivalent of two courses per semester. (Labi, 2009)

As one compares these strikingly different models of campus life, it is noteworthy that pressure on U.S. universities to reduce "frills" and devote more attention to "basics" is coming at the same time that many European universities are increasing private funding in order to increase just such "frills" and services. But what continues to stand in stark contrast is the difference in teaching expectations between the two systems. As international partnerships, comparisons and rankings of universities develop added significance, the debate of the role, expectations, responsibilities and "productivity" of the faculty is likely to become a matter of moment.

Responses to the economic downturn in European countries, where universities are heavily dependent on government funding, reflect the outcome of varying governmental policies (Europe's Response to Economic Crisis, 2009). In Austria, for example, the recession is seen as an argument for the government to discard earlier promises of increased investment in higher education. In France, in contrast, there has been increased investment in universities, while in both Germany and Britain increased public investment in universities has been provided as part of a broad overall economic stimulus program.

The effect of the economic downturn on every university, from the wealthiest to the poorest, has been to turn our attention to rising costs, only to find that the attention of our various publics was already there. As the economic storm clouds gradually recede, we must not allow our attention to wander.

Institutional Changes

Changes in numbers of universities and colleges by category

In the United States, the total number of educational institutions grew from 4,096 to 4,276 over the course of the decade, with much of the increase coming from for-profit institutions; the total numbers of traditional non-profit institutions have changed relatively little over the decade. (Table 1)

Table 1

Educational Institutions	1999	2009
Public 4 year institution	615	640
Public 2 year institution	1092	1053
Private 4 year institution non-profit	1536	1534
Private 4 year institution profit	169	408
Private 2 year institution non-profit	184	113
Private 2 year institution profit	500	528
Total	4096	4276

Source: 1999-2000 Almanac. *The Chronicle of Higher Education.*
http://chronicle.com/free/almanac/1999/almanac.htm
2007-2008 Almanac. *The Chronicle of Higher Education.*
http://chronicle.com/free/almanac/2007/almanac.htm

For-Profit Universities and Colleges

The rapid rise of the for-profit university is one of the most striking features of the last decade (Ruch, 2001). These businesses — for so they are — regard students as consumers, faculty as "delivery people", and administrators as "bosses", and they have developed a highly successful market strategy. Such enterprises are not new, but their explosive growth in the last decade has greatly expanded their influence. The major higher educational commercial companies — the Apollo Group (University of Phoenix), Archer Education Group, DeVry Institute of Technology, Strayer University — are publicly traded, accredited and are eligible for Title IV federal funding. They, and similar institutions, offer a broad range of baccalaureate, master's and doctoral degrees. The University of Phoenix has almost 400,000 students and offers typically vocational, part-time programs, taught by part-time faculty (Newman, 2009). Hentschke has estimated (2004) that in addition to these giant companies, each having revenues in excess of $100 million per year, there are approximately 4,000 smaller for-profit institutions. These for-profit institutions serve in a growingly important educational niche, providing instruction attuned to local needs and employment opportunities, at a low cost generally in rented space in shopping malls and office blocks. They are low-overhead, high-volume educational "providers", and their students are disproportionately lower income and minority group members. Their students benefit from an emphasis not only on job training, but also on job placement. In the decade 1990-2000 the number of for-profit institutions grew by 112% (Hentschke, 2004), and it continued to grow in the following decade. The growth of these institutions tends to drive the price of postsecondary education closer to the institutional cost. In 2004 the average cost of a two-semester program was $6,940 at a for-profit institution, $17,026 at a public non-profit, and $23,063 at a private, non-profit institution. There is continuing debate over the future role and prospects for such for-profit institutions, mostly among the more traditional proponents of higher education. They ask whether the consumer-driven demand for services and expectation of "results for their money" may not overwhelm the hardheaded need for consistent standards and objectivity (Flanagan, 2002). For all these "academic" concerns, it seems likely that the for-profit institutions will continue to play a valuable role in meeting society's needs for skilled workers.

Students

The broad patterns of enrolment over the decade within the various categories of institutions (Table 2) show a steady increase in overall numbers, with notable growth in the proportion of women and a significantly greater growth in full-time, compared with part-time, students. Although the rate of enrolment growth in private institutions exceeded that in public, the private institutional share of total enrolment is still only about 25% of the total.

Perhaps the most significant change was the overall increase in enrolment of 18- to 24-year-olds, from 29.6% in 1999 to 39.1% in 2009. (Table 3)

Demographic changes and enrolment patterns

Consider, first, broad demographic trends and changes in student enrolment and graduation, access of various groups, such as women and underrepresented minorities, and trends in graduate study.

In the discussion that follows, I deal chiefly with the United States, but some of the policy implications raised by these trends and changes in the U.S. have implications for other national educational systems.

Table 2

Enrolment by Institutional Category	1999	2009	% Increase
Total	14,881,000	18,567,000	25%
Public	11,602,000	13,895,000	20%
Private	3,279,000	4,672,000	42%
Fulltime	8,449,000	11,757,000	39%
Part time	6,432,000	6,810,000	6%
Men	6,370,000	7,793,000	22%
Women	8,511,000	10,774,000	27%

Source: 1999-2000 Almanac. *The Chronicle of Higher Education*.
http://chronicle.com/free/almanac/1999/almanac.htm
2007-2008 Almanac. *The Chronicle of Higher Education*.
http://chronicle.com/free/almanac/2007/almanac.htm

Table 3

Enrolment % by institutional type, level of degree, sex, racial & national categories, and proportion of age group	1999	2009 (projected)
Public 4 year institution	40%	40%
Public 2 year institution	37%	36%
Private 4 year institution	21%	23%
Private 2 year institution	2%	1%
Undergraduate	86%	86%
Graduate	12%	12%
Professional	2%	2%
Total	14,367,520	18,475,000
Women	55.8%	53.8%
Minority	26.2%	NA
Foreign	3.2%	NA
Proportion of 18-24 year olds	29.6%	39.1%

Source: 1999-2000 Almanac. *The Chronicle of Higher Education*.
http://chronicle.com/free/almanac/1999/almanac.htm
2007-2008 Almanac. *The Chronicle of Higher Education*.
http://chronicle.com/free/almanac/2007/almanac.htm

Total numbers for college enrolment for 2009 are not yet available, the latest available data being for 2006. If one compares these 2006 data with those for 1996, the overall number of high school graduates has shown little change (Chronicle Almanac, 2009), growing only by some 32,000 students to a total of 2,692,000 (1999-2000 Almanac, 2000). Table 4 shows that, of this total, an increased proportion of male high school graduates enrolled in college; the percentage college enrolment of black high school graduates decreased slightly, while the percentage of white students increased slightly; and that of Hispanic students increased significantly, as did their overall percentage of the total college population.

Table 4

College Enrolment of Recent High School Completers	1996	2006
Male	60.1%	65.8%
Female	69.7%	66.1%
White	67.4%	68.5%
Black	56.0%	55.5%
Hispanic	50.8%	57.9%
Total:	65.0%	66.0%

Source: Table 267. 2007. U.S. National Center for Education Statistics, *Digest of Education Statistics*, annual.

Projected, as opposed to actual, enrolment and graduation rates for 2009 are, however, available, and I have used them in the tables that follow.

The overview of population trends, college enrolment and graduation rates in U.S. colleges and universities over the decade provides some encouraging trends, but gives a mixed picture of success between various groups.

The traditional U.S. college age cohort (18- to 24-year-olds) has undergone some change in overall composition.

The proportions of Asian, Black and Hispanic members within the 18- to 24-year-old population have all increased, that of American Indian members has remained essentially stable, while the total White proportion has declined (Table 5).

The college enrolment figures reflect these increases, and the relative increase in enrolment of all minority groups over the decade is striking (Table 6). The White non-Hispanic proportion of the enrolment showed a decline, though the overall enrolment numbers increased.

World population continued to increase during the first decade of the new millennium, though the rate of increase continued to decline, with several

Table 5

Population 18-24 Year Olds	1999	2009
American Indian	1%	1%
Asian	4%	5%
Black	14%	15%
White	67%	62%
Hispanic	14%	17%

Source: 1999-2000 Almanac. *The Chronicle of Higher Education.*
http://chronicle.com/free/almanac/1999/almanac.htm
2007-2008 Almanac. *The Chronicle of Higher Education.*
http://chronicle.com/free/almanac/2007/almanac.htm

Table 6

Enrolment by Racial Ethnic Group	1999	2009	% Increase
American Indian	137,600	176,300	28%
Asian	828,200	1,134,400	37%
Black-non Hispanic	1,505,600	2,214,600	47%
Hispanic	1,166,100	1,882,000	61%
White-non Hispanic	10,263,900	11,495,400	12%
Nonresident Alien	466,300	584,800	25%
Total	14,367,500	17,487,500	22%

Source: 1999-2000 Almanac. *The Chronicle of Higher Education.*
http://chronicle.com/free/almanac/1999/almanac.htm
2007-2008 Almanac. *The Chronicle of Higher Education.*
http://chronicle.com/free/almanac/2007/almanac.htm

European nations experiencing negative growth. In contrast, many developing African countries and several wealthy Middle Eastern countries continued to experience substantial growth (Chart 1).

Student Access

One consequence of the present economic downturn is the increased demand for student financial aid. Some universities and colleges have been able to increase their funding for such aid, partly by budget reallocation and partly by targeted fundraising. Cornell, for example, has mounted a fundraising campaign targeted at raising an extra $125 million for undergraduate financial aid, to allow it to increase its existing $130 million annual aid budget.

Chart 1

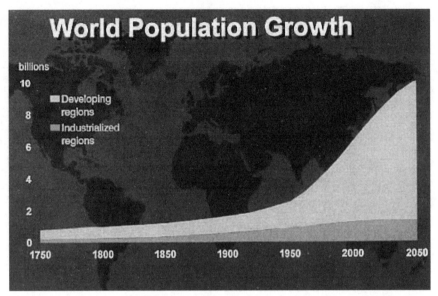

World Population Growth

billions

■ Developing regions
■ Industrialized regions

Source: http://www.canaryzoo.com/Geog1/world%20population%20growth%20map.jpg

Smaller and less well-endowed colleges and universities have been less able to support needy students, and many have had to reduce financial aid (Blankinship, 2009).

Meanwhile, reductions in state funding for public institutions have inflicted their own damage on financial aid, but plans for future federal funding promise to restore the value of federal financial aid.

These changes increase the financial pressures on needy students, and student borrowing has consequently doubled in the last 10 years (Schweber, 2009).

Graduation Rates

Graduation rates provide another measure of participation in higher education. The data show a marked difference in graduation rates between different types of universities and colleges and also among various racial and ethnic groups. (Table 7 and Table 8).

The "very high research activity" research universities (with a 72.8% freshman graduation rate) and the total private non-profit institutions (with a 63.8% rate) had far better graduation rates than all other categories of institution. It is not clear whether this is the result of recruiting more able students, or of more effective teaching, or other factors. But it is a feature whose implications need to be explored.

The changing enrolment pattern of various racial groups at all levels of higher education has led to significant improvement of educational attainment by all groups in almost all degree categories. Hispanic doctoral and professional degrees and Asian associate degrees are the exception, all exhibiting a very slight decline. (Table 8)

The graduation rates by racial/ethnic groups continue to show striking differences. (Table 9), with Asian students out-performing all the rest.

Table 7

6 Year Graduation Rates for Freshmen	2009
All	56.4%
Public	53.3%
Private nonprofit	63.8%
Private profit	48.2%
Res U v high res act	72.8%
Res U high res act	56.3%

Source: 2007-2008 Almanac. *The Chronicle of Higher Education.*
http://chronicle.com/free/almanac/2007/almanac.htm

Table 8

Educational Attainment by Racial Group	1999	2009
Associate Degree		
Asian	7.0%	6.8%
Black	6.9%	7.7%
Hispanic	5.0%	6.2%
White (non Hisp)	8.4%	9.1%
Bachelor's Degree		
Asian	22.7%	30.4%
Black	7.5%	12.6%
Hispanic	5.9%	8.8%
White (non Hisp)	13.9%	20.2%
Master's Degree		
Asian	9.4%	13.4%
Black	4.2%	4.3%
Hispanic	2.2%	2.4%
White (non Hisp)	6.5%	7.9%

Table 8 continued

Educational Attainment by Racial Group	1999	2009
Doctoral Degree		
Asian	3.1%	4.1%
Black	0.3%	0.5%
Hispanic	0.5%	0.3%
White (non Hisp)	1.3%	1.4%
Professional Degree		
Asian	2.7%	2.9%
Black	0.6%	0.8%
Hispanic	0.7%	0.6%
White (non Hisp)	1.7%	1.8%
TOTAL in millions:	175.2	194.3

Source: 1999-2000 Almanac. *The Chronicle of Higher Education.*
http://chronicle.com/free/almanac/1999/almanac.htm
2007-2008 Almanac. *The Chronicle of Higher Education.*
http://chronicle.com/free/almanac/2007/almanac.htm

Table 9

Graduation Rates by Racial/ Ethnic Group	1996	2000
All Total	54.4%	55.9%
American Indian	36.7%	38.3%
Asian	62.6%	65.2%
Black non-Hispanic	38.2%	40.4%
Hispanic	44.8%	46.7%
White non-Hispanic	57.2%	58.8%
Race unknown	52.1%	50.5%
Nonresident Aliens	58.0%	59.3%

Source: 1999-2000 Almanac. *The Chronicle of Higher Education.*
http://chronicle.com/free/almanac/1999/almanac.htm
2007-2008 Almanac. *The Chronicle of Higher Education.*
http://chronicle.com/free/almanac/2007/almanac.htm

The educational attainment of the U.S. population as a whole has also shown significant improvement over the ten-year period. (Table 10).

Table 10

Educational Attainment of Adult Population (highest level)	1999	2009
Associate's Degree	6.2%	7.4%
Bachelor's Degree	13.1%	17.2%
Graduate or Professional Degree	7.2%	10.0%

Source: 1999-2000 Almanac. *The Chronicle of Higher Education.*
http://chronicle.com/free/almanac/1999/almanac.htm
2007-2008 Almanac. *The Chronicle of Higher Education.*
http://chronicle.com/free/almanac/2007/almanac.htm

Doctoral students

The number of doctoral degrees conferred in the decade 1999-2009 increased by 6.8% (Table 11). The proportion of women receiving degrees grew steadily. Black and Hispanic recipients showed significant increases, whereas the percentage of Asian recipients declined. The largest percentage increases occurred in the sciences and engineering, with modest declines in education and social sciences. The overall percentage of U.S. citizens receiving doctorates in all fields declined from 64.8% to 59.0%, reflecting, presumably, the increasing numbers of international students.

Table 11

Doctoral Degrees Conferred	1999	2009
Total	42,705	45,596
Men %	58.5%	54.8%
Women %	40.6%	45.0%
Business	3%	3%
Education	15%	13%
Engineering	14%	16%
Humanities	13%	12%
Life Science	19%	21%
Physical Science	15%	16%
Social Science	16%	15%
US Citizens all fields %	64.8%	59.0%
Asian %	10.3%	5.9%

Table 11 continued

Doctoral Degrees Conferred	1999	2009
Black %	4.8%	6.3%
Hispanic %	3.8%	5.2%
White %	77.8%	80.3%

Source: 1999-2000 Almanac. *The Chronicle of Higher Education.*
http://chronicle.com/free/almanac/1999/almanac.htm
2007-2008 Almanac. *The Chronicle of Higher Education.*
http://chronicle.com/free/almanac/2007/almanac.htm

Social Conditions and Employment Prospects

Within the U.S. population, social conditions showed modest improvement. The poverty rate declined slightly, and the high school dropout rate declined significantly (Table 12).

Tertiary education is defined as "programs designed to provide sufficient qualifications for entry to advanced research programs and professions with high skill requirements". Unlike any other country except Canada among members of the OECD, the United States has a slightly higher percentage of "tertiary educated" individuals in the 25- to 64-year-old working population than the percentage of the same age group working in "skilled jobs" (Chart 1). If provision and growth of tertiary education are to be linked to particular needs for a skilled workforce, further expansion of higher education should then be linked to the growth in skilled jobs. Advocates for higher education will, of course, properly argue that the purposes of higher education are far more comprehensive than "job training".

In all OECD countries outside North America, the proportion of skilled jobs in the economy is markedly higher than the proportion of the working population with tertiary education. In the Netherlands, for example, 30% of the working population has enjoyed tertiary education, but over 50% of the

Table 12

Social Conditions	1999	2009
Per Capita Personal Income	$26,412	$36,276
Poverty Rate	13.5%	12.7%
High School Grads	2,840,170	3,186,940
High School Dropout Rate	10%	7%

Source: 1999-2000 Almanac. *The Chronicle of Higher Education.*
http://chronicle.com/free/almanac/1999/almanac.htm
2007-2008 Almanac. *The Chronicle of Higher Education.*
http://chronicle.com/free/almanac/2007/almanac.htm

Chart 2: Proportion of population in skilled jobs and proportion of population with tertiary education (2006)

The chart depicts the proportion of the 25-to-64-year-old working population in skilled jobs and the proportion of the 25-to-64-year-old population with tertiary education (2006).

■ Tertiary attainment (5B, 5A/6)   □ Skilled jobs (ISCO 1-3)

Large proportions of the workforce have moved into skilled jobs in OECD countries. Along with experience gained in working life, education provides a principal source of skills for the labour market. In OECD countries, the proportion of skilled jobs in the economy is generally larger than the potential supply of tertiary educated individuals. For countries in which work-based learning is central to occupational advancement, this difference is large. A broader initial skill base might require additional investment in higher education. In a few countries, tertiary attainment matches or marginally exceeds the proportion of skilled jobs, so that further expansion of higher education will to some extent depend on the growth of skilled jobs in the coming years.

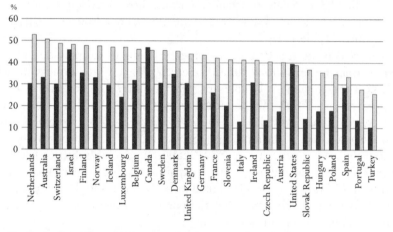

Note: For the United States, ISCO groupings 3 and 9 are not separated and thus distributed among remaining ISCO categories.
Countries are ranked in descending order by the proportion of the population in skilled jobs.
Source: OECD. Table A1.3a and Table A1.6. See Annex 3 for notes (*www.oecd.org/edu/eag2008*).
StatLink ▓▓▓ http://dx.doi.org/10.1787/401474646362

population occupies skilled jobs. The corresponding figures for Germany are 24% and 45% and for France, 26% and 42%. The increase in skilled jobs in most OECD countries in the last decade has been matched by corresponding increases in the participation in tertiary education. Comparison of younger and older age groups (Chart 2) thus show striking differences in educational attainment in most countries (though not in the U.S. and Germany). In France, Ireland, Japan and Korea, for example, there is a difference of 25 percentage points in rate of participation in tertiary education between the youngest and the oldest groups. The average participation rate in tertiary education in OECD countries is 33% among 25- to 40-year-olds, which suggests that overall participation rates will continue to rise.

Chart 3: Population that has attained at least tertiary education (2006)

Percentage, by age group

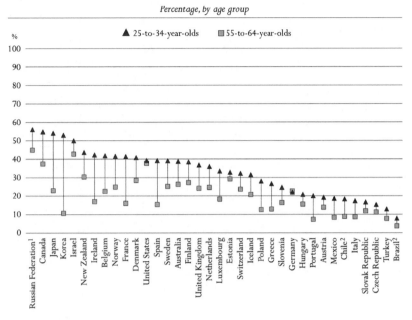

1. Year of reference 2002.
2. Year of reference 2004.
Countries are ranked in descending order of the percentage of the 25-to-34-year-olds who have attained tertiary education.
Source: OECD. Table A1.3a. See Annex 3 for notes (www.oecd.org/edu/eag2008).
StatLink ⬛⬛ http://dx.doi.org/10.1787/401474646362

On average in OECD countries, tertiary graduation rates increased by 15 percentage points over the 11 years between 1995 and 2006. In part these changes reflect structural change in the duration of degree programs (OECD, 2008).

These average graduation figures reflect wide differences between OECD member countries, however, ranging from 20% or fewer in Greece and Turkey to more than 45% in Australia, Finland, Iceland, New Zealand and Poland.

Faculty

The composition of the faculty shows the increase of women far exceeding that of men, as well as significant increases in recruitment of Asian and Hispanic members. In 1999, women constituted 35% of the total faculty. In 2009, they are projected to constitute 41%. (Table 13)

The increase of overall faculty numbers of 22.7% from 1999-2009 is only slightly less than the overall increase in the number of full-time students during the same period, 25%, suggesting that "productivity", whatever the precise definition, has not markedly improved or declined.

Table 13

Full-time Faculty Members by Race	1999	2009	Percent Increase
All	550,822	675,624	22.7%
Men	360,150	401,507	11.5%
Women	190,672	274,117	43.8%
Asian All	27,572	48,457	75.7%
Black All	26,835	35,458	32.1%
Hispanic All	12,942	22,818	76%
White All	468,518	527,900	12.7%
Race unknown	1,946	9,703	398.6%
Nonresident Aliens	10,853	28,057	158.5%

Source: 1999-2000 Almanac. *The Chronicle of Higher Education.*
http://chronicle.com/free/almanac/1999/almanac.htm
2007-2008 Almanac. *The Chronicle of Higher Education.*
http://chronicle.com/free/almanac/2007/almanac.htm

New Partnerships

In Europe over the last decade the Bologna process has allowed more than 40 countries to harmonize their academic calendars and degree cycles, anticipating the prospect of a European Higher Education Area by 2010. The creation of this area recognizes the positive educational value of international study in creating transferable skills and increased mobility for the graduate work force (Labi, 2009).

In contrast, most U.S. "study abroad" programs last less than a full year and are generally poorly integrated either into their home university's curriculum or into their host university's programs.

Critics of the Bologna process have raised important matters of policy. For example, the process has been criticized for encouraging "undemocratic" decision-making, for being closer in the UK-Irish model than to the traditional continental model, for inviting "privatization" of degrees, and for making the economic purposes of higher education more important than its traditional scholarly purposes.

But what the Bologna process has provided is a degree of standardization and reciprocity that has already created a new foundation for international cooperation and inter-institutional partnership, as yet unthinkable in the United States, where institutional autonomy and "academic freedom" have long been highly prized and fiercely defended. This autonomy generally resists any pressure for standardization, except to the extent that the right to award degrees is recognized by a process of regional review and accreditation. But even this relatively benign oversight is carried out by self-perpetuating bodies of academics, rather than appointed government officials or civil servants. Self-regulation is generally regarded by U.S. universities as synonymous with institutional autonomy.

In the Middle East there are now several successful examples of inter-institutional partnerships. In Qatar, for example, a newly constructed campus complex houses programs offered by Cornell in medicine, by Georgetown in foreign studies, by Northwestern in communication and journalism, by Texas A&M in chemical, electrical, mechanical and petroleum engineering, by Carnegie Mellon in computing and engineering and by Virginia Commonwealth in design. The independent programs are established and offered by faculty of the sponsoring institutions, which also award their own degrees to successful students. The arrangement is based upon 10-year contracts between the Qatar Foundation and the various institutions.

King Abdullah University of Science and Technology (KAUST), in which I must declare an interest, is the most ambitious of these international partnerships. It is an independently governed, coeducational, graduate level institution which will open its doors to some 360 M.S. and Ph.D. students in September 2009. Some 85 faculty have been appointed, and the university will offer degrees in 11 fields of study. KAUST is governed by an independent board of trustees and supported by a multi-billion dollar endowment, and is open to men and women from around the world. Its research and teaching are supported by partnerships and alliances with other major universities, including such institutions as University of California-Berkeley, Cambridge, Stanford, University of Texas at Austin and Imperial College London. It has research partnerships with a dozen or more international companies. My friend and former Michigan colleague, Fawwaz Ulaby, will describe this remarkable venture, in which he played a notable role (Chapter 11).

New private universities in Kuwait and elsewhere have become affiliated with American institutions: the American University of the Middle East, for example, is affiliated with Purdue (Mills, 2009). The American University in Kuwait has partnered with Dartmouth in a private response to the need for more university places in Kuwait, as the government-supported University of Kuwait reaches capacity. More than 100 new colleges and universities are opening in Saudi Arabia, including some that are private (Krieger, 2007).

Some established universities are also opening branch campuses in other countries within the same region. Two Turkish universities, for example — The Middle Eastern Technical University (ODTU) and Istanbul Technical University (ITU) — recently announced the opening of new campuses in Dubai, U.A.E. (*Hurriyet Daily News*, 2009).

Other inter-institutional partnerships are more precisely targeted. Columbia, for example, is building a network of six to eight research institutions in capitals around the world. These Columbia Global Centers, as they are called, are multidisciplinary in character and are intended to support faculty and student groups in collaborating on international projects. A centre has already opened in Beijing and others are planned for Paris and either Mumbai or Delhi (Labi, 2009). These centres will engage local universities, agencies and other organizations in international partnerships.

Even as such new international programs are being created, financial constraints have led to the closure of others. George Mason University will close its branch campus in the United Arab Emirates this year after financial, construction and recruitment difficulties (Mills, 2008). Its original plans were to establish a 2,000-student branch campus offering courses taught by George Mason faculty members and leading to a George Mason degree. The University of Illinois also has significantly reduced its ambitious "global campus" program (Labi, 2009).

Meanwhile, other international partnerships are taking root, including one in Dubai with Michigan State University and another in Abu Dhabi with New York University and MIT (Krieger, 2008). Abu Dhabi is also supporting an MBA program offered by INSEAD and a graduate program in public health sponsored by Johns Hopkins.

Increasingly, new international partnerships seem likely to rely on virtual networks, such as that developed in 2008 by the U.S. Agency for International Development (Lindow, 2008) in partnership with African universities. The Africa Education Commons, as it is called, is designed to promote cooperation between American and African institutions on projects involving education, economic development, food and health.

At least a dozen new Islamic universities have been opened in Sub-Saharan African countries in the last decade, sponsored and financed, in part, by charitable Muslim initiatives and foundations in other countries.

In India, foreign universities are not permitted to offer independent programs, but at least 130 foreign academic institutions (including 66 American and 59 British) have created partnerships with local, mostly private, unaccredited Indian institutions. Typically, the Indian institutions offer the first two years of instruction and the students then proceed to study on the foreign campus, from which they receive their degrees. These and similar arrangements have proved profitable revenue sources both for foreign partner universities and for investors in the Indian institutions. Western Michigan University, Purdue at Calumet, Marshall, and Union College have all participated in these partnerships, as has North Dakota State, which also has partnership programs in Sri Lanka, Malaysia and Thailand (Neelakantan, 2008).

Peking University has recently established a Joint Institute for Social Sciences with the University of Michigan and has an active partnership in gerontology, social work and policy planning with the University of Southern California (Hvistendahl, 2009).

The U.S. Department of Energy announced in 2007 a new partnership in bioenergy, involving the collaboration of 18 universities, seven national laboratories and several corporate partners in constructing three new research centres on bioenergy, each of which will receive $125 million.

Such international partnerships in both teaching and research seem likely to become more frequent, providing the benefits of pooled knowledge in addressing major regional needs and social concerns.

Governance and Management

Each of the areas of higher education we have reviewed — finances, institutions, students, faculty and partnerships — has undergone significant changes during the course of the last decade. In one major area, however, there has been almost no change: institutional governance and management. This stability is cause for satisfaction because governance by public-spirited lay boards, with the responsibility and authority for the conduct of academic affairs deliberately delegated to the faculties, has served universities well over the centuries. It has brought tangible benefits, not only to the universities and all their members, but also to the societies that support them.

The administrative pattern of internal management and institutional leadership has, however, been less effective. A decade after the expansive optimism of the new millennium and high aspirations of Glion I, the current economic downturn has affected all segments of society. Few universities appear to be dealing decisively and effectively with the grave financial difficulties that have arisen over the past year and continue to confront them.

The current economic crisis will require all universities to accommodate the new financial realities. And this will place a premium on effective governance and courageous leadership. The typical response to reduced income has been to distribute the impact by across-the-board budget reductions. Hiring freezes, salary cuts and construction caps are typically part of this avoidance-approach. It is thought to avoid even more painful choices; it limits faculty complaint, it reduces student uproar, it avoids confrontation and it "does the job". It produces a new balanced budget. It also sidesteps the most serious structural problems, it ignores inherent inequalities, it neglects differing contributions, it overlooks relative importance and meaningful priorities. Far from "doing the job", it may diminish the institution's capacity to pursue its longer-term goals. It represents, in short, an abdication of responsibility.

The alternative course is to use "financial exigencies" to make informed, though often difficult, choices and to do so in a way that promotes the long-term well-being of the institution. In the absence of major new sources of revenue over the next few years, choices will need to be made, and success will belong to those institutions whose boards and leaders are bold enough to make them deliberately and courageously.

PROSPICE

Adversity as Opportunity

I have attempted to give a thumbnail sketch of the development of higher education over the last decade. The changes that have taken place in both the United States and in Europe have been significant: in the former case they reflect much less central planning and coordination than in the latter, though some of the overall results are not dissimilar.

As we face the new decade, it seems increasingly probable that real economic recovery will be slow and that financial constraints may be a longer-term feature of higher education than we would have wished. We live in the anomalous situation where universities both compete for and contribute to the generation of public funding and private support. This is especially true because at the close of the first decade of the new millennium, we face a daunting range of social challenges, ranging from climate change to water management, from recession to deforestation and soil depletion, from poverty to epidemics, from energy to agricultural production. Serious as each is, and daunting as all are collectively, none can begin to be addressed without the skills embodied and practised within the universities, and without the particular blend of creativity and reflection which are the distinctive products of our institutions.

In this situation, it seems to me useful to consider together three broad policy questions:

- In financial terms, are we becoming so expensive in relation to other social needs that we jeopardize our own support?
- In educational terms, how can we become better in what we do?
- In societal terms, how can we be more useful to society in the vast range of services we provide?

These are large, difficult and controversial questions, and there may well be so many differences among our many institutions and systems that no common answers are possible. Yet to fail to address these questions would be to deny the very critical study universities exist to promote. To address them courageously could lead to innovation, and perhaps even to radical change.

Consider first, then, the difficult and controversial question of costs. Former U.S. Education Secretary Margaret Spellings, commenting on the report of the Commission on the Future of Higher Education, has declared:

Our universities are known as the best in the world. And a lot of people will tell you things are going just fine. But when 90% of the fastest-growing jobs require postsecond-

ary education, are we satisfied with "just fine?" Is it "fine" that college tuition has out-paced inflation, family income, even doubling the cost of health care? Is it "fine" that only half of our students graduate on time? Is it "fine" that students often graduate so saddled with debt they can't buy a home or start a family? None of this seems "fine" to me. Not as a policy maker, not as a taxpayer, and certainly not as the mother of a college sophomore (Rhodes, 2006).

Jared Diamond, whose best-selling book Collapse: How Societies Choose to Fail or Survive, published at mid-decade, used comparative historical methods to explore the decline and collapse of societies, concluded that the root problem leading to collapse was overpopulation and thus, exhaustion of the carrying capacity of the environment.

Diamond's analysis made it clear that it was important to distinguish biological survival from cultural survival. Societies can have the most admirable cultural values — love of freedom, peace and democratic rights, for example — but still become extinct.

It seems to me we face comparable challenges in our present situation. We can still embrace admirable academic values, defend academic freedom, insist on institutional autonomy, maintain the societal benefits and personal rewards of creative scholarship, liberal education and professional training, but if our appetite for funding overwhelms the carrying capacity of our environment, we, too, may be headed for decline. One has to ask whether we may now be approaching such a point in some of our best universities and colleges. In state after state, food programs for the hungry, health care for the sick, and public services to communities are now being reduced to the point of real hardship. It may be that society will no longer choose to support institutions where the total annual cost of tuition, room and board amounts to as much as $60,000 for an undergraduate student. If one regards the student as being in residence on the campus for 30 weeks of the year, that tuition, room and board would amount to $2,000 per week of residential instruction, or a total cost to the student of some $167 per hour of instruction. It will be argued, of course, that these are crude estimates and that they conceal many hidden factors. No doubt they do, but we must be willing to explain the subtleties and complexities of the fundamental issues they involve. We must also be ready, I think, to explain why we are constantly appealing for donor support in order to allow us to give full financial aid to students when, in some cases, their families are earning as much as $180,000 a year.

It is easy, of course, to reply that academic excellence is expensive. But does excellence accept any bounds to its appetite, or does it require unlimited support to pursue unlimited aims by unlimited methods? I submit that this Glion group is one of the few that has the ability to look at the larger financial picture and to talk in a collegial way about some of the practical funding issues that this theoretical question raises.

Let me explain what I mean. Schweber (2009) has described the University of Wisconsin at Madison as having 30,000 undergraduates, who can choose from among 161 majors and 35 certificate programs. But, in addition to this huge undergraduate program, in 2005 the university employed 9,100 in university research programs, had partnerships with 218 companies and generated $764 million in research-related revenue for the state of Wisconsin. It also consumed half of the state's appropriation for higher education. Now Wisconsin has 12 other public universities and colleges, enrolling some 175,000 students. The success of Madison in generating research revenue, Schweber argues, comes chiefly from the natural sciences, and he asks whether these should be favoured and supported at the expense of other areas. Even to raise such a question will be regarded as heresy, or even blasphemy, within the academic community. But if, as now seems possible, the financial stress within the universities is not simply a short-term phenomenon, we shall have to confront just such painful questions.

Of course, costs cannot be separated from the pattern and scope of instruction. In instructional terms, we have to ask the question "How much is enough?" For example, how many courses are required to provide a satisfactory range of choices for an undergraduate program in a contemporary English Department? Should it be 50, or should it be 100, or should it be 200? How many graduate courses are necessary? How many courses, do you suppose, a large English Department offers each year?

At one Ivy League university it is 140 undergraduate courses and 35 graduate courses. At a large Big Ten university it is 153 undergraduate courses. The numbers I have quoted are not necessarily unreasonable, and we must ask the same questions for every discipline, from psychology to civil engineering. What is needed is to confront the question.

Also, in instructional terms — how many faculty members are necessary to provide a balanced undergraduate and graduate program, not only for undergraduate majors, but also for those students in general education? For example, the chemistry department at one large state university in California has 111 faculty members and graduated 1,000 majors last year. Other science departments graduate fewer baccalaureate students each year than they have faculty members. What is the appropriate faculty-student ratio?

In professional and personal terms, we need to ask comparable questions about cost. Why is it, for example, that teaching loads at the nation's leading universities have declined from an average of two per semester, when some people here were active faculty members, to one per semester now? Has something changed? Has research productivity, for example, become strikingly higher? Has teaching notably improved? Why in Europe do professors teach roughly twice as many weekly credit and contact hours as those at leading universities in the United States? These are painful questions and ones that we should discuss, if they are to be discussed at all, in a gathering such as this, rather than have others discuss them for us.

In institutional terms, we have to ask: "Must a university take in every aspect of human knowledge and of human interest in order to pursue excellence? For example, is Princeton an inferior university because it chooses not to have a medical school and has decided not to include a law school? Is CalTech a lesser university than, say, UC-Berkeley, because it chooses to be less comprehensive? Is Chicago a lesser institution than, say, the University of Illinois because it is highly selective in the range of programs it offers?"

Some will argue that if particular universities have already embraced a comprehensive mission, it is too late to change. That has particular relevance, of course, in the case of land grant universities, which were created on the assumption of breadth in certain areas. It is not, however, the case in most universities. The question of the growingly expansive offerings of many universities is one that we need to address. Are there any bounds to institutional aspirations to provide the most comprehensive knowledge?

The voices of academic leaders have been strangely muted concerning these major choices. An honourable exception is Mark Yudof, president of the University of California (Hebel, 2009). Yudof asks whether new models of financing and operating the great public research universities should be developed. He argues that it is vital for the U.S. to invest in human capital, because that is the essence of economic and competitive advantage for the United States. He asks whether radical review of our current "delivery model" and our method of conducting research is not now urgently needed. Of our delivery model he concludes "it's awfully expensive because it's so hands-on. It works. It's great quality. But can we deliver a high quality education with a higher student-faculty ratio? Can we shorten up the time to degree?...We need to look at the delivery system, and we need the faculty to look at it because they're the experts." He also argues that if we are to build our research capacity and nurture those who can both create and convey knowledge, we need some measure of research productivity.

A few of our faculty colleagues have argued for just such a "paradigm-shift", its urgency sharpened by the present financial stress, together with widespread hiring freezes and layoffs.

"End the University as We Know It", reads the title of an op-ed article in the New York Times (27 April 2009) by Mark Taylor, chairman of the religion department at Columbia. "Graduate education is the Detroit of higher learning," he concluded. "Most graduate programs... produce a product for which there is no market, and develop skills for which there is diminishing demand... all at a rapidly rising cost... The dirty secret of higher education is that without underpaid graduate students to help in laboratories and teaching, universities couldn't conduct research or even instruct their growing undergraduate populations."

Among the radical remedies proposed by Taylor to address this "crisis" were the abolition of permanent departments, the imposition of mandatory retirement and the abolition of tenure. These remedies will commend themselves to few within the academic community, but we need to consider responsible alternatives. And we should honour those who are bold enough to confront our present situation.

Perhaps the greatest service that the Glion gathering could perform is to use our experiences in different educational settings to grapple with some of these larger issues, and so make some meaningful proposals. To do so at this moment would be particularly appropriate. In almost every area of society, recalibration is presently taking place because of our current economic distress. If it is true that "sweet are the uses of adversity", we should use our present adversity creatively, not passively, or carelessly. With bold and thoughtful leadership, universities can emerge stronger from the present economic turmoil and can better serve society.

But education has never owed its success only to money. Excellence may be present even in the most Spartan classroom; imagination may blossom even in the poorest place, though the increasing sophistication of the equipment required to translate discoveries into designs and convert insights into benefits makes that less and less likely in science and technology. But whatever the outcome of the debate over costs, there is a second question that we in the academy must confront: How can we do better with what we have in what we choose to do? How, given the already vast resources that we enjoy, can we be more effective in our chosen role of teaching, research and service to society?

Part of the answer to that question involves the proportion of the population served by our universities and colleges. Listen again to former Education Secretary Margaret Spellings: "... times have changed. Nearly two-thirds of all high-growth, high-wage jobs created in the next decade will require a college degree, a degree only one-third of Americans have. Where we once were leaders, now other nations educate more of their young adults, to more-advanced levels than we do."

I believe we have to address the issue raised by Ms. Spellings. Should the student population continue to rise as a percentage of the college age group? What should society set as its goal? Should it be roughly 50% of the college age group, which it now is in the U.S.? Or should it, perhaps, be 75%, or even 100%? Can everyone benefit from some college experience? Can society benefit from everyone attending college? And what should be the distribution among types of institutions? What do universities themselves have to say on this particular issue? What should we, as a Colloquium, conclude? In the end, who decides? Is it the marketplace? Is it elected officials? Is it the universities?

Performing better with what we already have also involves the richness of the student experience. Some of our universities — those centres of creativity and agents of discovery — are now becoming so compartmentalized and sub-divided that the common discourse on which both learning and discovery depend is constrained and inhibited. How best can we liberate the departmentalized mental energy and segregated creative power of our institutions? What were once bold experimental teaching styles, creative alternative learning modes and common course initiatives have, in far too many institutions, fallen victim to competing interests and become casualties to disciplinary protectionism. How can we rekindle the light of common learning in our increasingly specialized institutions; how can we demonstrate anew the unique benefits of the *community* of learning in addressing the needs of society?

These are matters not only of style, but far more of substance. Perhaps collegiality, like youth, is never what it once was, but the fragmentation of the curriculum and the atomization of research make it increasingly challenging to comprehend, still more to address, the great overarching social issues of our time, from climate change to poverty, that sprawl across the guarded boundaries of our disciplinary territories.

This fragmentation is reflected in the change in student attitudes over the recent decades. Since the 1970s, for example, the percentage of freshman students saying they desire to develop a meaningful philosophy of life has plummeted from 86% to 45%, while those who express enthusiasm for cleaning up the environment has waned by half to 20% (Rhodes, 2006).

There is one other aspect of quality that is related to the costs of our activity and the levels of our tuition. The public understands that higher education is not a production-line activity but instead reflects the individuality that lies at the heart of the best teacher-student relationships. But there seems also to be a nagging public concern about what appears to be a decline in commitment to teaching, an increasing proportion of our students taking more than four years to graduate, and a growing emphasis on the part of institutions on buying the brightest freshman students with merit awards. These concerns have been forcefully articulated in several recent independent reports, and they have reinforced the calls for "standards", "quality controls", published graduation rates, and broader transparency.

These calls for accountability have been echoed by some employers, who have criticized the lack of critical ability in recent graduates. No simple tests can measure the quality of our "output", but we need to take seriously the increasing public concerns for quality and accountability. If we in higher education are unwilling to address quality and performance, others, less qualified — the federal or state governments, for instance — may do it for us. That would not be good, either for our universities, or for our students. We should be prepared to demonstrate our performance by criteria, preferably of our own choosing, which are themselves open to scrutiny.

In the urgent priority we must devote to matters of great financial consequence, who is to speak to these no less-consequential questions of substance,
scope and effectiveness? Who better than this group here in Glion? How, I
ask, can we become better — much better — in what we already choose to do?
How can we harness our now segregated talent into a common discourse that
will enliven everything we do and enrich everything we study?

And then the final question: How can we better serve society in the vast
range of services we provide? From medical services to food production, from
education to industry, from art to government, from energy supplies to environmental systems, universities already provide essential public service, sup-
plying professional practitioners, providing scholarship, research and development, and educating enlightened citizens and discerning leaders in every field.
But is there any way we can more effectively tap the universities' great reser-
voirs of learning and expertise to grapple with some of society's macro-prob-
lems: say, failing schools, or the HIV-Aids epidemic, or sustainable agriculture
or renewable resources or alternative energy sources? We have federal grants
and industrial partnerships for well-defined projects. What we lack is some
substantial articulation of our national and international expertise to broader
issues of society. Even to ask the question is to contemplate the difficulty, perhaps even the impossibility, of the task.

There is, perhaps, one model that is worth consideration. In 1862, at the
height of the American Civil War, or the War Between the States, Abraham
Lincoln signed into law the Morrill Act, which granted to each state federal
lands, which could be either developed or sold to raise funds for the creation
and endowment of land grant universities to equip the nation to respond to
the social and agricultural upheavals of the Industrial Revolution. These institutions were to provide a broad education in "agriculture and the mechanic
arts... in order to promote the liberal and practical education of the industrial
classes in the several pursuits and professions of life." This practical aspect of
higher education was seen as supplementing the historic offerings of earlier
colleges and universities. The mission of these land grant universities was
expanded by the Hatch Act of 1887 to establish agricultural experiment stations and by the Smith-Lever Act of 1914 to create an extension service, by
which the results of these "agricultural experiments" and new agricultural
skills could be carried to farmers and homemakers in rural areas of every
county in the country by "cooperative extension" agents, whose work was supported by both state and federal funds.

The work of these land grant universities transformed the nation, providing
the foundation for the agricultural revolution that made the United States the
major food supplier to the world and providing new graduates, new knowledge
and new impetus to every area of national life. The universities that Lincoln
created now account for 25% of all the nation's baccalaureate graduates and

60% of the doctorates. Can we devise some larger "extension system" that will create the same beneficial impact for the age in which we now live?

These questions of cost, performance and public service are fundamental to our universities. Should we not grasp the financial adversity that now confronts all our institutions, indeed all our nations, as an opportunity to address the most profound social problems that confront our world? Can we use our present constraints to think anew, not only of our costs, but also of our performance and our contribution to society?

Some will respond that the problems are too complex, that our resources are too modest, that other tasks are too pressing. But listen again to Lincoln: "The dogmas of the quiet past are inadequate to the stormy present. The occasion is piled high with difficulty, and we must rise to the occasion. As our case is new, so must we think anew."

This symposium is devoted to "thinking anew," to innovation. Can we and our graduates rise to Lincoln's challenge, as did his countrymen 147 years ago? To address that question, to devise a new, workable model, might be the greatest innovation of all.

Universities existed throughout most of the last millennium, as they will, I trust, exist through this. The crucial question is how effectively their work and their graduates can contribute to the momentous challenges that now confront the world's peoples. And that will depend in large measure on the creativity and boldness of those entrusted with the leadership of our institutions. If ever there was a need for innovation, it is here, within our own universities. Only then can they make a proportionate contribution to creating an innovation-driven society.

REFERENCES

1999-2000 Almanac. (2000). *The Chronicle of Higher Education*. Retrieved from http://chronicle.com/free/alamanac/1999/almanac.htm

2007-2008 Almanac. (2008). *The Chronicle of Higher Education*. Retrieved from http://chronicle.com/free/alamanac/2008/almanac.htm

(6 April 2009). How Are State Budget Cuts affecting Spending for Higher Education. *University Parent Media*. Retrieved from http://www.universityparent.com/2009/04/06/how-are-state-budget-cuts-affecting-spending-for-higher-education

Bergman, K. (13 January 2004). Stanford University Program on Energy and Sustainable Development receives grant from BP. *Stanford News Service*. Retrieved from http://news.stanford.edu/pr/2004/bpgrant114.html

Blankinship, D. G. (12 March 2009). More bad news on campus: Scholarships drying up. *Associated Press*. Retrieved from http://abcnews.go.com/US/wireStory?id=7064642

Blumenstyk, G. (3 October 2008). The $375-billion Question: Why Does College Cost So Much? *The Chronicle of Higher Education*. Retrieved from http://chronicle.com/weekly/v55/i06/06a00101.htm

Blumenstyk, G. (23 January 2009). Report on Spending Trends Highlights Inequities in Model for Financing Colleges. *The Chronicle of Higher Education*. Retrieved from http://chronicle.com/weekly/v55/i20/20a01601.htm

Carlson, S. (16 January 2009). Moody's Forecasts Stiff Challenges, Especially for Private Colleges in the Next Year. *The Chronicle of Higher Education*. Retrieved from http://chronicle.com/free/v55/i19/19a01401.htm

Chronicle Almanac. (2009). For original source: *The Digest of Education Statistics, 2007*. Tables and Figures, Table 191: College enrollment and enrollment rates of recent high school completers, by sex: 1960 through 2006.

Cronin, J. & Horton, H. (22 May 2009). "Will Higher Education Be the Next Bubble to Burst?" *The Chronicle of Higher Education*. Retrieved from http://chronicle.com/weekly/v55/i37/37a05601.htm

Diamond, J. (2005). Collapse: How Societies Choose to Fail or Survive, Penguin Group, New York

Drucker, P. F. (1997). Interview: Seeing Things as They Really Are. *Forbes*, 159, pp. 122-28

"Europe's Responses to Economic Crisis". (20 February 2009). *University World News*. Retrieved 2 June 2009 from http://www.universityworldnews.com/article.php?story=20090220085540843

Fischer, K. (12 December 2008). Terrorist Strikes Are Unlikely to Keep U.S. Colleges Away from India. *Chronicle of Higher Education*. Retrieved from http://chornicle.com/weekly/v55/i16/16a02102.htm

Flanagan, E. (16 June 2002). Higher Ed, Inc.: The Rise of the For-Profit University. *Journal of Higher Education*. Retrieved from http://findarticles.com/p/articles/mi_hb172/is_4_73/ai_n28927541/

Hebel, S. (1 May 2009). We Can't Go On Like This. *The Chronicle of Higher Education*, Retrieved from http://chronicle.com/weekly/v55/i34/34a00401.htm

Hentschke, G. (Spring 2004). U.S. For-Profit Postsecondary Institutions — Departure of Extension? *International Higher Education*. Retrived from http://www.bc.edu/bc_org/avp/soe/cihe/newsletter/News35/text009.htm

Hirsch, W. & Weber, L. E. (Eds). (1999). *Challenges Facing Higher Education at the Millennium*, The Oryx Press, Phoenix, AZ.

Hurriyet Daily News. (13 June 2009). Economists Discuss Vertical Trade Model. Retrieved from http://arama.hurriyet.com.tr/arsivnews.aspx?id=11855407

Hvistendahl, M. (13 February 2009). Renewed Attention to Social Sciences in China Leads to New Partnership With American Universities. *The Chronicle of Higher Education*. Retrieved from http://chronicle.com/weekly/v55/i23/23a03501.htm

Krieger, Z. (14 September 2007). Saudi Arabia Puts Its Billions Behind Western-Style Higher Education. *The Chronicle of Higher Education*. Retrieved from http://chronicle.com/weekly/v54/i03/03a00101.htm

Krieger, Z. (28 March 2008). An Academic Building Boom Transforms the Persian Gulf. *The Chronicle of Higher Education*. Retrieved from http://chronicle.com/weekly/v54/i29/29a02601.htm

Labi, A. (6 February 2009). What's Tasty, Yellow, and Proves Nothing? *The Chronicle of Higher Education*. Retrieved from http://chronicle.com/weekly/v55/i22/22a00602.htm

Labi, A. (27 February 2009). Germany Provides Higher Education Without the Frills. *The Chronicle of Higher Education*. Retrieved from http://chronicle.com/weekly/v55/i25/25a01801.htm

Labi, A. (3 April 2009). Darwin's Economic Theory. *The Chronicle of Higher Education*. Vol 55, 30. p. A20.

Likins, P. N. (1998). Corporate partnerships: what's in it for the university? *Columbia News Service*. Retrieved from http://www.columbia.edu/cu/21stC/issue-3.1/likins.html

Lindow, M. (31 October 2008). New Virtual Network Links African and U.S. Universities. *The Chronicle of Higher Education*. Retrieved from http://chronicle.com/weekly/v55/i10/10a03801.htm

Masterson, K. (6 February 2009). Research and Inventions Earn Big Bucks for American Universities. *The Chronicle of Higher Education*. Retrieved from http://chronicle.com/weekly/v55/i22/22a01601.htm

Mills, A. (25 July 2008). U.S. Universities Negotiate Tricky Terrain in the Middle East. *The Chronicle of Higher Education*. Retrieved from http://chronicle.com/weekly/v54/i46/46a00104.htm

Mills, A. (22 May 2009). New Private Universities in Kuwait Pin Their Hopes on U.S. Partners". *The Chronicle of Higher Education*. Retrieved from http://chronicle.com/weekly/v55/i37/37a02401.htm

Neelakantan, S. (8 February 2008). In India, Limits on Foreign Universities Lead to Creative Partnerships. *The Chronicle of Higher Education*. Retrieved from http://chronicle.com/weekly/v54/i22/22a00104.htm

Newman, M. (14 May 2009). For-profit growth predicted if U.S. giant buys UK's BPP. *Times Higher Education*, Retrieved from http://www.timeshighereducation.co.uk/story.asp?storycode=406516

OECD. (2008). *Education at a Glance*. Retrieved from http://www.oecd.org/edu/eag2008

Petrie, M. (6 July 2007). Universities to Share in New Energy Centers. *The Chronicle of Higher Education*. Retrieved from http://chronicle.com/weekly/v53/i44/44a02004.htm

Rhodes, F. H. T. (24 November 2006). After 40 Years of Growth and Change, Higher Education Faces New Challenges. *The Chronicle of Higher Education*. p. A18.

Ruch, R. S. (2001). Higher Ed, Inc: The Rise of the For-Profit University. Johns Hopkins Press, Baltimore

Schweber, H. H. (13 February 2009). In Rough Seas, Flagships Could Use a Course Correction. *The Chronicle of Higher Education*, Retrieved from http://chronicle.com/weekly/v55i23/23a04301.htm

Taylor, M. (26 April 2009). End of the University as We Know It. *The New York Times*. Retrieved from http://www.nytimes.com/2009/04/27/opinion/27taylor.html

The Glion Declaration. (1998). *The University at the Millennium*, The Glion Colloquium, Geneva.

PART I

•••••••••••••

General Discussion of Innovation

CHAPTER 1

The Next decade,
a Challenge for technological
and societal Innovations

Luc Weber

"It is not the strongest of the species that survive, nor the most intelligent, but the one most responsive to change." Charles Darwin

PREAMBLE

About 25 years ago, the world entered a period that we can call — although it is not brutal or quasi-instantaneous, but progressive — a revolution, which is rooted in political and economic, as well as scientific and technological forces. This revolution has brought increasing prosperity to the developed world and allowed many other countries not only to take off, but also to become economic partners on an equal footing. Today, the same world is fighting one of its worst financial and economic crises. The political, social and economic impacts of both events are deep and will, we believe, contribute to changing dramatically the face of the world over the decades to come. But this crisis offers a great opportunity to leaders in governments and business, as well as to researchers and other intellectuals, to make the world better than it would have been if recent trends had continued.

Since the Renaissance, the main aspiration of populations has clearly been to find a better life than their ancestors, that is a better standard of living, greater security and less uncertainty, better health standards, more enriching professional activity and, for many, to live in a society that is more just and is based on ethical values. In other words, people desire economic development, that is economic growth plus something which, together with growth, contributes to prosperity and well-being. This burst of prosperity is very positive for humanity. However, and the crisis has reminded us of this in a dramatic fashion, it has become increasingly important to make sure that the develop-ment is globally sustainable, that is politically, socially, environmentally and economically sustainable; neither should we forget the many other very trou-bling situations, such as conflicts, poverty and disease, around the world (Weber, 2008).

The roots of the current revolution and of the crisis are to be found in var-ious powerful and interdependent forces that will be briefly identified and described. But one force of particular interest to us in this chapter is innova-tion. Innovation can be roughly defined as a new way of doing something: a new product or service, a new process to produce and/or deliver it, or a new organization. Innovation implies change, in order to take full advantage of existing knowledge. In their own jargon, economists are using the concept of the technology frontier, which, in order to encompass societal innovations, should be broadened to technological and **organizational** frontiers, organiza-tional being used here to focus both on structures (static) and processes (dynamic). In a static environment, innovation depends on the implementa-tion of existing knowledge that defines the technological and organizational frontier. In a dynamic world, it is possible to push this frontier out thanks to research and to the development of human capital through education. How-ever promising they are, many discoveries and inventions made possible by research may remain unexploited. Innovation is the art of turning them into a reality.

This first contribution on the topic of the colloquium *"Innovation and the Research University"* is meant to convey three messages, which will be exposed and developed in two sections and a first conclusion:

- Knowledge and innovation are key to a sustainable prosperity for mankind.
- The frontier to human prosperity depends in fact on hard and life sci-ences, as well as on innovative technologies, but also increasingly on what we shall call societal sciences, that is on social sciences and humanities, and on social innovations that can be derived from them.
- And, by way of conclusion, the responsibility of science policy and uni-versities to create the right environment to encourage social sciences and humanities to play fully the role expected of them in today's world.

THE REVOLUTION OF THE LAST 25 YEARS AND ITS CAUSES

Since World War II, and in particular during the last quarter-century, the world has experienced profound changes, which will certainly be considered as a real revolution by economic historians a few decades from now. The origin of this revolution whose impact is as important as the French political revolution at the end of the 18th and the industrial revolution in the late 18th and early 19th centuries, is to be found in the growing economic, military and scientific supremacy of the United States after World War II and accelerating scientific and technological progress, notably in information and communications technologies, as well as in life sciences. Another key factor was the progressive liberalization of world trade and the creation, in 1957, of the European Common Market, which became the European Union in 1993. The full potential of these various events was unleashed with the fall of the Berlin wall 20 years ago, and the following implosion of USSR that marked the end of the Cold War. Without any immediate impact, the slow opening of China in the early 1970s — the so-called "ping pong" diplomacy of April 1971 — that followed the catastrophic Cultural Revolution, now has immense consequences for the world. And, when examining these events, we should also keep in mind that the world's population has been growing at an increasingly faster rate since the beginning of the 19th century, increasing relatively recently by 1 billion people every 12 years to reach 6.8 billion today, whereas the first billion was reached only 200 years ago.

Today's world is not only globalized, but is the witness of the emergence of gigantic, new economic powers, mainly in Asia, but also in Latin America, which have become part of the global supply chain for services and manufacturing. One of the most important impacts of these developments is that the standard of living has increased considerably, not only in the "Old World" of Northern America, Europe, Oceania and Japan, but also in many countries in Asia, Latin America and the Arabian Peninsula. Furthermore, we are witnessing the emergence of new economic superpowers, in particular, but not only, China and India. Economic activity is moving globally and quickly, which requires the majority of world citizens to run faster in order to stay in place (Friedman, 2005). In other words, the world has become increasingly competitive: there is competition to maintain market positions and to gain new markets, to attract economic activities (industrial and services) and for cheap production locations, for cheap natural resources and energy, and for financial capital, as well as for well educated and experienced human resources (brains).

There are basically two opposite responses to competition. One is to try avoiding it by embracing a protectionist attitude at country or business levels. But there is a price to pay: the gains of trade are not fully exploited and the allocation of resources is not optimal; moreover, considering the forces of competition, such an attitude cannot last forever and the "wake-up call" might be painful. The alternative and positive attitude is on the contrary, to increase competitiveness! For firms and public organizations, this implies minimizing the cost of bringing goods and services to the potential consumers/

beneficiaries, while responding to their changing needs and taste and reacting to the supply of competitors or acting as if the competition was high. For governments and nonprofit voluntary organizations, it means creating a good environment for citizens and firms.

Knowledge creation and dissemination, as well as innovation, are keys to promoting competitiveness. Economists working on growth theory and/or human capital development have shown two important, strongly related phenomena. First, knowledge, which is embedded in human capital and created by research, has become a means of production as important as labour and capital (see for ex. Atkinson, 1983, or Psacharopoulos & Woodhall, 1985). Innovation, which is drawn more or less successfully from knowledge and the changes it implies, is the engine of growth. Second, innovation is all the more indispensable for a country the closer the country is to the "technology and organizational frontier" (Aghion & Cohen, 2004). Indeed, countries that are still far from the technology and organizational frontier can use the technologies developed in more advanced countries, whereas countries that are near the frontier are bound not only to innovate, but to push the frontier out thanks to research and better education. In other words, scientific progress and education are the best sources of new solutions to contribute to prosperity; however, it is a necessary, but not a sufficient condition for further progress, because potential advances have to be correctly implemented by business leaders and governments.

It is necessary to put scientific progress and its applications, technological or other, into perspective. They have indeed contributed to many good changes, but also to negative ones, and also to changes that appear difficult to categorize as either good and bad, notably as this might depend on the utilization made or even the point of view of the observer. Among the positive aspects, we note the rapid increase of the global standard of living and development of many traditionally underdeveloped countries. Moreover, knowledge societies mean better education, more interesting jobs, longer lifespans, less vulnerability to illness and poverty and a more enriching societal environment.

However, economic development, combined with a fast-growing population, has in particular provoked an over-utilization of non-renewable resources and has serious environmental consequences. It has also increased the income disparity between rich and poor countries and between individuals within countries. One cannot avoid also reflecting on the absurd contrast between the consumption pattern of the well-off in rich countries and those of the poor, in poor as well as in rich countries. No doubt these huge inequalities are giving birth to political instability and to terrorism. Finally, globalization is pushing firms to become global and gigantic and to be more concerned by value for shareholders than by citizens-consumers' real interest. Yet, huge firms are notably less innovative than smaller ones and are exaggeratedly driven by markets shares and profits, largely in response to the short-term requirements of financial markets.

In addition to that, even if it not necessarily a direct cause of economic development and of globalization, the world is suffering from many problems for which there are no apparent solutions or which are even deteriorating further. There are still many dictatorial and corrupt or unstable political regimes (mainly, but not only, in Africa), some of them posing a threat (e.g. North Korea), local tensions and wars (e.g. in the Middle East). Intercultural-ethnic-religious tensions are also growing, which are the source of great misunderstanding and of open or hidden conflicts, and this can also give additional roots to terrorism. Hunger is far from being eliminated and could even spread further. Pure water, as well as agricultural land, is becoming scarce, or is even used to cultivate cereals for producing alternative fuels to oil. Many chronic diseases like malaria are far from being eradicated and viruses are dangerously mutating, increasing the fear of a devastating pandemic. On the education front, even today many youngsters do not have access to basic schooling, let alone professional or tertiary education.

Last, but not least, the emergence of new economic powers is contributing very strongly to a displacement of the production of goods and services from developed countries to low salary countries with a high reservoir of workers (East Europe, China and India, Brazil and others). But, most importantly, many of these countries do not restrict themselves to producing low tech — low-quality products with a technology borrowed from developed countries — but invest heavily in human capital in order to be able to innovate, contrary to what was considered the right policy not very long ago. Considering the size of their populations, their eagerness to increase their standard of living and their capacity for change, it is understandable that the old world is worried about its own competitiveness, all the more so as its populations is ageing and about to diminish and given that their well developed social security systems are not only costly, but also reducing the willingness to work and to invest — on the whole impeding economic dynamism. Following Paul Kennedy (1989), one can even wonder if the old world is not going to lose its knowledge and economic supremacies in the quarter-century to come.

THE FINANCIAL AND ECONOMIC CRISIS

The above developments were focused at the trend over many decades. But today, most if not all the attention is focused on the financial and economic crisis that is deeply affecting the whole world. The banking (and insurance) system has suffered a destruction of capital estimated by the *Economist* (2009) at three trillion dollars, due to wrong economic policies, insufficient regulation and exaggerated usage of new financial products and the cupidity of a few thousand bankers, financiers and traders who had lost their sense of reality and ethical values. Inevitably, the destruction of wealth and reduction of income in the financial sector have directly affected the real economy. Industrial production and international trade diminished dramatically in the last quarter of 2008 and first quarter of 2009, contributing to the generalization of the crisis. This extraordinary situation condemned central banks and governments to take strong and extraordinary measures to save what could still be saved in the financial sector, to provide huge amounts of liquidity to respond to some of the absolute basic borrowing requirements of the economy, to support other sectors of the economy on the edge of collapsing, in particular the U.S. car industry, and to compensate for the insufficient private demand to avoid a terrible surge of unemployment and enterprise failures.

Policy-makers in central banks and governments benefited greatly from macroeconomic theories developed since the 1930s and implemented Keynesian and monetary instruments with a scope and intensity that were unimaginable a year before. Thanks to these measures, the heavyweight countries that have a real impact on the world economy, in particular the United States, the United Kingdom and China, prevented the collapse of the world economy. Today, the free fall of the economy has been stopped and there are signs of a timid recovery. But what the situation will be in six months, two, five or ten years is very hard to predict. In the short term, that is one to two years — the prediction capacity of econometric models has been reduced because they are based on a econometric representation of the economy over the past 20 years or more, which obviously does not include such a deep crisis. Moreover, the crisis was so serious and the measures so dramatic that we can expect that it will take a couple of years before the world economy finds itself again in a situation that can be considered normal. Probably the biggest challenge ahead will be to reduce the exploding budget deficit (expected to reach 12-13% of GNP in the United States and United Kingdom in 2009) and to control the upsurge of public debt. In the worst case, a few traditionally fragile countries could default unless supported by the IMF or other organizations. And a country like the United States, which is far too big to be supported, will have to pay very attractive interest rates to convince its traditional creditor countries, China and Japan, to continue buying state bonds. Moreover, almost all other countries will have to decrease expenditures and increases taxes. This will contribute to slowing down the recovery, not to speak of the negative consequences of reduced public expenditures. Many observers also believe that the dollar will fall as creditor countries will increasingly diversify their holdings in favour of other currencies and because, for the United States, it is an attractive policy to increase competitiveness and decrease the real value of the debt. And, if by any chance, the recovery is stronger than expected, there is also a risk that demand exceeds potential output, which would induce inflationary pressures. The policies implemented by the central banks are raising similar threats: higher inflation is unavoidable if they do not withdraw a large part of the additional liquidities they put into the system or if they continue to conduct a policy of cheap money.

OLD VS. NEW WORLDS

Last but not least, it is time to differentiate the long-term developments between different regions of the world, more precisely to look at the specific situation of the old world facing the emergence of new gigantic economic powers. Indeed, the old world is increasingly challenged, not to say threatened, by the emerging countries that not only have a competitive hedge to produce low technology products thanks to their immense reservoir of cheap labour, but are increasingly capable of innovating and producing high-tech products thanks to a huge effort in education and research. More and more countries are realizing that the "Chinese" model, characterized by a voluntary effort to develop a knowledge society thanks to huge investments in education and research on top of an abundant and relatively cheap labour force, is paying dividends. This strategy of forcing the development of the knowledge society, although the country could satisfy itself in taking advantage of great masses of still cheap labour, is now being imitated by many other countries in Asia, as well as in Latin America and in some Arabic countries. In other words, these countries are imitating the occidental model of good education and research that contributed so much to the prosperity of North America and Europe. This is also the same old world that promoted free trade for industrial products and which is now faced with the fact that most of the mass industrial production has deserted their lands. Economists have always agreed that these changes of structure are part of the growth process, but originally, these changes would take place within the country (jobs lost in one industry were replaced by jobs created in another industry in the same country). But, today, the new jobs are created in neighbouring countries and most often in another part of the world. The old world is condemned to produce very sophisticated or exclusive (luxuries) industrial products and to develop the service industries like banking, insurance, trading, consultancy, where it has still a competitive hedge.

THE IMPORTANCE AND SCOPE OF INNOVATION

As observed above, knowledge creation and dissemination, as well as innovation, are playing a key role in the wide-ranging revolution that is deeply transforming the world. In particular, it explains why the development of countries like China and India is so rapid and why the old world, with its decreasing, ageing and well paid population, must more than ever count on knowledge and innovation to secure its high standard of living. We believe that the sudden and deep financial and economic crises will not modify the situation. On the contrary, the fight to keep the economy moving and very soon to absorb the long-term negative consequences of all the strong measures that have been taken will even reinforce the pressures to develop new knowledge and innovation. More than that, some aspect of the roots of the crisis will — or at least should — be the object of deep reforms; the post-crisis era should give a much greater importance to government regulation and to the respect of professional and ethical values; moreover, stakeholder value should be an objective for firms as important as shareholders' value. This is in particular the aim of the United Nations Global Compact about Corporate Citizenship in the World Economy. The ultimate aim should be to promote **global sustainability**, that is a development that can last economically, politically, socially and environmentally (Weber, 2008) and in which the citizen-consumer is the ultimate aim of economic activity, the producer being only a means to this end.

The number of objects that deserve great attention if one is really concerned with improving the state of the world is impressive. The World Economic Forum has recently worked on it by setting up approximately 70 councils of experts to address the most important challenges facing the world in a collaborative and integrated way (WEF, 2009). These councils debated two questions: what is the state of the world on a specific issue? and what needs to be done to improve the state of the world on a specific issue? The non-exhaustive list of objects is: alternative energies, challenges of gerontology, chronic diseases and malnutrition, climate change, corporate governance, corruption, demographic shifts, economic imbalances, ecosystems and biodiversity loss, energy security, faith, food security, fragile states, future of transportation, gender gap, global governance, global trade regime, healthcare systems, HIV/AIDS, human equality and respect, illicit trade, international legal system, migration, negotiations and conflict resolution, pandemics, role of sport in society, skills gap, social entrepreneurship, systemic financial risk, terrorism, proliferation and weapons of mass destruction, urban management, water security...

This list speaks for itself: as argued before, improving the state of the world requires as much policies inspired by the social sciences and humanities — that we suggest calling societal sciences — as policies drawn from hard and life sciences [1]. As noted before, most of the economic development of the past quarter-century came through innovation in industry and a couple of services.

---

1 We observe that some purist English-speaking scientists like to reserve the word "science" for hard and life sciences.

Considering that many societal problems were neglected before the crisis, our conviction is that it would be essential today to broaden the search for new knowledge and innovation in order to contribute to solving these societal questions. In short, knowledge creation and dissemination, as well as innovation, should be all-inclusive to promote the long-term prosperity of nations, developed and developing. All the traditional scientific disciplines are concerned, but the place that has to be occupied by social sciences and humanities like economics, law, sociology, political sciences, history, philosophy, religious sciences, linguistics and their derived disciplines like anthropology, comparative literature, business should play a much bigger role.

As for scientific progress, innovation requires a capacity for change. This implies that government, public administration, board and management of firms, the leadership and stakeholders of other organizations, national or international, as well as individual citizens, are willing to change and/or have the capacity to convince or impose a decision on their organization. As for innovation in science and technology, innovation in societal sciences seems to be less painful in the United States than in Europe and Asia. Even if we cannot draw a generalization from a specific case, the way the federal government and Federal Reserve Board decided to implement totally new instruments to fight the crisis is certainly worth noting.

This increased expected role of societal sciences raises the serious question of the development and reputation of soft sciences vis-a-vis hard sciences. Universities with a high reputation are exclusively or in majority active in life sciences, medicine, applied and fundamental sciences. The size of their budget is determined by that specialization, and rankings of world universities are clearly biased in favour of those institutions. All this would be acceptable if it did not draw the other disciplines down. There is even a widespread fear that some of these soft disciplines are too critical of the establishment.

Societal sciences are not "cheap" (scientific) disciplines. The matter they are studying is quite different from the world of nature, but also immensely complex, among others because the human factor plays a key role. Indeed, human beings are making decisions on the basis of incomplete information and do not always act rationally; therefore, human behaviour is often difficult to predict. Knowledge is also strongly based on scholarship (erudition) and in general less formalized into universal theories; it is also often regional. Moreover, social sciences are sensitive to philosophical ideas and political positions. This explains why there is much more room for diverging positions and burgeoning ideas. However, the diversity of opinion in social sciences and humanities is real wealth. The brutal realization last year that markets do not always self-regulate is a strong example. In other words, any *pensée unique* is bound to perish some day, as it impoverishes itself in refusing to take into account critics and alternative proposals.

BY WAY OF CONCLUSION: CONSEQUENCES
FOR SCIENCE POLICY AND UNIVERSITIES

Inspired by economics and social sciences, this contribution can be summarized with two strong statements. First, globalization and the climate of increasing competition over the last quarter-century, as well as the severe financial and economic crisis, demand more innovation for rich countries to keep a high standard of living or for emerging countries to continue developing. The incapacity of approximately half the countries of the world to succeed in taking off should be a concern for all developed and developing countries. Second, scientific and technological innovation are indeed a key pillar to economic prosperity in the old world and emerging countries; but it is far from sufficient; at least three sets of problems or difficulties require a much greater investment in societal innovation: the rapid expansion of recent decades is not sustainable for ever due to the overexploitation of natural resources and of the environment; too many countries are left out of prosperity, cannot satisfy all their basic needs and are particularly suffering from instability and conflicts; finally, many manmade political, economic and social systems are not sustainable. The financial and economic crisis is just one example of what eventually happens if one does not pay enough attention to the sustainability of a system and/or of its development, not to speak about the rise of Nazism in Germany in the 1930s rooted in the preceding very severe economic crisis. Obviously, if science and technology can contribute to responding to many of these challenges, societal sciences, that is social sciences and humanities, also have a very important role to play.

This role to be played by societal sciences should be of direct concern to universities and those responsible for science policy. Indeed, it is already partly the case, but more could and should be done. In other words, we make a plea that the development of social sciences and humanities should be a priority of science policy and university institutions. As other contributions in this book are more directly focused on the role of universities, we shall remain very brief.

As is the case for science and technology, social sciences and humanities have a great record of seminal works in all sorts of subjects and their best figures are probably as well known as the best scientists. They have also contributed to developing instruments capable of solving problems. The best example today is certainly the successful intensive use made by governments and central banks of theories developed by Keynes and Friedman respectively more than 70 and 50 years ago.

The main weakness of social sciences and humanities is that their specialists are mainly working in separate disciplinary silos and according to their own curiosity and motivation. They have little incentive to spontaneously join forces with colleagues from other disciplines and too often to work on societal issues. However, we have strongly argued before that society expects today that societal sciences are more involved, when necessary with sciences and technologies, in contributing to solving societal problems. This will be possible only if one is able to better balance curiosity-driven and individual work and teamwork. We believe that soft sciences would gain in maturity if researchers increasingly work together within the limits of their discipline and, better, with other disciplines. The problems to solve are indeed multi-disciplinary. Therefore, transdisciplinary and, even better, interdisciplinary work have to be strongly promoted.

Bringing social sciences and humanities to a greater maturity should be a priority for science policy and universities, comprehensive ones or specialized in social sciences. This important objective should be pursued essentially with measures of a financial and organizational nature. Regarding finance, social sciences and humanities should be better funded in money terms and the funding programs should entail the right incentives to encourage the specialists to work together both on curiosity-driven projects and societal questions.

The organizational question is more at the level of institutions. They should in particular launch long-term research projects or create temporary ad hoc research centres to give researchers the opportunity to spend some of their time with researchers from other disciplines in order to slowly develop the pleasure of working on broader topics and the right "savoir-faire". Universities should also envisage adapting their organizational structure to lower the existing barriers between faculties or departments; the ultimate aim is to create a flatter organization with less compartments. This requires clearly strong steering by the leadership of the institution, with the support of adequate committees. To facilitate restructuring, financial incentives to change appears often as more efficient than moral suasion.

To conclude with this brief description of the measures that should be taken to increase the contribution of societal sciences to sustainable development and to solve societal problems, we would like to mention two additional points. First, regarding technological innovation, progress towards a better societal organization requires a broad partnership between universities, governments, business and other organizations concerned. Even if this seems obvious, there is even a much bigger effort to make in this respect than for technological innovation.

Second, but not least, Europe, Asia and Latin America should grant more autonomy to their universities. The world rankings of universities show unambiguously that the immense majority of the best performing institutions are also those that enjoy the greatest autonomy. In other words, there is strong correlation between the degree of autonomy and performance (Aghion *et al*, 2009). And, contrary to what might be thought at first view, autonomous universities are those that are the most responsible and responsive towards society as the system of rewards and sanctions ensure that they have to be accountable to their sponsors, the State, their students, donors and partners. With little or no autonomy, institutions are placed in a vicious circle that condemns them to wait for instructions and to take as few initiatives as possible.

REFERENCES

Aghion, P. & Cohen, E. (2004). *Education et croissance*, La Documentation française, Paris.

Aghoin, P. *et al.* (2007). "Why Reform Europe's Universities?", Bruegelpolicybrief Nb. 4 (Sept), Brussels.

Aghion, P. *et al.* (2008). Higher aspirations: An agenda for reforming European Universities, Bruegel Blueprint Nb. 5, Brussels.

Aghion, P. *et al.* (2009). The Governance and Performance of Research Universities: Evidence from Europe and the U.S., National Bureau of Economic Research, Cambridge.

Atkinson, G. B. J. (1983). *The Economics of Education*, Hodder and Stoughton, London.

Friedman, T. L. (2005). *The World is Flat, A Brief History of the Twenty-first Century*, Farrar, Straus and Giroux, New York.

Gourley, B. (2008). *Real World, real People: a Purpose beyond ourselves in the 21st century*, IAU 13th General Conference, Utrecht. http://www.unesco.org/iau/conferences/Utrecht/presentations/Gourley.pdf

Huntington, S. P. (1996). *The Clash of Civilizations and the Remaking of the World Order*, Simon & Schuster, London.

IMD. (2008). *IMD World competitiveness yearbook*, Institute for Management Development, Lausanne.

Johnson, W. (2008). *Higher Education and Innovation: The Good, The Bad, and the Unknown — An Industry Perspective*, IAU 13th General Conference Utrecht. http://www.unesco.org/iau/conferences/Utrecht/presentations/Johnson.pdf

Kennedy, P. (1989). *The Rise and Fall of the Great Powers*, Vintage, New York.

Porter, M. E. & Schwab, K. (eds). (2008). *The Global Competitiveness Report 2008-2009*. World Economic Forum, Geneva.

Lambert, R. & Butler, N. (2006). *The Future of European Universities, Renaissance or decay?* Centre for European Reform.

Madison, M. (2001). *L'économie mondiale, une perspective millénaire*, Etudes du Centre de Développement, OCDE, Paris.

Mustar, P. & Penan, H. (2003). *Encyclopédie de l'innovation*, Economica, Paris

OECD (2008). *Education at a Glance 2008*, OECD Indicators, Paris.

Psacharopoulos, G. & Woodhall, M. (1985). *Education for Development, An Analysis of Investment Choices*, A World Bank Publication, Oxford University Press.

The Economist (2009). "Rebuilding the Banks", 16 May.

The World Bank (2002). *Constructing Knowledge Societies: New Challenges for Tertiary Education*, Directions in Development, the World Bank, Washington D.C.

The World Bank (2008). *World Development Indicators*, the World Bank, Washington D.C.

United Nations Global Compact: Corporate Citizenship in the World Economy. (2000) http://www.unglobalcompact.org

Weber, L. (2008). "The Responsibility of Universities to promote a sustainable society" in chap. 20 (pp. 229-243) Weber & Duderstadt (eds), *The Globalization of Higher Education*, Glion colloquium Series, Economica, London, Paris, Geneva.

World Economic Forum (2008). *The Global Agenda 2009*, Geneva. http://www.weforum.org/pdf/globalagenda.pdf

CHATER

Technological Innovation in the 21st Century

Charles M. Vest

THE INNOVATION IMPERATIVE

The early years of the 21st century have found the U.S., Europe and Asia increasingly committed to technology-based innovation as the road to economic prosperity. Every CEO has had a catchphrase to this effect on his or her tongue. Etsuhiko Shoyama of Hitachi says "Ceaselessly Innovate", and Sam Palmisano of IBM says "Innovate or Abdicate".

Many speakers and observers have quoted a poem attributed to Richard Hodgetts:

> *Every morning in Africa a gazelle wakes up.*
> *It knows it must outrun the fastest lion or it*
> *Will be killed.*
> *Every morning in Africa a lion wakes up.*
> *It knows it must outrun the slowest gazelle*
> *Or it will starve.*
> *It doesn't matter whether you are a lion or a*
> *Gazelle — when the sun comes up, you'd*
> *Better be running.*

Now all of this connotes that the world is in a hurry, and for good reason when it comes to technology, its development, marketing, acceptance, and economic and social impact. After the automobile was introduced as a consumer product in the early part of the 20th century, it took 55 years to create and penetrate markets such that 25% of the U.S. population had one in their household. In those days, 55 years was essentially a lifetime. Another society-changing consumer innovation was the telephone. It took 35 years to reach

25% of the U.S. population, and 35 years was essentially a working lifetime. By the time the personal computer came along, it took about 16 years until 25% of the U.S. population had one, and it took only 8 years for the World Wide Web to achieve this penetration (Council on Competitiveness, 2005).

So when we say that the impact of technology is accelerating, we are speaking truth. But the key word here is "impact". The automobile, telephone, personal computer and World Wide Web are prime examples of world-changing, empowering technologies that drove economic advancement. There also is an interesting evolution from the automobile that initially had its primary impact in the United States to the World Wide Web that had almost instantaneous *global* impact. The clear progression is from national and slow to global and fast. Furthermore, there also is a distinct path from big and mechanical to small and electronic.

These observations get to the heart of the innovation imperative. From the perspective of a company or an industry, the implications are very clear. Most companies set goals such as 20-40% of their business to come from products developed in the last two or three years. The specific goal and speed of introduction naturally depend on the product sector. The stakes are high: fall behind in innovations that continuously improve your product or expand your product range, and you are out of business.

But there is a deeper level of importance to innovation and speed. When I was a graduate student in about 1965, one of my friends was studying for a Ph.D. in electrical engineering. One day his professor said to him: "I think that in the future, telecommunications and computing are going to merge somehow. You should think about this." When you read this, please put your mind in the frame of 1965, and you will see that this was a radical prediction. My friend took that advice and he is a very successful person today.

In other words, combining telecommunications and computing was not just an incremental improvement, it was the deeper kind of innovation — one that changed society by empowering and enabling all manner of things. Fast forward to today; our world is under enormous financial stress. As we move beyond this crisis, we must rebuild an economy based on the production of real goods and services that are of real value. The Holy Grail we seek is the next major enabling and empowering technology — the 21st century equivalent of Information Technology. Somewhere the spark of this innovation is forming in someone's mind. Innovation is the process by which it will be developed, made real, and brought to the marketplace. I have no idea what the next major enabling technology will be or where it will be spawned, but there are some things we can learn about the environment that may encourage its development.

To initiate an exploration of innovation's future, let me suggest four facts, three consequences, and one principle. I will add to this list an irony.

The four facts are: People everywhere in the world are smart and capable; science and technology advance relentlessly; globalization is a dominating reality; and the Internet and World Wide Web are democratizing forces.

The three consequences are: Individuals must innovate; companies must innovate; and nations and regions must innovate.

The principle is: competition drives excellence and innovation.

And finally, the irony is that in the 21st century cooperation and competition reinforce each other.

THE U.S. INNOVATION SYSTEM 1945-2009: A BRIEF HISTORY

There is value in understanding where we have come from, as long as we don't assume that what worked in the past will, without modification or replacement, work in the future. With that caveat, let me trace the outline of America's innovation system since World War II. During most of this period, the U.S. had a comparative advantage because it developed a strong S&T base and coupled it to a free-market economy that was in turn built on a base of democracy in a diverse society. But there also was a clear policy basis that enabled scientific and technological advancements.

In November 1944, President Franklin Roosevelt wrote a letter to Vannevar Bush, who was then on leave from MIT serving as head of the Office of Scientific Research and Development (OSRD). His role was to mobilize U.S. science and industry to serve the war effort. In his letter, Roosevelt stated that U.S. science had contributed mightily to a pending Allied victory. He then asked Bush to form a committee and tell him how the U.S. science community could work in peacetime to secure the nation's economic vitality, health and security, just as it had advanced national interests in the war. Nine months later, Bush submitted his now famous report, *Science — the Endless Frontier* (Bush, 1945). This report made four fundamental recommendations:

1. Universities should be the primary national infrastructure for doing basic research;
2. Federal dollars supporting university research should do double duty by procuring research results and simultaneously supporting the education of the next generation of engineers, scientists and doctors;
3. Research grants should be awarded to university investigators on the basis of technical and intellectual merit; and
4. A National Science Foundation should be established to further these ends.

The Bush recommendations may be "old hat" today, but this was a profound and rather radical vision at the time. However, as we look at this from the vantage point of the early 21st century, we should note two implicit assumptions about economic development. The Bush model is *linear* and *laissez-faire*. It is linear in that it more or less assumes that there is a straightforward progression from basic research to applied research to product development and then to the marketing of goods and services. Basic research would be done in universities. Applied research would be done in some mix of universities and industry. Product development and marketing would be the sole province of industry. It was *laissez-faire* in the sense that it assumed that industry would scan the research results from universities, select the important results and then commercialize them as products or services. Neither government nor industry would be expected to select research topics or guide research programs.

What emerged from the Bush approach was the U.S. Innovation System that created new knowledge and technology through research, educated young men and women to understand and create this new knowledge and technology, and moved it to market as new products, processes and services. This system was an enormous success from any perspective. Economists generally believe that about half of U.S. economic growth since the War was due to technological innovation, much of which originated in research universities.

During the period from 1945 to roughly 1985, America's public and private research universities grew to excel and set the world standard. American companies dominated many product domains. Large corporations were dominant, especially those based on mass production. Many large companies also developed outstanding central research laboratories that attracted outstanding university graduates, conducted outstanding pure and applied research, and contributed to the "S&T commons" through the technical literature and professional meetings. Then two tectonic shifts occurred in the 1980s and, 90s.

Suddenly, Japanese companies dominated the consumer-manufacturing sector, and U.S. companies could not effectively compete with them. Japanese advances in quality, throughput and product cycle times were astonishing. Indeed, the Japanese Total Quality Movement was the major innovation in the world in the 1980s. It changed everything. It is important to note that this was not a purely technological innovation; rather, it was about organization, discipline, quantitative and statistical approaches, and social motivation.

U.S. and European corporations responded through painful, fundamental and permanent transformations. Downsizing, process management and quality control became central. But most relevant to this history of innovation, corporate R&D was dramatically changed and merged with product development. Many companies emerged strong and globally competitive, but the U.S. Innovation System had changed.

During the latter stages of this transformation, a second tectonic change occurred; in some sense it happened just in time. Namely, American entrepreneurship expanded explosively, driven by information technology made possible by the microprocessor revolution and the Internet. The rapid advance of biotechnology also played a major role.

The broad thrust of U.S. corporate innovation and R&D seems to have changed on a decadal time scale. The 1970s was the golden age of central corporate research laboratories. Absorbing and transforming R&D into product development dominated the 1980s, as already mentioned. In the 1990s, companies became concerned that although they were now competitive and adept at incremental improvement, they were not generating sufficient amounts of basic innovation, so they began to acquire it by purchasing high-tech start-up companies that often had been spawned by research universities. In the first decade of the 21st century, a more globally integrated open innovation system began to form. The linear model implicit in the Bush vision was breaking down and being replaced by a more complex, faster, nonlinear regime.

There was a similar decadal evolution of university research and education that paralleled this. The 1970s was the golden age of the "engineering science revolution", an approach that emerged largely from the wartime work at MIT's Radiation Laboratory and the Manhattan Project. A base of science supported a new way of teaching and practising engineering. This movement from engineering as an empirical, "handbook" activity to one based on design and development from first scientific principles was essential to the new "high technology" world. In the 1980s, many universities began to respond to the manufacturing crisis by moving design, manufacturing, and computer science to centre stage, and by introducing joint management/engineering programs. The 1990s saw an explosion of university emphasis on life sciences, more interdisciplinary work, and more direct engagement in use-inspired research and commercialization. This continued into the early 21st century.

The nature of the challenges facing humankind in the early 21st century will lead, as has been noted, to more use-inspired research in universities. A word about this concept is in order. One of the great technological achievements of the 20th century was the development of the transistor at Bell Labs. Bell Labs in those days had one of the most impressive staffs of engineers and physical scientists ever assembled. They made many contributions to the basic understanding of the physical world. The technical staff had much opportunity to think and explore important problems and to publish their work in the open literature. Because of this flexible and open environment, an "urban legend" has grown up that the transistor resulted from unfettered basic research. The fact is that it was the result of a carefully planned and executed R&D program. The people who contributed to it were often doing very basic work, but there was a specific goal of creating a solid state device to replace the vacuum tube. This is a prime example of use-inspired basic research.

In 1997, the late Donald Stokes of Princeton University explored how the flow of knowledge to product had changed from the linear, *laissez-faire* approach of Vannevar Bush's *Science — the Endless Frontier* (Stokes, 1997). He found a very useful framework to help answer this question: a two-dimensional plot in which the vertical axis displays the answer to the question: "Is the research motivated by the quest for fundamental understanding of the natural world?" and the horizontal axis displays the answer to the question: "Is the research motivated by consideration of use of the results?" Stokes thereby referred to pure basic research as residing in the "Bohr Quadrant" because it is motivated only by the desire to understand nature. He considered research to reside in the "Edison Quadrant" if only a practical result is sought. The "Pasteur Quadrant" contains research that has the dual motivation of increasing fundamental knowledge and being driven toward a practical application. This, of course, refers to Louis Pasteur's seminal scientific work that developed fundamental knowledge of microbiology in order to reduce disease.

Many of the challenges we face today regarding energy, climate, sustainability, clean water, food, medicine and healthcare must both advance the state of knowledge of physical and biological science, but also drive toward technological solutions. Indeed, the term *technological innovation* refers to an extension of use-inspired research; it is an activity that either discovers or designs new technologies and systems and moves them along a pathway to practical applications or introduction to the marketplace.

INNOVATION AND GLOBALIZATION

Most observers seem to agree that innovation is the key to many advances in human welfare, and certainly to economic vitality. For much of modern history, innovation was largely a local or national activity, building or improving factories, distribution systems and businesses. Indeed, prior to World War II nations prospered largely on the basis of geography, natural resources, capable labourers and military might. This local or national centricity has long since passed from the scene in most developed nations. There are many reasons for this, but among them certainly are the roles of inexpensive long-distance travel and shipping, the global flow of information via the Internet and World Wide Web, and the geographic spread of talent and knowledge generation. From the business perspective, labour costs, intellectual property policy and especially tax policy should be added to these factors. The whole innovation scene is changing rapidly and is not well understood, but its relentless globalization is very clear.

Two indispensable input variables for innovation are a workforce well educated in engineering and science and expenditures on R&D. These are not sufficient conditions, but certainly are necessary. Even a cursory look at the available data indicates that the distribution of engineering and science degrees around the world has changed dramatically during the last two decades. The headline indicator is the rise of engineers educated in China, and across Asia in general. For examples, in 1983, the U.S., Japan and China each graduated approximately 75,000 bachelor-level engineers. By 2002, the U.S. production of bachelor-level engineers dropped to about 60,000 while the production in Japan rose to 100,000 engineers, and the production in China rose to 250,000. The trend can be expressed in an even more meaningful way by the fact that today about 4.5% of U.S. college and university graduates earn degrees in engineering, about 12% of European university graduates are engineers, and across Asia about 20% are engineering majors (National Science Foundation, 2008). This is a colossal redistribution of the talent base required for innovation.

There has been a similar rapid shift in the global distribution of R&D expenditures by both government and industry. The fact is that the total annual expenditures on R&D are now spread almost evenly around the developed world, with about one third each in North America, Europe, and Asia.

This spread of the potential for innovation has been amplified by the deployment of the Internet and the World Wide Web. As Thomas Friedman famously wrote: "The world is flat," and globalization has "accidentally made Beijing, Bangalore and Bethesda next-door neighbors," with many jobs being "just a mouse click away". (Friedman, 2006). Although Friedman's analysis woke many from their lethargy about the modern world, this is only part of the story, although a very important part. Others have argued that it is not true that location no longer matters, because the power of regional innovation clusters such as Silicon Valley and Route 128 is still important. These local clusters often are enabled by the proximity of small companies and corporate laboratories to research-intensive universities.

The quest to understand the evolution and probable future course of innovation has spawned considerable scholarly study and publication during the last several years. Henry Chesborough, then at the Harvard Business School and now at the University of California at Berkeley, introduced the term *open innovation* to characterize what goes on in most large companies today, i.e. to be competitive they must integrate the best ideas no matter where they originate, in other countries, in other companies or laboratories, and often even in competing organizations. This is part, but not all of the reason that corporations are opening R&D laboratories in many different countries to be close to and able to tap into organizations worldwide (Chesborough, 2006). And every industry works day-to-day in fear of not recognizing and grasping "disruptive technologies", the game-changing ideas and technologies that Clayton Christensen has so clearly expounded in his 1997 book, *The Innovators Dilemma* (Christensen, 1997).

Related ideas are developed in John Hagel and John Seeley Brown's analysis, *The Only Sustainable Edge*, although they place great emphasis on the development of deep disciplinary capabilities within corporations as well as good connectivity with other companies and organizations. They also point to the need for constant learning across networked enterprises (Hagel & Seely Brown, 2005). I also note the research of Michael Piore and Richard Lester, which points out two important institutional capabilities, *analysis* and *interpretation*. In this context, *analysis* refers to the ability to form a rational, discrete, quantitative basis for decisions. This is essential for innovative product development and productivity gains. But they find that interpretation is the heart of true innovation. Here *interpretation* encompasses exploiting ambiguity, imagining alternative pathways and endpoints, and the creative removal of constraints (Piore & Lester, 2004).

Judy Estrin, former Chief Technical Officer of Cisco and highly successful entrepreneur, has recently assessed the *innovation ecosystem* of the United States and concluded that there are numerous indications that it is declining. She finds an increasing focus on the near term and an attenuation of free-spirited openness that defined America. Her analysis delineates the nature and characteristics of organizations and leaders that innovate well. She urges a return to long-term, adventurous perspectives that can enable technology and business to interact to produce and market new goods and services in the global economy (Estrin, 2009).

The public perception of innovation is often focused on small, flashy IT-related technologies or web tools. However, as implied in the preceding discussion, innovation is necessary at all scales. In the United States and elsewhere, we are faced with a need to innovate on a massive scale to deal with the production, storage and distribution of electrical energy. This is a very complex problem because of the variety of technologies that need to be improved, eliminated or discovered, and because of the scale of deployment and infrastructure required. One must add to this the huge corporate investments in existing infrastructure and the major role that must be played by government policy and investment at the federal, state and local levels. Some have called for a national technology roadmap to the next generation energy system. But, in my view, this problem is too large and complex, and too rich in opportunities for new game-changing discoveries and developments, to begin mapping a detailed technology pathway. Weiss and Bonvillian have recently written a book, *Structuring an Energy Technology Revolution*, in which they propose a roadmap not directly to specific technologies, but rather a roadmap for innovation that recognizes both the uncharted nature of technology and the government roles in policy-making and research (Weiss & Bonvillian, 2009).

Finally, it is clear that a variety of modes of global cooperation will be needed to address innovation associated with energy. The fundamental reasons are that the geopolitical stakes in energy resources and distribution are extremely high, and that the underlying issues of climate change and sustainability are global.

INNOVATION: WHAT IS NEXT?

As noted above, the core of the industrial innovation system in the U.S. has changed substantially about every decade. In the 1970s, central corporate research laboratories dominated; in the 1980s, corporate R&D was transformed and absorbed into a new style of product development in response to the challenge of Japanese consumer manufacturing; in the 1990s, large companies acquired innovation by buying start-up companies often spun out from research universities; and in the early 2000s, open innovation has begun to play a major role.

Several things suggest that we may see another shift in the U.S. innovation system:

1. The scientific basis of new technologies will increasingly come from the life sciences and information technology;
2. Macro-scale systems challenges, especially energy, will drive innovation in the coming decade;
3. Some believe that the venture capital system is becoming too risk averse and may not be appropriate to the large-scale issues that badly need innovation;
4. Globalization of R&D investments, education and high-quality workforce will continue apace;
5. Economic growth probably requires a new enabling technology to play a role analogous to that played by IT and the World Wide Web during the last decade; and
6. We will need some truly transformative breakthroughs and disruptive new technologies in order to address many of the global grand challenges such as energy, healthcare and security.

I do not know what the future actually holds, but I will briefly address four factors that may be involved in the next stage of innovation: evolution of the current system, education, prizes, and large-scale web interaction.

There is an almost universal movement to improve education in science, mathematics and engineering at the primary and secondary level. Asian countries in particular have set contemporary standards in this regard in order to strengthen the base for technology, innovation and 21st-century economic competition. It is likely that information technology also will play a role in increasing the knowledge base, reasoning abilities and scientific skill sets of young people. But innovation requires more than this important base; it requires abilities of imagination, synthesis, open-ended problem solving, and the elusive quality of creativity.

Much of future innovation in the U.S. context will likely continue to be carried out through the informal and loosely coupled system of universities, companies and governments that has dominated since the end of World War II. But this system may be augmented or readjusted to tackle large-scale 21st century challenges. For example, a 2004 U.S. National Academy of Engineering report chaired by James Duderstadt suggested the formation of a set of *Discovery Innovation Institutes* to be located on the campuses of research-intensive universities (National Academy of Engineering, 2005). They would be intended to conduct engineering research and innovation at a larger scale than is typical for universities today and that would have direct linkages and responsibility to industries. These continuous linkages to relevant industries would provide guidance to use-inspired research and would increase the efficiency and effectiveness of movement of new ideas, discoveries and technologies into the commercial sector. Such institutes would be especially suitable to complex, large-scale and long-lived challenges such as energy.

In higher education there are many experiments underway to foster and enhance innovation capacity and new modes of thought. *Olin College of Engineering*, outside Boston, has operated now for seven years with a nontraditional, design-oriented curriculum and an organizational structure without the usual disciplines. Finland is constructing an entire new, large-scale institution, *Aalto University*, which will combine technology, economics, and art and design. It will be established in 2010 by merging programs from three existing universities, but it will afford an opportunity to rethink and reformat curricula and build a community of scholars with a new collective perspective. Singapore is establishing a new university in partnership with MIT that will also be focused heavily on science, engineering, information systems and architecture with a special emphasis on the role of design, broadly defined. Opening in 2011, it is explicitly intended to be part of a new ecosystem for producing innovations and new products.

In California, *Singularity University* is the working name of a joint effort by NASA, Google and several leading thinkers such as Ray Kurzweil to bring together students from the emerging disciplines of nanotechnology, biotechnology, and information technology. The purpose will be to cross educate them in these fields and prepare them to attack the great challenges of our times. The working name is an allusion to Kurzweil's theories expounded in his book, *The Singularity is Near* (Kurzweil, 2005). The hypothesis of this book is that many new technologies will follow exponential growth models like the well-known Moore's Law, and therefore change far more rapidly and transformatively than our traditionally linear thinking leads us to expect, thereby rapidly giving us the tools to solve huge societal problems. Whether or not this somewhat Utopian view is correct, this approach will provide a rich tool set and experience base for 21st-century innovators.

Another intriguing attempt to unstick the innovation system to achieve large goals is the work of the X-Prize Foundation. In 1996, the Foundation offered the $10 million Ansari X-Prize to the first private, i.e. non-governmental, group to achieve human space flight, rigorously defined. This prize was won in 2004 by *SpaceShipOne* designed by Burt Rutan and financed by Paul Allen. But the point here is that not only was the goal achieved, but the financial prize money was highly leveraged by the various competing groups, thereby accelerating investment of both financial and intellectual resources to push technology forward.

The X-Prize Foundation, chaired by Peter Diamandis, is expanding this concept to several other areas of technological challenge that require levels of innovation that do not appear to be forthcoming from the usual industrial or governmental systems. Their goal is to spur innovation to solve problems and leverage financial and intellectual resources of contest entrants to move technology forward. The best known of their extant programs is the Progressive Automotive X-Prize to build an automobile that achieves 100 mpg or equivalent. The prize-winning automobile must pass all U.S. highway safety standards, carry four passengers, have an acceptable manufacturing plan and have consumer appeal. 111 entrants have qualified for the competition.

There are many emerging, web-based platforms for developing and using the collective input of large numbers of people to forge new ideas, solve problems and, in a broad sense, innovate. An obvious example is *Wikipedia*, and the creation of many special purpose wikis following its example. The U.S. intelligence community has even applied this new collective tool to the production of intelligence estimates. *Roseta.org* is a website that enables thousands of people around the world to play a massive computer game the real purpose of which is to use their collective brain power to solve very complex problems of protein folding and bimolecular design.

A direct use of IT to enable innovation is the IBM *InnovationJam* conducted by IBM to innovate in its organization and product line. First held as a virtual discussion among its worldwide employee base, it is now conducted not only with IBM employees, but with thought leaders in many other companies and organizations. A topic is set for consideration, and participants can log into the conversation over a multi-day period. There is a rigorous process for narrowing down lines of thought and specific suggestions until a finite set of actionable recommendations is established. IBM indicates that its 2008 Jam lasted 90 hours and involved 90,000 log-ins and 32,000 posts. Participants came from 1,000 companies across 20 industries.

CONCLUSION

The U.S. Innovation System has been highly successful for over 60 years and it has been replicated in many countries around the world. This has helped fuel a global rise in economic power and quality of life. But, as a result of this globalization, the system must now be transformed in ways that are not yet clear. Such transformation is demanded by the changing base of science that supports technology, and by the scale and importance of such worldwide challenges as food, water, energy, healthcare, climate change and security. This paper has presented a sampling of the experiments and thinking that are beginning to drive transformations in national and global innovation ecosystems.

REFERENCES

Bush, V. (1945). *Science — The Endless Frontier: A Report to the President on a Program for Postwar Scientific Research.* Reprint, 1990, Washington, DC: National Science Foundation.

Chesborough, H. (2006). *Open Innovation: The New Imperative for Creating and profiting from Technology.* Boston, MA: Harvard Business School Press.

Christensen, C. M. (1997). *The Innovators Dilemma: When New Technologies Cause Great Firms to Fail.* Boston, MA: Harvard Business School Press.

Council on Competitiveness. (2005). *Innovate America: National Innovation Initiative Summit and Report.*

Estrin, J. (2009). *Closing the Innovation Gap: Reigniting the Spark of Creativity in a Global Economy.* New York: McGraw Hill.

Friedman, T. L. (2006). *The World is Flat: A Brief History of the Twenty-First Century.* New York: Farrar, Straus and Giroux.

Hagel III, J., & Brown, J. S. (2005). *The Only Sustainable Edge: Why Business Strategy Depends on Productive Friction and Dynamic Specialization.* Boston, MA: Harvard Business School Press.

Kurzweil, R. (2005). *The Singularity is Near: When Humans Transcend Biology.* New York: Viking Press.

National Academy of Engineering. (2005). *Engineering Research and America's Future: Meeting the Challenges of a Global Economy.* Washington, DC: The National Academies Press.

National Science Foundation. (2008). *Science and Engineering Indicators,* National Science Board, Washington, DC.

Piore, M. & Lester, R. K. (2004). *Innovation: The Missing Dimension.* Cambridge MA: Harvard University Press.

Stokes, D. E. (1997). *Pasteur's Quadrant: Basic Science and Technological Innovation.* Washington, DC: Brookings Institution Press.

Weiss, C. & Bonvillian, W. B. (2009). *Structuring an Energy Revolution.* Cambridge, MA: MIT Press.

CHAPTER 3

Community Engagement as Social Innovation

Ellen Hazelkorn [1]

The world needs more social innovation — and so all who aspire to solve the world's most vexing problems... must shed old patterns of isolation, paternalism and antagonism and strive to understand, embrace and leverage cross-sector dynamics to find new ways of creating social value. (Phills Jr, 2008, p. 43)

THE CHANGING GLOBAL DISCOURSE

In 1992, Francis Fukyama reflected in *The End of History and the Last Man* on the transformative events signified by the collapse of the Berlin Wall. He argued that

What we may be witnessing is not just the end of the Cold War, or the passing of a particular period of post-war history, but the end of history as such: that is, the end point of mankind's ideological evolution and the universalization of Western liberal democracy as the final form of human government.

Although he disputes this interpretation, Fukyama's (2007) arguments were widely construed as a defence of unregulated market capitalism and American strategic hegemony. Coupled with rampant global economic growth during what became known as the "naughties", there was an almost universal adoption of the view that the cyclical nature of "boom and bust" was now at an end. But that was before September 2008, and the collapse of Leh-

1 Many thanks to Pamela Eddy, Marek Rebow, John Donovan, Steve Konkel, Catherine Bates, Howard Newby and Eva Egron-Polak for their helpful comments, and Evin McCarthy for the diagrams. All errors are mine.

man Bros. As Eric Hobsbawm (2008) has recently stated, "the belief that the market will always regulate itself and will help the economy produce socially optimal results or even maximum growth... is as extreme [as the view of]... a totally state-run planned economy in the Soviet systems. Both rightly failed." Today Keynesianism is enjoying a rebirth as the pendulum swings, and calls to nationalize the "commanding heights of the economy" are coming not just from the Left.

Higher education is not immune from this ideological battle. Much has been written about the marketization of higher education, the need to adopt/ adapt commercial business practices to public sector organizations, and the student as consumer or client. Robert Birnbaum's book, *Management Fads in Higher Education*, poked fun at the distinction between management innova- tion as a "truly good idea" and a fashion. Discussing the differences between business and higher education, Birnbaum (2000, p. 215) quoted the view: "If we could just run our universities as General Motors is managed, most of our educational problems would vanish." Today this adage may have a different meaning.

There is no doubt it has suited higher education to argue that academic research or knowledge production is critical to economic growth because this has underwritten substantial hikes in public expenditure. Today higher edu- cation tops many government policy agendas, and is considered a vital ele- ment of the productive economy rather than social expenditure. Yet regard- less of governance structure, more demands are being placed on higher education. In return for increased financial support, governments want more accountability regarding student learning; in return for more funding, govern- ments want more income-generation; in return for greater support for research, governments want to identify "winners"; and in return for valuing HE's contribution to society, governments want measurable outputs.

Has higher education become a victim of its own propaganda? Three differ- ent examples:

The rising popularity and obsession with global rankings of universities and the establishment of world-class universities are having positive and perverse effects. They appear to provide a simple way to gauge the talent-catching and knowledge-producing capacity of higher education, and assess value-for- money, especially important in difficult economic circumstances. But we know that measuring the wrong things can produce distortions — as people react to that which is rewarded/valued. Even in relation to scientific research, rankings can do great damage. They value some disciplines and research more than other work, and distort the focus of research towards that which is more predictable and easily measured. Yet, many HE leaders are as culpable as their policy colleagues in basing their ambitions and strategies on global rankings.

Similarly, the concept that higher education is the "engine" of the economy rather than an integral part of the education-research-innovation ecosystem has reinforced a linear or fordist model of science-push innovation. This has led to the idea that reductions in public funding of higher education could be compensated by commercialization, patents and licensing. But as Mowery *et al.* (2001) demonstrates only seven U.S. universities had a net return from patenting (that is offsetting the costs incurred in preparing and getting patents), over 90% of the returns were linked to a handful of patents (less than five for most universities) and nearly all these patents were in human life sciences (linked to the pharmaceutical industry). Moreover, as the OECD (Santiago *et al.*, 2008, 102-103) argues, too much emphasis on IPR may be contrary to public policy because it raises the cost of knowledge to users. The focus should be enabling greater knowledge diffusion through open science.

A recent Irish government announcement is another illustration of the tendency for *magic bullet* solutions. Trinity College Dublin (TCD) and University College Dublin (UCD), the two "highest ranked" Irish universities, will develop an "innovation corridor". They plan to create 300 new businesses and 30,000 jobs, based on an investment of €650 m from government, industry and private funding. Using MIT as an exemplar, the proposed €650 m will be over 10 years, whereas MIT invested €485 m in 2008 alone. It averages 20-25 HPSU per year. This means that the Irish initiative aims to create 25% more start-ups than MIT with approximately 13% of the investment (Jordan, 2009).

Can the new global economic reality provide the opportunity to move away from hyperbole and provide the opportunity to reassert a sustainable relationship between higher education and the wider community? In a growing number of countries and regions, higher education, in partnership with city government, business and civic organizations, has formed new social organizations in the realization that successful cities and mega-regions are "focal points of innovation and creativity" (OKC, 2009). Many cities have now openly embraced the concept of building a "creative alliance" between specialized clusters of higher education and research institutes interacting with enterprise and civil society, exchanging ideas and personnel, as the best way to attract and retain talent and investment. Rather than cities seeing higher education simply as employers and the latter viewing cities as mere locations, there is a growing realization of mutual benefit and added value.

This paper argues that community engagement — a vital component of HE's third mission — can be a sustainable force of innovation, and provide a model of "research engagement with society and public engagement with research" (Mulder, 2009).

SOCIAL INNOVATION AND
NEW KNOWLEDGE PRODUCTION

For most of the 20th century up to today, innovation has been associated with science, engineering and technology, despite the fact that many well-known innovations occur through changes in business processes, e.g. Google, UPS, Virgin and Apple. An important exception is made by the creative and cultural industries which have managed in recent years to demonstrate a close connection between themselves and innovation in the wider economy. Heretofore, when the humanities, creative arts and social sciences have been included in R&D budgets it is usually as "last-minute concessions to dogged lobbying" (Cunningham, 2004), but with significantly less funding. NESTA, the U.K.'s National Endowment for Science, Technology and the Arts — along with similar organizations in other countries — has played an important role in providing evidence that innovation performance is strongest for industries with the highest spending on creative industry products as a percentage of their output. Richard Florida (2002) has built on these ideas to argue that cities which embrace the creative and cultural industries are much more likely to attract and retain high-skilled, high-spending talent, with all the spin-offs that such a population seeks and demands. But, in addition to the specific illustration of the economic effect of spend on creative products and services, the compelling argument and evidence have helped open up a much broader debate on innovation and how change happens in society and the economy.

Michael Mumford defines social innovation as "the generation and implementation of new ideas about how people should organize interpersonal activities, or social interactions, to meet one or more common goals" (2002, p. 253). While S&T innovation has tended to be located within the market economy, social innovation takes place in daily life, in social relationships and behaviour and in the home and is, therefore, not trapped by any standard measures of economic activity. In recent decades, there has been a growing focus not just on new products but on new services, ways of organizing ourselves, society and work, and through new social movements. For example, whereas the principle of production has traditionally been oriented towards increasing capacity, rising consumer consciousness has helped re-orient the supply and distribution chain to respond to real-time consumer demand (e.g. H&M fashion). The role of the consumer has changed dramatically from a passive to an active player, not only navigating but even shaping the product line and the services (e.g. Google, LEGO). Organizations that fail to embrace this new paradigm are forced to compete unsuccessfully on price — losing out to cheaper labour markets in Eastern Europe and Asia. Those left standing "have recognized that it is their capacity to provide bespoke services — with products being reconceptualised as part of a service — and above all their capacity to innovate on which their future depends" (Murray *et al.*, n.d., p. 4).

Another distinguishing characteristic and objective is that social innovation aims to create social value for the wider community rather than for personal profit. According to Phills Jr. *et al* (2008, p. 39), social innovation is "truly social only if the balance is tilted toward social value — benefits to the public or to society as a whole — rather than private value — gains for entrepreneurs, investors and ordinary (not disadvantaged) consumers". Examples range from the establishment of the International Monetary Fund or the United Nations, the establishment of the Boy Scouts, open source software or the introduction of flexible working schedules and maternity/paternity leave. Drawing on Benjamin Franklin's legacy, Mumford (2002) describes how minor modifications within social organization can exert a decisive influence. Initiatives as diverse as a subscription library, the police force and fire department, paper currency, paving and lighting, a hospital and the University of Pennsylvania are all examples of "acting on and manipulating function role relationships, restructuring these relationships to achieve new goals or to allow old goals to be met more efficiently".

The Fair Trade movement is a more recent example. It has grown exponentially from a moral rebuke of free trade into a worldwide movement and organization certifying, labelling, distributing and selling a wide range of products, e.g. coffee, chocolate, bananas, cotton and other products. Its dynamic reconstruction of the value chain links peasant farmers with consumers in a determined effort to ensure fair prices to the producers, protect against child labour, create international certification and ensure sustainable agriculture. The real success of Fair Trade has been to transform it from a fringe activity to a brand that cities and towns themselves have sought to embrace and highlight as a demonstration of ethical values — in the belief/realization that this is important for its own citizenry and tourists. Corporate social responsibility fulfils a similar role; companies like the Body Shop, Ben and Jerry's and Patagonia have "regarded their businesses both as a vehicle to make money and as a means to improve society" (Vogel, 2005, p. 28) — albeit others might cynically argue CSR has proven to be a good marketing tool.

These different initiatives illustrate Charles Leadbeater's contention that "production for the masses is being replaced by production by the masses". In his book, *We-think*, Leadbeater (2009, p. xxi) described how this new social and organizational landscape is also altering the way in which ideas are diffused:

Scientific research is becoming ever more a question of organizing a vast number of pebbles. Young scientists especially in emerging fields like bioinformatics draw on hundreds of data banks; use electronic lab notebooks to record and then share their results daily, often through blogs and wikis; work in multi-disciplinary teams threaded around the world organized by social networks; they publish their results, including open source versions of the software used in their experiments and their raw data, in open access online journals.

This description mirrors what Gibbons *et al* have been saying about the new production of knowledge.

The progression from simple to complex — from disciplinary to inter/ multi-disciplinary — knowledge, has been reflected in the emergence of new disciplines, methodologies and ways of thinking, transforming knowledge economies and the way in which knowledge is actually created. Whereas traditional knowledge production, often referred to as Mode 1, was disciplinary or "curiosity-oriented" usually conducted by individuals in secluded/semi-secluded environment, "socially robust" or Mode 2 knowledge is created within an expanded context of being useful. No longer confined to the university, it is interdisciplinary and conducted in active engagement and collaboration with society — the wider community, civil society, industry, and the region (Gibbons *et al.*, 1994). Mode 1 research achieves accountability and quality control through the peer-review process, while Mode 2 achieves accountability and quality control through social accountability and reflexivity. Mode 2 moves the site of problem formation, investigation, discovery and resolution into the public realm or "agora". The "agora is the space in which societal and scientific problems are framed and defined, and where 'solutions' are negotiated. It is the space, par excellence, for the production of socially robust knowledge" (Gibbons, 2002, p. 59).

This transformation of knowledge production from something directed by individual academics to an activity directed by external agencies mirrors the transformation in the state's role — but not its authority — from provider to regulator, and from sole to partial financier of knowledge. There are now alternative and competitive sources of knowledge production — toppling the privilege of the "ivory tower". Arguably, knowledge has become democratized in the sense that more people are aware of the issues and are social actors in the application of knowledge. In other words, knowledge has "ceased to be something standing outside society, a goal to be pursued by a community of scholars dedicated to the truth, but is shaped by many social actors under the conditions of the essential contestability of truth" (Delanty, 2001, p. 105).

It is within this context that there is a growing understanding that the world's "grand challenges" require collaborative solutions and inter-locking innovation systems. They are not bound by borders and disciplines, but require bi-lateral, inter-regional and global networks to tackle.

Interdisciplinary thinking is rapidly becoming an integral feature of research as a result of four powerful 'drivers': the inherent complexity of nature and society, the desire to explore problems and questions that are not confined to a single discipline, the need to solve societal problems, and the power of new technologies (CFIR, 2004, 2).

Grand challenge problems are of economic and social importance, and include: Environment/Climate, Energy, Human health and healthcare delivery, Food, Water, Security, and Urban infrastructure.

Mode 2 research shares many of the characteristics of social innovation — the former being a form of the latter. Both require a unique approach to problem-defining and problem-solving involving shifting roles and relationships between the various partners, who most effectively come together from different sectors and experiences as partners rather than adversaries. "In principle, many people accept the trend of dissolving sector boundaries; in practice, however, they continue to toil in silos" (Phills Jr, 2008, p. 42).

'THINK & DO' [2] NETWORKS

Higher education has, for a number of decades, especially in the U.S., been involved in the movement for civic engagement. Recent initiatives include thematically linked learning communities, community-based research, collaborative projects, service-learning, mentored internships, reflective experiential learning and study abroad — with a focus on drawing meaning and understanding from direct experience, critiquing theory in light of this practice, and then evaluating practice in light of the new knowledge. Campus Compact [3] is a network of over 1100 HEIs — no longer just in the U.S. — which seek to bridge the town and gown divide.

The concept being promoted in this paper takes this initiative to another level, building on the triple helix mode of innovation. It involves the establishment of "Think & Do" fora which bring together actors from civil society, the state and state agencies, and higher education to mobilize and harness knowledge, talent and investment in order to address a diverse range of problems and need through co-ordinated action. Rather, sustained, embedded and reciprocal engagement is defined as learning beyond the campus walls, discovery which is useful beyond the academic community and service that directly benefits the public. Two developments from Ireland, both in their early stages, suggest how social innovation can inject a new way of thinking about "let[ting] knowledge serve the city". [4]

---

2 Northeastern University World Class Cities Partnership, (n.d.) "Global Impact on a Local level" presentation. See also http://www.policyschool.neu.edu/news/index.php?nid= 114&navyear=2009
3 http://www.compact.org/
4 Vision of Portland State University, U.S.

In 2008, the **Dublin Creative Alliance** was formed as collaboration between four Dublin region Local Authorities, four Higher Education Institutions, State Agencies, Business and the Not-for-Profit sector, and championed by Dublin City Council (DCC). Recognizing the benefit in maximizing collective capacity beyond individual capability, the Creative Alliance is premised on the understanding that as economic activity has gone global, cities now compete on global terrain for talent and investment. Thus the Creative Alliance aims to help identify, discuss, recommend, distribute and implement solutions in response to the challenges that Dublin faces as an International Competitive City Region. Its aims are:

1. A committed leadership with a unified vision and a critical mass of influence.
2. A clear vision of the unique strengths and future potential of the city.
3. An excellent 3rd and 4th level sector that is internationally competitive.
4. A City Region that is supportive of innovation and enterprise through education, business and civic leadership.
5. A strong accessible information, communications and transport network.
6. An open, merit-based, tolerant and inclusive society that promotes well-being.
7. The delivery of projects in support of agreed objectives.

The concept builds upon and is linked to similar initiatives being developed under the World Class Cities Partnership Initiative, the Open Cities Initiatives, and the OECD Higher Education in Cities and Regions project. It shares some characteristics of the classic triple-helix model, but goes beyond technology transfer or "tri-lateral initiatives for knowledge-based economic development" (Etzkowitz & Leydesdorff, 2000) to create a new boundary crossing organization to solve civic challenges as the diagram below illustrates.

Rethinking The Triple Helix

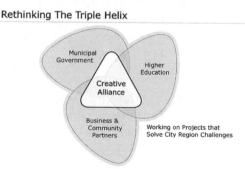

Underpinning the strategy is a recognition that mutual benefits derive from a multi-dimensional, collaborative and distributive model to problem solving. We believe that by unifying resources, working on projects that solve our City Region challenges and delivering on these projects, that we can place Dublin as a creative and influential International City Region.

The organizational model for identifying, developing and implementing initiatives is depicted by the following diagram. The numbered circles are aligned to seven of the projects thus far identified (see below):

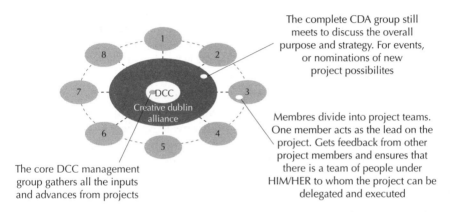

The complete CDA group still meets to discuss the overall purpose and strategy. For events, or nominations of new project possibilites

Membres divide into project teams. One member acts as the lead on the project. Gets feedback from other project members and ensures that there is a team of people under HIM/HER to whom the project can be delegated and executed

The core DCC management group gathers all the inputs and advances from projects

Thus far, the Creative Alliance has selected a number core projects which involve all partners in various permutations and include:

1. *Innovation Dublin*: Public events showcasing innovation and creativity in Dublin [5].

2. *Economic Action Plan* for the Dublin City Region that includes City Indicators to benchmark Dublin's performance internationally prioritizing the actions agreed in the plan.

3. *Public Identity*: To build a distributed citizenship model that would get Dubliners passionate about contributing to their city via discussion forums, events, web presence, and project initiatives.

4. *Branding Dublin*: To develop a branding strategy for Dublin as an internationally competitive and creative city so as to attract investment and talent.

5. *Network Mapping*: To identify the formal and informal cross-agency/ cross-sectoral alliances and linkages that exist across key players in Dublin in order to capture existing and potential knowledge net-

---

5 See http://www.innovationdublin.ie.

works and information flows and benefits that accrue as well as weaknesses or gaps in participation or the networks.

6. *UniverCities*: An alignment of the teaching and research programmes of universities with the challenges of managing and planning for the future of the City.

7. *Institute for the Twentyfirst Century* will be an Institute for post-graduate learning focused on design innovation and inter-professional collaboration to identify solutions to the challenges facing the city.

Another example is being developed by the Dublin Institute of Technology in association with Dublin City Council (DCC) and the Health Services Executive (HSE). Together they have formed a non-traditional partnership to develop an Environmental Health Sciences Institute (EHSI). Usually collaborative partnerships involve several HEIs as the core cluster, which then liaise with stakeholder groups which operate in an outer circle of influence. EHSI is different in so far as the core is the triangular partnership between an academic institution, the largest local authority in Ireland (DCC) and the national organization responsible for providing health and personal social services for everyone living in Ireland (HSE). The proposal aims to co-locate scientists, technologists, social scientists, city planners, policy-makers and public health/environmental health professionals to form an interdisciplinary, collaborative research platform in order to:

1. Inform environmental health policy, planning, decision-making;
2. Develop practical solutions to environmental health problems;
3. Study the impact on the health of vulnerable populations and facilitate investments to reduce the burden of chronic disease and injuries.

Rather than simply being members of stakeholder or focus groups, city and health professionals will actively participate in scoping and setting the research road-map and as end-users, through involvement of city residents, to test and validate the applicability of the analysis and the "solutions". EHSI will exploit the academic-professional interface, and facilitate researcher mobility, DCC/HSE staff development and re-training, technological development, outreach and knowledge transfer activities. The following diagram places users, researchers, practitioners/professionals, and policy-makers at the centre of the research road-mapping process.

This inter-institutional, non-traditional collaboration is a model for the integration of policy-makers, researchers and practitioners. It aims to drive more public engagement with research and research engagement with society in such a way as to enable the uptake of research questions from the city and health authorities into the research agenda of the academic partners, and to improve civil society's access to and uptake of research findings. By involving

User Centred Research Process

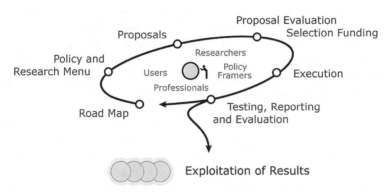

the two key stakeholder groups — the city council on behalf of the citizens and the health service directly in the process, EHSI aims to create a new form of science communication, one in which the end-user and civil society are active participants rather than passive consumers.

COMMUNITY ENGAGEMENT AS SOCIAL INNOVATION

John Voelcker (2006, p. 44) says "it takes more than a fancy new gadget to make life better". That's why the examples above suggest how the principles of social innovation can help transform the way in which higher education interacts with its stakeholders and the wider community through the formation of new boundary-crossing organizations. Drawing upon Mumford's (2002) account,

- Social innovation may occur when people, particularly people with somewhat atypical backgrounds, build structured institutions to secure informal, naturally occurring relationships of value;
- Social innovation is underpinned by networks of community, enterprise and elite support;
- Social innovation may not require complete solutions but rather timely, more limited solutions that address key issues while laying an organizational foundation for more long-term efforts;
- Social innovation may, at times, lay a foundation for subsequent technical advances;

- Social innovation requires marshalling, and effective management of financial resources;
- Social innovation often involves a willingness to consider new ways of structuring long-standing social relationships;
- Social innovation may, at times, involve a redefinition of roles and role relationships to address the equity concerns of various parties; and
- Social innovation may be self-reinforcing and highly iterative, requiring committed engagement by all the stakeholders.

These characteristics are present, in different degrees, in both the Creative Alliance Initiative and the proposed Environmental Health Sciences Institute: they aim to overcome the diffusion of skills and experience amongst key actors and across different sectors, the lack of involvement of end-users or the community in framing both the agenda and the solutions, and the "neglect of the needs of deprived [or vulnerable] groups within urban society" (Moulaert, 2009, p. 15). Rather than seeing innovation as the result of a discovery process that is commercialized, it is viewed as a complex iterative process involving an array of stakeholders and (end) users — from the private/public sector and/ or wider civil society — coupled with feedback loops and market linkages. This approach challenges the traditional linear model, which tends to view the user as a passive rather than active participant.

Success in both initiatives depends on the extent to which innovation occurs in the social relations between the organisations, as well as transforming the way in which needs are identified, road-mapped and problem-solved. Identifying the requisite mechanisms to reconcile tensions between institutional and collaborative loyalties, which are often not in conflict when all is going well but may be challenged when difficulties arise, is important. The organizational, management and governance practices and processes are critical in building true communication channels between the stakeholder groups, including the wider community. This requires people who can think outside the box, and whose contribution to new knowledge ill-fits the type of metrics promulgated by global rankings. Thus, another essential element, vital in the audit culture in which we live, is to find appropriate indicators to measure, assess and reward community engagement, creativity and social innovation in order to incentivise the academy and other professionals, assuage investor-confidence and inform the public. This is critical because a major handicap for faculty engaging in new forms of knowledge production is that tenure/promotion and prestige still rewards Mode 1 outputs. If we truly embrace Boyer's (1990) four scholarships, this would not be an issue.

While "service" has been one of the three pillars of higher education (the other two being education/teaching and research), these initiatives push the envelope of community engagement beyond volunteerism and campus compacts to embed the principles of social innovation to rethink the relationship between higher education and its community. Social innovation principles have the potential to transform our understanding of knowledge transfer beyond the traditional HE-industry partnership, science parks and economic clusters. While social innovation is generally viewed as a process occurring within the community, what is proposed here is not a magic bullet but a new way of configuring higher education's relationship with its stakeholders. New thinking and effective boundary-crossing organizations are vital, especially in tough times.

REFERENCES

Birnbaum, Robert. (2000). *Management Fads in Higher Education. Where They Come From. What They Do. Why They Fail*. San Francisco: Jossey-Bass Inc. Publishers.

Boyer, Ernest L. (1990). *Scholarship Reconsidered. Priorities of the Professoriate*. Princeton: The Carnegie Foundation for the Advancement of Teaching.

CFIR — Committee on Facilitating Interdisciplinary Research. (2004). *Facilitating Interdisciplinary Research*. National Academy of Sciences, National Academy of Engineering, Institute of Medicine. Retrieved 31 July 2009, from http://books.nap.edu/openbook.php?record_id=11153&page=2

Cunningham, Stuart. (2004). The Humanities, Creative Arts and the Innovation Agenda, in Brad Haseman, Sue-Anne Wallace & Rod Wissler (Eds), *Innovation in Australian Arts, Media and Design: Fresh Challenges for the Tertiary Sector*. Flaxton: Post Pressed.

Delanty, Gerard. (2001). *Challenging Knowledge. The University in the Knowledge Society*. Buckingham: The Society for Research in Higher Education and Open University Press.

Etzkowitz, Henry & Leydesdorff, Loet. (2000). "The Dynamics of Innovation: From National Systems and 'Mode 2' To a Triple Helix of University-Industry-Government Relations", Retrieved 16 May 2009 from: http://users.fmg.uva.nl/lleydesdorff/rp2000/.

Florida, Richard. (2002). *The Rise of the Creative Class*, New York: Basic Books.

Fukyama, Francis. (1992). *The End of History and the Last Man*. New York: Free Press.

Fukyama, Francis (2007). The history at the end of history, *The Guardian*. Retrieved 3 May 2009, from http://www.guardian.co.uk/commentisfree/2007/apr/03/thehistoryattheendofhist

Gibbons, M., Limoges, C., Nowotny, H, Schwartzman, S., Scott, P. & Trow, M. (1994). *The new production of knowledge*. London: Sage.

Gibbons, Michael. (2002). Engagement as a Core Value in a Mode 2 Society, in Svava Bjarnason & Patrick Coldstream (Eds.), *The Idea of Engagement. Universities in Society*. Association of Commonwealth Universities. London: Association of Commonwealth Universities, pp. 48-70.

Hobsbawm, Eric (2008). Quoted by Alastair Bruce, Global financial crisis is the "end of the era" for capitalism, *MSN Money*, 7 November. Retrieved 3 May 2009, from http://money.uk.msn.com/investing/articles/morecommentary/article.aspx?cp-documentid=10465208

Jordan, Declan. (April 2009). Research — Opinion, *Innovation*, p. 10.

Leadbeater, Charles. (2009). *We-Think. Mass innovation, not mass production*. London: Profile Books.

Moulaert, Frank. (2009). Social Innovation: Institutionally Embedded, Territorially. (Re)produced in Diana MacCallum, Frank Moulaert, Jean Hillier & Serena Vicari Haddock (Eds.), *Social Innovation and Territorial Development*. Farnham: Ashgate Publishing Ltd, pp. 11-24.

Mowery, D.C, Nelson, R., Sampat, B.V. & Ziedonis, A.A. (2001). The growth of patenting and licencing by US universities: an assessment of the effects of the Bayh-Dole Act of 1980, *Research Policy*, 30: 70-119.

Mumford, Michael D. (2002). Social Innovation: Ten Cases from Benjamin Franklin, *Creativity Research Journal*, 14:2,253-266.

Murray, R., Mulgan, G. & Caulier-Grice, J. (n.d.). "How to Innovate: The tools for social innovation", Draft, NESTA, pp. 1-41.

OKC — Office of Knowledge Capital. (2009). *Melbourne: Australia's Knowledge Capital*. Presentation to The Dublin Creative Alliance, April.

Mulder, Henk & Steinhaus, Norbert. (2009). *Public Engagement with Research and Research Engagement with Society (PERARES)* research funding proposal, FP7, unpublished.

Phills Jr., James A., Deiglmeier, Kriss & Miller, Dale T. (Fall 2008). Rediscovering Social Innovation, *Stanford Social Innovation Review*, pp. 34-43.

Santiago, P., Tremblay, K., Basri, E. & Arnal, E. (2008). *Tertiary Education for the Knowledge Society*, vol. 2, Paris: OECD.

Voelcker, John. (2006). Creating Social Change. 10 Innovative Technologies, *Stanford Social Innovation Review*, Summer, pp. 44-53.

Vogel, David. (2005). *The Market for Virtue: The Potential and Limits of Corporate Social Responsibility*, Washington D.C.: Brookings Institution Press.

PART II

•••••••••••••

Agents of Innovation

CHAPTER 4

Curiosity and the Transformative Impact of Fundamental Scientific Research

Jean-Lou A. Chameau and Carol S. Carmichael [1]

"Never doubt that a small group of thoughtful, committed citizens can change the world; indeed, it is the only thing that ever has." — Margaret Mead.

OVERVIEW

Starting with the rise of Silicon Valley in the 1960s and 70s, the different stakeholders associated with U.S. research universities have emphasized and nurtured the relationship between scientific research and technological innovation taking place at these universities and economic development. The perceived importance of this relationship was reinforced by the Bayh-Dole Act, the decline of the large corporate research laboratories, the emergence of clusters of innovation and the rise of venture capital.

In a study of invention reports at Columbia University, Stanford University and the University of California, researchers found that the nature of

1 **Acknowledgements:** We would like to express our appreciation to Carver Mead for helpful and enjoyable discussions on Caltech and its culture. They have had strong influence on the first author since he became the president of the institute. We would also like to thank Fred Farina, director of Caltech's Office of Technology Transfer, and his predecessor, Larry Gilbert, for their work in creating a national model for university technology transfer while bringing Caltech innovations to the marketplace.

emerging areas of research, especially genetics and computer software, along with court decisions on patentable research results, contributed significantly to the expansion of university patenting and licensing activities. The passage of Bayh-Dole, they concluded, served to "accelerate and magnify trends that already were occurring" (Colyvas *et al.*, 2002).

The first part of this paper addresses the most recognized forms of technology transfer engendered by university research. It summarizes several studies examining the direct evidence of innovation inspired by university research such as patents, licences, start-up companies and other forms of economic spillover effects. These are all important measures and reflect a great success story that is emulated globally in both developed and emerging economies.

However, these measures don't adequately capture the contributions of university research to innovation. Several studies of the informal or indirect effects reveal a much more complicated "innovation eco-system". The foundation of this system is built upon fundamental, curiosity-driven scientific research and led by a relatively small number of institutions that create the conditions where "unconventional" people can make discoveries that have a disproportionate impact on society.

The final part of this paper uses a Caltech case study to illustrate the intangible, yet profound, impact curiosity and fundamental research can have on innovation and quality of life (including economic aspects). Such stories lead us to believe that a national "innovation eco-system" needs universities like Caltech that are driven by fundamental, curiosity-driven scientific research, and must include mechanisms to support and leverage the unusual characteristics of some of the best minds in the world. We will conclude with a few remarks on this "Caltech model".

SCIENCE AS A DRIVER FOR INNOVATION

The expectation for a return on the public investment in scientific research has catalyzed a cottage industry for analysts and researchers interested in documenting the tangible contributions of research to economic development. Several studies included here describe the extent to which inventors draw upon publicly-supported research and the role faculty inventors and their institutions play in the broader innovation ecosystem. Studies show that the involvement of faculty inventors in the innovation process beyond the university walls, as entrepreneurs or consultants to startup firms, is essential to successful technology transfer. And the more eminent the researcher and the home institution are, the more likely this occurs.

Inventors draw heavily upon the results of publicly-supported scientific research. One way to assess the contribution of public science to innovation is to examine the citation linkage between U.S. patents and scientific research papers. Narin *et al.* (1997) examined 100,000 patent-to-science references and found:

- 73% of the papers cited by U.S. industry patents are based on public domain science; only 27% are authored by industry scientists; and
- The reliance on U.S.-based scientific papers by inventors (with U.S. Patents) increased dramatically, with the citations to U.S. papers tripling between 1987 and 1994 (the increase in patents during that period was only 30%).

They found that inventors show a strong preference for science conducted in their own country, with "local" publications exceeding those from other countries by a factor of two to four. And the cited papers are, in general, "... quite basic, in influential journals, authored at top-flight research universities and laboratories, relatively recent, and heavily supported by NIH, NSF, and other public agencies" (Narin, Hamilton & Olivastro, 1997).

Faculty inventors develop the results of basic research both within and outside the university. Thursby *et al.* (2009) examined a sample of over 5,000 patents involving faculty members at Research I universities. Their study addressed some interesting questions about the "outside" activities of faculty inventors, including concerns about university technology transfer policies and technology "going out the back door" of the university (Link, Siegel & Bozeman, 2007). What this study found, instead, was evidence of legitimate faculty activity leading to economically useful results. They found that:

- 62% of the patents involving faculty members were assigned solely to the university.
- 26% of faculty patents were assigned solely to firms.

The faculty patents that were assigned to firms tended to be "more incremental" (less transformative) than those assigned to universities. Nearly one-third of those patents assigned to firms were to firms which identified the faculty inventor as a principal. The authors concluded that the assignment of faculty inventions to firms is primarily the result of consulting and not faculty inventors circumventing university policy (J. Thursby, Fuller & Thursby, 2009).

THE UNIVERSITY IN THE INNOVATION ECO-SYSTEM

Numerous studies have found that proximity to the talent and technical resources of leading research universities is a key factor in technology-oriented economic development. Michael Porter identified the competitive advantage of such "clusters", with some of the most successful ones being Silicon Valley in California or Boston's Route 128 (Porter, 1998, 2007). It isn't surprising that most startups locate geographically close to the universities where the faculty-inventors reside. The success of such startups in moving an innovation into the marketplace may be due, in part, to the role of tacit knowledge embodied in the inventor that is not easily communicated through formal patent and licensing documents (Di Gregorio & Shane, 2003; J. Thursby *et al.*, 2009). According to one study, faculty/university led startups are "disproportionately successful" among startup firms and some universities generate more of these new businesses than their competitors. In 1998, nearly 70% of the 2,578 faculty/university startups created since 1980 were still in operation (AUTM, 1998).

One reason other firms may locate within a regional cluster is to gain strategic advantage, for example, through the placement of key individuals within an innovation network (Colyvas *et al.*, 2002). The importance of geographic proximity, however, likely varies with the type of research and its relevance to the technology base of an industry sector. In one study of innovations among 66 firms in 7 manufacturing industries, the researchers found that geographic proximity was less important for those innovations that drew upon basic research (Mansfield, 1995). For applied research, they concluded that close location was important to support face-to-face interaction between academic and industrial researchers (Mansfield, 1995).

An increasing number of universities have established technology transfer organizations to facilitate the movement of intellectual capital from the campus into the marketplace, especially since the passage of the Bayh-Dole Act in 1980. Researchers at the Kauffman Foundation expressed concern about the goals and expectations of technology transfer activities: whether technology transfer organizations are gatekeepers focused on revenue maximization or facilitators of commercialization. These different goals have implications for innovations with longer- versus shorter-term potential, or for innovations "that might be highly useful for society as a whole, even if they return little or nothing in the way of licensing fees". They worry that an over-emphasis on licensing revenue may lead many universities to overlook innovations important to society as a whole (Litan, 2007).

Some studies provide insight into the effectiveness of various university approaches to technology transfer. A case study of 11 inventions in software and molecular biology from Columbia University and Stanford, for example, provides some insight into the role of technology transfer organizations (Colyvas *et al.*, 2002). They found that such organizations were not critical for making contacts with industry, marketing the inventions, or inducing industry interest. They were useful, however, in making arrangements for licensing, facilitating the patent application process, and defining/protecting the university interests.

Di Gregorio and Shane (2003) examined the variation in startup activity among 101 research universities (including 89 of the top 100 research universities, by research expenditures, accounting for 85% of the patents assigned to universities in the U.S.). They found little or no effect from university incubators, internal venture capital funds, the level of local venture activity, or the commercial orientation of the university research. They found a strong influence on startup activity from university policies related to equity investments and inventor share of royalties. They found that higher inventor-shares of royalties correlated with lower rates of startup company formation. "Intellectual eminence" of the university significantly predicts startup activity in that it attracts resources to establish companies (by reducing perceived risk associated with "asymmetric information" about inventions). They concluded that "better quality researchers are more likely to start firms to exploit their inventions" (Di Gregorio & Shane, 2003, pp. 210-212).

'CROSS-BOUNDARY' INTERACTIONS IN THE INNOVATION ECO-SYSTEM

Numerous studies and reports on the contributions of fundamental scientific research to innovation and economic development acknowledge that a focus on patents, licences and startups is incomplete and would grossly underestimate the value of basic science· in the innovation ecosystem. The development of science and engineering talent for the workforce, open scientific publications, conferences and consulting are just a few ways science diffuses into the broader economy. Another way to think about the contribution of fundamental scientific research is through the natural give and take between basic and applied research, between science and technology.

Stokes (1997) coined the term "Pasteur's quadrant" for "use-inspired" basic research, reframing the relationship between scientific understanding and technology, and suggesting a way to renew the compact between the scientific community and the public that supports it. Stokes argues that research in "Pasteur's quadrant" will lead to support for pure research because as "the emergence of goal-oriented basic research within a scientific field strengthens the case for public investment, it also strengthens the case for public investment in the pure research that will enhance the capacity of the field as a whole to meet the societal goals on which it bears" (Stokes, 1997, p. 104).

Use-inspired research may support the "co-evolution" of science and technology in emerging science-based fields. Murray (2002) set out to examine such co-evolution in the field of tissue engineering. In a study of the 56 patents and 158 papers associated with tissue engineered cartilage, she found little overlap in scientific and technological networks in this field, but significant "cross-boundary" ties not captured formally in patents and papers. This co-evolution occurred through key scientist involvement in patenting and technology development, the creation of startup companies, consulting and informal science advising and mentoring (Murray, 2002).

Studies of industrial research and development (R&D) managers support the idea that fundamental- and use-inspired scientific research contribute significantly to the innovation process. In a study of R&D managers from 66 firms in seven manufacturing industries, researchers found that scientific research provided new theoretical and empirical findings as well as new types of instrumentation "essential to the development of a new product or process" (Mansfield, 1995). They found that approximately 10% of innovations from the industry sample could not have been developed or completed without recent academic research. And when asked to identify key researchers, the firms' top R&D managers most frequently cited "world leaders" in science and technology (Mansfield, 1995).

In the Carnegie Mellon Survey on Industrial R&D, researchers attempted to assess the contributions of public science to industrial R&D (Cohen, Nelson & Walsh, 2002). Using data obtained from over 1,000 industrial R&D managers in 1994, they found "... [t]his conception of a more interactive relationship where public research sometimes leads the development of new technologies, and sometimes focuses on problems posed by prior developments" (Cohen et al., 2002). Public research contributed about equally as a source of ideas for new projects and for information needed to complete projects:

- 31.6% of the R&D managers indicated that university or government research was the source for new ideas or projects.
- 36.3% of the R&D managers indicated that university or government research provided information used in the completion of a project.

Researchers in industry and in the academy share similar perceptions of the relative importance various forms of knowledge transfer have on innovation. Cohen et al. (2002) asked industrial R&D managers about the importance of public research to a recently completed "major" R&D project. A survey of faculty in mechanical and electrical engineering at MIT asked about the relative importance of various mechanisms for knowledge transfer (Agrawal & Henderson, 2002). We have placed results from the two studies into the table below (Table 1). Though drawn from very different study designs and sample sizes, the results show similarities nonetheless.

Faculty consulting is important for technology transfer, but some forms of consulting may actually support the development of new insights and technologies. Perkmann and Walsh (2008) describe three types of faculty consulting and their relationship to innovation in firms: opportunity-driven, commercialization-driven and research-driven. Opportunity-driven consulting builds upon knowledge commonly held in the academic community, is generally short-term and plays little role in innovation as it focuses on solving

Table 1

MIT Faculty Survey (n = 68) (Agrawal & Henderson, 2002)		Industrial R&D Managers Survey (n = 1229) (Cohen *et al.*, 2002)	
Consulting	26%	Informal Information Exchange (conferences, consulting, meetings)	31-36%
Publications	18%	Publications and Reports	41%
Recruitment of Graduates, Collaborative Research	12-17%	Recruitment of Graduates, Joint/ cooperative Ventures	17-21%
Patents and Licensing, Co-supervising Students, Informal Conversations, Conferences	<9%	Licences and Personnel exchanges	<10%

immediate problems as opposed to proposing new ideas for development (Perkmann & Walsh, 2008).

Patent and licence documents often provide insufficient information to licensees to develop successfully inventions for the marketplace. To fill this information gap, faculty inventors engage in commercialization-driven consulting. Such consulting strives to "capture such latent knowledge" and is often motivated by the faculty inventors' desires to commercialize their own inventions (Perkmann & Walsh, 2008). Such consulting, as noted by Jerry and Marie Thursby and their colleagues, is essential for the successful commercialization of nearly three-quarters of inventions licensed from universities and may result in additional patents assigned to the licensees (J. Thursby *et al.*, 2009; J. G. A. Thursby, Jensen & Thursby, 2001).

Research-driven consulting, Perkmann and Walsh argue, forms a "circular relationship" between faculty members conducting fundamental scientific research and the industries that develop technologies. Perkmann and Walsh note the synergistic effect when "research is recursively intertwined with technological development." Faculty will be motivated to participate to obtain access to "research challenges, data, materials and instrumentation" and industry will gain insight into development opportunities. The authors predict that research-driven consulting would not shift academic research into applied areas and would "be practised mostly in Pasteur-type fields, i.e. those fields that combine fundamental scientific understanding with practical usage considerations" (Perkmann & Walsh, 2008).

EXTRAORDINARY PEOPLE IN THE INNOVATION ECO-SYSTEM

The studies discussed in this paper and common sense tell us that faculty inventors and researchers conducting scientific research are essential components of our national innovation ecosystem. Over the past decade or so the decline in U.S. students studying engineering and science has been alarming. It is a concern for our national competitiveness in a technology driven world which requires a technologically savvy workforce. From the standpoint of innovation per se, it leads us to think about whether innovation is driven by a large number of engineers and scientists, or a smaller number of truly creative, game-changing scientists and engineers. It reminds us of a favourite quote from Margaret Mead:

"Never doubt that a small group of thoughtful, committed citizens can change the world; indeed, it is the only thing that ever has."

What conditions lead to game-changing innovation? What allows researchers to take the risks they need to break through conventional understanding with insight that creates new opportunities? In his long-term study of researchers in elite universities, Edward Hackett describes risk-taking as a choice between "answering research questions or forming research questions to answer; between studying phenomena or investing in the creation of phenomena to study and the means to do so." He said: "… the most intense and consequential competition in science is the competition to avoid competing" (Hackett, 2005).

It is ironic then, as some have noted, that one of the main methods for evaluating the creativity of scientific work is the peer review: pitting plausibility and validity (or conformity) against originality (Heinze, Shapira, Rogers & Senker, 2009). Several national groups lament the relatively low amount of exploratory, high-risk research in the U.S. public research portfolio and its implications for our innovation ecosystem (U.S. Committee on Prospering in the Global Economy of the 21st Century, 2007). And others have noted that mechanisms to foster university-industry research collaborations have a tendency, when spun off federal funding, to become more near-term and applied in focus (Feller, Ailes & Roessner, 2002).

Innovative people thrive in universities that share some important characteristics. One study examined the organizational context of research groups involved in 20 "creative events" in human genetics and nano-science/technology (identified through awards of prestigious prizes and a peer nomination survey) (Heinze et al., 2009). They found that a "combination of small work units in rich research contexts with requisite scientific variety" allowed the researchers to eliminate dead-ends, thereby improving the effectiveness of high-risk research. Other characteristics include:

- small groups composed of a highly selective community of scholars
- effective student-supervisor relationships;
- stable and flexible research funding; and
- multidisciplinary contact among those who share "mutual curiosity and interest".

They found that truly creative discoveries were made by "bright and curious minds" who had the freedom to define and pursue interests both within and outside of broadly defined or long-term research agendas (Heinze *et al.*, 2009). Let's turn now to a case study of one such bright and curious mind in the "right" institutional context. Carver Mead, the Gordon and Betty Moore Professor of Engineering and Applied Science (Emeritus) at Caltech, is interested in the fundamental properties of materials and their relationship to the design and development of a wide array of technologies. Winner of the National Medal of Technology in 2003, his story as a rural California native captivated in his youth by power plants and radio technology has been told by many (Brown, 2003; Kilbane, 2004; Spice, 2002). He arrived at Caltech in 1952 as an undergraduate and took mathematical physics from a young Richard Feynman and chemistry from Linus Pauling, whom Mead credits with helping him understand quantum mechanics. Since his arrival in 1952, Mead has helped shape and been shaped by the context of a small institution highly focused on fundamental science and technology research.

"... [Y]ou can sit down at any table in the Athenaeum [Caltech faculty club] over lunch and have a discussion with someone and you find out what the real fundamental things are in a particular field. And that, to me, is what sets this place apart from anywhere else" (Mead, 1996).

Mead studied the "detailed physics of the contacts between metals and semiconductors" and his insights led to the development of a new kind of transistor. When challenged by Gordon Moore of Fairchild Semiconductor (and later, Intel) to determine the smallest size possible for transistors, Mead not only predicted the size to be two orders of magnitude smaller than thought possible by other scientists in the field (0.15 micron versus 10 microns), he also realized that the challenge for future development of microchips would be the design of chips with millions of transistors (Kilbane, 2004). His innovative response was the development of an automated process for chip design, called very large-scale integration (VLSI), involving a "silicon compiler" that would chart the silicon circuit and plot the design to be etched on a silicon chip (Brown, 2003).

At Caltech, curious minds can meaningfully explore other disciplines, sometimes leading to the creation of new fields or academic programmes. In 1980, a new professor of chemistry and biology sparked Mead's interest in "neural stuff" and it relationship to computation in silicon, an interest that had its origins to a time in the late 1960s when Mead collaborated briefly with Nobel laureate and Caltech professor of biology Max Delbruck (on a study of nerves and lipid bilayer membranes). He and this new professor, John Hopfield — joined one year later by Richard Feynman — co-taught a course called the Physics of Computation. This course became a learning-laboratory of sorts in which they argued, reasoned and fermented ideas that became a course on neural networks for Hopfield, a course on neuromorphic analog circuits for Mead, and a course on physics and computation for Feynman (Mead, 1996).

This collaboration ultimately led to the formation of the programme in Computational and Neural Systems at Caltech involving faculty in cognitive and behavioral biology, electrical engineering and computer science. Mead says: "It's a really remarkable concentration of talent with quite a good shared vision [neuromorphic way of looking at systems]. That's really an amazing thing; I mean, at Caltech usually everybody goes their own way. We have no mechanism for corralling people at Caltech. Thank God, we don't have that mechanism. That's why I'm still here" (Mead, 1996).

But the knowledge and technology transfer process isn't a one-way street from the university to the marketplace. Like his interaction with Gordon Moore that provided insight into the scaling challenge in microchip design, Mead's collaboration with a variety of Silicon Valley firms fed his research curiosity. His discussion of his relationship to industry describes the type of use-inspired basic research advocated by Stokes in Pasteur's Quadrant:

"I've gotten most of my research issues, down through the years, from my interaction with Silicon Valley, but not because they told me to work on [particular projects]. It was because I was working with them and I could figure out, 'Gee, that's an interesting fundamental thing and they don't have time to look at it.' So I would go off and look at it, and then I'd go back to [someone like Gordon Moore] and say, 'Hey, I did this and this and this.' "Oh, that's interesting.' So there was always a good mutual back-scratch" (Mead, 1996).

Mead's curiosity in the scientific underpinnings of technology is matched by his entrepreneurial talent. His work on "neurally-inspired chips" found its way into several innovative technologies and associated spinoff companies, including touchpad systems (Synaptics), digital hearing aids (Sonic Innovation) and high-fidelity imaging systems (Foveon). His ability to get students interested in his research has resulted in the creation of more than 100 high-tech companies by his former students (Kilbane, 2004)!

THE CALTECH MODEL

As noted earlier, the philosophy for technology transfer at many universities is based on either a "home-run" or revenue maximizing model or a "volume" model, with the latter focusing on the number of innovations and the speed at which they are commercialized (Litan, 2007). Carl Schramm, President and CEO of the Kauffman Foundation, places Caltech in the "Big Five" of an elite group of institutions involved in technology transfer:

"... Just five schools, in fact, constitute the elite of the technology transfer world. They are Berkeley, Caltech, Stanford, MIT and Wisconsin. The list of universities reporting new discoveries changes from one year to the next, but each of these five schools consistently garners around 100 patents per year. Not every patent becomes the basis of a business, of course, but some do. And what is remarkable about the five schools above is that, in addition to producing new ideas, they consistently rank at the top of the list of universities in terms of how many businesses are built around the technologies created in their labs. Along with teaching and doing research, they seem to be in the business of inventing companies" (Schramm, 2006).

Schramm argues that the Big Five's secret to technology transfer success is that they (1) "treat business people as allies and equals;" (2) "encourage students to think about the business potential of their academic research;" and (3) resist "the temptation to monitor and regulate business relationships aggressively" (Schramm, 2006).

Many people not intimately familiar with the descriptive statistics of Caltech are often surprised to learn that it has only 295 full-time tenure-track faculty members, roughly 925 undergraduate students, and 1,200 doctoral students. Caltech scholars have garnered 32 Nobel prizes, 49 National Medals of Science and 10 National Medals of Technology. Our community also includes 105 members of the national academies of science and engineering.

The Caltech office of technology transfer (OTT) was established in 1995, much later than many of our peers. The OTT operating philosophy is based on trusting, collaborative relationships with the scientists so no extensive technology evaluation is needed. It supports our belief in the intrinsic value of the Caltech discoveries over revenue, encourages faculty and staff to pursue patents aggressively, and actively encourages start-ups founded with faculty inventions. Caltech scientists and engineers have, on an annual basis, filed 150-200 invention disclosures, been awarded 120-140 patents, licensed 40-50 inventions and established 8-12 new start-up firms.

These numbers suggest Margaret Mead is correct and that unusual talent is the key to extraordinary results. We should also note that even in the rarefied air of Caltech a number of faculty members repeatedly innovate at levels above the "average". In addition, faculty innovation is supported by critical contextual factors: access to first-class laboratories, outstanding students and post-doctoral fellows, and an environment that encourages curiosity driven research and interdisciplinary work.

Caltech faculty and students want to have an impact disproportionate to the size of the institution. We believe they do and the perception of the public at-large is that they do. Scientific discoveries with a transformative impact on knowledge and subsequent innovation are more than often conducted or at least inspired by unusual individuals. At the level of a nation, we believe it is critical to assure the portfolio of research investments include the support of organizations and programmes which nurture such individuals.

REFERENCES

Agrawal, A., & Henderson, R. (2002). Putting patents in context: Exploring knowledge transfer from MIT. *Management Science*, 48 (1), 44-60.

AUTM. (1998). AUTM Licensing Survey. Norwalk, CT: Association of University Technology Managers.

Brown, D. (2003). *Inventing Modern America: From the Microwave to the Mouse*. Cambridge, MA: MIT Press.

Cohen, W. M., Nelson, R. R. & Walsh, J. P. (2002). Links and impacts: The influence of public research on industrial R&D. *Management Science*, 48 (1), 1-23.

Colyvas, J., Crow, M., Gelijns, A., Mazzoleni, R., Nelson, R. R., Rosenberg, N. *et al.* (2002). How do university inventions get into practice? *Management Science*, 48 (1), 61-72.

Di Gregorio, D. & Shane, S. (2003). Why do some universities generate more startups than others? *Research Policy*, 32 (2), 209-227.

Feller, I., Ailes, C. P., & Roessner, J. D. (2002). Impacts of research universities on technological innovation in industry: evidence from engineering research centers. *Research Policy*, 31 (3), 457-474.

Hackett, E. J. (2005). Essential tensions: Identity, control, and risk in research. *Social Studies of Science*, 35 (5), 787-826.

Heinze, T., Shapira, P., Rogers, J. D. & Senker, J. M. (2009). Organizational and institutional influences on creativity in scientific research. *Research Policy*, 38 (4), 610-623.

Kilbane, D. (2004). Carver Mead: A trip through four eras of innovation. *Electronic Design*, Retrieved May 15, 2009 from: *http://electronicdesign.com/Articles/Print.cfm?ArticleID=8683*,

Link, A. N., Siegel, D. S. & Bozeman, B. (2007). An empirical analysis of the propensity of academics to engage in informal university technology transfer. *Ind Corp Change*, 16 (4), 641-655.

Litan, R. E., Mitchell, L. & Reedy, E. J. (2007). Commercializing university innovations: Alternative approaches. Unpublished Working Paper Series. Available at SSRN: http://ssrn.com/abstract=976005.

Mansfield, E. (1995). Academic research underlying industrial innovations: Sources, characteristics, and financing. *The Review of Economics and Statistics*, 77 (1), 55-65.

Mead, C. A. (1996). Interview by Shirley K. Cohen. Oral History Project. California Institute of Technology Archives. Pasadena, CA. Retrieved May 10, 2009 from *http://resolver.caltech.edu/CaltechOH_Mead_C* Unpublished manuscript.

Murray, F. (2002). Innovation as co-evolution of scientific and technological networks: exploring tissue engineering. *Research Policy*, 31 (8-9), 1389-1403.

Narin, F., Hamilton, K. S. & Olivastro, D. (1997). The increasing linkage between U.S. technology and public science. *Research Policy*, 26(3), 317-330.

Perkmann, M. & Walsh, K. (2008). Engaging the scholar: Three types of academic consulting and their impact on universities and industry. *Research Policy*, 37(10), 1884-1891.

Porter, M. E. (1998). Clusters and new economics of competition. *Harvard Business Review*, 77-90.

Porter, M. E. (2007). Understanding competitiveness and its causes Competitiveness Index: Where America Stands. Washington, D.C.: Council on Competitiveness.

Schramm, C. (2006). Five universities you can do business with. *Inc. Magazine*, February (Retrieved on May 1, 2009 from www.inc.com/magazine/20060201/views-opinion).

Spice, B. (2002). Carver Mead's career is based on practical problem-solving. *Pittsburgh Post-Gazette*. Retrieved May 15, 2009 from: *http://www.post-gazette.com*.

Stokes, D. E. (1997). *Pasteur's Quadrant*. Washington, D.C.: The Brookings Institution.

Thursby, J., Fuller, A. W. & Thursby, M. (2009). US faculty patenting: Inside and outside the university. *Research Policy*, 38(1), 14-25.

Thursby, J. G. A., Jensen, R. A. & Thursby, M. C. A. (2001). Objectives, characteristics and outcomes of university licensing: a survey of major U.S. universities. *Journal of Technology Transfer,* 26 (1), 59-72.

U.S. Committee on Prospering in the Global Economy of the 21st Century (2007). Rising above the Gathering Storm: Energizing and Employing America for a Brighter Economic Future. Washington, D.C.: National Academies Press.

CHATER

Industry as a Catalyst of Innovation

Wayne C. Johnson [1]

THE CHANGING LANDSCAPE

Success today hinges on our abilities to harness human potential, combine creativity with new knowledge and ensure economic impact is quickly derived from money spent on research. U.S. strength continues to lie in the ability to master innovation, but the future increasingly depends on our ability to also collaborate, optimize resources and align parties around common national agendas.

It is also clear that industry continues to be a critical force in the innovation equation, but the role that industry plays has changed dramatically over the last 30 years. Only through clear understanding how this innovation ecosystem has evolved over time can we hope to capture the true nature of sustainable success in the 21st century.

This paper reviews the evolution of the private sector's contribution to innovation over the last 40 years; it illustrates this shift through case study examples of successful innovation and extracts best practices as food for thought going forward.

Recent studies have indicated that the source of high-level innovations has changed considerably in two key ways. "First, large firms acting on their own account for a much smaller share of award-winning innovations, while innovations stemming from collaborations with spin-offs from universities and federal laboratories make up a much larger share. Second, the number of

1 The author would like to acknowledge, with gratitude, the assistance of Mr Dan Marcek in the preparation of this chapter.

innovations that are federally-funded has increased dramatically." (Block & Keller, 2008) The conclusion from this study is that the U.S. innovation system has become more collaborative in nature and federal funding now plays a more catalytic role.

A recent data analysis of the top 100 R&D awards over the past 40 years, conducted by the Information Technology and Innovation Foundation, indicates that a significant majority of these award-winning U.S. innovations in the 1970s came from corporations acting on their own.

Over the last two decades the majority of innovations have shifted and now come from partnerships involving universities, business and government, including federal labs and federally funded university research. The figures are 80% vs. 66% respectively. In sum, the innovation ecosystem is much more collaborative than it was several decades ago and the federal government is now playing a much more integral role.

There are several factors which have created this outcome: "(1) growing global competition is shrinking technology life cycles; (2) the complexity of emerging technologies is beyond the internal R&D capabilities of even the largest firms; (3) the expansion of R&D capability in more industries is causing R&D investments to spread vertically in high-tech supply chains, which increases the potential for the loss of value added from a single domestic economy; and (4) a growing number of nations are responding to these trends by implementing new mechanisms that increase the efficiency of R&D." (Tassey, 2007)

From an economic viewpoint, the period of the last 40 years has demonstrated the growing importance of scientific and other knowledge in the innovation process, while at the same time the sophisticated nature of technological advances increasingly requires close cooperation across multidisciplinary, possible geographically disperse, teams. In some ways, the old distinction between "basic science" and "applied science" has become obsolete, with proof of concept work being more the norm.

After World War II, the U.S. was dominated by large corporations. These oligopolies allowed higher levels of risk and subsequently investment in more radical and higher payoff technologies. In the 1950s and 1960s, this resulted in large central research labs in firms such as AT & T, General Electric, IBM, RCA and Xerox. However, in the period that followed, foreign firm competition, decreased government regulation, increased computerization, shifts in consumer preference away from standardized products and shifts in the financial marketplace to prioritize increasing short-term returns to shareholders, fundamentally changed the way long-term research was managed. Perhaps the biggest change was the closing down of corporate research laboratories or a significant reduction in in-house R&D budgets. Increased outsourcing and a need for external partnerships followed.

The innovation ecosystem was further impacted by changes in Federal Government policy and practice. Policies to increase the commercial impact of research (mostly in response to Japanese competition), the passing of the Bayh-Dole Act which allowed universities to commercialize research, investment programs such as the Small Business Innovative Research (SBIR) program, Advanced Technology Program (ATP), Manufacturing Extension Program (MEP), National Nanotechnology Initiative and SEMATECH are all examples that emerged during this period. They were then followed by similar examples from the Department of Energy (DOE) and the National Institute of Standards and Technology (NIST). The National Science Foundation (NSF) and the military supported a more decentralized system of university laboratories that build localized networks of collaboration with groups of industry partners. During this time NSF launched a series (17) of Engineering Research Centers which are interdisciplinary, located at universities and operated in close partnership with industry. (Block & Keller, 2008)

These various initiatives launched in the 1980s essentially coalesced into a system or "triple helix" of university-industry-government collaboration that has become central for innovation (Etzkowitz, 2003). This centrality of networks has played a major role in the effectiveness of the U.S. innovation process, and there are several reasons this approach has worked. First, the need to assemble all relevant forms of expertise under a single organization is impracticable and expensive. Second, the connections between the knowledge embodied in one or more organizations are most critical for the innovation process. The sparks produced when these different approaches combine facilitate effective new approaches (Hargadon, 2003).

THREE CASE STUDIES: NORTHEASTERN U. CENSSIS; UCSD CALIT2; EFTA

Looking at the role that industry plays in the innovation process, it is helpful to review Case Studies that illustrate why the private sector partnerships are critical for successful innovation. Three programs have been selected, each representing a different strategy for impacting innovation.

The first case study, the Northeastern University Center for Subsurface Sensing and Imaging Systems (CenSSIS), is an NSF-funded Engineering Research Center (ERC). This is an example of a long cycle (10 years) investment, with industry playing a key role from conception. The second case study, the University of California San Diego Calit2 — "A Systems Approach to the Future of the Internet and its Transformation of our Society" — involves a state-funded initiative based on an integrated strategy of complex partnerships. The third case study — Engineering for the Americas — illustrates far-sighted investments by the private sector in the creative side of the innovation ecosystem itself. This capacity-building initiative has worked to enhance the innovation ecosystem of the Americas by capacity-building in

engineering. Hemispheric competitiveness depends on technology and innovation — through EftA, governments, universities and industries have partnered to address systemic changes with economic results.

Center for Subsurface Sensing and Imaging Systems

The Northeastern University Center for Subsurface Sensing and Imaging Systems (CenSSIS) was awarded in 2000 by the National Science Foundation as
part of its Engineering Research Center (ERC) program. Funded in two por-
tions, the program will last 10 years and ultimately receive $37M from NSF.
Matching funds from the University total $12M over this period. Since its
inception eight years ago, it has been considered one of the most successful
examples of the ERC Program. Its beginning was less promising.

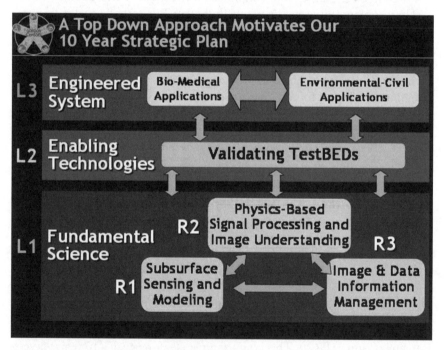

It started out as an unsuccessful proposal with feedback that Northeastern could
not expect to perform this level of research as an R2 school. Enter a new Dean of
Engineering and a committed corporate partner and that changed everything.

Alan Soyster was appointed Dean of Engineering in 1999. He came from
Penn State where he was a Department Chair. Assessing the NSF rejection
letter, he realized that Northeastern could not win a research program of this
scope alone and that he needed a core industry partner to drive the initiative.
Raytheon Company fit the bill.

Raytheon was a long-standing partner who hired many Northeastern engineering graduates and coops. Its President was an engineering alumnus and the subject area was core to its defence technology and recent interest in environmental sensing. Raytheon was also an aerospace contractor, familiar with how to win federally funded programs by delivering compelling proposals.

Addressing the concern that Northeastern did not have the capacity to perform all of the multidiscipline research, a strategy of partnership was developed wherein Boston University (acoustics), RPI (video imaging) and the University of Puerto Rico (satellite spectral imaging) were added to the team. The President of Northeastern also committed to invest $500,000 to seed the proposal.

For a medium-sized R2 university, this kind of activity represents a large gamble, but the clear role of Raytheon as proposal manager, research collaborator and contributor played a major role in winning the program. As important as winning the program was to the partners, however, it was the subsequent involvement by senior leaders from Raytheon and other industry participants that led to the outstanding string of successes that CenSSIS is known for today.

The goal of the Center was to revolutionize the ability to detect and image biomedical and environmental-civil objects or conditions that are underground, underwater or embedded within cells or inside the human body. A unified, multidisciplinary approach combining expertise in wave physics, sensor engineering, image processing and inverse scattering with rigorous performance testing to create new sensing system prototypes that are transitioned to industry partners for further development. Some of the most difficult and intractable problems in sensing and imaging involve detecting, locating and identifying objects that are obscured beneath a covering medium. Mapping pollution plumes underground, detecting a tumour inside the body, and identifying developmental defects in the interior of a multi-celled embryo all share the problem of distinguishing the effect of a dispersive, diffusive, and absorptive medium from the desired details of the subsurface structure and functionality. The problem is similar whether the wave probe is electromagnetic or acoustic, whether the medium is soil or tissue or whether the target is a land mine or a tumour.

Ultimately, to address the research barriers common to advanced biomedical and environmental-civil applications of subsurface sensing and imaging, CenCISS combined the four universities already mentioned with four affiliated hospitals and research institutions: Lawrence Livermore National Laboratory, Massachusetts General Hospital, Brigham and Women's Hospital and Woods Hole Oceanographic Institution.

Now fast forward to 2009. The CenSSIS program has received $37M from NSF as compared to the original estimate of $28M. In addition, a total of $12M in university matching funds has been achieved over the 8-year period. In 2006 a $20M gift from the Gordon Foundation was made to sustain R&D

infrastructure and create the Gordon Engineering Leadership Program. Over the 8-year period, corporate partners have won 11 R&D proposals totalling $40.4M from key agencies including Department of Homeland Security, DoD, NASA, Army SBIR, NIST and ALION. This represents a clear "Return on Investment" to the Center's industry partners. University partners have been successful in winning over $20M for additional research from NSF (IGERT), DHS, NIH, NIST and NIEHS.

The commercialization of Center technologies has provided additional revenues from: a portable confocal microscope for skin cancer detection; autonomous underwater vehicle; IR-based explosives detection; NVIDIA chip acceleration of tomosynthesis; new CT techniques to detect cardiovascular blockages and cell counting for reliable in vitro fertilization. There are currently 15 industrial members, including Raytheon, the Idaho National Engineering and Environmental Laboratory, AFOSR, Analogic, Lockheed Martin, Sloan Kettering Cancer Center, Mercury Computer Systems, Textron, Siemens and American Science and Engineering. Lastly, Raytheon Company has been awarded a Department of Homeland Security contact in excess of $400M based upon technology developed in the Center.

There are several conclusions that can be drawn from this set of accomplishments. One which has not been discussed is the importance of the excellent leadership of the PI from Northeastern, Michael Silevitch who has led the program from proposal to the current day. Not only have the research and commercial outcomes been spectacular, but so have the impacts on education. From K-12 outreach to opportunities for undergraduate research hundreds of students have benefited. The recent NSF IGERT grant in Puerto Rico continues this work.

Looking at the private-sector contribution, it is clear that the diverse group of partners has enriched the research outcomes and provided the marketplace grounding necessary for commercialization. Key to this success has been an industry-driven three-level strategy that enables the solution of diverse problems by coupling a tops-down approach that integrates fundamental science with enabling technologies and engineered systems. The industrial advisory board has played a key role from the first review, with hard-hitting SWOT analyses that were transformative to the program's success. The end result was that system applications were built around real world problems with biological-medical applications and environmental-civil applications.

California Institute for Telecommunications and Information Technology (Calit2)

The state of California took a noteworthy approach to innovation and collaboration early in the new century. In December of 2000, Governor Gray Davis proposed the creation of up to four California Institutes for Science and Innovation to be jointly funded with industry and having the goal of integrating research in California universities with industry and economic impact.

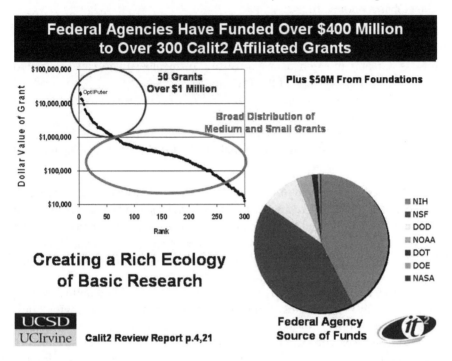

This state-level strategy was intended to "ensure that California maintains and expands its role at the leading edge of technological innovation in the 21st century" and to "give rise to world-class centers for strategic innovation that combine excellence in cutting-edge research with collaborations and training for our next generation of technological leaders". The subjects chosen were explicitly cross-disciplinary: biomedicine and bioengineering, nanosystems, telecommunications, and information technology. The price tag wasn't high. Each institute had to find private sector matching funds of at least twice the level of state support and had to be hosted by at least two campuses. (Kao, 2007)

Since that time, the California Institute for Telecommunication and Information Technology (Calit2) was formed. Calit2 has focused research on addressing large-scale societal challenges through a multidisciplinary approach intended to connect theory and ideas with partners in industry to accelerate innovation and encourage development of ideas. By striving to move beyond traditional research and integrate with practice, Calit2 has impacted real-world solutions in contexts ranging from large, established companies to start-up spin-offs.

From their website: Calit2 represents an experiment in inventing the university research environment of the future to continue to fuel innovation in the global economy. It:

- Builds horizontal links among departments to foster multidisciplinary studies.
- Creates research teams consisting of members who can be located anywhere because of the Internet.
- Supports involvement by faculty, students, industry, government and community partners.
- Enables prototyping in Calit2 "living laboratories."
- Provides technical professionals as the bridge between academia and industry.

Calit2 has demonstrated sustained success and the ability to act as a catalyst for impacting the California economy. Today UC San Diego and UC Riverside count over 350 faculty involved in Calit2 from over two dozen departments. Activities impact faculty, students and the community and are focused on integrating technology consumers and producers. Over $100M in building funding has allowed Calit2 to create "living laboratories" in areas of technical convergence.

Campus life has been greatly impacted due to the increased ability to integrate research into teaching. Students are now exposed to challenging questions faced in research facilities while faculty reaps the benefits of greater industry involvement (and the associated increase in support). Partnerships with industry have resulted in joint grant application, fellowships, internships, endowed Chairs, an emphasis on entrepreneurship in campus cultures and an expanded palette of intellectual pursuits.

But on the Industry side, returns are even more impressive. Myriad research centers and institutes have formed or become involved in Calit2 activities including networked systems, wireless communications, machine perception, microscopy and imaging, and structural genomics, to name a few.

From this traditional model, Calit2 also enables industry by providing access to state-of-the-art facilities, allowing industry to have access to unique resources and capabilities. Examples in this are the new clean rooms at UCSD, the *Leading Edge Photonic Laboratory* and the *Machine Perception Lab* in which company partners play visible, active roles in research areas of business import.

Calit2 has also continued to evolve industrial offerings in other areas. Today, cooperative test beds exist on power transistor tradeoffs, power amplifier tradeoffs, and digital signal processing tradeoffs and provide vendor neutral analysis opportunities and a forum for discussing shared problems. Other innovative efforts include a Nano-Bio-Info Innovation Library.

Outcomes have been impressive with Calit2 affiliated proposals winning over $400M in federal funding and another receiving $93M in Industry support. In one example, Qualcomm has invested over $22M in Calit2 projects, faculty and students.

Calit2 is an excellent examples of the successful strategy embarked on by Gov. Davis and committed to by the leaders and legislatures of California since. A culture of research integrated with economic outcomes is ideal and, through investment in these institutes, California has taken proactive action to ensure relevance of its universities, health of its industries, and a solid foundation for employment of the workers of their state.

Engineering for the Americas (EftA)

Innovation is not always about products and services. Innovative partnerships can also address more fundamental questions of workforce creation, talent formation, and the balance between the creative needs of industry and priorities of academe. This technical innovation example is concerned with exactly those issues: how can we develop an innovation ecosystem able to improve competitiveness while equitably managing opportunity?

Engineering for the Americas (EftA) is an initiative of technical capacity building in engineering for the hemisphere of the Americas in order to facilitate the attraction of foreign direct investment (primarily from multi-national companies), the stimulation of small technology based businesses by entrepreneurs, and creation of high-quality/high-salary employment in the region for socio-economic development.

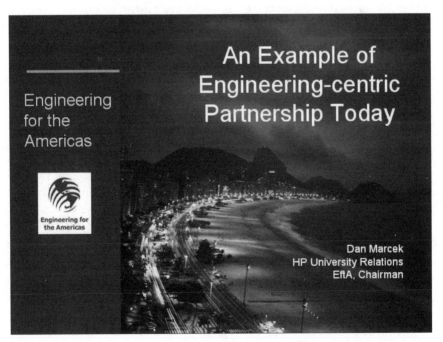

In collaboration with the Organization of American States (OAS), endorsement of this thrust was obtained from the Ministers of Science and Technology of the 34 countries in the Hemisphere, in November 2004. Through funds provided by the U.S. Trade Development Agency and several leading corporations (Hewlett-Packard, Cemex, Microsoft, National Instruments), a major conference was held in Lima at the end of November 2005, bringing together leaders from academia, industry, governments, and NGOs to discuss technical capacity-building in the Hemisphere and to lay plans for its implementation (for example through loans and grants from the International Financial Organizations — IFOs).

A Provisional Executive Committee has been established to pursue the recommendations and plans from the conference, including the organization of workshops in the region, pilot projects, research and survey studies, and sustainable funding on engineering education, accreditation and quality assurance, as well as technological businesses and job-creation.

Since its creation in 2004, EftA has made great progress in solidifying interests among the countries of the Americas and in including stakeholders from all sectors and all geographies of the hemisphere. Enabled by multiple sources and totalling over $3M of invested and leveraged funding, EftA has embarked on a series of awareness-generating activities, invested in partnership outreach and development, and facilitated construction of proposals and ideas designed to harness the resources of the IFO world on behalf of engineering as a basis for sustainable social and economic development.

Engineering for the Americas Progress: Over the course its initial incarnation, the Provisional Executive Committee embarked on several activities including the creation of a strategic plan and activities in support of EftA objectives. The three core strategies and associated activities have been:

Engineering Education Improvement: EftA has produced and delivered workshops in support of educational improvement in Chile, the Dominican Republic and Peru. These workshops focus on the need for engineering curriculum to incorporate project-oriented lessons and address the needs of industry through lessons enhanced with practice and real world context.

EftA also sponsored and supported many education conferences and events including an entire track of the Global Colloquium on Engineering Education held in Rio de Janiero in October 2006. A partial list of conference participation includes annual meetings of ASEE '06, ASEE '07, GCEE '06, LACCEI '05, LACCEI '06, and UPDAI '06. Through these visibility-raising investments, EftA has elevated the discussion and brought focus to international engineering education collaborations throughout the hemisphere.

Accreditation and Quality Assurance: Acting as a catalyst, EftA created a partnership committed to founding a regional accreditation system for engineering in the Greater Caribbean. Panama, Jamaica and the Dominican

Republic aligned together to submit a proposal to the Inter-American Development Bank (IDB) *Regional Public Good* funding window in October of 2006. This winning proposal received nearly US$750,000 in IDB and partner support. Since 2007, countries of the Greater Caribbean are collaborating to improve the brand and credentials of the engineering graduates of their region.

Job Creation: EftA has worked to identify, engage, and involve local industry. One common challenge is the apparent disconnect between academia and industry in Latin America.

To address this issue, in 2007 EftA facilitated collaboration among the Deans of Engineering in Chile, Argentina and Brazil to create programs and curriculum around entrepreneurship to the engineering education experience in the Southern Cone. Together with their respective governments, industry, and broader community of universities, Argentina submitted a proposal to IDB on behalf of Chile and Brazil to establish a cross-border partnership in this area. In 2008, IDB awarded this project and nearly $2M in IDB and partner funding is now working to enhance education and shape a more entrepreneurial culture in the South.

Summary of EftA Accomplishments: Since the Ministers and other High Authorities committed to engineering as a pathway to sustainable opportunity in the Lima Plan of Action, Engineering for the Americas has made great progress in creating collective understanding of the importance of engineers to economic health and the critical nature of engineering education to future national competitiveness.

Engineering for the Americas established a comprehensive partnership, established political will within the hemisphere of the Americas, engaged with constituents and development finance organizations, and succeeded in generating funding based on public-private partnerships and co-investment strategies.

EftA has catalyzed the discussion within the Development Finance community, with Ministers and governments, among educators, and with the enthusiastic support of Industry practitioners. Today, discussions of "Competitiveness" and "Innovation" include sensitivity about talent creation. Investments are being made to ensure a robust and healthy engineering community engages in creating the talent that our economies will need to succeed in a global market.

CONCLUSIONS & RECOMMENDATIONS

Since World War II, the evolution of research and innovation clearly points to an increasing need for collaboration between the industry, government and university sectors. The impact and selection of government funding is also critical. These "Open Innovation" models succeed only when there is a true partnership that delivers winning outcomes to all participants.

Recent work funded by the Kauffman Foundation and supported by the Sasakawa Peace Foundation, reviewed over 90 case studies of University-Industry partnerships in four countries: Japan, the U.K., Canada and the U.S. The report provides insights into an evolved understanding of business-university relationships:

- The process through which economic and social value is most likely to be added is through a partnership between industry and universities.
- The process of knowledge exchange that involves businesses and universities working together adds the most value: the old paradigm of fundamental research moving to applied research needs to be rethought.
- The metrics which encourage knowledge exchange need to reflect this understanding.
- The development of open innovation models will also require changes to how government measures the condition of university research.
- A need for knowledge transfer practice to work more flexibly and with speed in interacting with businesses (large companies and SMEs).
- The need to understand and support the relational as well as the transactional aspects of collaboration between universities and business; building trust and mutual understanding really matters and this takes time.
- The capacity and capability of business to interact with universities is just as important as the willingness and ability of universities to work with industry; universities need to take these variables into account when developing their own knowledge transfer strategies.

As the Kauffman-funded study illustrates, the new landscape of the global economy demands that we examine the processes at work to understand what strategies for competitiveness might work. This should be an ongoing process, part of a dialogue, wherein industry, academe and governments work together toward a common vision of national success. Clearly knowledge will be critical and talent creation is vital to economic results.

These case studies and many others have shown that collaborations really do work. Industry has proven to be catalytic in forming sustainable, relevant partnerships. Increasingly it is the holistic collaborations that master innovation and have lasting impact in the global market. Today, competitiveness and quality of life derive from success in innovation. At this we must excel.

REFERENCES

Block, Fred & Keller, Mathew. (2008) "Where Do Innovations Come From? Transformations in the U. S. National Innovation System 1970-2006. The Information Technology & Innovation Foundation". July 2008.

Etkowitz, Henry. (2003). "Innovation in Innovation: The Triple Helix of University, Industry, Government Relations." *Social Science Information* 42 (2003).

Hargadon, Andrew. (2003). "How Breakthroughs Happen — The Surprising Truth About How Companies Innovate". Cambridge, Massachusetts, Harvard Business School Press.

Kao, John. (2007). *Innovation Nation*. New York: Free Press.

Tassey, Gregory (2007). *The Technology Imperative*. Cheltenham, U. K. and Northampton, Massachusetts: Edward Elgar.

CHAPTER 6

National Innovation Policies: Governments as innovation agents of higher education and research

David D. Dill and Frans A. van Vught [1]

GLOBALIZATION AND INNOVATION

There is widespread agreement among economists that international forces have changed the nature of economic development (Soete, 2006). National markets have become increasingly interrelated, and goods, services, capital, labour, as well as knowledge, flow around the world seeking the most favourable economic conditions. Natural resources no longer provide a comparative advantage in economic growth. Instead, in internationally competitive markets, industrial innovation, defined as "the ability for firms and workers to move rapidly into new activities or to improve production processes" (Aghion, 2006, 2), becomes the principal means of sustaining economic growth and productivity.

Promoting innovation has in fact now become the principal means of economic growth in the leading nations. To better compete in a globalised economy, these countries focus increasingly on knowledge, creativity and technical innovation. In this new economic context, higher education and research organizations are becoming crucial objects of national policy. They form an

1 Excerpt from Dill, David D. and Van Vught, Frans A., eds. National Innovation and the Academic Research Enterprise: Public Policy in Global Perspective © 2009 The Johns Hopkins University Press. Reprinted with permission of The Johns Hopkins University press.

essential component of the knowledge economy and therefore are increasingly addressed by newly adopted national innovation policies.

Governmental actors in many countries appear to have comparable motives for developing and implementing national innovation policies. National policy-makers refer to the growth and importance of the "knowledge society" (Santiago, *et al.*, 2008) in which knowledge is *the* crucial production factor. The creation, transfer and application of knowledge are now perceived by policy-makers to be the primary factor influencing further social and economic development. Policy-makers also refer to the processes of globalization and increasing international competition in which the capacity to make use of new knowledge provides important strategic benefits. The creation, dissemination and application of knowledge have now come to be regarded as the essential conditions for the international competitiveness of regions, nations and even whole continents. Therefore they have become the focus of policies at sub-national, national and supranational levels (World Bank, 2007).

As a consequence, over the last several decades many governments have adopted national innovation policies designed to strengthen the innovative capacity of universities and research organizations. These institutions, which are primarily funded by public sources, are now perceived by policy-makers to be one of the few remaining mechanisms government can employ to influence international competitiveness.

NATIONAL INNOVATION SYSTEMS

During the 1980s, a new approach to the economics of innovation emerged that has become known as the National Innovation Systems (NIS) perspective. This perspective emphasises the interactive character of the generation of ideas, scientific research and the development and introduction of new products and processes. The NIS approach adopts an explicit policy orientation, and has been internationally promoted by organizations such as the OECD, the World Bank and the European Commission (Balzat, 2006). The NIS perspective now informs the national policies of many developed nations and has altered their traditional higher education and research policies.

Economic research has discovered that academic institutions play a critical role in NIS and, if anything, their influence on technical innovation has grown over time (Mowery & Sampat, 2004). However, the NIS research emphasised that while the "hard" outputs of academic research — publications and patents — are important for innovation, equally significant are "softer" knowledge transfer processes, including the hiring of new science and engineering Ph.D. graduates, whose added expertise is a primary means of transferring academic knowledge to industry (Cohen, Nelson & Walsh, 2002). In direct contrast to the linear assumptions of the traditional "science-push model", the NIS perspective emphasizes the influential role of linkages among the various actors and organizations that participate in the overall innovation process (Edquist, 1997; Nelson, 1993). While these linkages do include formal knowledge transfer arrangements between universities and industry, such as science parks and joint university-industry research ventures, they also include the many channels of communication such as meetings and consulting by which knowledge is exchanged. Finally, a critical difference between the NIS perspective and traditional higher education and research policy is the NIS perspective's emphasis on the importance of framework conditions: the governance processes, regulations, incentives and underlying beliefs that shape innovative behaviour (Balzat, 2006).

Over the last 20 years, the NIS perspective has influenced national reforms in higher education and research policy in many nations (Laredo & Mustar, 2001; Lundvall & Borrás 2004; Rammer, 2006). One version of the NIS perspective aims at promoting innovation within the existing institutional context of higher education through national and state-level incentive programs for basic research in fields deemed critical to future industrial innovation, such as biotechnology, information and communication technology (ICT), medical technology, nanotechnology, new materials and environmental technologies. A second, more systemic and laissez faire version of the perspective, focuses on changing the framework conditions of higher education institutions to promote innovation. This latter approach involves changes in higher education governance processes and legal frameworks; the development of new yardsticks for the evaluation of academic research activity; and the adoption of new incentives to promote the transfer of academic research to society, an issue not traditionally considered part of higher education policy. Examples of this approach include changes in the laws governing IPR (intellectual property rights) and academic labour markets; the introduction of competitive market forces into higher education systems; the transformation of institutional financing of research into competitive research funding; the deregulation of university management; the evaluation of academic research ex post, utilizing new performance indicators; novel initiatives to strengthen and reform doctoral research education; as well as a number of incentive schemes designed to encourage more effective university-industry linkages.

The NIS perspective and its proposed reforms clearly challenge a number of the traditional academic beliefs regarding the necessary unity of teaching and research and the essential incompatibility of basic and socially useful research (Martin, 2003). Not surprisingly, the NIS perspective has provoked controversy within the academic community. However, it appears that many governments (and supranational systems like the European Union) are developing "policy strategies" that are clearly based on this perspective. We will address these "policy strategies" in the next section.

POLICY STRATEGIES

In the present international context, governments are seeking to redesign their systems of higher education and research and to adapt them to the new demands of globalisation and competitiveness. For this they employ certain "policy strategies", i.e., processes in which policies are related to policy-objectives with the intention to realize these objectives. Generally speaking these policy strategies appear to consist of some combination of the basic notions of market coordination and central governmental planning.

The coordinative capacity of the market mechanism is well known. In a free market with perfect competition, prices carry the information on the basis of which decisions are made with respect to demand and supply. However, the model of the perfectly competitive free market often is not realistic. In reality one has to allow for transaction costs, scale effects, less than perfectly informed actors, less than perfectly mobile production factors, and non-homogeneous goods. In addition, high barriers to entry to a market may provide existing organizations with monopoly power, or competition may take place by means of mechanisms other than prices (e.g., quality or reputation). In short the perfectly competitive free-market mechanism seldom is a realistic option for policy-makers (Teixeira et al., 2004; Weimer & Vining, 2005).

But central governmental planning clearly also has its drawbacks. Central governmental planning is an approach to public-sector steering in which the knowledge of the object of steering is assumed to be firm; the control over this object is presumed to be complete; and the decision-making process regarding the object is completely centralized. In reality governmental actors are unable to form comprehensive and accurate assessments of policy problems and to select and design completely effective strategies. In addition, governments are unable to monitor and totally control the activities of other societal actors involved in a policy field and run the risk of non-compliance, inefficiency and nepotism (Lindblom, 1959; Van Vught, 1989).

A "third way" thus has to be found and this is what governments in many nations appear to be seeking. These third ways are specific combinations of the two basic notions of the free market on the one hand, and of central planning on the other. They are "policy strategies" that show a set of "policy characteristics", i.e., a number of features that are the result of the relative emphasis on market coordination and central planning, and that create the specific appearance of these policies. A recent comparative study on national innovation policies shows that in general terms two major categories of policy strategies can be distinguished (Dill & Van Vught, 2009).

Prioritization Strategies

The first and largest category of policy strategies is formed by those policies that can be described as *prioritization strategies*. These policies show characteristics like foresight analyses in the science and technology sectors, priority allocation and concentration of resources, and quality assessments of research outputs. In doing so, they reflect continuation of the notions of central planning.

For example, in Australia both the Commonwealth and the state governments have engaged in research priority setting, emphasizing areas of science that will enhance economic competitiveness. In Canada the governments have attempted to define and fund Centres of Excellence in areas deemed strategic to the country's prosperity. In Finland the national technology agency TEKES explicitly funds university research programs in a number of technology fields that are assumed to be priorities of the Finnish policy of industrial development. In the Netherlands the national Innovation Platform has selected a limited set of "national key-areas" in which both fundamental research and knowledge transfer should be increased. The Foresight Assessments begun in the U.K. in the early 1990s were one of the earliest prioritization strategies in research funding. Even in the U.S., the president's National Science and Technology Council has recently defined a number of interagency research programs in areas of strategic importance to the national economy, and a number of the states are now identifying and funding academic research in specific technical fields with the expectation of stimulating economic growth.

These prioritization strategies also include national efforts to assess the quality of research outputs. The Research Assessment Exercises (RAE) have been a major driver of the significant changes in U.K. university behaviour. Similar, if less ambitious, efforts to link general university funding for research to government-determined output measures are also being experimented with in Australia, as part of the Institutional Grants Scheme, in Finland with performance-based contracts, and in the Netherlands with the so-called "Smart Mix" program.

Competition Strategies

The other category of innovation policies places an emphasis on market forces. These *competition strategies* show policy characteristics, such as emphasizing competitive allocation of research-related resources, encouraging entrepreneurial university behaviour, deregulating the university sector and encouraging multiple sources of funding for higher education and research. As such these strategies reflect a greater reliance on market coordination.

The pre-eminent example of this strategy is the U.S. federal science policy with its emphasis on a national market composed of rivalrous private and state-supported universities, its limited federal control, and its competitive allocation of funding through a set of overlapping research agencies. But many other governments are also experimenting with competition strategies, for example, by allocating less money for research via institutional block grants or general university funds and providing more resources via research councils and competitive grant schemes. For example Australia, Canada, Finland, Germany, Japan and the Netherlands have adopted a competitive approach to strengthening research doctoral training, either through competitive national fellowships to support Ph.D. students or through competitive grants for the development of selected graduate or research schools, or both. Australia is also utilizing competitive funding for the allocation of university research facilities; Canada and Finland for the allocation of well-funded faculty chairs; and Germany for funds designed to identify and support university "excellence". The U.K. is attempting to further diversify the funding base of their universities by offering competitive "third sector" funding to promote greater knowledge transfer between universities and industry. Similarly, Canada and several of the U.S. states competitively award matching funds for research facilities and research projects as a means of inducing private industry to participate in and financially support university research.

The State Supervising Model

Although the prioritization and competition strategies that have developed as part of governmental innovation policies can be clearly distinguished, neither is a clear-cut specimen of the respective notions of market coordination or central planning. Rather, the two strategies are both examples of the "third way" mentioned previously. The two strategies in this sense can be interpreted as manifestations of the "state supervising policy model" (Van Vught, 1989). This model is a combination of market coordination, which emphasises decentralized decision-making by providers and clients; framework setting; and supervision by government. In the general policy model of state supervision, the influence by governmental actors is limited. Governments do not intrude into the detailed decisions and operations of other actors. Rather, a certain level of autonomy of these actors is respected and their self-regulating capacities are acknowledged. Governments in this policy model see themselves as the providers of the regulatory, financial and communicative frameworks within which other actors can operate, and as the supervisors of these frameworks.

However, the setting and supervision of governmental policy frameworks in this model can nevertheless have major impacts on the behaviour of other actors. By introducing certain general quality assessment instruments or financial allocation mechanisms into their national policy frameworks, governments are able to strongly steer higher education and research systems without introducing detailed regulation. The differences between the prioritization and competition strategies previously mentioned reflect the levels of impact governmental policy frameworks have on these systems. The policy characteristics of the prioritization strategy clearly show a higher level of guidance and restriction than the competition strategy.

POLICY IMPACTS

The innovation policy strategies employed by national governments appear to have a number of direct effects on the behaviour of universities, thereby producing discernable changes in overall national higher education and research systems. International forces as well as the market competition introduced by these new policies have led to major reforms in the organization of publicly supported universities. Universities in many countries are now being encouraged by government to adopt a more corporate type of organization, with a stronger central administration, better ties to external stakeholders, and greater independence in the management of their internal affairs — a form well illustrated by Clark's (1998) concept of the "entrepreneurial university".

Research

The growing emphasis on competitive strategies for higher education and research has affected the internal research allocations of universities. The typical reaction of individual universities to the national innovation policies is to increase the quality and size of their successful research fields and hence to focus and concentrate their academic efforts in certain specialized areas. The outcomes of these institutional specialization and concentration processes, of course, differ according to the conditions of the various institutions. Previous academic performance, the affiliation of top-level researchers, and, in particular, the financial resources of a university are factors that are of crucial importance when developing an institutional research profile. But the general effect appears to be a trend within universities toward "focus and mass", toward specialization and concentration.

The new policies also appear to be making universities more productive in their output of publications and graduates, as well as in their patenting and licensing activities. In Australia and the U.K., this improvement has also occurred in universities newly designated after the abolition of the binary line, but the recent evidence from the U.K. suggests that any closing of the performance gap between the old and new universities brought about by these new policies has now slowed if not ended (Crespi & Geuna, 2004). This analysis also suggests that the adoption of performance-based research funding creates a one-time shock to the overall system, which initially motivates increased research productivity in all universities eligible for the funding, but over time is most likely to lead to an increased concentration of research in those institutions with richer resources, larger numbers of internationally recognized academic staff, and established reputations (Soo, 2008).

Marked improvements in the organization and management of higher education and research activities and programs are another impact of the national innovation strategies. It is likely that this improvement is due not only to the policies reviewed above, but also to the general reductions in funding for publicly supported universities that have occurred in conjunction with the massification and expansion of higher education in most countries (Williams, 2004). As a consequence, universities in a number of countries have necessarily become more highly motivated to pursue alternative sources of revenue for their research programs and, therefore, have been required to develop the internal management processes necessary to survive in this competitive market.

A possible negative impact of the new policies is the diminishment of research support in particular fields, often in unanticipated ways. Historically, the social sciences and humanities have received substantially lower levels of research support than have the basic sciences, medical sciences, and engineering. The current concern with national innovation and economic development, as well as the new policies of academic research, further disadvantage research in the "softer fields". Less obvious, however, is the potential negative impact that the strong emphasis on research programs in the applied sciences and technology along with performance-based funding can have on the support for research in some basic science subjects, such as chemistry, physics, and mathematics, which serve as the critical foundation for many technical and applied fields (Cohen, Nelson & Walsh, 2002). In the U.K. the concentration of research funding brought about by the RAE has led many universities to reduce or eliminate basic science departments that do not receive the highest rating. In the United States, despite a recent initiative by the National Science Foundation to increase funding for the basic sciences, shifts in research priorities by the large, mission-oriented agencies like the Department of Defense and NASA (the National Aeronautics and Space Administration), which fund significant amounts of academic basic research, may still result in reduced funding in foundational science fields. These concerns suggest that the more competitive and dynamic environment of higher education and research, which the new policy strategies helped create, may now require national governments to take more active steps to define particular subjects as in the national interest and to assure that these fields receive adequate support for research and (doctoral) education.

Knowledge Transfer

A major impact of the national innovation policies is that knowledge transfer has become an accepted and valued element of the general mission of most universities. Despite initial reluctance and even controversy in some institutions, significant changes in university culture have occurred over the last decades, with the development of a more entrepreneurial and utilitarian orientation to both university education and research programs. Universities now increasingly focus on their potential role as regional partners in innovation "clusters"; they develop programs with business and industry; they open up technology transfer offices; they offer consultancy and training activities in order to assist entrepreneurs in making use of new knowledge; and some even adopt their innovative character as an institutional identity. In Europe a group of "entrepreneurial universities" have organized themselves into a cooperative network, the European Consortium of Innovative Universities (ECIU).

As with publications and doctoral students, there clearly are increases in knowledge transfer activity by higher education institutions, as indicated by the numbers of patents, licences, and industrial start-ups. A much debated topic in the context of knowledge transfer is policies on intellectual property rights (IPR). The original changes in the IPR legislation in the United States — the Bayh-Dole Act — were motivated by a desire to speed knowledge-to-market; therefore, patent and licensing rights were re-allocated to universities through new laws designed to increase university incentives for knowledge transfer. The policy was never expected to create a major new source of funding for higher education and research institutions. But with the growing competition for academic research funding, universities are now more aggressively seeking research revenues from other sources and, in many instances, have interpreted new IPR legislation as an exhortation to "cash in" their research outcomes. The available evidence, however, suggests that most universities are at best breaking even and many are suffering net losses from their investments in technology transfer offices and affiliated activities. While many universities see their technology transfer expenses as a necessary investment that they expect to bear significant fruit over time, Geiger's (2007) research in the United States suggests that over the longer term the institutions that do reap some financial benefit from patenting and licensing are the most highly ranked and best known research universities. But even in these institutions there tends to be a ceiling as to the amount of such revenue that can be earned.

One unintended impact of public policies emphasizing IPR as a means of stimulating academic knowledge transfer is their influence upon the core academic processes. By increasing incentives for universities to patent and license their discoveries as a means of raising revenues, some theoretical results and research tools that have traditionally been freely available to other scholars and researchers are now being restricted. This constriction of open science may in fact lessen the economically beneficial "spillovers" to society that are a primary rationale for the public support of basic academic research. Policies intended to provide incentives for knowledge transfer, therefore, have to be designed with particular care to maintain the benefits of open science.

Research on sources of innovation in industry raises additional questions regarding the emphasis of national knowledge transfer policies on the "hard" artifacts of academic research (Cohen, Nelson & Walsh, 2002). Patents and licences are influential on innovation and profits in a relatively small number of industries and technical fields, biotech being the most prominent example. This reality helps explain the natural ceiling on patenting and licensing revenues that Geiger (2007) discovered in leading U.S. universities. More influential for most industries are the "softer" knowledge transfer processes, such as publications, meetings, the use of consultants, and the hiring of new Ph.D. graduates (Cohen, Nelson & Walsh, 2002; Agarwal & Henderson, 2002). As Geiger (2007) notes, public policies that emphasise the "hard" outputs of academic research are, therefore, likely to undersupport knowledge transfer beneficial to society. In the policies implemented by the European Commission and by a number of the E.U. member states, the emphasis on patenting and licensing appears to be more limited than in the United States. Instead the knowledge transfer focus is largely on the exchange of people, the increased production of research doctorates, and the stimulation of start-up firms. This European approach to knowledge transfer is "softer" than the U.S. focus on licensing and patents, but, as a first comparative study shows (Van Vught, 2007), not necessarily less effective. Despite less effort in terms of invention disclosures and patent applications, the E.U. countries execute more licences and create more start-up firms (but have less patents granted) than the United States.

Institutional Diversity

Reviewing the policy impacts discussed before, an interesting question is whether there is an overall diversification effect at the level of the *system* of the higher education and research as a result of the various reactions by higher education and research institutions to their altered framework conditions. The introduction of market forces and greater competition into higher education should, according to economic theory, lead not only to greater productivity in research outputs, but also to greater allocative efficiency for society as universities are required to respond more effectively to the needs of their various research patrons.

Because of its distinctive national policies, the U.S. higher education and research system has long been considered a system with substantial diversity in quality, with highly ranked academic research concentrated in a minority of its universities. About a third of the U.S. universities conduct more than two-thirds of federal academic R&D in addition to graduating over two-thirds of research doctorates. In contrast, the national policies of many European countries were designed to achieve a certain homogeneity in performance among publicly supported universities. The general impact of the new policies is to concentrate academic research and Ph.D. training in a smaller number of institutions, as well as in universities in economically advantaged regions. In Finland the government has made a public commitment to concentrate research and Ph.D. training in a few comprehensive universities. In Denmark the recent mergers in higher education and research intend to concentrate quality, volume and investment capacity. In a number of other countries national innovation policies have clearly been designed to create a group of "world-class universities". The RAEs in the U.K. and the Excellence Initiative in Germany are obvious examples.

Although there is clear evidence of increased research concentration, there is little empirical support for the view that the new policies are encouraging a diversity of university roles and missions. These policies certainly stimulate universities to engage in international competition, but they provide insufficient incentives for the development of true system diversity. While global market forces as well as government-designed prioritizing and competition strategies have been effective in helping differentiate a class of international research universities, the existing policies appear inadequate for steering the majority of a country's universities into constructive roles as part of a national higher education and research system. Academic autonomy is such that scholarly norms and values have become major drivers of institutional homogeneity. The forces of academic professionalism and the eagerness to increase individual and institutional academic reputations impel all universities in the new, more competitive environment to imitate one another rather than to diversify their missions and profiles.

All universities try to recruit and employ the best scientists, i.e., those scholars with the highest recognition and rewards, the highest citation impact scores, and the largest numbers of publications. In order to be able to do so, they need to increase their research expenditures (since the research context attracts scholars), creating a continuous need for extra resources. Given their wish to increase their reputation, universities also try to attract the most talented students. They use selection procedures to find them, but they also offer grants and other facilities in order to recruit them, again leading to a continuing need for additional resources. The major dynamic driving all universities is therefore an increasingly costly "reputation race" (Van Vught, 2008) in which universities are constantly trying to show their best possible academic performance and in which they have a permanent hunger for financial revenues. In this sense Bowen's famous law of higher education still holds "... in quest of excellence, reputation and influence... each institution raises all the money it can... [and] spends all it raises" (Bowen, 1980, 20).

The result of these forces is that the new policies for higher education and research have not yet engendered the allocative efficiency for society that they were expected to achieve. In the concluding section a strategy will be suggested for addressing this problem.

A NEW INNOVATION POLICY STRATEGY

The national innovation policies adopted by many nations have positively affected the productivity of higher education and research in most countries and have encouraged a more entrepreneurial culture within universities, particularly in the development of active processes of knowledge transfer. At the same time these policies also reveal a number of limitations. The apparent positive relationship between adoption of elements of the competition strategy and academic research performance may not be linear, and the actual impact of the increased research outputs on technical innovation and economic development has yet to be fully established. Furthermore, the new policies may be encouraging a costly race for world-class reputations among higher education institutions, a race that relatively few can win and that diminishes the diversity in higher education and research missions most beneficial to society.

We would suggest that these weaknesses of current public policies appear to be symptoms of market and government failures associated with inadequate information on the performance of both universities and related public policies. In the more competitive political environment now shaping higher education and research, what is needed in our view is a new innovation policy strategy. Such a strategy would focus less on the identification and prioritization of promising technology fields (i.e., the prioritization strategy) or on stimulating competition between higher education and research institutions (i.e., the competition strategy), but would focus more on the provision of information to enhance university performance. It would be a strategy of policy learning.

In our view, policy learning consists of three elements: a continuous search for better/new policies, a process of trial and error, and the gaining of experience and results under real-world conditions. Policy learning, in this sense, is the "deliberate attempt to adjust the goals and techniques of policy in response to past experience and new information" (Hall, 1993, 278). It implies the search for more effective policies through the application of existing policies. It combines application with analysis and, thus, focuses on learning.

A policy learning strategy underscores the necessity of providing valid, publicly accessible information on the performance of higher education and research organizations. Learning can only take place if the access to knowledge is a public good, open to all participants in the process and if no specific ownership of information exists. The policy learning strategy is therefore clearly related to the concept of "open innovation" (Chesbrough, 2003) and the Open Source approaches to software and information, in which ownership and protection of information are seen as restricting the circulation of knowledge and the consequent social benefits for society. A learning policy strategy, therefore, would stress the importance of public provision of information about higher education and research performance and about the effectiveness of public policies to stakeholders in order to stimulate learning and change.

A traditional role of government is to provide information in strategically important policy areas to help the public evaluate socially beneficial behaviour (Majone, 1997). However, the increased economic value of academic research, higher education graduates, and university reputation has motivated development of a worldwide industry of publications designed to provide information on university rankings and program quality. The U.S. News and World Report pioneered the publication of university quality rankings for students in 1983. But more recent rankings, such as the Shanghai Jiao Tong University rankings (commenced in 2003), the Times Higher Education Supplement rankings (commenced in 2004), and Ph.D. rankings by the commercial firm Academic Analytics in the United States (commenced in 2005), have focused more explicitly on institutional research performance and worldwide university reputation. These rankings provide extra stimuli for universities and governments to clamber up the global ladder of university reputation. The measures employed in these league tables represent the private interests of those who design them, and the validity and reliability of their indicators of research performance are highly debatable (Dill & Soo, 2005; Van der Wende & Westerheijden, 2009). In the new worldwide competitive market that confronts higher education and research, there is a need for more valid "signals" of higher education and research performance, i.e., information-oriented public policies designed to assure a more efficient rivalry among universities as they vie to better serve society (Dill, 1999). The recent, E.U.-funded project to develop a mechanism to "map" the higher education landscape by providing a multi-dimensional classification of higher education institutions is a first answer to this need (Van Vught, 2009a).

The Open Method of Coordination (OMC), as it is being applied in the innovation policy of the European Union (the "Lisbon Strategy"), offers another creative example of an information-based policy. The OMC assumes that coordination of national policies can be achieved without the transfer of legal competences or financial resources to the European level. It works through the setting of common goals; translating these into national policies; defining explicit, related performance indicators; and measuring and comparing the performance of these policies. With regard to national innovation, performance measurement takes place by using standardized indicators for benchmarking processes and progress monitoring as well as by means of peer reviews of the outcomes (European Commission, 2000; Bruno, Jacquot & Mandin, 2006; Gornitzka, 2007).

The OMC clearly is an arrangement that promotes policy learning among the E.U. member states. Its basic idea is to create, in a two-level structure of jurisdictions, systemically organized mutual-learning processes. At the level of the E.U., the member states evaluate their various policy performances according to the joint objectives set and the indicators agreed upon. In the variety of experiences, "good practices" are identified and their diffusion is supported. The coordination of the process is largely in the hands of the European Commission, which analyses the progress reports of the member states, identifies good practices, suggests recommendations for each member state and drafts an overall report that must be approved by the European Council (the heads of state or government of the member states and the president of the European Commission). Though the European Commission cannot make mandatory recommendations, it nevertheless plays a crucial role in organizing the process by suggesting common goals, collecting and analysing information, and drafting recommendations. The OMC stimulates the member states to experiment with different policies, evaluate their outcomes, and then identify good practices. It is a process of mutual learning, coordinated at the level of the European Commission, but with substantial flexibility and openness for the national governments (Van Vught, 2009b).

The E.U. experience with the OMC is usefully compared with the lack of comparable information-oriented policies to promote mutual learning among the U.S. states. The National Science Foundation provides extensive data on science and technology in the U.S. system and federal science agencies subsidize the research doctoral rankings conducted by the National Academies of Science. But the federal government has not formally supported the provision of systematic comparative data on the innovation performance of the 50 states similar to the European Innovation Scoreboard (latest version: European Commission, 2008a) or provided comparative data on the performance of U.S. universities similar to the European "progress toward the Lisbon objectives" reports on research and higher education (E.C., 2008b, 2008c). Nor has it provided related indicators or incentives for policy learning that would help guide the rapidly increasing investments in academic science and technology by many U.S. states. In order to prevent inefficient university regulation at the state level and promote mutual learning about effective innovation practices among states, the European approach to innovation policy learning deserves serious attention in the U.S., as well as in other federal systems of higher education.

In summary, the policy strategy of policy learning provides a potentially valuable and important supplement to the policy strategies of prioritization and competition, the two strategies that are so far still dominant in national innovation policies. The policy learning strategy assumes a minimal level of policy heterogeneity and therefore is particularly appropriate for multi-level political systems, like federal states and the European Union. But as suggested in Finland, with its emphasis on regional diversification, mutual learning is applicable in unitary nation states as well. Finally, the heterogeneity of policy contexts also offers a new and interesting means of addressing the issues of university autonomy in different higher education and research systems, and the inequalities regarding global academic competition. In diversifying their policy contexts in order to stimulate policy learning, national governments may create different conditions for different categories of universities and hence allow some of these institutions to really compete at the international platform of academic reputation, while other institutions are stimulated to develop more national or regional profiles. National governments that take global competition processes seriously and accept the fact that the capacity to create, disseminate and apply knowledge is of crucial importance in these processes may, in this sense, find important extra strategic advantages in developing their ability to learn.

Public policies designed to strengthen national innovation and its contributions to economic development need to focus on promoting mutual learning among universities, their various patrons, and policy-makers in the different strata of multi-level governance. For this to occur, governments need to invest in information-based policies that provide to the many stakeholders of the universities valid and reliable information on higher education and research performance as well as comparably objective information on the social costs and benefits of public policies intended to enhance academic research, improve the quality of graduates, and boost knowledge transfer.

REFERENCES

Aghion, A. (2006). A Primer on Innovation and Growth. Bruegel Policy Brief: www.bruegel.org

Agarwal, A. & Henderson, R. (2002). Putting Patents in Context: Exploring Knowledge Transfer from MIT. Management Science 48(1): pp. 44-60.

Balzat, M. (2006). An Economic Analysis of Innovation: Extending the Concept of National Innovation Systems. Cheltenham, U.K.: Edward Elgar.

Bowen, H. R. (1980). The Costs of Higher Education. San Francisco: Jossey-Bass.

Bruno, I., Jacquot, S. & Mandin L. (2006). Europeanization through its Instrumentation: Benchmarking, Mainstreaming and the Open Method of Coordination... Toolbox or Pandora's Box? Journal of European Public Policy, 13(4): pp. 519-536.

Chesbrough, H. W. (2003). Open Innovation, the New Imperative for Creating and Profiting from Technology. Boston: Harvard Business School Press.

Clark, B. R. (1998). The Entrepreneurial University. Oxford: Pergamon Press.

Cohen, W. M., Nelson R. R. & Walsh, J. P. (2002). Links and Impacts: The Influence of Public Research on Industrial R&D. Management Science 48: pp. 1-23.

Crespi, G. & Geuna, A. (2004). The Productivity of Science. Science and Technology Policy Research Unit (SPRU), University of Sussex. http://www.sussex.ac.uk/spru/documents/crespiost2.pdf.

Dill, D. D. (1999). Academic Accountability and University Adaptation: The Architecture of an Academic Learning Organisation. Higher Education 38(2): pp. 127-154.

Dill, D. D. & Soo, M. (2005). Academic Quality, League Tables, and Public Policy: A Cross-National Analysis of University Ranking Systems. *Higher Education* 49(4): pp. 495-533.

Dill, D.D. & Van Vught, F.A. (eds.) (forthcoming, 2009). *National Innovation and the Academic Research Enterprise: Public Policy in Global Perspective*, Baltimore: the John Hopkins University Press.

Edquist, C. (1997). *Systems of Innovation: Technologies, Institutions and Organisations*. New York: Francis Pinter.

European Commission. (2000). *Development of an Open Method of Co-ordination for Benchmarking National Research Policies: Objectives, Methodology and Indicators*, Working Document, SEC (2000) 1842. Brussels: EC.

European Commission. (2008a). *European Innovation Scoreboard 2008, Comparative Analysis of Innovation Performance*, www.proinno-europe.eu/metrics

European Commission. (2008b). *A More Research-Intensive and Integrated European Research Area*, Science, Technology and Competitiveness Key Figures Report 2008/2009, Brussels: Directorate-General for Research.

European Commission. (2008c). *Progress Toward the Lisbon Objectives in Education and Training, Indicators and Benchmarks 2008*, Commission Staff Working Document based on SEC (2008) 2293, Brussels: Directorate-General for Education and Culture.

Geiger, R. L. (2007). *Technology Transfer Offices and the Commercialisation of Innovation in the United States*. Paper presented at the CHER Conference, Dublin, Ireland, 30 August - 1 September.

Gornitzka, Å. (2007). *The Open Method of Coordination in European Research and Education Policy: New Political Space in the Making?* Paper presented at the CHER Conference, Dublin, Ireland, 30 August - 1 September.

Hall, P. A. (1993). Policy Paradigms, Social Learning and the State: The Case of Economic Policymaking in Britain. *Comparative Politics* 25: pp. 275-296.

Laredo P. & Mustar, P. (2001). *Research and Innovation Policies in the New Global Economy: An International Comparative Analysis*. Cheltenham, UK: Edward Elgar

Lindblom, C. E. (1959). The Science of Muddling Through. *Public Administration Review* 19: pp. 79-88.

Lundvall, B-Å. & Borrás, S. (2004). Science, Technology, and Innovation Policy. In J. Fagerberg, D. C. Mowery, & R. R. Nelson (eds.), *Oxford Handbook of Innovation*, pp. 599-631. Oxford: Oxford University Press.

Majone, G. (1997). The New European Agencies: Regulation by Information. *Journal of European Public Policy* 4(2): pp. 262-275.

Martin, B. R. (2003). The Changing Social Contract for Science and the Evolution of the University. In A. Geuna, A. J. Salter & W. E. Steinmuller (eds.), *Science and Innovation: Rethinking the Rationales for Funding and Governance*, pp. 7-29. Cheltenham, UK: Edward Elgar.

Mowery, D. C. & Sampat, B. N. (2004). Universities in National Innovation Systems. In J. Fagerberg, D. C. Mowery & R. R. Nelson (eds.), *Oxford Handbook of Innovation*, pp. 209-239. Oxford: Oxford University Press.

Nelson, R. (1993). *National Innovation Systems: A Comparative Study*. Oxford: Oxford University Press.

Rammer, C. (2006). Trends in Innovation Policy: An International Comparison. In U. Schmoch, C. Rammer & H. Legler (eds.), *National Systems of Innovation in Comparison: Structure and Performance Indicators for Knowledge Societies*, pp. 265-286. Dordrecht: Springer

Santiago, P., Tremblay, K., Basri, E., & Arnal, E. (2008). *Tertiary Education for the Knowledge Society*. OECD: Paris.

Soete, L. (2006). Knowledge, Policy and Innovation. In L. Earl & F. Gault (eds.), *National Innovation, Indicators and Policy*, pp. 198-218. Cheltenham: Edward Elgar.

Soo, M. (2008). *The Effect of Market-Based Policies on Academic Research Performance: Evidence from Australia 1992-2004*. Ph.D. diss., University of North Carolina-Chapel Hill.

Teixeira, P., Jongbloed B., Dill D. D. & A. Amaral. (Eds.) (2004). *Markets in Higher Education: Rhetoric or Reality?* Dordrecht: Kluwer.

Van Vught, F. A. (ed.). (1989). *Governmental Strategies and Innovation in Higher Education*. London: Jessica Kingsley.

Van Vught, F.A. (2007) *Knowledge Transfer in the European Union*. Paper presented at the CHER Conference, Dublin, Ireland, 30 August - 1 September.

Van Vught, F.A. (2008). Mission Diversity and Reputation in Higher Education. *Higher Education Policy* 21(2): pp. 151-174.

Van Vught, F.A. (ed.) (2009a). *Mapping the Higher Education Landscape, Towards a European Classification of Higher Education*, Dordrecht: Springer

Van Vught, F.A. (2009b). The EU Innovation Agenda, challenges for European higher education and research, *Journal of Higher Education Management and Policy*, Vol. 21/2, forthcoming.

Weimer, D. & Vining, A. R. (2005). *Policy Analysis: Concepts and Practice*. Upper Saddle River, NJ: Pearson Prentice Hall.

Van der Wende, M. & Westerheijden, D. (2009). Rankings and Classifications: the Need for a Multidimensional Approach. In Frans van Vught (ed.), *Mapping the Higher Education Landscape, Towards a European Classification of Higher Education*, Dordrecht: Springer

Williams, G. (2004). The Higher Education Market in the United Kingdom. In P. Teixeira, B., B. Jongbloed, D.D. Dill & A. Amaral (eds.) (2004) *Markets in Higher education: Rhetoric or Reality?* Dordrecht: Kluwer.

World Bank. (2007) *Global Economic Prospects: Managing the Next Wave of Globalisation*, Washington DC: The World Bank.

PART III

• • • • • • • • • • • • •

National and Regional Innovation Strategies

CHAPTER 7

Innovation strategies of European universities in the triangle of education, research and innovation

Georg Winckler

THE TRIANGLE AND ITS HISTORY

Education was first

In Europe, the first university started in Bologna in 1088 as "universitas magistrorum et scholarium", a community of teachers and students. Its legitimacy was derived from a humanistic program; its activities consisted in providing general and professional education.

As an example of the mission of a medieval university, I may cite the charter of the University of Vienna, founded in 1365 as one of the oldest universities in Europe. The charter states first that the university should strengthen the Christian faith. Then, it continues lengthily that the university should serve (1) the public good ("res publica"), (2) the judicial equity ("equitas iudicii"), and (3) human reasoning ("humanus intellectus"), as well as rationality ("ratio"). Accordingly, the University of Vienna, as other universities, was divided into the four classical faculties. There were three "higher" or "professional" faculties: the faculty of theology (strengthening faith), of medicine (public good) and of law (judicial equity). The "lower" faculty of artists, as the fourth faculty, was devoted to general education. There, reasoning and rationality were taught through grammar, logic, the art of rhetoric, arithmetic, geometry and astronomy/astrology. In the British universities which remained so medieval for so long, and which were copied by the old colleges in the U.S., it was clear that their main purpose was education too. They wanted emancipation through education and aimed at forming a civil society. Students should be transformed into learned and "honourable" gentlemen.

Then came scientific research

Conducting scientific research at a university is a goal which explicitly emerged only in the 18th century. However, this goal was not accepted by universities without resistance, since at that time, universities were mostly occupied in debating theological themes, an outcome of the reformation and counter-reformation of the preceding centuries. As a consequence, besides training doctors and lawyers, the universities then excelled in theology and philosophy, but not in the sciences. An open issue of the 18th century was how to get universities engaged in developing the sciences.

Take the case of the University of Vienna once again. The strengthening of the sciences was introduced by a decree from above: the Empress Maria Theresia simply nationalized the university in the 1770s and ousted the Jesuits who dominated the previously autonomous university. On the advice of the Dutch scientist and doctor van Swieten, she ordered that the university should expand in the sciences, especially in the faculty of medicine.

France took another, more radical approach. During the French revolution, on the suggestion of the Talleyrand commission of the Assemblée Nationale in 1791, it was stated that, on behalf of progress, universities should be closed and substituted by "écoles spéciales". These institutions, later called "grandes écoles", served the purpose of educating the needed technocratic cadres to help strengthen the state by public investments and to defend a nation at war. The Ecole Polytechnique, founded in 1794, is a part of the French Ministry of Defence even today. Strengthening civil society through universities was not an aim to be pursued. Research activities were mostly placed in specific research institutions, e.g., in the CNRS. As a consequence, many universities were closed, even in Germany during the Napoleonic era (e.g. Erfurt, Cologne and others).

The idea of a true research university was developed later in Prussia. The first important contribution in this direction came from Kant in his booklet *Fakultätenstreit*, first published in 1798. He argued that, especially in the "professional" faculties of theology, medicine and law, the teaching of prescriptions should be replaced by philosophical, scientific reasoning, thus giving the faculty of philosophy, the former faculty of artists, not a lower, but a superior rank within the university. In creating the Berlin University in 1810 as "universitas litterarum" by Humboldt and others, and no longer as "universitas magistrorum et scholarium", the legitimacy of the university was changed from humanism to philosophical speculation (Lyotard, 1979, ch. 9). The search for truth, for new knowledge, constituted the very purpose of a university. The university was perceived as the meta-subject of the unity of knowledge, of all the sciences, hence as "universitas litterarum".

It is not a surprise that, as a consequence, the bachelor and master programs were totally abolished. Only doctoral programs were offered by the Humboldtian universities, since doctoral education could be ideally combined with searching for the truth. Each university had to follow this speculative idea of a research university, otherwise it would not be regarded as a true university. Until the early 20th century, diploma studies in Germany were only offered at technical universities which were originally modelled according to the French Ecole Polytechnique. Only during the last 100 years, especially during the Nazi Regime, diploma studies got generally introduced at universities in order to meet the practical demands of a more and more industrialized society, going along with a steep increase in the number of students.

In the 1890s and then especially in the first half of the 20th century, U.S. universities started to implement the Humboldtian idea of a research university. Yet their approach was pragmatic. They put the Ph.D. programs on top of the British, medieval study structure. This pragmatism, driven by no political planning at the federal level, allowed a diversification of the U.S. university system preparing it (a) for the recent massification of higher education and (b) for a strong research intensification at some universities. Today, among the 4,000 to 5,000 US higher education institutions, most of them are purely teaching institutions. There are only 200 to 300 research intensive universities, granting Ph.Ds. In contrast, in Continental Europe where the Humboldtian idea influenced so many university reforms at the national level during the 19th century, there are about 1,000 Ph.D.-granting universities, not counting those in Russia or in the Ukraine. In addition, the university system in Continental Europe remained nationally fragmented, fostering national university cultures and national academic careers. According to a survey of the E.U. Commission, still today in the E.U., 97% of the academic staff of universities had employments only in the country in which they received their Ph.Ds. Of course, the Bologna-Process as well as the emergence of the European Research Area aim at overcoming these national fragmentations in higher education and research.

Finally: Innovation

Innovation is a buzz-word of the last ten years. It emerged from an economic debate, stressing the importance of innovation for growth and jobs in a globalized world. The economic growth in Europe after World War II was mainly seen as a result of a successful imitation. The failure to surpass the U.S. during the last 20-30 years was attributed to the lack of innovation activities in Europe (see Aghion & Howitt, 2006). Thus, replacing imitation strategies by an innovation agenda became a strong political program of the E.U., and inspired the so-called Lisbon Strategy of 2000. Research, supposed to generate innovation activities, should reach 3% of GDP by 2010.

At first, universities were hardly mentioned in the various strategy papers of the E.U. However, that has changed during recent years, especially due to the efforts of the E.U.-Commission. At the meeting of the European Council during the British E.U. Presidency at Hampton Court in October 2005, the then British Prime Minister, Tony Blair, stressed the need for modernized universities as agents of innovation. The E.U. Commission, having launched this debate already in 2003 (see, especially, "The Role of Universities in the Europe of Knowledge", [European Commission, 2003]), responded to the Hampton Court request of the European Council by "Delivering on the Modernisation Agenda for Universities: Education, Research and Innovation" (European Commission, 2006). However, many E.U. member states, apart from general commitments and declarations, did not allow the E.U. Commission to push this issue further after the Hampton Court meeting, since they regarded the implications of this agenda, especially the better financial dotations of universities, as a national concern only. Given this division of responsibilities, the evolution of the university system in the E.U. is still today mainly driven by various national political interests.

To summarize: When discussing the new role of European universities in the triangle of higher education, research and innovation, one needs to be aware of the fact that there are different historical, legal and political layers to the debate. The continuity of old ideas, the persistence of history and the dominance of the interests of nation states seem to thwart any far-reaching European plan in which universities would play a more effective and more entrepreneurial role in this key triangle of the 21st century.

TOWARDS A COMMON UNDERSTANDING IN EUROPE: COMBINING 'OPEN SCIENCE' WITH 'OPEN INNOVATION'

'Open Science'

Despite the different national pasts of universities in Europe and despite the deeply rooted national interests which still seem to drive the evolution of the European university system, new and common concepts for the working of universities in the 21st century have emerged. This emergence of new concepts reflects, on the one hand, the common values and traditions of universities, especially their common mission to provide public goods. In the Magna Charta Universitatum, signed in Bologna 1988, the set of common values of European universities is recorded. On the other hand, due to various E.U. programs (ERASMUS scheme for the mobility of students, E.U.'s framework programs) and due to the effects of creating a common market in Europe, the networking and collaboration among European universities increased during recent decades. That created a dynamism which started to foster new common ideas. The various joint meetings of European universities are witness to this development.

One increasingly shared concept among European universities is the notion of "open science". "Open science" means that the bulk of new knowledge should be generated and disseminated rapidly by giving up the rights over using this knowledge. It is assumed that the existence of "open science" will facilitate the generation of further knowledge, will help students to be equipped with the best knowledge and will allow the latest insights to be more easily fed into the innovation system. The benefits of "open science" are explained by the huge positive external effects it creates. This in turn justifies the principle that research and education at universities should be basically regarded as public goods and be financed by public money, a tradition which is strongly rooted in the political culture of many European countries.

Of course, there is an incentive problem: How to reward the researchers so that they give up their rights over new knowledge via rapid publication? This incentive problem can be solved by designing specific reputational, hierarchical and monetary rewards within the university (which, in Europe, implies changes from a still feudal to a meritocratic system).

'Open Innovation'

A second concept receiving more and more acceptance in Europe is the concept of "open innovation" (see, e.g., H. Chesbrough *et al.*, 2006). "Open innovation" is defined by H. Chesbrough as "a paradigm that assumes that firms can and should use external ideas as well as internal ideas, and internal and external paths to market, as they look to advance their technology" (p. vii). Clearly, the more universities pursue the idea of "open science" and the more firms follow the paradigm of "open innovation", the more intensive will be the formal and informal interactions between universities and business.

Universities have accepted that collaboration with business, up to a certain level and dependent on the subject area, increases scientific productivity. They have left the ivory towers of academia. Of course, when dealing with business, the universities should take into account how university-business relations will influence status and funding systems within a university; for a critical account see, e.g., L. Manjarrez-Henriguez *et al.* (2008). As a consequence, universities need to design institutional strategies of how to best benefit from interaction with business and from the private revenue streams it generates there.

Against this background, today's universities can be defined as effective institutions managing "open science" and linking "open science" with "open innovation" of firms. Institutional strategies, based on the mission and profile of a university, are required. Institutional policies of quality assurance should make sure that academic values are maintained. Given the widespread non-observability of academic output, universities are challenged to solve intricate principal-agent problems in creative work. Optimal designs of the reputational, hierarchical and monetary rewards are needed.

Universities as autonomous institutions

During recent decades, it has become quite clear that universities cannot solve these principal-agent problems and cannot come up with consistent institutional strategies when managing "open science" and linking this to "open innovation", if they remain a dependent part of national ministerial bureaucracies. To meet the challenges of more and more globalized knowledge societies, universities need academic, organizational, staffing and budgetary autonomy so that they can adopt their own profiles and missions, and choose appropriate governance structures in order to be "fit for purpose". Institutional autonomy should also allow the universities to be more active, more effective and more entrepreneurial at the global, European and regional level. Universities should no longer act within the national context only.

Due to various European activities, including the Bologna Process, and due to various regional initiatives, universities are now aware that they are not just a medium of the nation state. Now, European universities are prepared to participate in a more European education of their students, a consequence of the increasing Europeanization of labour markets. They now engage more in research and innovation activities at the European level. Successful participation in the programs of the European Research Council and, soon, in EIT activities, bring reputation-enhancing benefits and scientific rewards. In addition, universities are now also more willing to become innovative engines within their region. As a consequence, the institutional diversification of the European university system will more and more follow the diversified needs of the European knowledge society and knowledge economy. In the Europe of the next decades, the universities will be less shaped by national interests, but will more and more respond to upcoming European and regional interests.

INNOVATION STRATEGIES OF EUROPEAN UNIVERSITIES

Regional innovation

Particularly since the oil shocks of the 1970s, it has become evident that universities can substantially contribute to a sustainable regional development. Universities can help in making regional industry more globally competitive. This point has been studied extensively by the OECD which reports on various institutional and regional strategies, policies and activities in order to offer a good understanding of the drivers of and the barriers to the regional engagement on universities, see OECD, 2007.

According to the OECD, there are several key factors for success of regional policy initiatives involving universities as stakeholders: (1) formal and informal interconnections with all actors at the regional level, including local governments, regional development agencies, industry and enterprises, (2) political support to undertake major actions for innovation, especially support for upstream strategies, consisting in attracting the relevant world-class work force, e.g., researchers and attracting the financial means to invest in specific educational and research infrastructures, (3) addressing major societal needs of regions so that general political support is maintained and (4) the use of E.U. Structural Funds where applicable.

Interesting case studies include the regions of Värmland/Sweden, Twente/ Netherlands, the Region of Valencia/Spain, North East of England (Durham Newcastle, Teesside) and the cross border initiative in the Oresund region/ Denmark and Sweden. In Twente/NL and in the North East of England older heavy industrial areas got transformed into modern ones, whereas, e.g., in Värmland/Sweden an industrial base was established around agriculture.

In all these cases, the mismatch between the industrial and academic profile of a region could be overcome. Although regional innovation activities of European universities are now starting to impress, all the cited cases cannot match the well-known Taiwanese example of Hsinchu. There, a thriving computer industry is located around an industry-science-park, consisting of more than 100,000 employees, and a university focusing on electrical engineering, computer sciences and computational business administration only.

E.U.-wide innovation strategies

In general, according to the European Commission, universities have failed to use their innovation potential (see van Vught [2009], chapter on E.U. higher education policy). Barriers to the better use of their potential are: uniformity and egalitarianism with national university systems, national fragmentations, too much mono-disciplinarity, lack of lifelong learning, lack of entrepreneurship of graduates, too high dependency on the state with too little autonomy for the universities and too much regulation. In research, there is too little world-class excellence.

This far-reaching critique leaves open the question of how this shortage in they supply of innovation activities can be overcome: by bashing universities and pushing them to supply more activities or by pulling universities by a strong European innovation demand (See Edler & Georghiou, 2007)? In fact, one can argue that the poor outcome concerning innovation activities of European universities, besides some interesting cases of regional innovation, results from a non-existing cross-border innovation demand in Europe. There are only national innovation demands, at low levels, duplicating efforts again and again in the field of sustainable energy, ICT, climate change and so on. No member state of the E.U. wants to be left out when it comes to do research in relevant innovation fields. As a consequence, either no agreements on cross-border innovation demands are reached or, if there are agreements, a complex, bureaucratic cooperation structure is set up which deters the world-class research centers in Europe from participating.

The so-called Aho Report (European Communities, 2006), another document of 2006 which responded to the 2005 Hampton Court request of the European Council, pleaded for the creation of European-wide innovation-friendly markets with a strong innovation demand. An independent High Level Coordinator should be appointed to orchestrate European action. Actions are especially needed on regulation standards, public procurement and intellectual property rights. Creating a European, cross-border innovation demand would be especially important in e-Health, Pharmaceuticals, Energy, Environment, Transport and Logistics, Security and Digital Content. A "Pact for Research and Innovation" should drive the Agenda for an Innovative Europe. Europe, it is reported, must break out of old, national structures and expectations.

At the European level, there have been some developments since 2006 which pick up the recommendations of the Aho Report. Joint Programming, Technology Platforms and Joint Technology Initiatives are new key words of the R&D policy of the E.U. The Innovative Medicine Initiative, e.g., has a budget of 2 billion Euro, 1 billion coming from industry, 1 billion from the European Commission. However, issues of lack of full cost recovery, of sharing patents and the complexity of cooperation structures remain, making these initiatives not sufficiently attractive for universities. Perhaps a new, less complex and more excellence-related path of development may be pursued by the EIT when the first four Knowledge and Innovation Communities (KICs) in the field of ICT, climate change and sustainable energy will be created in 2010. The size of money involved in the EIT activities, however, is limited. It will be less than what in the U.S. one institution (MIT) received as innovation demand by only one federal agency in one year: In 2006 MIT received US$639.5 million from the Department of Defense (World Almanac 2008, p. 125).

FINAL REMARKS

The activities of European universities in the triangle of education, research and innovation are still driven by the interests and bureaucracies of the European nation states. However, there are new trends. The common university values, the readiness to meet the challenges of the 21st century by managing "open science" and linking this to "open innovation", the search for institutional autonomy and the effects of emerging common markets generate a dynamism which may well create a new and diversified university structure in Europe, with more effective institutions, being more open to regional or cross-border innovation. Hopefully, the current economic crisis will not revitalize national interests and impede these new trends.

Greater linkage between the instruments of the European higher education policies and of European research policies, on one hand, and national policies, on the other hand, are needed. Such linkages would foster continuity in the strategic development of a university's teaching, research and innovation activities.

REFERENCES

Aghion, P. & Howitt, P. (2006). "Appropriate Growth Policy: A Unifying Framework. Joseph Schumpeter Lecture", *Journal of the European Economic Association*, pp. 269-314.

Chesbrough H. *et al.* (Eds). (2006). *Open Innovation, Researching a new Paradigm*, Oxford University Press.

Edler, J. & Georghiou, L. (2007). "Public procurement and innovation — Resurrecting the demand side", *Research Policy*, Vol. 36/7, pp. 949-963.

European Commission. (2003). *The Role of Universities in the Europe of Knowledge*, COM (2003), 58 final, 5 February 2003, Brussels.

European Commission. (2006). *Delivering on the Modernisation Agenda for Universities: Education, Research and Innovation*, COM (2006), 208 final, 10 May 2006, Brussels.

European Communities. (2006). *Creating an Innovative Europe, Report of the Independent Expert Group R&D and Innovation*, appointed following the Hampton Court Summit and chaired by Mr. Esko Aho (Aho-Report), Brussels.

Lyotard, F. (1979). *La condition postmoderne*, Paris: Editions de Minuit.

Manjarrez-Henriguez, L., Gutirrez Gracia, A. & Vega Jurado, J. (2008). "Coexistence of university-industry relations and academic research: Barrier to or incentive for scientific productivity". *Scientometrics*, vol 76/3, pp. 561-576.

OECD. (2007). *Higher Education and Regions. Globally Competitive and Locally Engaged*, Paris.

Van Vught, F. (2009). "The EU innovation Agenda: Challenges for European Higher Education and Research", *Higher Education Management and Policy*, Vol. 21/2.

World Almanac. (2008). *The World Almanac and Book of Facts*. New York: World Almanac Books, A Reader's Digest Company.

CHAPTER

Team Players to Shape our Future: Do our Students Learn the Right Skills?

Ralph Eichler

E ducation is the key for success and welfare of a country. Figure 1 shows the correlation between the wealth intensity and the number of citations in scientific journals. Switzerland is among the top nations. It has a special, so-called dual education system (Figure 2). From age 16 onwards, the majority of our young people receive practical training in a company, and a minority of only about 20% (Figure 3) attend senior high school, which provides the entry ticket to one of our universities. This system is different from many other countries, but it is an effective tradition and generates the lowest unemployment rate among young people in Europe.

DEMANDING BASIC EDUCATION

ETH Zurich is a 154-year-old technical university with degree programs in architecture, engineering and science. At the beginning of their studies, the students have to go through a demanding basic education — mathematics, physics and chemistry — before concentrating on their field of choice. Among the faculty members and the students there is a large number of foreign people. This is done intentionally as a small country has to recruit from an international pool of talent. It also gives our students exposure to different cultures and, last but not least, it generates an element of competition. But the question remains: do our students learn the right skills?

The global community today is confronted with complex, long-term tasks that are the core business of universities. To meet these Great Challenges, such as climate change, energy conservation, clean mobility, ageing population and sustainable food production, we need excellent interdisciplinary research and highly skilled scientists and engineers. In the world of science, national borders do not exist; researchers work in international groups in order to achieve the best results.

THE ARCHITECTS — PLANNERS OF SUSTAINABLE CITIES

One Great Challenge for architects is the sustainable planning of future cities — cities with a population larger than the size of Switzerland — which means more than approximately seven million. Architects not only have to design houses and streets, but also have to involve the dynamics — which means they have to understand the interplay of the flows of people (mobility), of energy, water, and the flow of waste. It needs the skills of an artist, the know-how of a designer and knowledge of the physics of energy in order to achieve optimal solutions for different climate zones. Architects should also understand the social behaviour of different cultures.

It is thus clear that modern education needs the exchange of global knowledge and knowledge of different cultures. The best way to achieve this exchange is through the mobility of people — of people who are eager to learn and who want to shape our future.

THE ENGINEERS — DEVELOPERS OF HIGH-TECH SYSTEMS

Engineers have built the modern world around us. Mobile phones, computers, cars, planes, power plants and many other technical products are proof of this. For example, we had a period in Switzerland about 100 years ago when all the trains, tunnels and dams in the Alps were constructed by engineers educated at ETH Zurich.

Today, engineers design high-tech systems, but sometimes, although these products are top class, they are too expensive for developing countries. An example of this is the hybrid car with a conventional engine and an electric motor in addition. The team responsible for this at ETH Zurich — Professor of Mechanical Engineering Lino Guzzella, together with his students — designed an intermediate energy storage with compressed air, driven by a conventional engine filled during breaking. In the successive acceleration of the car this stored energy is recuperated, and therefore it is possible to save 20 to 30% of gasoline.

THE SCIENTISTS — TEAM PLAYERS FOR FUTURE SOLUTIONS

Due to the worldwide ageing population and the corresponding development of medical technology, collaboration between engineers and medical doctors is becoming more and more important. ETH is very active in this field and plans to enlarge its activities even further. Also quantum science has a long tradition at ETH. And the great masters and Nobel laureates Albert Einstein, Erwin Schroedinger and Wolfgang Pauli spent part of their scientific career in Zurich. But what comes next? The quantum computer, quantum cryptography or the single electron transistor in commercial products? Involved are physicists, electrical engineers and computer scientists — they are the team players for future solutions.

SCIENCE — AN ADVENTURE FOR YOUNG PEOPLE

Where are the adventures for young people today? The North Pole has already been discovered, men have been to the Moon. But I am convinced that science can still fascinate young people. It offers really true adventures of a different kind — to discover unknown territory through hard work. We are curious to understand the big bang, the beginning of our universe. We are looking for answers to questions such as what dark energy and dark matter are made of. And, although we know the structure of proteins, we do not know the dynamics of life. Or, for example, what do the 10^9 proteins do in a cell? We still are not able to design a computer with the power of our brain and an energy consumption of less than 50 Watt. Real life problems are the most difficult to understand because they need input from many different disciplines.

The question remains: how to attract the best talents in this worldwide contest? ETH Zurich assigns to its students tasks that are a mixture of adventure and competition. Adventure is a driver for discoveries, and competition a motivator for top-quality performance — and an attraction for creative young people in scientific technologies. Research projects like a soccer game for micro-robots on a mm^2 playing field, or a self-directed sailing boat to cross the Atlantic Ocean — such projects and many others inspire the pioneering spirit and evoke visionary dreams.

MODERN EINSTEINS ARE NEEDED — FOR INTERDISCIPLINARY AND INTERNATIONAL TEAMS

We need a lot of Einsteins to face these challenges — but modern Einsteins! He was a genius and discovered new physical theories, and without them no particle accelerator would run today. But he also was an individualistic scientist working alone in his study. In fact, he was not a big team player. Today however, we need to train scientists and engineers who can work together and who are able to cross the boundaries of their original disciplines. Modern Einsteins must not only have a high-class, scientific education, but also social competence — for instance, they have to be able to communicate with people of different disciplines and cultures.

Interdisciplinary projects demand enlarged skills that can only be acquired in several stages. We have learnt over the years how to judge the quality of projects in specific disciplines, and we know how to make a career in a specific discipline — that is tradition and business as usual. Therefore, it is my strong belief that it is mandatory to first become a champion in one discipline. But the second part of an academic education has to deal with students having to learn to talk to people from neighbouring disciplines. For example, a physicist should be able to understand a biologist and vice versa. Or a civil engineer should know the scientific problems of a chemist. More than mere curiosity should drive scientists to find a solution for a scientific problem. They should also dedicate themselves to finding solutions to one of the world's Great Challenges. We need both of them!

PROJECT LEADERS LEARNING FROM PRACTICAL EXPERIENCE

I have described the example of the architects in the field of city planning, now I give you another example: most IT projects fail, not because of technology, but because of the lack of understanding of the customer's needs (but also the customer does not always know his or her needs). In addition, software projects often involve people who are located in geographically different places. Therefore, we also need good project leaders, who monitor the different tasks, the time schedule and the budget as well. Is this something you can learn in a theoretical lecture? Not really; because one also has to practise it. ETH students have founded a company called "ETH Juniors". The management consists of eight people who acquire jobs from the industry for students. One out of ten inquiries to the industry was successful. And this is an example for a training in patience and endurance. Last year, they had a turnover of a million Swiss francs.

ETH Zurich provides the basics and support to all these "soft skills". Every student has to select from a broad line-up of topics from our department of Management, Technology and Economics and from the department of Humanities, Social and Political Sciences. There are lectures about management abilities, the history of science, Asian history and culture, or behaviour sciences, just to name a few.

BUILDING A BETTER WORLD — RELYING ON SCIENCE AND TECHNOLOGY

Besides becoming a champion in his or her academic field, the student should obtain a broader view of our planet. As I said, we need modern Einsteins — with innovative scientific ideas and social skills. My hope goes in the direction that globalization will preserve some of the cultural differences between nations. By respecting each other, we will build a better world. For this ambitious plan we have to rely on science and technology.

THE ROLE OF HUMANITIES AND SOCIAL SCIENCES

So far, I have emphasized science and technology. Physics is a way of thinking. Each complex problem is cut into sub-problems, which can be solved. The art is to identify these solvable and therefore simplified sub-problems. Other disciplines are now also starting to use this method. One example for this is that recently, a researcher at ETH modelled the behaviour of the crowd in Mecca during the pilgrimage. Instabilities of the crowd could be predicted from measurable quantities during the stable phase: mathematical language and statistics therefore enter into social sciences.

A fascinating problem is to understand human language. The difficulty is made obvious by the poor performance of language translation by machines. The ultimate goal is the machine translation of a joke and a machine laughing automatically at the right spot. This is so difficult to achieve because you have to understand the culture and history of a country. And there is also an emotional component, too. It is so complex, because it is much more than a pure linguistic masterpiece.

FUNDAMENTAL INVARIANTS

The question is if we can parameterize the culture of a country? It needs about 15 years for a child to become familiar with the basics of its own culture, religion and established prejudices. I believe that the deep truths of our world are the invariants, the similarities in religions and cultures. Fundamental truths are usually independent of time. These invariants are the research subjects a physicist is interested in. Once these invariants are known, the remaining parameter space of a cultural system or even civilization will be much smaller.

Figure 1: Wealth intensity versus citation intensity

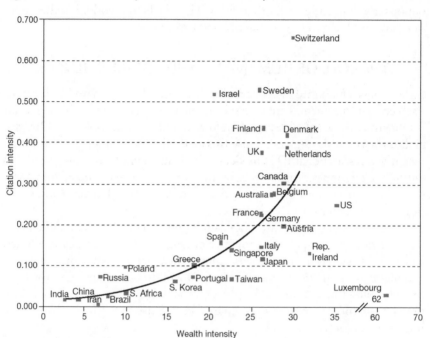

Figure 2: The Swiss dual education system

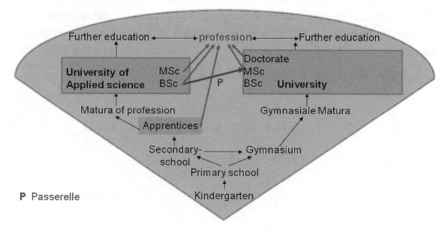

Figure 3: Upper secondary school graduation rates in 2005

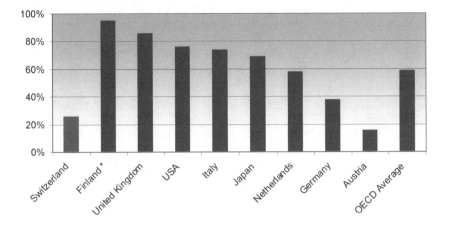

Upper secondary school graduation rates (ISCED 3A), 2005 (or latest data)

CHAPTER 9

The Innovation Society: Canada's Next Chapter

Heather Munroe-Blum [1]

The story of Canada's innovation strategy begins with two key measurements:

1. Since 1990, Canada has ranked first fully eight times in the United Nation's Human Development Index, which examines health, education and income indicators to assess overall quality of life (United Nations Development Programme, 1990-2007/08).
2. In 2008, Canada placed 13th out of 17 peer countries in innovation (Conference Board of Canada, 2008).

The tale is one of a great divide: how to protect the quality of life measured in the first index by tackling the problem captured in the second. This chapter examines Canada's innovation performance and strategies, and suggests some actions needed to turn Canada into a sustained Innovation Society. While emphasis is placed on the role of universities, they are not usefully considered in isolation. In today's hyperconnected world, innovation unfolds as part of local, national and international ecosystems. Universities, government at all levels and businesses interweave their benefits via primary roles, with NGOs, community groups, arts organizations and others all contributing to the process of innovation.

1 I would like to acknowledge, with gratitude, the contributions of my colleague, Susan Murley, Ph.D., Director of Strategic Communications, McGill University, in the preparation of this chapter.

There are many different definitions of innovation, but those that best capture its essence, I think, see innovation as a dynamic system, one that results
not just in new products but also new ways of doing things along an iterating
cycle with multiple players in the process. For example, in *Growing Ontario's
Innovation System: The Strategic Role of University Research*, innovation is
defined as, "the development of new knowledge and ideas, new processes and
new methods, and applying these for economic and societal benefit" (Munroe-Blum, 1999), and that definition, though a decade old, still holds.

THE CREATORS OF INNOVATION

Before analysing Canada's unique innovation system and assets, I would like
to set the stage by quickly sketching some primary factors that lay the groundwork for a healthy innovation system:

- A highly educated, creative and adaptable workforce: Today, the talent pool needed for innovation to flourish runs far deeper than scientists and engineers, and includes managers, lawyers, designers and
  experts in the arts and culture. Creativity, multilingualism, entrepreneurship and international perspective are also key skills.
- Strong regional clusters that are globally connected: For all the buzz
  around Thomas L. Friedman's "flat" world, local clusters and city cor-
  ridors remain vital to innovation. According to Richard Florida,
  10 mega-regions, which together have only 6% of the world's population, "account for 43% of the planet's economic activity and more
  than half of its patented innovations and star scientists" (Florida,
  2008). To become globally competitive, the best innovation strategy
  is built on collaboration with key partners, a high degree of activism
  and aspiration, and constant benchmarking of progress against
  national and international peers. Interestingly, this most often still
  entails the assembling of a critical mass of niche expertise locally but
  connected outward. High-profile international collaborations such as
  the Human Genome Project have been driven by distributed clusters
  of outstanding biomedical, genomics and computational teams, generally in universities and research institutes, but also in industry labs,
  connecting clusters of smart people to harness their collective
  strength for economic and human advantage.
- A strategic policy and business environment that encourage industry
  innovation in proximity to research universities: Multiple factors foster business innovation, such as access to venture capital, the availability of experienced managers and mentors for start-ups, an intelligent
  regulatory environment, indirect and direct government incentives in

support of business R&D, visionary procurement policies and progressive intellectual property protection frameworks.

• Research excellence as measured by the top international standards
and fluid knowledge exchange: Highly qualified talent emanating
from globally competitive research universities provides an absolutely
vital foundation for promoting innovation in regions and countries,
but alone it is not enough. To put knowledge to work, all players in
the innovation system must interact proactively to build strong connections and trust.

• A mindset open to innovation: The importance of culture and attitude cannot be underestimated. Cities and centres will thrive in this
globally driven market, where business, government and academic
communities are incented to be competitively oriented, entrepreneurial and cognizant of the direct line between innovation, prosperity and quality of life.

CANADIAN INNOVATION STRATEGIES

The mid-1990s were a rather grim period for research in Canada, due to an
economic downturn. A drop in the competitiveness of funding programs for
university research and post-secondary education in general led quickly to a
loss of some of Canada's top talent across fields as wide-ranging as theoretical
astrophysics, economics and genetics. However, governments quickly recognized the importance of supporting R&D at the dawn of the Information Age
and began developing strategies that focused squarely on attracting and
retaining top talent, reinvesting in research, and viewing universities and
business R&D as major contributors to innovation and economic productivity. In the mid-1990s, the Government of Canada, with the collaboration of
key university and industry leaders and advisory groups such as the National
Advisory Board on Science and Technology, began to formulate a new strategy — one focused on "the creation of a more effective, integrated innovation
system" (Government of Canada, 1996).

Science and Technology for the New Century (1996) laid the groundwork for
Canada's ensuing innovation strategies, focusing on boosting partnerships and
cooperation among universities, governments and business to encourage
knowledge exchange. The federal government saw itself in "a new role: that
of information analyst, knowledge disseminator and network builder". The
1996 strategy also emphasized return on investment, through increased
emphasis on accountability, performance evaluation, coordination and smart
management. For the first time, there was recognition that institutions and
the governments of Canada's provinces must also choose their research/inno-
vation niches. New funding programs such as the Canada Foundation for

Innovation, established in 1997, required universities to develop overall "institutional" research and academic strategies. Benchmarking of research and innovation indicators across jurisdictions within Canada, and between Canada and other nations, began in earnest. For example, *Growing Ontario's Innovation System* (Munroe-Blum, 1999) was the first comparison of university research policy and related innovation performance indicators across the large Canadian provinces. Also in 1999, the Conference Board of Canada published its first annual Innovation Report.

With its economic house back in order, the Government of Canada started in the later 1990s to heighten investments in university research, with much of the money targeted to creative new programs designed to support "pillars" of research excellence (people, infrastructure, operating support and indirect research costs) and to promote intersectoral partnerships. Programs such as the Networks of Centres of Excellence and the new Canada Foundation for Innovation (CFI) strongly encouraged collaboration across sectors. The CFI granted only 40% of a project's budget, requiring institutions to find the other 60% through their provincial governments, the private sector, foundations, their own investment and other sources such as philanthropy.

From 1996 to 2001, gross expenditures on R&D in Canada grew by an average of 10.77% each year, led by growth in the information and communications technology sector (before the dot-com bust) and the biopharma sector, along with an influx of government research funding to higher education. [2] In the decade from 1997 to 2007, federal investments in university research started to make up for the lost years of the early to mid-90s, growing by an average of 11% annually in constant dollars (Association of Universities and Colleges of Canada [AUCC], 2008).

CURRENT SCIENCE, TECHNOLOGY AND INNOVATION STRATEGIES

In November 2006, Canada's federal government launched its most recent economic plan, *Advantage Canada*. Among other goals, it has aimed to upgrade the skills of Canada's workforce through post-secondary education and to maximize the value of Canada's public sector research "by focusing on

---

2 In comparison, the United States saw annual growth in gross expenditures on research and development of 7.08% and the U.K. 5.48% for this same period (real dollars). Information has been compiled from the statistics provided by the Government of Quebec's Institut de la statistique, the Association of Universities and Colleges of Canada (AUCC) *Momentum* report and Robert Dugal's article on "Pharmaceutical Research Investment". Note that the AUCC publishes a figure of 8.8% annual growth for Canada, but this figure is in constant dollars.

excellence and increased linkages with the private sector" (Government of Canada, 2006). The government built on the economic strategy with the release approximately six months later of *Mobilizing Science and Technology to Canada's Advantage* (Government of Canada, 2007). By promoting excellence, choosing priorities, encouraging partnerships and enhancing accountability, the science and technology strategy is designed to position Canada for global leadership. The agenda identifies three imperatives to fortify Canada's competitive advantage:

- An Entrepreneurial Advantage: "Canada must translate knowledge into commercial applications that generate wealth for Canadians and support the quality of life we all want."
- A Knowledge Advantage: "Canadians must be positioned at the leading edge of the important developments that generate health, environmental, societal and economic benefits."
- A People Advantage: "Canada must be a magnet for the highly skilled people we need to thrive in the modern global economy with the best-educated, most skilled and most flexible workforce in the world."

Mobilizing Science and Technology to Canada's Advantage targets four broad fields as federal priorities, and the Science, Technology and Innovation Council (STIC), created in 2007 as an advisory board to the federal government, later recommended specific areas as sub-priorities:

- "Environmental science and technologies
  Sub-priorities: Water (health, energy, security); cleaner methods of extracting, processing and using hydrocarbon fuels, including reduced consumption of these fuels.
- "Natural resources and energy
  Sub-priorities: Energy production in the oil sands; Arctic (resource production, climate change adaptation, monitoring); biofuels, fuel cells and nuclear energy.
- "Health and related life sciences and technologies
  Sub-priorities: Regenerative medicine; neuroscience; health in an aging population; biomedical engineering and medical technologies.
- "Information and communications technologies
  Sub-priorities: New media, animation and games; wireless networks and services; broadband networks; telecom equipment" (Industry Canada, 2008).

Given the significance of science, technology and innovation to regional competitiveness and the benefits of seeding priorities and quality locally to enhance competitiveness at the national and international levels (Munroe-Blum, 1999), many of Canada's provinces have also formulated their own productivity and innovation strategies. They share common characteristics with each other and with *Mobilizing Science and Technology to Canada's Advantage*: increasing commercialization and knowledge exchange, intensifying excellence in research, attracting and fostering talent, and nurturing regional clusters.

In addition to substantial new provincial research support, the federal government's strategies have prompted new competitively allocated university research investments in four pillars:

- Talent: To attract and retain the best faculty, the Canada Research Chairs (CRC) program, created in 2000, supports 2,000 chairs for both established and emerging research stars through an annual budget of $300 million. [3] More than 30% of CRCs have been recruited from outside Canada. Applications are currently underway for 20 Canada Excellence Research Chairs (CERC), proposed via STIC and established by the federal government in 2008 to attract the world's best researchers in the government's priority areas related to science, technology and innovation. The Canada Graduate Scholarships program (established 2003) and Vanier Canada Graduate Scholarships (established 2008) both aim to attract top-level graduate talent. The Vaniers, which are worth a competitive $50,000 per year, are open to international as well as domestic graduate students, to attract the next generation of researchers to Canada. These scholarships, along with the CRCs and CERCs, are beginning to reverse an unproductive period of natural protectionism where provincial (state) and federal governments had barriers to international recruitment.

- Infrastructure: Reflecting, perhaps, Canada's particular constitutional idiosyncrasies, support for university research housing and major infrastructure fell between the cracks of provincial responsibility for post-secondary education and federal responsibility for the lion's share of university research. To strengthen cutting-edge research infrastructure, therefore, the Canada Foundation for Innovation has committed almost $4.5 billion to date for more than 6,000 projects at 129 institutions. Building on this as well, in its 2009 budget, the Government of Canada announced an impressive additional $2 billion in "stimulus funding" to upgrade facilities and infrastructure at universities and colleges.

- Research Operations: Over the past decade, federal and many provincial governments have raised the level of operating funding through research granting councils and other agencies. The Government of Canada has also invested $840 million in Genome Canada since the

---

3 All figures are in Canadian dollars unless otherwise noted.

program's establishment in 2000, to support genomics and proteomics research projects, again with an emphasis on stimulating partnerships and collaborations.

- Indirect Costs: In 2001, the federal government began to cover a percentage of universities' indirect costs or "overhead", though Canada still has a long way to go to keep pace with the U.S. and the U.K. Currently, the universities in Canada that perform the most research unfortunately receive the lowest percentage of return on their significant indirect costs.

CANADA'S INNOVATION PERFORMANCE TODAY

The previous decade has seen not only significant investments to promote innovation and the development of strategic frameworks, but also a new focus on measuring innovation and productivity indicators and beginning to benchmark, albeit selectively, against national and international peers. *Canada's Science, Technology and Innovation System: State of the Nation 2008*, released by the Science, Technology and Innovation Council (STIC) in May of 2009, represented significant progress in creating a baseline for understanding where Canada stands and will allow a monitoring of progress over time on key performance indicators. And numerous organizations, both governmental and independent, such as the Conference Board of Canada and the Institute for Competitiveness and Prosperity, are closely tracking Canada's performance, analyzing weaknesses and proposing solutions. The Government of Canada has commissioned reports from several governmental and advisory bodies, including STIC's aforementioned report, the Competition Policy Review Panel's *Compete to Win* (2008), and the Council of Canadian Academies' *Innovation and Business Strategy: Why Canada Falls Short* (2009).

The proliferation of reports, which recognize Canada's plentiful assets, sends a strong coordinated signal that there is a serious need to improve competitiveness. There is a renewed energy for Canada to transform itself into an Innovation Society. Rather than summarize each report individually, I will draw on these and other sources to provide an overall picture of Canada's innovation performance.

The collective analysis shows that, despite a sincere commitment to enlarge innovation and R&D capacity, Canada has made only "modest improvement", remaining a "solid, middle-of-the-road performer" (STIC, 2009). Canada has not yet reached the OECD average of gross expenditures on R&D (GERD). GERD as a percentage of GDP (R&D intensity) fell from its peak of 2.09% in 2001 to 1.89% in 2007, placing it 12th out of OECD countries (OECD, 2008c and d). In fact, Canada was one of only six OECD members who saw a fall in research intensity since 2001. The Conference

Board scores Canada a "D" in innovation, ranking it 13th of 17 countries. In fact, to put per-capita income on par with the U.S. in 15 years (assuming the U.S. stays constant), Canada will have to quadruple its productivity growth (Conference Board of Canada, 2008).

Why the lackluster results in the face of real efforts to turn Canada around and preserve its quality of life? What are the factors influencing Canada's innovation performance? Certainly the nation faces some unique challenges in shaping a coherent innovation system, though it also boasts great assets. Canada's reputation and quality of life draw talented people from across the world. Internationally, Canada as a nation is well respected, seen as safe, honest and "family friendly". For the last three years, the world's most trusted companies have been based in Sweden, Germany and Canada, according to the 2009 *Edelman Trust Barometer*.

A central structural hurdle is Canada's population density, one of the lowest in the world. Its population of 33 million is spread out over the world's second largest country by area (Central Intelligence Agency, 2009), with a widely varied geography, a broad range of natural resources and very distinctive regional cultures. While the nation has developed some vibrant clusters (energy in Alberta; aerospace in Quebec; biotech and life sciences in Quebec, Ontario, Saskatchewan, and B.C.; information and communications technology in many provinces, to name just a few), its geography makes it difficult to connect these local initiatives to form the mega-regions that drive growth. Canada's status as a federation also hinders strategic coordination. As noted, research, for example, is a dominantly federal responsibility, though given the importance of R&D to regional growth, many provinces also have their own innovation/S&T strategies and funding mechanisms. Education is a provincial responsibility, though the federal government funds national scholarship programs.

Despite the difficulties that geography and a complex federated system raise, Canada's higher education system has developed quality institutions with varied missions: from those focused on a regional agenda to internationally ranked universities driving national and international innovation. According to the World Economic Forum's *The Global Competitiveness Report 2008-2009*, "[Canada's] educational system gets excellent marks for quality", with its scientific research institutions ranking fourth internationally (Porter & Schwab, 2008). Canada's researchers perform admirably in both the number and quality of publications. With only 2.8% of the population of OECD countries, Canada produces 4.8% of OECD publications (Government of Canada, 2007). Its Average Relative Impact Factor, a measure of "the national rate of publication in highly cited journals relative to the average international rate of publication", ranks sixth in the OECD (STIC, 2009). And it boasts a rate of international co-authorship fully double the world average (AUCC, 2008).

Canada leads OECD countries in the percentage of the population aged 25 to 64 who have completed some form of higher education (OECD, 2008a). However, while Canada's college graduation rates rank first in the OECD, only 24% of Canada's working-age population holds a university degree, a rate that lags 11% behind the U.S. (OECD, 2008a). In terms of Ph.D. graduates, the talent pool that dominantly drives the innovation economy, Canada places second-last amongst 17 peers in terms of number of Ph.D. graduates in 2006 per 100,000 population aged 20 to 39 (Conference Board of Canada, 2008). The education system possesses the capability to graduate more advanced degrees, but the receptor capacity of businesses in hiring or otherwise benefiting from these graduates remains problematic. "Canada's private sector does not provide strong enough incentives for students to strive for advanced S&T and business management skills. Canadian firms across most industries hire fewer university graduates as a percentage of their total workforce than do their counterparts in the United States, particularly fewer Ph.D. graduates" (Government of Canada, 2007). Canadian universities are attracting more international doctoral students than ever before, but since 2001, fewer are staying (AUCC, 2008), possibly because attractive employment opportunities are lacking.

Canada's business demographics hold part of the answer to this puzzle. Canada has a huge proportion of small- and medium-sized enterprises (SMEs), many successful nationally, but relatively few companies large enough or innovative enough to achieve and sustain a stable global profile. Some of those it had, such as Nortel and Alcan, no longer serve this role. SMEs traditionally conduct less R&D than larger corporations, and typically will not if they are not led by technologically and scientifically literate managers. The composition of Canada's R&D landscape demonstrates this. On average, businesses in OECD countries conduct 69% of a nation's R&D; Canadian businesses conduct 54%. As a result, Canada relies much more heavily on research stemming from universities than do other countries. Universities in Canada perform 36% of total R&D, much higher than the OECD average of 17% (OECD, 2008c). And Canada's business expenditures on R&D (BERD) sat at just 1.03% of Canada's GDP in 2007, two-thirds of the OECD average of 1.56% and about half the U.S. rate (OECD, 2008c).

The underlying reasons for the low business investment in research, apart from the high number of SMEs, are still being teased out. Preliminary research from a number of analyses, however, suggests the influence of the following factors:

- Industries centred around natural resources, of which Canada has a large proportion, have been been traditionally less R&D intensive. However, competing with emerging economies in today's world requires that natural resource-based companies have the capacity to utilize high-tech identification and extraction processes, develop value-added products and manage complex social and political systems that foster environmentally friendly and socially responsible corporate behaviour.

• Historically, Canada has been a "branch plant" economy in sectors such as the auto and pharmaceutical industries, with R&D tending to take place in headquarters located outside of the country. Again, times are changing, and research is now more distributed globally, regardless of the location of head office. Canada has had some success in attracting multinational investment in biotechnology and aerospace research, to name two sectors.

• Canadian industries invest less in capital equipment, particular in information and communications technologies (ICT), which have been shown to drive innovation. Canadian firms tend to be, "with notable exceptions... technology followers, not leaders" (CCA, 2009), notwithstanding an early commitment on the part of the federal government to, "make Canada the most connected nation in the world" through building access to the Internet (Manley, 1999).

• Access to venture capital, particularly later-stage, is limited.

• Numerous analyses of Canada's innovation problem also point to a lack of "business ambition" in certain sectors, such as manufacturing, what the Canadian Council of Chief Executives called, "a culture of complacency... a sense that good is good enough" (Canadian Council of Chief Executives, 2008).

While the situation may sound dire, in fact there are some real rays of hope. Notwithstanding the branch plants, Canada's large number of SMEs tells the story of an entrepreneurial people who roll up their sleeves and start businesses wherever they see a niche. Canadian companies also have a good track record in creating new-to-market products (OECD, 2007). What is lacking is the support, knowledge and capacity to develop the critical mass to allow these innovative small businesses and smart ideas to compete internationally and remain Canadian. BERD, or any aggregate R&D spending measurement, also doesn't capture the full picture of innovation. The Canadian automotive sector, despite R&D expenditures that are about one-seventh the level of their American counterparts, is nonetheless more productive, due to process innovations not captured in BERD statistics (CCA, 2009).

In recent years, analyses have moved from blaming universities for insufficiently commercializing the products of their research to focusing Canada's innovation problem closer to the private sector. In fact, the problem is really that the country has not sufficiently mobilized the innovation system. Canada requires a leveraging of talent and innovation across sectors. The low level of business innovation suggests insufficient productive collaboration of universities, governments at the city, state and national levels, and industry. The World Economic Forum's *The Global Competitiveness Report 2008-2009* notes a lower level of business-university collaborations, and the OECD's *Science, Technology and Industry Scoreboard 2007* shows that only 11.8% of large Canadian firms collaborate in innovative activities with institutions of higher education, compared with 52.8% of large companies in Finland, the world leader. [4]

Encouraging is the fact that the share of Canadian university R&D financed by business is one of the highest in the world (OECD, 2008d) and the value of research contracts more than doubled from 1999 to 2006 (AUCC, 2008). Seemingly, a contradiction exists: Canadian companies are willing to sponsor research in universities, but it would appear that truly collaborative partnerships are not as prevalent as would be ideal. As the Science, Technology and Innovation Council points out in its recent report (2009), more study is needed to understand the reasons why.

THE WAY FORWARD

Canada stands at a crossroads. It has taken large steps toward becoming an Innovation Society, but other nations are leaping forward faster. The new U.S. administration has a coherent vision for higher education, research and innovation and the will to achieve it. The competitive pressure from Canada's southern neighbour has already provoked fears of a new brain drain, but may instead have the positive effect of spurring the country to greater action. Noted American science policy advisor, James Duderstadt, has noted that while it can take, on average, a decade or more to build a research program of significance, just two to three years of neglect can stifle it. After all, momentum is hard to build, and to lose it is tragic.

So how can Canada quickly refine its strategy to become an innovation leader? What specific actions should it take? In broad terms, for Canada to succeed in this new global environment, all the key players in Canada's innovation ecosystem must collaborate. Canada is not big enough to accommodate one country, 10 provinces and three territories acting in isolation or actively working against each other, all hoping to capture the attention of institutions and regions around the world.

The core of any innovation strategy should be talent and knowledge, and in these areas Canada possesses a solid foundation to build on. In terms of talent, Canada is starting to move away from old-school thinking, that intellec-

---

4 Data for Canada includes the manufacturing sector only, and some differences in the survey methodology used in Canada mean that the true percentage of university-industry partnerships may not be fully captured. Nonetheless, the gap is striking.

tual protectionism that concentrates on only home-grown skills development. The federal government's new Canada Excellence Research Chairs and Vanier Scholarships provide an opportunity to attract high-level international stars and stars-in-training. In addition to initiatives to attract skilled people, Canada also needs to foster connections with students, faculty and business leaders who leave the country. A recent OECD study advises that, "The mobility of researchers... is not necessarily a zero-sum game in which receiving countries gain and sending countries lose" (OECD, 2008b). There exists an opportunity to advance distinctive international networks in areas of Canadian strength and continue to derive benefit from the flow of ideas and the uptake of new technologies and processes that speed innovation.

As well, we need to broaden our ideas of leadership, and ensure that organizations are growing more "distributed leadership", in which roles are shared across a group fluidly, according to the capabilities of individual members, allowing the best approaches to come forward. Increasingly, universities can support the development of global citizens, people who are comfortable moving freely across cultures and borders, who are scientifically and technologically literate, with nimble minds, tolerant attitudes and facility in more than one language.

As elsewhere, Canada must continue to invest in both basic and targeted research at levels that will allow the country to keep pace with, and in some fields lead, the G7. The right funding mix across the four pillars of research support (talent, infrastructure, operating and indirect costs) will help make the most of investment. Paradoxically, the influx of superb new talent to Canada, thanks to new programs such as the Canada Research Chairs, the Canada Foundation for Innovation and the Knowledge Infrastructure Program, has had the effect of stretching thin operating funding for research and discovery. Ongoing dialogue across levels of government and academia, as well as a real-time assessment of changing needs, will be required to ensure that the balance most conducive to innovation and retaining talent can be found.

Federal, provincial and business strategies, as well as the recent benchmarking reports referenced above, identify the need not only to fortify knowledge and talent, but to harness these assets to address the country's stubbornly persistent problem of business innovation; perhaps through a more constructive form of competetive federalism. And this problem isn't ours alone. Worldwide, nations are struggling to identify the best mechanisms to open up knowledge exchange across sectors. The issue is not straightforward because, at its heart, it is about social capital, what the OECD calls, "the norms and networks facilitating co-operation either within or between groups" (Box, 2009). The complex social context of innovation includes the different cultures in industry versus academia and goverment, interactions between people with distinct agendas, and levels of trust among the various actors. Outreach and communication among all players in Canada's innovation ecosystem will be a start.

Aside from "soft" mechanisms to address co-operation, governments can also establish better frameworks to promote business innovation. For example, the Canadian government currently provides the richest government support of business R&D as a percentage of GDP of 13 OECD countries (STIC, 2009). With the highest level of support, however, Canada is getting some of the poorest results — a level of BERD well below the OECD average. The answer to this puzzle may be found in the nature of the support. Approximately 90% of government assistance is indirect, through non-refundable tax credits (STIC, 2009), and recent studies are suggesting that "subsidies [i.e. direct support] have a greater impact on small firms' R&D expenditures than those of large firms" (Box, 2009). Given the large concentration of SMEs, reviewing the balance of indirect and direct government aid to business R&D would be strongly advisable.

More direct support of business R&D would also allow governments to target a percentage of investment to their defined priority fields, as it currently does with academic research. The shared platform would provide a sense of common purpose for industry-university-government partnerships. We are missing the opportunity to forge strategic collaborations that would integrate cutting-edge knowledge, talent and research from universities into business and government in a way that creates and sustains results.

Happily, Canada is not just looking within its own borders for partnerships. Though Canada does not have a national framework for international research, it did launch the International Science and Technology Partnerships (ISTP) program in 2005 to advance international networks and fund international research projects with commercial potential. Over the last few years, the federal government has also negotiated individual bilateral agreements with countries such as India (2005), Israel (2006), China (2007) and Brazil (2008). But the future of high-impact international partnerships, I believe, lies in a new model: one where high performers in the key innovation sectors in Canada — from industry, government and universities — work in targeted partnerships with the key sectoral players in peer countries. Close competitors become close collaborators. The Canada-California Strategic Innovation Partnership, or CCSIP, is piloting this new model.

CCSIP was formed in 2005 to mobilize bilateral collaborative research, development and delivery in the two "innovation-intensive" regions of Canada and California. This is *not* the usual researcher-to-researcher collaboration. The CCSIP partnership champions new paradigms of cooperation and focuses on innovative areas with market potential that are strengths for both jurisdictions: stem cells and regenerative medicine, information and communications technologies, advanced transportation and energy, nanotechnology, infectious diseases, venture capital, intellectual property, and the development of highly qualified personnel (Canada-California Strategic Innovation Partnership).

I see CCSIP as a promising model of research partnership because it takes an effective national strategy and makes it global. The partnerships revolve around the shared priorities and strengths of each jurisdiction, providing a focus for investment and connection. The joint initiatives are time-limited, jointly funded and have champions on the ground in both jurisdictions. This makes it easy to quickly identify and act upon critical research questions that align with industry needs. Because governments are involved from the ground up, they are motivated to smooth out obstacles and adjust policies to speed along results. And perhaps most importantly, CCSIP establishes a network of the most critical players — the organizations and people that, when brought together, are most likely to jumpstart innovation.

CONCLUSION

Talent, research excellence, knowledge exchange, international connections — what could be missing to create the unbeatable strategy that will turn Canada into an Innovation Society? As your parents or teachers might have told you, attitude is everything. To most Canadians, innovation or productivity gaps are issues too abstract to capture their imagination, especially since the quality of life here is still strong. As well, Canada has experienced some buffering of the impact of the current economic turbulence owing in part to the smart regulatory framework governing the banking industry in Canada. As Robin V. Sears (2007) says in his informing and entertaining article, "Bridging the Political Productivity Gap", the, "not unreasonable query of the average Canadian," is: "If we are doing so badly why are we doing so well?"

But unless they heed the warning signs of recent benchmarking reports, Canadians risk losing the wonderful quality of life that has pushed the country to the top of the Human Development Index for so many years. Canada needs a new coherent vision, uniting the country behind a national dream of innovation, as it were. Together, Canadians can interweave wealth creation with strong social values, balancing concern for environmental impact, global health, and addressing growing disparities for the disenfranchised with innovation, education, economic stability and growth.

Today, Canada is prosperous. Will it be tomorrow?

REFERENCES

Association of Universities and Colleges of Canada [AUCC]. (2008). *Momentum: The 2008 Report on University Research and Knowledge Mobilization*. Canada: Association of Universities and Colleges of Canada.

Box, Sarah (2009). *OECD Work on Innovation: A Stocktaking of Existing Work*. STI Working Paper 2009/2. Organisation for Economic Co-operation and Development.

Canada-California Strategic Innovation Partnership. http://www.ccsip.org/. Accessed 25 May 2009.

Canadian Council of Chief Executives. (2008). *From Common Sense to Bold Ambition: Moving Canada Forward on the Global Stage*. Submission to the Competition Policy Review Panel. http://www.ic.gc.ca/eic/site/cprp-gepmc.nsf/vwapj/Canadian_Council_Chief_Executives.pdf/$FILE/Canadian_Council_Chief_Executives.pdf

Central Intelligence Agency. (2009). "Canada". *The World Factbook*. CIA. https://www.cia.gov/library/publications/the-world-factbook/geos/ca.html#Geo. Accessed 25 May 2009.

Competition Policy Review Panel. (2008). *Compete to Win*. Ottawa: Government of Canada.

Conference Board of Canada. (1999). *Building the Future: 1st Annual Innovation Report*. Ottawa: Conference Board of Canada.

Conference Board of Canada. (2008). *How Canada Performs: A Report Card on Canada*. Executive Summary (PDF) and full report (web). Ottawa: Conference Board of Canada. http://www.conferenceboard.ca/HCP/default.aspx

Council of Canadian Academies [CCA]. (April 2009). The Expert Panel on Business Innovation. *Innovation and Business Strategy: Why Canada Falls Short*. Abridged version. Council of Canadian Academies. http://www.scienceadvice.ca/documents/(2009-04-29)%20Report%20in%20Focus%20-%20Innovation.pdf

Dugal, Robert. (1 April 2001). Pharmaceutical Research Investment. *Canadian Chemical News*. http://www.allbusiness.com/north-america/canada/789057-1.html.

Edelman International. (2009). *Edelman Trust Barometer 2009: The Tenth Global Opinion Leaders Survey*. Edelman International. http://www.edelman.com/trust/2009/docs/Trust_Book_Final_2.pdf

Florida, Richard. (15 June 2008). The Buffalo Mega-Region: Bigger Than We Know. Buffalo, New York: *The Buffalo News*.

Government of Canada. (1996). *Science and Technology for the New Century: A Federal Strategy*. Ottawa: Government of Canada.

Government of Canada. (2006). *Advantage Canada: Building a Strong Economy for Canadians*. Ottawa: Government of Canada.

Government of Canada. (2007). *Mobilizing Science and Technology to Canada's Advantage*. Ottawa: Government of Canada.

Industry Canada. (2 September 2008). Minister of Industry Accepts S&T Strategy's Sub-Priorities Recommended by the Science, Technology and Innovation Council. Ottawa: Government of Canada. http://www.ic.gc.ca/eic/site/ic1.nsf/eng/04160.html

Institut de la statistique. Dépenses intra-muros de R-D (DIRD), Québec et autres provinces ou régions canadiennes, pays de l'OCDE, Union européenne, G7 et certains pays hors OCDE, 1996 à 2008 (M$ US courants, PPA). Québec : Gouvernement du Québec. http://www.stat.gouv.qc.ca/savoir/indicateurs/rd/dird/dird_ocde_ppa.htm

Institute for Competitiveness and Prosperity. (2009). *Opportunity in the Turmoil: Report on Canada 2009*. Toronto: Institute for Competitiveness and Prosperity.

Manley, John. (1999). Canada and the Internet Revolution: Connecting Canadians. A speech made to the 1999 annual meeting of the Trilateral Commission in Washington, D.C. http://www.trilateral.org/annmtgs/trialog/trlgtxts/t53/man.htm

Munroe-Blum, Heather, with Duderstadt, J. & Davies, Sir Graeme. (1999). *Growing Ontario's Innovation System: The Strategic Role of University Research*. Ontario.

Munroe-Blum, Heather & MacKinnon, Peter. (2009) Canada's innovation deficit. *Policy Options*. Quebec: Institute for Research on Public Policy.

Organisation for Economic Co-operation and Development [OECD]. (2007). OECD Science, Technology and Industry Scoreboard 2007: Innovation and Performance in the Global Economy. OECD Publishing.

Organisation for Economic Co-operation and Development [OECD]. (2008a). *Education at a Glance 2008*. OECD Publishing.

Organisation for Economic Co-operation and Development [OECD]. (2008b). *The Global Competition for Talent: Mobility of the Highly Skilled*. OECD Publishing.

Organisation for Economic Co-operation and Development [OECD]. (2008c). Main Science and Technology Indicators/Principaux indicateurs de la science et de la technologie. Volume 2008/2. OECD Publishing.

Organisation for Economic Co-operation and Development [OECD]. (2008d). *OECD Science, Technology and Industry Outlook 2008*. OECD Publishing.

Porter, Michael E. & Klaus Schwab (2008). *The Global Competitiveness Report 2008-2009*. Geneva, Switzerland: World Economic Forum.

Science, Technology and Innovation Council [STIC]. (2009). *Canada's Science, Technology and Innovation System: State of the Nation 2008*. Ottawa: Government of Canada

Sears, Robin V. (2007). Bridging the Political Productivity Gap. *Policy Options*. Quebec: Institute for Research on Public Policy.

United Nations Development Programme. (1990 through 2007/08). Human Development Reports. New York: Palgrave Macmillan.

CHAPTER 10

Singapore: successful in research, striving for innovation

Bertil Andersson, Tony Mayer and Jeffrey Nadison [1]

INTRODUCTION

Across the World, governments subscribe to the thesis that investment in research is a worthwhile public good for a number of reasons. Such investments are generally predicated on the view that research will lead directly to innovation and, hence, to wealth and employment creation. This "linear" model is an over-simplification of a complex reality in which there are innumerable feedback loops. However, in broad terms, it is a truism that investment in research should support and encourage economic development and whilst sometimes not leading directly from one to the other, nevertheless it provides the essential "substrate" on which innovation grows.

Singapore, whose name translates as the "Lion City", is a unique state in the modern World and one which has experienced extraordinary economic growth over its 44 years of existence. In its economic development and, more lately, in its research development, it has certainly lived up to its name with a ferocious commitment to drive its economic development forward. This has been based on its basic nature and geography as a World entrepôt to which has been added a burgeoning economic sector (according to some measures, it now ranks only behind London and New York and ahead of Hong Kong in terms of trade volumes), a substantial tourism industry and, last but not least, a thriving manufacturing sector. Recognizing that, faced with competition

1 Acknowledgements: We wish to thank Mme Ho Hwee Shi, Jan for all her help with the diagrams and figures and in formatting this paper.

from major players such as China, the latter sector has to evolve from one based on low employment costs to one which can provide high value goods, the Singaporean government has fully embraced the concept of the knowledge-based economy. As part of this aim, the government has lived up to its soubriquet to push forward to become one the World's poles of expertise of high level research. This has happened since the start of the millennium and Singapore is now playing in the top league for research, deservedly so given the huge public investment in research that has been made over the past decade.

The achievements are impressive, especially considering that Singapore is a geographically very small country with a population of only 4.5 million inhabitants. Furthermore, unlike city states of the past, it lacks a geographical hinterland. This is a unique situation and one which was recognized by Singapore's founding father and long-time Prime Minister, Lee Kuan Yew, when he has talked about the necessity to develop a global hinterland to compensate for its geographical disadvantage. Certainly nothing is more global than research.

The country has some natural advantages in terms of its vibrant, multi-cultural and cosmopolitan society with a strong business community, a strong work ethic and with its main language of administration and business being today's *lingua franca*, English. Furthermore, it is able to take advantage of its geographical position in South East Asia and act as a bridge between the rising economic powers of China and India; forming a cultural linkage between "the West" and "the East". In some respects it may be termed "Asia-'lite'."

A STRONG EDUCATION SYSTEM

Singapore benefits from having a strong school education system that provides the "raw material" for the universities, for employers and for the Singaporean "research project". Indeed Singapore ranks among the best Asian nations in terms of having the best brains in mathematics. The 2007 Trend in International Maths and Science Study (TIMSS) conducted by Boston College, U.S., puts Hong Kong, Singapore and Taiwan students scoring best in mathematics and with the best science students coming from Singapore, Taiwan, Japan and Korea.

However, one notable feature of the Singaporean educational system is its very vocationally minded approach and it is from such a base that one might discern some of the difficulties that we deal with later in this paper.

GLOBAL AND HISTORICAL COMPARISONS

Singapore has used these advantages effectively to propel itself forward in research to become a leading player in what is now a multi-polar World of

Asia, Europe and North America. Previously, there has been a tendency to look at World economy in terms of Europe and the U.S., including also Japan. However, historically this may not be a true picture as shown by Madison in his 2003 Statistical analysis for the OECD when he compared GDP figures for the major regions of the World over the past 300 years (see Table 1).

Table 1: Estimates of the percentage contribution to Global GDP, 1700-2003

	1700	1820	1952	1995	2003
China	22.3	32.9	5.2	11.1	15.1
India	24.4	16.0	4.0	4.6	5.5
Japan	4.1	3.0	3.4	8.1	6.6
Europe	24.9	26.6	29.3	23.8	21.8
United States	0.1	1.8	27.5	21.2	20.6

Source: Madison, A. (2003). The world economy: historical statistics. Paris, France: Development Centre of the Organisation for Economic Co-operation and Development.

In other words, in the historical long-term we have been part of a multi-polar World and may be returning to this "ground state" for global economies in the 21st century. Working through successive 5 year plans, Singapore has set itself a very ambitious target of 3% for both public and private investment in GERD (gross domestic expenditure on research and development) within its GDP by 2010. If this target is achieved, and there is every likelihood of this happening, then Singapore will join an elite group of countries with this or a higher GERD investment level, i.e. Finland, Israel and Sweden. It is noteworthy that this is the same ambitious target as that set for itself by the European Union within the Lisbon Process. However, the likelihood is that Singapore will succeed, while the E.U. has already acknowledged that this target is beyond its current capacity. Figure 1 shows recent trends in the development of GERD in selected countries.

DEVELOPMENT OF THE SINGAPOREAN RESEARCH SYSTEM

Singapore has an added advantage of having a well integrated Government system and where there is a strong inclination to take and plan for the longer view. Currently, the most recent quinquennial plan for Science and Technology is ending (2006-2010) and the Government is actively planning for the next five years. During the current plan period, there has been an impressive additional investment of $S13 billion (€6.5 billion) which may be compared with the E.U. Framework Programme which has an expenditure of just over €7 billion per annum for a population some 100 times larger than that of

Figure 1: R&D intensity (GERD as % of GDP) in the major world regions, 1995-2007

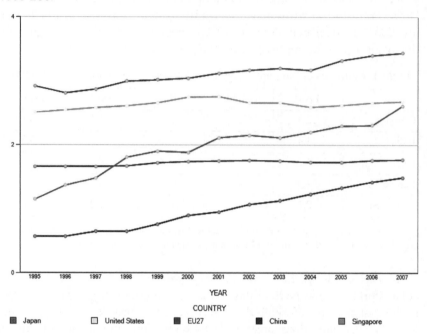

YEAR

COUNTRY

■ Japan   □ United States   ■ EU27   ■ China   ■ Singapore

Source: OECD, Main Science and Technology Indicators 2009-10.

Singapore. This investment has been principally apportioned between the Agency for Science, Technology and Research (A*STAR) Institutes and the universities (see Figure 2), with for the latter, the introduction of very competitive schemes such as that for Research Centres of Excellence (RCEs) with an investment level of $S150 million each over 10 years and with around five Centres being created in the first five-year period, other highly competitive and strategic funding and the highly prestigious National Research Foundation's (NRF) Research Fellowships for young and very talented post-doctoral researchers. In fact, the Plan saw the creation of the NRF within the Prime Minister's Office to oversee this investment in research in the higher education sector. It is noteworthy that the NRF's mandate is not simply the funding of excellence, but to do so with one eye on the ultimate benefit for the Singaporean economy. It is also noteworthy that part of the investment is to the Economic Development Board as part of its activities to stimulate research coupled with inward investment.

Singapore has rapidly developed its university sector to be research-intensive and should be proud that its two major science and technology universities rank within the top 100 in the World, according to the latest *Time Higher*

Education/QS rankings. Now there is an advanced plan to create a fourth university to cater for an increased entry cohort of up to 30% and which will also be devoted to science, technology and design.

Figures 2 and 3 illustrate the structure of the Singaporean research "ecosystem" and its academic research performers.

Figure 2: Singapore: Research Funding Ecosystem

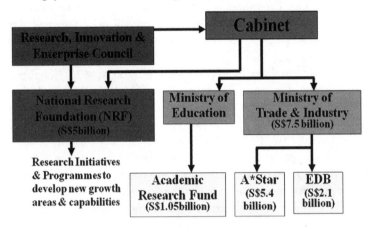

Figure 3: Singapore's Higher Education Institutions — the main research performer

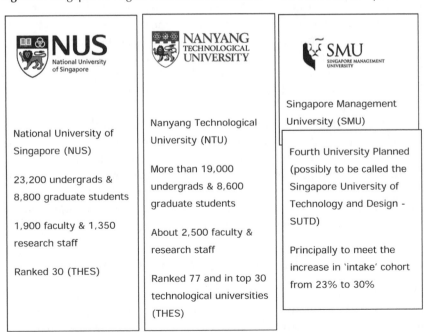

IMPORTING TALENT

Singapore has developed a tradition of importing talent in a number of ways. This is partly because of the difficulty of attracting Singaporeans themselves into research and may be demonstrated by the origins of the intake of students into the universities. At the undergraduate level, 20% of the students are incomers to Singapore (coming principally from its neighbours — Indonesia and Malaysia). This rises sharply to 60% at the postgraduate level including 80% undertaking Ph.D.s (many of the latter come from China, as well as those coming from other parts of the World on the very generous SINGA scholarships).

This unprecedented and massive research investment in global terms has served to attract top research talent into Singapore through both the A*STAR institutes and the universities. In the latter case, this comes from the recruitment policies of the universities and from the NRF funding schemes, especially the RCE, which demands the bringing in of top, senior researchers from overseas. In this manner, Singapore has been able to "leap-frog" into the top level of World research. For example, the RCE on the Earth Observatory of Singapore, based at NTU, has catapulted Singapore overnight from a place with virtually no Earth Sciences into a centre having some of the World's leading researchers in seismology, tectonics and volcanology.

It is this pro-active recruitment at the very top levels coupled with what may be termed "institutional recruitment" that has propelled Singapore into this upper echelon of World research. Through partnerships and direct recruitment, Singapore has brought in an impressive list of institutions including MIT, Stanford and Cornell Universities from the USA, Imperial College London and Cambridge University from the UK, the Technical University of Munich, Germany, ETH Zurich, Switzerland, INSEAD from France and Technion, Israel.

Coupled to this has been the ability to attract top level technologically based multi-national companies and again the list is impressive: General Electric, EADS, Rolls-Royce, Siemens, Robert Bosch, Infineon, Panasonic, Novartis, GlaxoSmithKline to name but a few. These companies provide high quality employment, but they are also attracted by the availability of a highly educated and "research-savvy" work force and the very positive and company friendly business environment that has been created.

INNOVATION — SOME GLOBAL COMPARISONS

Having demonstrated the rapid rise of Singapore in the "research league" and its very sound educational base, one also needs to examine the innovation record of the country as the third side of the so-called "knowledge triangle".

Figure 4: Examples of major infrastructure investment to house the A*STAR institutes: On the left is Biopolis and on the right is the recently opened Fusionopolis, both at the One North academic and research complex

Biopolis   Fusionopolis

As shown in the above paragraph, Singapore is a natural home for high technology industry. It is also a centre of economic endeavour and entrepreneurialism and its citizens are business-minded. Singapore ranks as having one of the most business-friendly environments with full intellectual property protection. In terms of Global Competitiveness measures, Singapore ranks in fifth place and yet the technological innovation process falls below the high standards of research and research investment.

We have looked at a number of international comparisons as part of a study into the promotion of commercialization of research, specifically that at NTU.

In terms of Global Competitiveness, as shown in the Global Competitiveness Report, 2008-2009, World Economic Forum, Geneva 2008, Singapore ranks fifth in the World (the highest of any Asian country and moving up two places from the 2007-2008 survey behind the USA, Switzerland, Denmark and Sweden). The upward progression of the overall ranking is a result of a strengthening across all aspects of the institutional framework. Singapore is placed among the top two countries for the efficiency of all of its markets — goods, labour, and financial — ensuring the proper allocation of these factors to their best use. However, if one examines the innovation factors themselves in this study, the picture is much more uneven — Singapore drops to 11th place for innovation factors and patents per million of population (see Table 2).

Although substantial gains can be obtained by improving institutions, building infrastructures, reducing macroeconomic instability, or improving

Table 2: 2008-9 Global Competitiveness Index Rankings — Top Ten Performers

	Overall 2008-9		Basic Requirements		Efficiency Enhancers		Innovation Factors		Patents/ Mil. Pop1.
	Rank	Score	Rank	Score	Rank	Score	Rank	Score	Rank
United States	1	5.74	22	5.50	1	5.81	1	5.80	2
Switzerland	2	5.61	2	6.14	8	5.35	2	5.68	6
Denmark	3	5.61	4	6.14	3	5.49	7	5.37	14
Sweden	4	5.58	6	6.00	9	5.35	6	5.53	8
Singapore	5	5.53	3	6.14	2	5.52	11	5.16	11
Finland	6	5.50	1	6.18	13	5.51	5	5.53	4
Germany	7	5.46	7	5.96	11	5.22	4	5.54	9
Netherlands	8	5.41	10	5.81	7	5.38	9	5.20	13
Japan	9	5.38	26	5.36	12	5.22	5	5.65	3
Canada	10	5.37	8	5.84	5	5.44	16	4.96	10

the human capital of the population, all these factors eventually run into diminishing returns. The same is true for the efficiency of the labour, financial and goods markets. In the long run, standards of living can be expanded only with **technological innovation**. Innovation is particularly important for economies as they approach the frontiers of knowledge and the possibility of integrating and adapting exogenous technologies tends to disappear. Although less advanced countries can still improve their productivity by adopting existing technologies or making incremental improvements in other areas, for countries such as Singapore, which has reached the "innovation stage" of development (Porter and Schwab define three stages of economic development, largely correlated to national per capita GDP. These stages — or economic phases are: a. Factor-Driven Economies, b. Efficiency-Driven Economies, and c. Innovation-Driven Economies. Singapore, with a per capita GDP of US$35,163 is in this third stage) this approach is no longer sufficient to increase productivity. Firms in countries such as Singapore must design and develop cutting-edge products and processes to maintain a competitive edge. This requires an environment that is conducive to innovative activity, supported by both the public and the private sectors. In particular, this means sufficient investment in R&D, the presence of high-quality scientific research institutions, extensive collaboration in research between universities and industry, and the protection of intellectual property. The other key pillar for ensuring innovation competitiveness is a sophisticated financial market.

There is now concern expressed in Government circles about the low out-put of innovation as measured by start-ups and income for the higher educa-tion sector. Whilst 11th position is still very creditable, one has to ask what the reasons are for this comparative failure. Is it cultural or is it systemic? We believe that one may discount the latter given the encouragement to move to innovation and the very business friendly conditions that prevail.

Table 3 illustrates the position of Singapore within the Global Competi-tiveness Survey by components of the "innovation factors".

Table 3: Global Competitiveness Index Rankings — Innovation Factors

Performance Factors	Singapore's position/134
Quality of Education System	2
Quality of Math and Science Education	2
Secondary Enrolment	21
Tertiary Enrolment	31
Quality of Science and Research Institutions	13
Availability of Scientists and Engineers	12
University — Industry Research Collaboration	5
Foreign Direct Investment in Technology Transfer	1
Intellectual Property Protection	2
Brain Drain	13
Capacity for Innovation	19
Quality of Management Schools	7
Availability of Venture Capital	12

Source: The Global Competitiveness Report 2008-2009, World Economic Forum, Geneva, Switzerland 2008.

Innovation — cultural issues

Low Kim Cheng Patrick identified four obstacles or impediments that tended to discourage the setting up of businesses among Singaporeans. These were being overly compliant, being too "left-brained", over-pampering and the fear of failure. Low suggested that Singaporeans need to make a "paradigm shift", adopt a "backpack mentality", embrace globalized thinking and networking and tapping into their own rich cultural diversity.

National cultures can be described according to the analysis of Geert Hof-stede. These ideas were first based on a research project into national culture differences across subsidiaries of a multinational corporation (IBM) in 64 countries. Subsequent studies by others covered students in 23 countries, elites in 19 countries, commercial airline pilots in 23 countries, up-market consumers in 15 countries, and civil service managers in 14 countries. Together these studies identified and validated four independent dimensions of national culture differences, with a fifth dimension added later.

Such an analysis leads to interesting results when comparing Singapore with small, developed economies such as Denmark, Hong Kong, Israel and Ireland (see Figure 5).

Figure 5: Comparison of cultural factors related to Innovation between Singapore and a selection of small developed countries

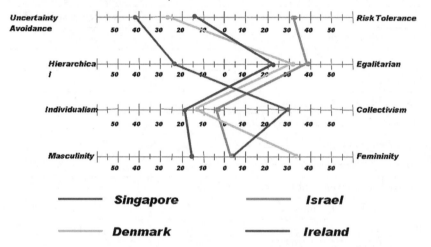

Source: Variables derived from Geert Hofstede's National Cultural Differences IBM Dataset.

It is informative to note that Singapore is significantly the most risk avoidant of the states considered, hierarchical and more prone to collectivism. This is further emphasized when combining both the Hofstede analysis and the WEF Capacity for Innovation Ranking. Again, this results in similar conclusions when comparing Singapore against the average figures for the top, middle and bottom third of the countries ranked (see Figure 6).

Turning now to patent statistics, the overall picture shows that, despite giving what appears to be a reasonably healthy income stream, it is one that could be considerably improved.

In analysing the situation further, especially in terms of the output from the academic institutions in terms of the Global Competitiveness Report, one sees that, in comparison with the U.S., the usual benchmark, patents per million of population are 89.3 for Singapore against 261.7. Looking at a comparably sized country with an enviable innovation record, Israel, the figure is 158.1. (see Table 4)

Figure 6: Capacity for Innovation Ranking — Comparison of Singapore against the top, middle and lower third of the rankings

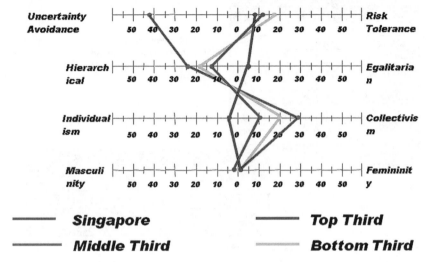

——— **Singapore**   ——— **Top Third**

——— **Middle Third**   ——— **Bottom Third**

GCR Capacity for Innovation: In your country, companies obtain technology (1 = exclusively from licensing or imitating foreign companies, 7 = by conducting formal research and pioneering their own new products and processes)

Source: Variables derived from Geert Hofstede's National Cultural Differences IBM Dataset, Rankings from the Global Competitiveness Report 2008-9, World Economic Forum.

A particularly telling statistic is that the top research performers in Singapore (all the A*STAR institutes plus the National University of Singapore and the Nanyang Technological University) **collectively** created only as many start-ups as the top U.S. academic institutions such as Harvard or Stanford and have fewer start-ups than the relatively small but very research-intensive California Institute of Technology (CalTech). In fact, one can extend this comparison further to include the Canadian universities in British Columbia and Toronto (see Table 5).

Despite the encouragement of the system to create value from the research investment, there still seems to be an "innovation deficit" within the Singaporean research system. How can this be addressed?

Evidence from interviews

A series of interviews with NTU faculty members was conducted during Spring 2009 which showed up a series of perceived impediments to innovation within NTU. A simple cluster analysis was undertaken of the notable comments "harvested" during the interviews. The cluster of highest frequency

Table 4: International comparison of patent production/population

Global Competitiveness Report	
Top Performers 2007	Patents/Mil Pop
Taiwan, China	270.4
United States	261.7
Japan	260.0
Finland	160.4
Israel	158.1
Switzerland	141.8
Korea, Rep	130.9
Sweden	116.6
Germany	109.4
Canada	100.9
Singapore	89.3

Government spending
on university R&D has yet
to realize an economic
return one year on

National Survey ofR&D in Singapore 2007		
Aggregate results: all Higher Education Institutions		
	Actual	PerMil.Pop
Granted Patents	67	15.2
License Revenue	$560,000	
Salaries	$1,120,000	

Sources: Global Competitive Index 2009; NRF R&D National Survey, 2007

Table 5: Comparison of the Academic Output of Start-up Companies in Singapore and selected leading North American Institutions

Name of Institution	2007 Start-ups
Singapore Academic and Research Institutions (Nanyang Technological University/ National University of Singapore/A*STAR Research Institutes)	8
California Institute of Technology (CalTech)	11
Georgia Institute Of Technology	9
Harvard University	6
Massachusetts Institute of Technology	24
Stanford University	6
University of British Columbia	5
University of Toronto	8

related to culture and risk aversion. Without exception, these comments were shared as examples of impediments to innovation and are highly consistent with the ideas cited in the work of Low Kim Cheng. These quotes indicate that a challenge to innovate in Singapore may be the tendency to avoid "disruptive development" arising from new ideas.

Following in order of importance were comments about a perceived dilemma concerning the need to publish to secure tenure-ship versus withholding public disclosure to be able to maintain some competitive advantage with commercialization of IP in mind. Typical of this sentiment is the following quote:

"Key Performance Indicators (KPIs) drive all behaviour at the university. Professors still prefer to publish rather than patent in order to fulfil requirements to secure tenure".

The third most prevalent type of comment concerned collaboration. Generally, interviewees suggested that collaboration across disciplines on campus is limited and acknowledge that much more is needed. Several interviewees discussed the need for "translators" to build bridges across disciplines as a means of overcoming this limitation. The following quote expresses well this idea:

"There is a vital role to play for 'translators' between 'links in a value chain', i.e., between pioneering research, applied research and applications development. The individual 'links', as pools of domain expertise, tend to be narrowly focused but deep. This often hinders progress as concepts move from theory to commercial reality as the 'warlords' in each domain 'fiefdom' tend not to share a common lexicon".

The frequency of these comments is shown in Figure 7 and again they demonstrate a cultural rather than a systemic problem.

In recognizing this problem and in trying to provide a new incentive to change academic habits, the NRF has introduced a new scheme to encourage the universities to develop new and more pro-active measures to encourage more entrepreneurial thinking by faculty members. These include provision for each university to establish an "Enterprise Board" to manage a generous Innovation Fund totalling some $S25 million which supports entrepreneurship education, technology incubators and "entrepreneurs-in-residence" to promote the commercialization of university technologies. Within the enterprise support structures, the fund provides for Proof-of-concept grants; Technology incubation schemes; Early-stage venture funding; support for Disruptive Innovation (DI) incubators; and Special innovation overheads from research grants.

While all these measures are to be welcomed, there still remains the cultural resistance to be overcome. Perhaps, ultimately, it has to be recognized that this is a long-term process and that only with a profound cultural shift will Singapore be able to take full advantage of its far-sighted vision to fund research as a major tool of economic development. Given the nature of Singaporean society as it has developed over the past 40 years, this is something for which the Government has to take responsibility. Financial incentives and the provision of entrepreneurial training can only go so far without endeavouring to change the mindsets of the technocracy within the country.

Figure 7: Frequency of Unsolicited Interview Comments on Innovation Processes at NTU, 2009

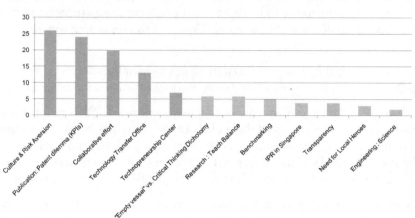

CONCLUSION

Despite the far-sighted decision to treat research investment as a key part of economic development and its commitment to a knowledge-based economy, the Singaporean government still struggles to reap the rewards of this policy in encouraging increased risk-taking and the development of an entrepreneurial academic society. However, it has to be recognized that the policy of research investment, based on a first class education system, has paid off in allowing Singapore to very rapidly leap-frog into the top echelons of World science and to attract high class, technologically-based inward investment and to provide the infrastructure to support this advanced economy. However, it must also be recognized that the whole research-innovation "enterprise" is still very young and that it may have been over ambitious in expecting its innovation returns to match that which could be expected from more "mature" systems. Nevertheless, there does appear to be difficulties in developing a truly entrepreneurial approach in terms of high technologically based innovation emanating from its academic institutions. Now it has to address how to change mindsets in its quest to economic advancement and to maximize the return on the investment made on behalf of its citizens for their future benefit.

REFERENCES

Hofstede, G. (1994) Cultures and Organisations: *Software of the Mind. Intercultural cooperation and its importance for survival*, Successful Strategist Series, London: HarperCollins.

Martin, M. O., Mullis, I. V. S., & Foy, P. (with Olson, J.F., Erberber, E., Preuschoff, C. & Galia, J.). (2008). Chestnut Hill, MA: TIMSS & PIRLS International Study Center, Boston College.

TIMSS (2007) International Mathematics Report: Findings from IEA's Trends in International Mathematics and Science Study at the Fourth and Eighth Grades

TIMSS (2007) International Science Report: Findings from IEA's Trends in International Mathematics and Science Study at the Fourth and Eighth Grades

Low Kim Cheng, Patrick. (2006). Cultural obstacles in growing entrepreneurship: a study in Singapore. *Journal of Management Development*, Vol 25,2 pp. 169-182.

CHAPTER 11

KAUST: An International, Independent, Graduate Research University

Fawwaz T. Ulaby

INTRODUCTION

Education, research and economic development are among the highest priorities established by King Abdullah for Saudi Arabia. An equally important overriding priority for him is the development of women for greater participation in the workforce. According to UNESCO, women make up 58% of the total student population of Saudi Arabia, and yet only 16% of the Saudi workforce (excluding foreign workers) is made up of Saudi women. To advance his agenda, the King has increased support for higher education tenfold over the past two years, and promises to maintain it at that level for the next ten years. This year he authorized funds for the construction of two new university campuses, both for women, at approximately $10 billion each. He has also boosted the government outlay to all of Saudi Arabia's 20 other universities.

While this new level of funding will likely improve the quality of higher education and make it available to a greater segment of Saudi society, its focus is primarily on undergraduate degree programs and the professional schools (medicine, business, engineering, etc.). King Abdullah's pride and joy is KAUST (King Abdullah University of Science and Technology), not only because it carries his name, but also because it is envisioned as a model for the global research university of the 21st century. The initial concept of KAUST as an elite, relatively small, international, financially independent, graduate university (Figure 1) was introduced to King Abdullah (under a different name) by a small group of advisors in June 2006. Today, only three years later, construction of its $10 billion campus is almost complete, most of its research facilities are in the final stages of acceptance testing, many of its initial cadre of faculty are in the process of moving themselves and their families to Saudi Arabia, and all plans are on schedule for opening day on 5 September 2009. KAUST's incoming class is expected to be ~400 graduate students.

Figure 1: The KAUST concept

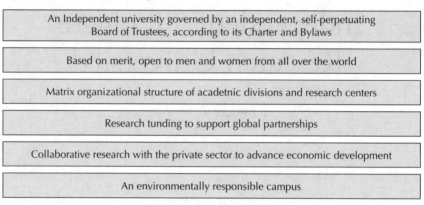

An Independent university governed by an independent, self-perpetuating Board of Trustees, according to its Charter and Bylaws

Based on merit, open to men and women from all over the world

Matrix organizational structure of acadetnic divisions and research centers

Research tunding to support global partnerships

Collaborative research with the private sector to advance economic development

An environmentally responsible campus

PERSONAL CONNECTION

My personal involvement with KAUST started during the concept formulation stage in the spring of 2006. I later participated in several KAUST-sponsored programs, primarily as an advocate and advisor. In May 2008, I accepted a formal appointment with KAUST as its Founding Provost and the first member of its academic faculty. Exactly one year later, I resigned from KAUST and returned to the University of Michigan. I provide this background to place in context the material contained in this presentation, most of which will be factual information about the story of KAUST to date, but often intermingled with personal observations and lessons learned. In brief, my association with KAUST was a unique and exhilarating experience, very rewarding, highly demanding and certainly memorable.

THE KAUST MISSION IN BRIEF

Whereas King Abdullah has been the financier and driving force behind the establishment of KAUST, and Minister Naimi, chair of its Board of Trustees, has been its chief guide and archangel, Frank Rhodes has been KAUST's spiritual leader and mentor. Frank's role is most evident in his articulation of KAUST's academic philosophy, through both its Bylaws and Articles of Governance. KAUST's mission (Articles of Governance, 2008) is captured by the following excerpt:

The University exists for the pursuit and advancement of scientific knowledge and its broad dissemination and benevolent application. As a world-class research university, King Abdullah University of Science and Technology will be a catalyst for diversification of the Kingdom of Saudi Arabia to a knowledge-based economy. By these means, the University serves not only the Kingdom of Saudi Arabia, but also the larger region and the world.

Independent in its character, international in its membership, scientific and technological in its focus, the University provides graduate-level instruction, awards masters' and doctoral degrees, undertakes advanced research, and collaborates with other organizations in pursuit of its purposes.

Members of the Faculty are dedicated to research, teaching, and the advancement and application of knowledge. As such, they have an obligation not only to their scholarly professions and the University but also to their students and the larger society. This obligation requires an environment of openness and free inquiry, if the University is effectively to serve the public interest. The Articles of Governance are intended to nurture and support that environment, and thus to promote the well-being and effectiveness of the University.

As the Bylaws state: "Within the University, the faculty members shall enjoy the academic freedom and freedom of research available in international universities, and shall use such freedom and rights to boost the students' knowledge in their fields of specialty, improve their scientific competencies and skills, and develop and enrich knowledge." The Faculty shall have a fundamental role in University governance pursuant to mechanisms set forth in Article II, Article V, and such policies, consistent with the Articles of Governance, as the University shall from time to time establish.

ACADEMIC INFRASTRUCTURE

The birth of KAUST is characterized by two overriding features: speed and parallel development.

KAUST Speed

From breaking ground in October 2007 to completion by August 2009, the 20-month-long, $10-billion construction project of the KAUST campus is nothing short of monumental in size, scope, environmental quality, complexity and speed. Realization of the physical infrastructure (Figure 2) — which included 3,000 housing units for faculty, staff and students and all of the usual services of a small town (schools, health clinic, shopping mall, entertainment centres, restaurants, etc.) — could not have been possible had it not been for the heroic efforts of a highly experienced group of about 200 engineers and managers that was seconded to KAUST by ARAMCO. That said, we also know that buildings and laboratory facilities are only a necessary, but not sufficient condition for establishing a viable research university. The heart of an academic institution is its people — the faculty, staff and students, and its soul is the collective academic environment that defines its values, relationships and expectations.

In the spirit of democracy and self-governance, we (academics) are accustomed to an environment in which all significant (and all too often even insignificant) decisions are made through a lengthy process involving committees, meetings and more meetings. Moreover, under common circumstances, when we assume academic administrative positions, we move into fully operational systems capable of functioning autonomously, with or without us. KAUST started from scratch, which is both an opportunity and a challenge. When I was appointed as KAUST's chief academic officer, I was a chief of a tribe of one, myself. I had no academic staff of any stripe or description, not even a secretary. And yet, I was expected to create the critical mass that will soon evolve into a world-class research university (Figure 3). With the help of and active participation by several American and European universities, I managed to recruit Division Chairs (equivalent to deans), some

Figure 2: Main KAUST campus

Figure 3: Fast facts about KAUST

Language of Instruction: English

Initially, KAUST will have 400 grad students; at maturity **2,000** (1000 master's and 1000 Ph.D. students)

Initially, KAUST will have ~ **100** faculty members, building to 250 at maturity

Full research community at KAUST will consist of **1,500** people (not including students)

At maturity, the KAUST community will have **20,000** residents

50 faculty, directors of multidisciplinary research centres, librarians, registrars, admission officers, budget managers, etc.

We also developed degree programs, admission and graduation requirements, faculty and staff policies, and created offices to support student services, arts programs, symposia and workshops, and many of the activities commonly enjoyed on academic campuses.

Throughout the recruiting process, many colleagues expressed concern and scepticism about KAUST's ability to attract accomplished faculty and highly promising graduate students. The question often asked by many is: "How are you able to convince highly successful professors to leave their well-established, secure positions at prominent universities and move to a hitherto unknown, unproven university, in a country that does not have the history or tradition of academic research?" KAUST's attraction consisted of three important ingredients:

- World-class research facilities, supported by a group of highly qualified technicians and engineers. From one of the fastest supercomputers in the world to the latest instrumentation for nanofabrication and characterization, KAUST offers its faculty and graduate students unparalleled capabilities.
- Ample funding to support research activities.
- Attractive compensation packages, including housing and other benefits.

It is significant that in addition to recruiting a cadre of superb faculty and staff, KAUST recruited some 400 graduate students, from 60 different countries, all on par, in terms of academic qualifications, with those attending graduate programs at top U.S. and European universities.

Parallel Development

When executing a complex project, some of its tasks may be carried out in parallel, while others may require sequential programming. Because of the time pressure — and the absence of academics in the early stages — KAUST could not afford to obey the sequential programming logic. In 2007, several strategic plans were developed to design KAUST's academic infrastructure, but they were led by different teams with limited coordination between them. Stanford Research Institute (SRI) was contracted to define the research directions that KAUST should support (Figure 4), on the basis of both relevance to Saudi Arabia and significance as a frontier area of science and technology. The Washington Advisory Group contributed a plan that specified which academic disciplines and degree programs KAUST should offer, and how to recruit faculty through partnerships with U.S. and European universities. Independently, KAUST contracted with several academic and industrial institutions to acquire designs and specifications for state-of-the-art experimental facilities that can support MRI, nanofabrication, gene sequencing, and similar types of instruments. Also, a teraflop supercomputer was procured from IBM. In an ideal scenario, such disparate but interdependent strategic plans and contractual arrangements would be fully integrated, necessitating extensive coordination and multiple iterations. Unfortunately, that was not the case, so one of the major challenges at KAUST was to figure out how to integrate or realign the individual parts of the overall academic puzzle so that they become compatible elements of a coherent whole.

EXPECTATIONS AND VULNERABILITIES

To its advantage, KAUST possesses two critical ingredients for success: financial resources and highly dedicated staff. I have no doubt that KAUST will succeed in realizing its stated mission of becoming a world-class research university in the not-so-distant future. How well it succeeds and how quickly it realizes its mission will depend on a third, equally important, ingredient, namely its academic leadership. KAUST has many supporters, within and outside Saudi Arabia, but it also has its detractors. KAUST is viewed by a segment of Saudi society as a threat to accepted social norms. While KAUST will not likely have to face the financial challenges that many universities around the world are now facing, its Board of Trustees and academic leaders will be constantly challenged by how to mediate the wide array of highly conflicting perspectives held by its many stakeholders, from lifestyle and gender-related issues to academic freedom and freedom of speech.

Figure 4: KAUST research thrusts

Biosciences and
Bioengineering

Industrial biotechnology
Microbial bioremediation
Agricultural biotechnology
Sustainable aquaculture

Regional environmental bioscience
Red Sea marine environmental science
and engineering

Health science and technology

Applied Mathematics and
Computational Science

Materials Science
and Engineering

**Polymers and membranes,
Nanomaterials**
Carbon and bioprocessed nanomateria
Photovoltaic applications

**Catalytic chemistry materials for
high-stress environments**

Ressources, Energy and
Environment

REFERENCE

Articles of Governance. (2008). King Abdullah University of Science and Technology, Thuwal, Saudi Arabia. pp. 1-2.

CHAPTER 12

Transforming an Economy through Research and Innovation

Arif S. Al-Hammadi, Mohammed E. Al-Mualla and Russel C. Jones

INTRODUCTION

In the race to diversify their economies beyond oil and gas predominance, several Middle East Countries are moving to develop "knowledge-based" economies. Higher education, particularly in technical areas, and innovation are seen as key to making that transition. New higher education institutions are being built to implement this vision. In the United Arab Emirates, the Khalifa University of Science, Technology and Research (KUSTAR) is a primary example of these developments.

Building dynamic economies that are based on the creative application of human knowledge is currently an aspiration of all developing countries. The United Nations Development Program has conducted a number of studies of the Arab world's progress in developing the knowledge, skills and institutions needed to compete in today's global economy. Its 2003 report (UNDP, 2003) presented a comprehensive picture of the "knowledge deficit", and suggested needed reforms. Since then, the 22 countries of the Arab world have worked on reducing this deficit. A recent report (Lord, 2008) analysed what has been achieved, what has failed, and what remains to be done. The 2008 report concluded that Arab countries as a group have made significant progress when measured against their own histories. Significant success has been achieved in access to education, including new universities with global standards, and Arab governments have begun investing more in research and development.

As part of this effort to reduce the "knowledge deficit", the six Arab counties that form the Gulf Cooperation Council (GCC) have come to understand that they must diversify their current oil-based economies, investing some of today's income flow in economic diversification. In particular, these countries are focusing on developing "knowledge-based economies" by developing higher education programs that will provide the human capacity to initiate and support such new economic thrusts.

In this paper, we briefly discuss the efforts of the emirate of Abu Dhabi in transforming its economy into a "knowledge-based economy" and we use the establishment of Khalifa University of Science, Technology and Research (KUSTAR) as a case study for this effort.

ABU DHABI — TOWARDS A DIVERSE KNOWLEDGE-DRIVEN ECONOMY

Vision and Plan for Economic Development

The government of Abu Dhabi, the largest of the seven emirates that comprise the United Arab Emirates, has established an aggressive plan for diversification of the currently heavily oil-based economy (Government of Abu Dhabi, 2008). The vision for Abu Dhabi, currently being implemented, includes:

- Premium education for human capacity building.
- Research and development (R&D), leading to innovation.
- Commercialization of R&D results.
- Creation of a sustainable knowledge-based economy.

The plan for economic development of Abu Dhabi, aimed at implementation by the year 2030, has three major objectives:

Objective 1 — Reduce GDP volatility through diversification

Abu Dhabi will aim to reduce the volatility of overall economic and Gross Domestic Product (GDP) growth through diversification. Diversifying away from oil into other economic sectors will minimize the impact of oil price fluctuations and other shocks, ensuring more stable and predictable economic growth. In order to do this, Abu Dhabi will focus on capital-intensive, export-oriented sectors where the Emirate can have or build a competitive advantage.

Objective 2 — Enlarge the enterprise base

It is important to enlarge the enterprise base, both through the continued growth and expansion of large national champions, attraction of foreign direct investment in leading edge technology sectors, and through the stimulation of a more vibrant Small-Medium Enterprise (SME) sector. This will provide more meaningful opportunities for U.A.E. nationals, encourage innovation in higher value-added sectors, and mitigate the risk to the economy of shocks to larger enterprises. Coupled with the traditional support mechanisms — financial or technical — that could be offered to SMEs, it is expected that the revision of anti-trust laws, the removal of entry barriers into some economic sectors, and encouraging market-based competition mechanisms will encourage entrepreneurship and foster the SMEs sector growth.

Objective 3 — Enhance competitiveness

Abu Dhabi will enhance competitiveness and productivity. Not only will steps in this regard bolster the entrepreneurial SME sector, but it will also generate significant economic growth in an underperforming segment of the economy. By focusing on capital-intensive industries and internationally traded services and optimizing the workforce in low-productivity areas, companies will be able to make capital and labour work more efficiently, greatly increasing the overall competitiveness of the economy.

To illustrate the current heavy reliance on oil and the need for diversification, Figure 1 shows how enterprise contributions in Abu Dhabi compare with those in other economies. The planned diversification of the Abu Dhabi economy is set to reduce the dependence on oil GDP to 36% by 2030, as shown in Figure 2.

Figure 1: Enterprise Contribution to GDP (Government of Abu Dhabi, 2009)

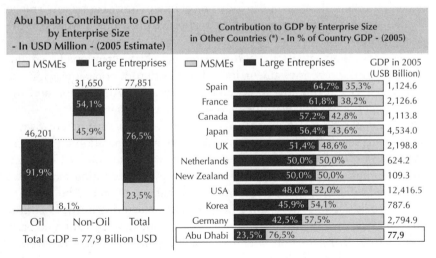

Figure 2: Target Abu Dhabi GDP (Government of Abu Dhabi, 2009)

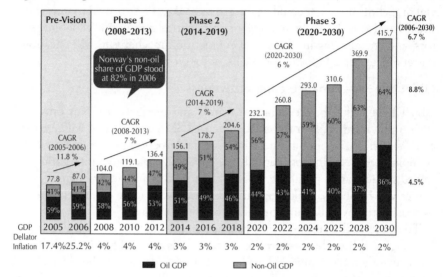

Strategic Initiatives

As already discussed, Abu Dhabi will build a sustainable and stable economy through the diversification and broadening of its enterprise base across a range of different sectors, and by taking steps to improve the competitiveness of the local private sector.

Elements of implementation of this vision include the creation of new educational institutions, investment in and acquisition of companies that are bringing diverse technological economic activities to Abu Dhabi, and the development of research activities and support mechanisms.

For example, Mubadala (2009) has been created as a government-owned company to develop new companies in Abu Dhabi. In operation for some six years, its portfolio of investments is currently valued at some $15 billion. Mubadala has, for example, purchased the chip manufacturing facilities of AMD, and will be moving significant parts of that operation to Abu Dhabi as part of the initiative of developing high-tech manufacturing in the U.A.E. It also is making investments in aerospace research and development, and parts manufacture, in association with the major expansion of U.A.E. airlines, including Etihad and Emirates.

Another example is the development of Saadiyat Island as cultural center, for both tourist attraction and local education purposes. The island will include five major cultural institutions: a branch of the Louvre Museum; a branch of the Guggenheim Museum; a National Museum named after the founder of the U.A.E., H.H. Sheikh Zayed Bin Sultan Al Nahyan; a Maritime Museum; and a Performing Arts Center.

On the education front there are a number of strategic initiatives. New York University (NYU)-Abu Dhabi is being established as a comprehensive liberal arts and sciences campus in Abu Dhabi (NYU-AD, 2009). New York University has long been committed to building its international presence, and had increased study-abroad sites to places such as Singapore, Accra and Buenos Aires. But the plan that has been developed for a comprehensive, residential liberal-arts and sciences branch campus in the Arabian Gulf, set to open in 2010, is in a class by itself. The NYU-Abu Dhabi project will see a flow of professors and students between New York and Abu Dhabi, allowing seamless transfers. The NYU-Abu Dhabi project meets several needs of the U.S. university, and simultaneously addresses a major goal of Abu Dhabi, to be identified as a hub of knowledge transmission and creation in the region, as well as attending to the need to build human capacity in its citizens and its significant expatriate population.

Another liberal arts branch campus has been established — the Paris-Sorbonne University-Abu Dhabi (2009). This a French-speaking higher education institution that aspires to attract not only the best students from the U.A.E., but also the best students from all over the Middle East and the world.

The Masdar initiative, spawned by Mubadala, includes three major thrusts: investments in alternative energy to initiate the follow-on to the petroleum years as a major part of the U.A.E. economy; development of a $22-billion demonstration city, Masdar City, which will be carbon neutral and be powered entirely by solar and wind energy; and establishment of the Masdar Institute of Science and Technology (2009), a graduate level specialty institution focused on research and education in alternative energies. The MIST is offering master's degree programs — and eventually doctoral programs — in engineering and science disciplines. Current programs are Engineering Systems and Management, Information Technology, Materials Science and Engineering, Mechanical Engineering, and Water and Environment. It is a research-driven institute being developed with the support and cooperation of the Massachusetts Institute of Technology (MIT). The MIST will be located in Masdar City.

In addition to higher education, Abu Dhabi government is also addressing school education. The Abu Dhabi Education Council (2009) was established in 2005 to develop education and educational institutions in the Emirate of Abu Dhabi, implement innovative educational policies, plans and programs that aim to improve education, and support educational institutions and staff to achieve the objectives of national development in accordance with the highest international standards.

As part of the initiative to develop schools of the highest international standards, the Institute of Applied Technology (2009) was founded in 2005. The
IAT offers Career-Based Technical Education (CTE), in English language, at
the secondary school level. The IAT has five campuses located throughout the
U.A.E.

KUSTAR — A CASE STUDY

Overview

Almost all of the above higher educational initiatives are branch campuses of
well-known international institutions.

The U.A.E. has created three home-grown higher education institutions at
the Federal level: U.A.E. University (2009), Higher Colleges of Technology
(2009), and Zayed University (2009). The main aim of these federal-level institutions is to provide as many U.A.E. nationals as possible with higher education.

However, the Abu Dhabi government has identified the need for a home-
grown university that caters for the elite and that is focused on building the
high caliber human capital needed for the economic development of the emirate as it evolves from an oil-based economy to a diverse knowledge-driven
economy. This need was addressed by the establishment of Khalifa University
of Science, Technology and Research (2009).

KUSTAR was established to address the full chain starting from undergraduate education, to graduate education, to research and development, and even
to incubation and spin-off of companies.

In what follows we give a more detailed description of KUSTAR and its
plans to address the needs of Abu Dhabi government and the U.A.E.

History

KUSTAR has been built on the strong base of a predecessor institution, the
Etisalat University College (EUC). Established in 1989 in Sharjah, EUC has
offered engineering programs in the telecommunications area in three degree
tracks: Communications Engineering, Computer Engineering, and Electronics Engineering. Having graduated some 500 engineers over the past two
decades, EUC has populated the technical and leadership ranks of the telecommunications sector of the U.A.E. As the Sharjah campus of KUSTAR, it
currently enrols 350 students in its undergraduate and graduate programs.

KUSTAR was established by Royal Decree in 2007, and merged with EUC.

Vision and Mission

Vision: To be a leading international center of higher education and research
in technology and science.

Mission: KUSTAR is an independent, non-profit, coeducational institution, dedicated to the advancement of learning through teaching and research and to the discovery and application of knowledge. It pursues international recognition as a world-class research university, with a strong tradition of inter-disciplinary teaching and research and of partnering with leading universities around the world.

The University endeavours to serve the Emirate of Abu Dhabi, U.A.E. society, the region and the world by providing an environment of creative enquiry within which critical thinking, human values, technical competence and practical and social skills, business acumen and a capability for lifetime learning are cultivated and sustained. It sets itself high standards in providing a caring, rewarding and enriching environment for all of its students and staff. It ensures that its graduates, on entering the workplace, form a superlative cadre of engineers, technologists and scientists, capable of making major contributions to the current and future sectors of U.A.E. industry and society as leaders and innovators.

The University insists on the highest world-class standards of academic excellence in all that it does. It complements other universities in the region by providing, in its chosen areas of activity, the best teaching and research available in the region. It strives to meet demands for expansion while never compromising on quality.

Governance

The senior governing bodies of KUSTAR are the Board of Trustees and the Board of Governors. The prime responsibility of the Board of Trustees is the formation of the higher policy of the University as well as any further duties in accordance with the decree setting up the University. The Board of Governors is the executive governing body, responsible for matters including the finance and property of the University. It is specifically required to determine the educational character, vision and mission of the University and to set its general strategic direction.

The Chairman of the Board of Trustees is His Highness General Sheikh Mohammed bin Zayed Al Nahyan, Crown Prince of Abu Dhabi and Deputy Supreme Commander of the U.A.E. Armed Forces.

Academic Organization

KUSTAR is developing four colleges:

- Engineering.
- Management and Logistics.
- Health Sciences.
- Sciences.

In addition it has an Institute of Homeland Security, and plans to develop more such institutes.

The Sharjah Campus offers the following undergraduate and graduate degree programs:

- Bachelor in Communications Engineering.
- Bachelor in Computer Engineering.
- Bachelor Electronics Engineering.
- MSc by Research (Communication, Computer, or Electronics Engineering).
- MSc in Information Security (planned start in Fall 2009).
- PhD in Engineering (planned start in Fall 2009).

The Abu Dhabi Campus admitted its first class of students to the foundation year in Fall 2008. This class, plus additionally admitted direct entry students, will inaugurate the following engineering programs in the Fall of 2009:

- BSc Communications Engineering.
- BSc Computer Engineering.
- BSc Electronics Engineering.
- BSc Aerospace Engineering.
- BSc Mechanical Engineering.
- BSc Software Engineering.
- BSc Biomedical Engineering.

Additional programs will be introduced each successive year at the Abu Dhabi Campus: Civil Engineering and a Post Baccalaureate Premedical Program in 2010; Medical School and two additional engineering programs in 2011; and four new engineering and science programs each year from 2012 through 2015. The potential new programs to be developed include:

- Electrical Engineering.
- Avionics Engineering.
- Manufacturing Engineering.
- Materials Engineering.
- Industrial Engineering.
- Mechatronics Engineering.
- Energy Engineering.
- Environmental Engineering.
- Construction Engineering.
- Chemical Engineering.
- Bioengineering.
- Mathematics.
- Physics.

- Chemistry.
- Biology.
- Logistics Management.
- Supply Chain Management.
- Crises Management.
- Homeland Security.

Enrolment Projections

The Sharjah Campus, providing a center of excellence in telecommunications, is expected to grow from its current enrolment of 350 to approximately 450. It plans to move from male-only to coed, and to expand enrolments in its masters and doctoral programs substantially.

The Abu Dhabi campus will have some 300 students enrolled in seven programs in the Fall of 2009, and will grow to some 3400 students by 2020, distributed as shown in Table 1 below.

Table 1: Enrolment Projections by the Year 2020

College	Students by 2020
Engineering	1560
Medical	480
Management	480
Science	480
Post Graduate	400

Faculty

World-class faculty members are being recruited to provide challenging education to the KUSTAR students, and to conduct leading edge research. In keeping with standards at other world-class research-driven universities, KUSTAR faculty members will spend approximately half of their time on research. Teaching loads will be two to three courses per academic year. This pattern will require some 500 faculty members by 2020.

Collaborations with top world universities are being developed to assist in faculty recruitment, as well as in facilities development and research initiation.

Research and Development

KUSTAR is a research-driven university. This is emphasized by the explicit inclusion of the word "research" in the name of the University. This is also reflected in KUSTAR's vision and mission statements.

The research goal of KUSTAR is to conduct globally competitive research. The University pursues a research strategy that addresses the balance of basic and applied research, emphasizes the value of collaborative and interdisciplinary research, and takes into account the global and national trends and the needs of government, industry, business and the community.

KUSTAR is recruiting faculty and research staff with a proven international track-record of conducting and managing competitive research. Faculty and researchers are provided with an environment conducive to research. Policies and procedures are designed to be flexible and supportive, teaching loads are set to allow for research-active faculty to spend at least half-time on research, and support services such as fund management, contracts, exploitation of intellectual property rights, and knowledge transfer and enterprise, are provided.

Research activities within KUSTAR colleges are organized into centers/groups. These tend to be interdisciplinary and are fully supported to become internationally recognized.

Both undergraduate and graduate students are involved in research and independent study and are equipped with the capability to extend their understanding beyond what is covered in their curriculum.

KUSTAR is currently working on establishing links and partnerships with world-class research universities, groups and laboratories to instigate relevant joint research projects and exchange arrangements.

In addition, a Research & Development Center with state-of-the-art facilities and resources is being developed with a range of key partners. The mission of this center is to promote the economic development and competitiveness of Abu Dhabi and the U.A.E. by fostering innovation, technology transfer, and entrepreneurship. The R&D Center will identify and focus on the development of science and technology clusters that are most relevant to Abu Dhabi and the U.A.E.

One of the focus areas that has already been identified is the Information and Communication Technologies (ICT) area. KUSTAR has successfully formed a partnership with British Telecom (BT) and the Emirates Telecommunication Corporation (ETISALAT) to establish the Etisalat-BT Innovation Center at KUSTAR. This will be the first industry-led center in the Middle-East concentrating on ICT next generation networks, systems and services.

Another area of focus that has been identified is Nanotechnology. KUSTAR has formed an advisory panel from eminent nanotechnology and nanoscience academics and experts. The panel is currently working on a proposal for forming a world-class Nanotechnology and Nanoscience center at KUSTAR.

High performance and parallel computing is also an important area of focus. KUSTAR has recently signed an MoU with Intel to collaborate on this area.

KUSTAR is also discussing the establishment of an Aerospace center with Mubadala and other leading companies in this area of focus.

Other discussions are ongoing to attract well established R&D technology institutions and companies. The R&D center will also incubate new innovative technology start-ups.

The establishment of the R&D Center and its strong links with the academic colleges will have many benefits to KUSTAR. The center will build on the strengths of KUSTAR's research and graduate studies to support the relevant clusters within the center. In return, the center will enhance, influence and inform KUSTAR's research and teaching by providing faculty and students with opportunities to interact with potential users of the outcomes of the research and potential employers of graduates. In addition, the center will enhance the chances of faculty to attract research funding by providing them with collaboration opportunities with government, industry and business. The center will also provide faculty and students with access to its facilities and its services for funds managements, project management, and knowledge and intellectual property rights management. The center will also present students and graduates with internship and employment opportunities.

All the research and development activities of KUSTAR will be supported with an outreach program to foster greater understanding by the general public of the benefits and applications of research.

Facilities

The Abu Dhabi operation of KUSTAR is currently comfortably housed in new temporary facilities on Abu Dhabi Island. These facilities will be adequate for two to three years, at which time the growth of enrolments and research activity will require a move to a new, purpose-built campus. Land has been designated for that campus, in the education sector of the new 2030 national capital development, near the Abu Dhabi airport.

The permanent campus is being designed to include the following state-of-the-art facilities, including:

- Academic classroom and laboratory buildings for the engineering, management and logistics, and science colleges.
- Purpose-built Medical School building.
- Research and Development laboratories building.
- Administration Building.
- Multi-purpose Buildings/Student Hub (Book Store, Coffee Shops/ Restaurants, Shops, Printing/copying services, Laundry, Library, Student Union. Post Office, ATMs, etc.), Mosque, Sports/Recreation Building and fields.
- Conference Center.

- Museum of Technology.
- Student and Staff Accommodation.
- Car Park.

In addition to development of a physical campus, KUSTAR is leading the formation of a major broadband computer network in the U.A.E. The Emirates Advanced Network for Research and Education (ANKABUT) is a dedicated advanced network connecting academic and research institutions at a speed of 10 GB/S at the core and 1GB/s at the access level. It will initially connect 28 sites at public colleges, universities and schools with one another and to Internet2 in the U.S. It facilitates research collaboration by providing access to databases and supercomputers, and teaching collaboration through rich multimedia content and high-definition video conferencing.

CONCLUSION

Countries throughout the GCC region, and beyond in the Arab world, are striving to develop diverse economies which allow them to compete effectively in today's global economy. Much of the effort is appropriately directed to education and associated activities which aim toward building "knowledge-based" economies.

The Emirate of Abu Dhabi has embarked on a particularly enlightened and aggressive program of economic development, aimed at transforming its current oil-based economy to one based on knowledge and innovation. It is making substantial investments in higher education, particularly in engineering and science, to develop the human capacity to accomplish this transition. KUSTAR will play a major role in Abu Dhabi's journey towards a diverse knowledge-based economy.

REFERENCES

Abu Dhabi Education Council. (2009). http://www.adec.ac.ae/en, Date accessed 5/8/09.
Government of Abu Dhabi. (2008). *Abu Dhabi Economic Vision 2030*, November 2008.
Higher Colleges of Technology. (2009). http://www.hct.ac.ae/, Date accessed 5/8/09.
Institute of Applied Technology. (2009). http://www.iat.ac.ae/, Date accessed 5/8/09.
Khalifa University of Science, Technology and Research. (2009). http://www.kustar.ac.ae/main/, Date accessed 5/8/09.
Lord, Kristin M. (2008). *A New Millennium of Knowledge?* Saban Center at Brookings, Analysis Paper Number 12, April 2008. Washington D.C.: The Brookings Institution.
Masdar Institute of Science and Technology. (2009). http://www.mist.ac.ae/home/index.aspx, Date accessed 5/8/09.

Mubadala Development Company. (2009). http://www.mubadala.ae/, Date accessed 5/8/09.

New York University — Abu Dhabi. (2009). http://nyuad.nyu.edu/, Date accessed 5/8/09.

Paris-Sorbonne Université — Abu Dhabi. (2009). http://www.sorbonne.ae/sites/psuad/Pages/default.aspx Date accessed 5/8/09.

U.A.E. University. (2009). http://www.uaeu.ac.ae/, Date accessed 5/8/09.

United Nations Development Program. (2003). Arab Human Development Report 2003, "Building a Knowledge Society", http://www.arab-hdr.org/publications/other/ahdr/ahdr2003e.pdf, Date accessed 5/8/09.

Zayed University. (2009). See http://www.zu.ac.ae/main/Date accessed 5/8/09.

CHAPTER 13

Research and Innovation in Latin America

Juan Ramón de la Fuente [1]

ECONOMIC OVERVIEW

While Latin America has achieved relative economic stability and growth over the past decade (37.7% for 1998-2008), as the global financial struck the productive sectors of the economy through a drop in demand from the industrialized countries, declining remittances from abroad and falling commodities prices, in 2008 it grew 4.3%.

Latin America is a very diverse region. Some countries have entered the crisis in a relatively favourable position, whereas others are suffering more from the external shock. Whatever outcomes at country level, overall GDP will decline this year.

In any case, despite prudent fiscal policies and reduction of macroeconomic vulnerabilities in recent years, its economy has not been without problems. Volatility, inflation and policy reversals in various countries explain, at least to some extent, their unequal development.

From a global perspective, Latin America is not only not catching up; it is falling relatively further behind. In 1996-2006 it grew 34.6%, lower than East and North-East Asia (62.5%), South and South-West Asia (73.5%) and even Africa (57.8%) (The World Bank, 2008).

In a highly competitive global environment that is increasingly driven by knowledge and innovation, Latin America lags behind. This paper reviews some of the reasons why, particularly those related to education as well as R&D, and suggests some ideas for taking remedial action.

1 President, International Association of Universities. Former Rector of UNAM, Mexico. Simón Bolívar Professor, University of Alcalá, Spain.

Twelve Latin American countries were selected, together with Spain and Portugal (to be able to talk of Iberoamerica, when appropriate) as well as four countries from other regions: Canada, Korea, Australia and the United Kingdom, for international comparisons to provide a context for framing some of the analysed variables, and to follow the methodology from previous works published in Spanish that used these countries for similar analyses (CINDA, 2007).

GROWTH AND INNOVATION

Jamil Salmi from the World Bank has suggested that the technological change residual, often referred to as "the residual of our ignorance", the problem-solving "mystery variable" would explain why economies such as Brazil, Chile or Mexico, when compared with the Republic of Korea's, which had roughly similar endowments of capital and labour 30 years ago, subsequently grew at very different rates (Rodríguez, 2008). However, the linkage between innovation indicators and economic performance is not all that clear.

Innovation has typically been analysed as a determinant of productivity growth, but not so much as a determinant of overall growth. The central question is what the effect of innovation on long-term development is. Classic innovation-related variables refer to expenditures on research and development, patents, foreign investment, technology licensing, etc., whereas labour has been measured usually through education, skills and experience.

How is it that the equation composed by capital, labour and innovation determines development?

Rapid-growth economies have invested heavily in research and development — India, for example, relying more on publicly financed R&D, and China relying more on acquiring technology developed elsewhere. By contrast, Latin America clearly has done neither, and the investment gaps caused by these lags are important in explaining the relative differences in economic growth and mid-class prosperity.

How does innovation improve productivity that leads to economic growth? A variable defined as total factor productivity (TFP) which can be understood as the factors beyond capital and labour that enable an economy to increase production output, focuses on changes in productivity related to education, training and technology, among others (Baier, 2006).

Compared with other regions, how does Latin America fare in the strength of TFP? The most obvious comparison is with East Asia. Evidence has been found that as much as half the growth in Korea or Taiwan, for example, was due to TFP. And by making comparisons with Latin America, it has been suggested that TFP is a significant factor in the East Asian Tigers' much-better performance (Figure 1). Over the past 25 years, Latin America experienced lower growth rates than them.

Figure 1: Growth and TFP Š Latin America compared with orher regions

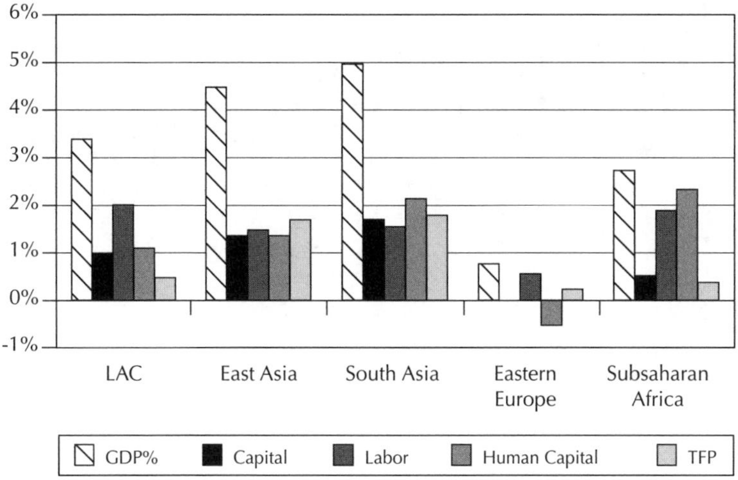

Source: IDB, 2006.

While the lower growth in Latin America can be explained by several factors, the poor contribution of human capital seems to be a shackling of growth potential in the region.

There is also evidence that having a more educated workforce leads to higher growth. While recent research that focuses on quality rather than quantity of education gives support to the complex and sometimes controversial relationship between human capital and economic growth, population with at least tertiary education in countries such as Mexico, Chile and Brazil is significantly lower than in most OECD countries (Figure 2).

Higher education enrolment between 2000 and 2005 grew faster in Brazil (12%), Venezuela, Chile and Colombia (6-8%) than in other countries. However if one looks at public expenditure in tertiary education, as well as R&D expenditure as percentage of GDP, it is clearly less than that of other countries that have achieved a higher Human Development Index as defined by UNDP (Table 1). In fact, it reflects as well in the number of researchers by country, patents granted and what has been described as global competitiveness measured by variables such as infrastructure and technological readiness (Figures 3-5).

Figure 2: Population that has attained at least tertiary education (% by age group)

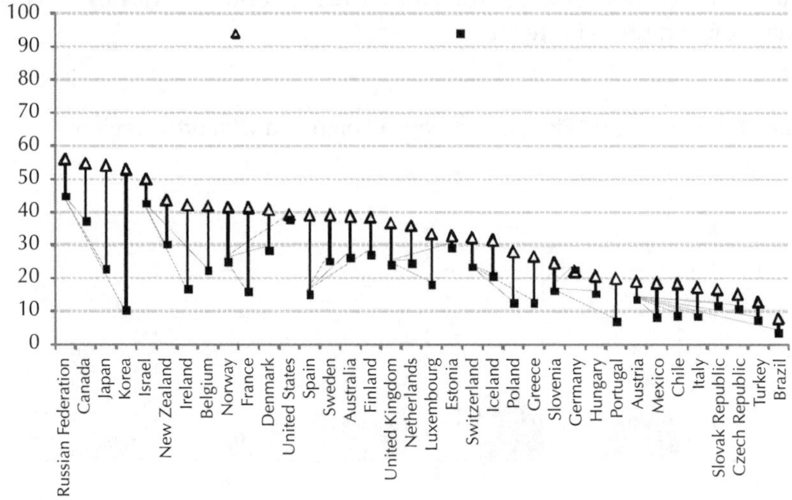

Source: OECD, 2008.

Table 1

			UNDP, 2007 Š 2008				
COUNTRY	GDP per capita (PPP US$)	Public expenditure in education (% GDP)	% of Public expenditure in tertiary education	R&D expenditure (% GDP)	Researchers per 1 million inhab.	Patents granted per 1 million inhab.	Human Development Index
AUSTRA	31.794	4,7	25	1,7	3.759	31	0,962
CAN	33.375	5,2	34	1,9	3.597	35	0,961
SPA	27.169	4,3	20	1,1	2.195	53	0,949
UK	33.238	5,4	..	1,9	2.706	62	0,946
KOR	22.029	4,6	13	2,6	3.187	1113	0,921
POR	20.410	5,7	6	0,8	1.949	14	0,897
ARG	14.280	3,8	17	0,4	720	4	0,869
CHI	12.027	3,5	15	0,6	444	1	0,867
URU	9.962	2,6	20	0,3	366	1	0,852
CRC	10.180	4,9	..	0,4	..	..	0,846
MEX	10.751	5,4	17	0,4	268	1	0,829
PAN	7.605	3,8	26	0,3	97	..	0,812
BRA	8.402	4,4	19	1,0	344	1	0,800
VEN	6.632	..	..	0,3	..	1	0,792
COL	7.304	4,8	13	0,2	109	..	0,791
DOM	8.217	1,8	..	..	..	..	0,779
PER	6.039	2,4	11	0,1	226	..	0,773
ECU	4.341	1,0	..	0,1	50	0	0,772
BOL	2.819	6,4	23	0,3	120	..	0,695

Figure 3

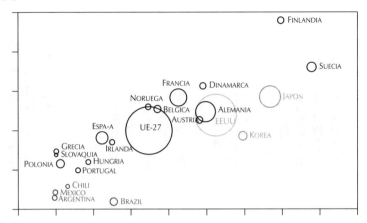

Figure 4

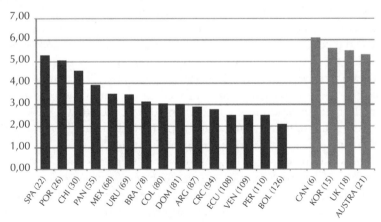

Source: World Economic Forum, 2008.

Figure 5: Global Competitiveness: Technological Readiness

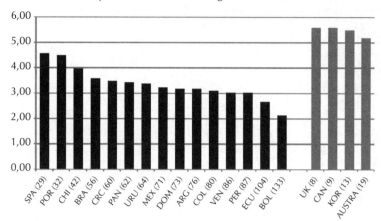

Source: World Economic Forum, 2008.

TECHNOLOGY AND RESEARCH

Technology by itself provides no magic. Successful countries at the times of "knowledge economy" are those that have proved able not only to produce knowledge and use technology efficiently, but to have long-term public policies to strengthen higher education and research.

Productive workers have been defined as the "missing link" between innovation and productivity since not just highly trained scientists and engineers are needed for innovation. For this reason, Latin America is a region to be called upon to innovate on how it educates approximately 100 million young people (15-24 years old) who are enrolled in its school systems and will demand further education in the next years (IESALC/UNESCO, 2008).

The formation of human capital at the primary, the secondary and tertiary levels remains a central and critical issue in the region.

As previously mentioned, innovation is by no means limited to formal R&D efforts. Knowledge creation also comes by constantly trying to improve hands-on productivity. However, research is the first step in innovation. Discoveries in basic knowledge are often first published in scientific and technical journals. It is therefore useful to compare Latin America's output of scientific journal articles with the outputs of other regions and countries (Figure 6). Another long-term problem has been the lack of international visibility of Latin American journals and the fact that relatively few scientists in the region publish their results in higher impact journals (Figure 7).

Figure 6

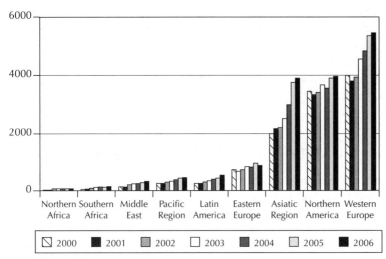

Source: SCIlago, 2008.

Figure 7: International visibility of scientific journals by region of publication

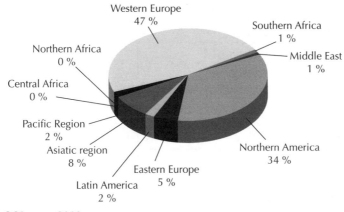

Source: SCImago, 2008.

Patent-related culture is also limited and there is little experience in development work required to convert discoveries into practical applications and finding concrete marketable opportunities.

In summary, Latin America is behind the global technological frontier and that is a reason why some believe that it can therefore obtain greater economic benefit if using knowledge that already exists rather than trying to create new knowledge. But this assumption may be misleading. To create new knowledge may have many indirect positives externalities in addition to the direct economic benefits and, in any case, it is compatible with the notion that it is also important to acquire and use new knowledge created elsewhere.

Innovate or abdicate seems to be the dilemma for less-advanced economies that aspire to become part of knowledge-based growth dynamics. Thus, basic research cannot be eluded if national innovation systems are to be developed (Salmi, 2009).

UNIVERSITIES AND PRODUCTIVE PROCESS

Some Latin American universities are the main incubators of created knowledge and thus, constitute the fundamental components of those incipient national innovation systems. Government and university research labs are the main actors of the process of creating knowledge in Latin America and although productive enterprises are becoming an increasingly important segment and it is very desirable as they are the main appliers of new knowledge, company spending on R&D remains largely insufficient (Table 2).

Table 2: Company spending on R&D*

Place	Country	Punctutation**
1	Switzerland	6.0
2	Japan	5.8
3	E.U.	5.8
31	Brasil	3.9
39	Spain	3.7
53	Portugal	3.3
64	Chile	3.1
66	Colombia	3.1
71	Mexico	3.0
81	Argentina	2.9

* World Economic Forum, The Globla Competitiveness Report 2008-2009
** X 139 countries = 3.4

At the global level, multinational corporations typically drive the creation and dissemination of applying knowledge, and it is now estimated that these corporations carry out more than half of all global R&D.

Functional links between universities and private firms are another issue that contributes to explain large differences in growth and innovation between Latin America and other regions. Some of the most productive and best ranked universities, such as those in México (UNAM), Sao Paulo (USP) and Buenos Aires (UBA), have both high research productivity and growing links with industry.

Nevertheless a related issue, on which Latin America has also lagged behind, has to do with the process and prospects for commercialization of knowledge. Some purists still believe it is not a good idea to think about patents and commercialization, as basic research is conceptualized and undertaken where the creation of new scientific and technical knowledge is financed primarily trough public expenditure. However this perspective is no longer the dominant viewpoint. University autonomy is not threatened but strengthened by alliances with productive sectors, provided there are appropriate legal frameworks.

Public policies to promote mechanisms ranging from tax incentives to the construction of science parks are very much needed, as is the creation of incubators to encourage interactions between publicly funded scientists and the private sector. This interaction benefits societies at large. Where scientists lack experience or business acumen, instruments and policies are needed to provide social benefits by translating ideas into valuable enterprises. That is what knowledge economy is all about.

Publicly funded incubators can serve a wide range of roles, from matching scientists with businessmen who can help develop business plans to helping them to get permits, find employees, and obtain financing support for start-up operations. Many other regions are doing precisely that, and it also explains why they are steadily forging far ahead.

THE NEXT STEPS

In an innovation-driven global society, to become a major player, Latin America has a long but not unachievable agenda to pursue.

Much dedication needs to be focused at enhancing basic and secondary education, but also on advanced skills and tertiary education as well; and clear, long term policies to create, transfer and acquire knowledge are very much in need to develop better environments for both public and private sectors spending on R&D.

Countries such as Argentina, Brazil, Chile, Costa Rica, México and Uruguay with strongest universities, higher scientific productivity and better infrastructure must continue to lead the way and, despite economic recession, investments in these critical issues must continue.

Further finance and transfer policies to enhance collaboration with industry and private companies are also in order.

Internationalization of higher education institutions must be actively promoted, as is networking with other universities and research institutions. High-quality joint degree programs in specific fields are promising strategies as well.

In the end, national policies for such a diverse set of countries will be needed, but general guidelines based on successful experiences elsewhere and some of the concepts discussed hereby may be helpful.

REFERENCES

Baier, S. L., Dwyer, G. P. & Tamura, R. (2006). *How Important are Capital and Total Factor Productivity for Economic Growth?* Economic Inquiry 44: 23-49.

CINDA. (2007). Centro Universitario de Desarrollo. *Educación Superior en Iberoamérica, Informe 2007*. Santiago de Chile.

IESALC/UNESCO. (2008). International Institute for Higher Education in Latin America and the Caribbean. *Tendencias de la Educación Superior en América Latina y el Caribe*. Caracas, Venezuela.

IDB. (2006). Inter-American Development Bank. *Education, Science and Technology in Latin America and the Caribbean*. Washington, D.C. http://www.iadb.org/sds/doc/

OECD. (2008). Organization for Economic Co-operation and Development. *Education at a Glance*. Paris.

Rodríguez, A., Sahlman, C. & Salmi, J. A. (2008). *Knowledge and Innovation for Competitiveness in Brazil*. WBI Development Studies. The World Bank, Washington, D.C.

Salmi, J. (2009). *The Challenge of Establishing World-Class Universities*. Washington, D.C.: The World Bank,

Scimago. (2008). Scimago Research Group. Journal Indicators & Ranking. Spain. http://www.scimago.es/

SJTU. (2008). Shanghai Jiao Tong University. *Academic Ranking of World Universities 2008*. http://www.arwu.org/

The World Bank. (2008). World Development Indicators. Washington, D.C.

The World Bank. (2009). Latin America and the Caribbean Regional Brief. June, http://www.worldbank.org/

THES (2008). The Times Higher Education World University Rankings 2008. http://www.timeshighereducation.co.uk/

UNDP. (2007-2008) United Nations Development Programme, Annual Report 2008. http://www.undp.org/

World Economic Forum. (2008). The Global Competitiveness Report 2008-2009. Davos. http://www.weforum.org/

PART IV

•••••••••••••

Innovation Strategies
at the Institutional Level

CHAPTER 14

The Research University as Comprehensive Knowledge Enterprise: A Prototype for a New American University

Michael M. Crow

While the Glion Colloquia have brought university leaders together to exchange perspectives on an array of critical issues confronting higher education, perhaps none is more imperative to consider than the role of the research university in an innovation-driven society. Research universities are the primary source of the new knowledge and innovation that drives the global economy and provides those of us in advanced nations with the standard of living we have come to take for granted (Atkinson & Blanpied, 2008; Blakemore & Herrendorf, 2009). The intrinsic impetus to advance innovation distinguishes the research university from other institutional forms in higher education. Indeed I seek to redefine the research university as a *comprehensive knowledge enterprise committed to discovery, creativity and innovation*. If we do not embrace what has been termed "perpetual innovation" — and by this I mean innovation in products and processes and ideas, as well as in the institutional design of knowledge enterprises themselves — not only the outcomes of academic research but also our collective standard of living will decline, and opportunities for the success of future generations will be diminished (Atkinson, 2007; Crow, 2007a, 2008a; Kash, 1989; McPherson *et al.*, 2009).

Despite the critical niche that research universities occupy in the global knowledge economy, however, institutions committed thus primarily to innovation restrict the potential of their contribution unless they explicitly embrace a broader societal role. Innovation inevitably flourishes in a number of organizational settings, such as corporate research and development laboratories, but with their complex institutional missions spanning teaching, research and public service, universities should feel compelled to construe their research enterprises in a context of engagement and purpose. We mistakenly assume that the intellectual objectives of our institutions, especially in terms of scientific and technological research, are automatically and inevitably aligned with our most important goals as a society. The challenge in this context is therefore one of institutional design — about reinventing knowledge-producing enterprises to create institutions that understand and respond to their multiple constituencies and advance broader social and economic outcomes (Kitcher, 2001; Sarewitz, 1996; Sarewitz & Pielke, 2007). If research universities are to create knowledge that is as socially useful as it is scientifically meritorious, in areas as broad and complex as social justice, poverty alleviation, access to clean water, sustainable development and technological innovation, they must integrate their quest to advance discovery, creativity and innovation with an explicit mandate to assume responsibility for the societies they serve (Bok, 1982; Duderstadt, 2000; Kerr, 2001; Kitcher, 2001; Rhodes, 2001).

But our academic culture is not outcome-driven and instead values knowledge for its own sake. The proliferation of increasingly specialized knowledge that universities produce brings diminishing returns on investment as its impact on the world is measured in smaller and smaller ratios. But there is no reason why universities must confine themselves solely to the analysis of increasingly specialized knowledge. In our valorization of basic research, motivated solely by curiosity rather than with any higher purpose in mind, we lose sight of the potential for application when research is use-inspired (Kitcher, 2001). This is not to posit a dichotomy between basic and applied research — both are crucial, and in many cases the boundary between them is so permeable as to be meaningless (Stokes, 1997). In our accustomed effort to produce abstract knowledge, however, many research universities have lost sight of the fact that they possess the capacity to advance desired outcomes or to create useful products and processes and ideas with entrepreneurial potential (Geiger, 2004; Schramm, 2006). Prestige will always attach to the pursuit of the unknown, but I would argue that we must reprioritize our practices and rethink our assumptions if we are not to minimize the potential contributions of academic research.

Other manifestations of institutional responsibility might include a commitment to the production in sufficient numbers of scientists and engineers and artists and philosophers and economists and doctors and lawyers — in short, the human capital from which we draw our future leaders in every sector (Committee on Prospering in the Global Economy of the Twenty-First Century [U.S.], 2007). Our institutions would further also embrace ambitious and multifaceted public outreach and engagement programs dedicated to societal advancement and regional economic development.

With my formulation of the research university as a "comprehensive knowledge enterprise", I seek to underscore the potential inherent in the concept of "enterprise", through some strange elitist logic generally wholly lacking in discussions about higher education. In this context I advocate the designation "academic enterprise", representing an entrepreneurial academic culture that inspires creativity and innovation — the intellectual capital that is the primary asset of every college and university. Generally associated with the private sector, the spirit of enterprise is critical to the advancement of innovation (Schramm, 2006). My focus on enterprise is deliberate because since becoming the president of Arizona State University in July 2002, I have been coordinating an effort to reconceptualize a large public university as a competitive academic enterprise dedicated to leading the vanguard of innovation while simultaneously addressing the grand challenges of our era (Crow, 2007b). At ASU we have undertaken the task of pioneering the foundational model for what we term the "New American University" — an egalitarian institution committed to the topmost echelons of academic excellence, inclusiveness to a broad demographic, and maximum societal impact (Crow, 2002; "A New American University," 2008).

In the following I consider the New American University model at length and offer an account of the reconceptualization of Arizona State University, initiated in 2002, as a case study in institutional innovation in higher education. My objective is also to establish a context for subsequent discussion of the fundamental design flaws in our knowledge enterprises. These intrinsic flaws obstruct progress toward the integration of knowledge with action. In speaking of research universities as knowledge enterprises, my objective is also to underscore the potential for differentiation between institutions. Research-grade universities are but one of a number of institutional types in American higher education, but even institutions so categorized need not be cut from the same cloth. As the lead architect in the design of a new class of large-scale multidisciplinary and transdisciplinary institutions and organizations at the forefront of education and research during the past two decades, both at Columbia University, where I most recently served as executive vice provost, and now in Arizona, I recognize that while institutional design requires considerable investment of time and effort and is not without challenge because of inherent sociocultural barriers, new designs offer new ways of shaping and examining problems and advancing questions through cooperation between large numbers of groups, programs, and initiatives. It is the inherent and fraught complexity of these various dimensions to the research university, as well as their interaction and interplay, that is the context of this assessment and analysis.

TOWARD INSTITUTIONAL INNOVATION
IN RESEARCH UNIVERSITIES

An objective analysis of our knowledge enterprises undertaken with sufficient perspective — perhaps from the distance of the Oort Cloud, as suggested by James Duderstadt (2005) — discloses a number of fundamental design flaws. We face challenges of unimaginable complexity, but rather than learning to understand and manage complexity in the academy, we perpetuate existing organizational structures and restrict our focus with the entrenchment of disciplines and ever-greater impetus toward specialization. Our universities remain static if not entirely ossified, disinclined to evolve in pace with real time, and focused primarily on their advancement of abstract knowledge. The organizational frameworks we call universities — this thousand-year-old institutional form — have not evolved significantly beyond the configurations assumed in the late 19th century, nor have new designs come to the fore that accommodate change on the scale we are witnessing or address the challenges associated with the attendant increases in complexity. The problem of scale is an important dimension to analysis and endeavour that has not been sufficiently examined. I believe we do not understand either the implications of scale or how to shape questions at an appropriate scale in order to advance society and our institutions.

In order to conceptualize a model for the institutional design of knowledge enterprises, I extrapolate from a fundamental distinction explored by the polymath Herbert A. Simon in his 1969 book, *The Sciences of the Artificial.* Through his exploration of the categories of the natural and the artificial, Simon suggests the possibility for radical reconceptualization in our knowledge enterprises. His analysis underscores the distinction between the natural and artificial worlds, referring by the term "artificial" to objects and phenomena — artifacts — that are man-made as opposed to natural. He terms knowledge of such products and processes "artificial science" or the "sciences of design". While artificial science more broadly refers to our use of symbols — the "artifacts" of written and spoken language — the most obvious "designers" of artifacts are engineers. But his usage of the term is broad and everyone is a designer who "devises courses of action aimed at changing existing situations into preferred ones". The natural sciences are concerned with how things are, as he puts it, and the artificial sciences with how things ought to be. Artificial science — or design science — determines the form of that which we build — tools, farms or cities alike — but also our organizational and social structures (Simon, 1969). For our purposes we enlist Simon's concept to underscore the potential for differentiation in the structure and organization of knowledge enterprises. The redesign of an institution represents a process as focused and deliberate and precise as the knowledge production of scientists, engineers, and other scholars. From a design perspective and with the objective of optimal outcomes in mind, we may begin to assess the design flaws inherent in our existing knowledge enterprises and posit new models for their improvement, such as the New American University (Crow, 2008b).

The evolutionary trajectory of universities in the Western world can be modeled as a process visualized along two axes. The x-axis represents the scale of the institution, with scale meaning more than just size. Scale in this usage refers to the *breadth of functionality*, which measures more than just the number of disciplines studied. If the institution is a comprehensive knowledge enterprise such as the New American University, it will be committed to the traditional missions of teaching, research and public service, but in addition will advance innovation and entrepreneurship. Scale thus refers to both the intellectual, or pedagogical, and functional breadth. The y-axis, meanwhile, reflects the institution's *conception of itself* as an evolving, entrepreneurial entity. At the low end of the y-axis, we have what organizational theorists call conserving institutions, those that are inwardly focused, risk-averse and concerned primarily with self-preservation. At the upper end are entrepreneurial institutions, those willing to adapt, innovate and take risks in rethinking their identities and roles. On a chart the New American University would thus appear in the curve in the upper-right quadrant reserved for leading-edge institutions designed to accommodate innovation, rapid decision-making and entrepreneurial behaviour (Crow, 2008a).

A CASE STUDY FOR THE NEW AMERICAN UNIVERSITY

With the implementation of the New American University model, beginning in 2002, Arizona State University has often been characterized as a "case study" in American higher education. Not only is ASU a new university, it is competing in an arena dominated by some of the most well-established and influential institutions in the world. Some institutions might perceive such case study status as problematic, but for us the designation is not only appropriate but entirely welcome because through our reconceptualization we have deliberately positioned ourselves as an experiment in higher education at scale. *Newsweek* termed our reconceptualization "one of the most radical redesigns in higher learning since the modern research university took shape in nineteenth-century Germany" (Theil, 2008). And according to an editorial from the journal *Nature*, questions about the future of the contemporary research university are being examined "nowhere more searchingly than at Arizona State University" (26 April 2007). While the reinvention of the American research university has generated recommendations found scattered across the relevant specialized literature, the New American University model we are advancing was generally shaped through trial and error and our efforts at the application of common sense, in some measure initially inspired by the call for a "new university" articulated by Frank Rhodes (2001).

Differentiation through a process of design

The designation of Arizona State University as a case study in higher education derives in part from the intensive and ongoing process of perpetual institutional self-assessment and reconceptualization that we often refer to as the "design process". As set forth in the white paper "One University in Many Places: Transitional Design to Twenty-First Century Excellence" (2004), the objective of the design process is to build a comprehensive metropolitan research university that is an "unparalleled combination of academic excellence and commitment to its social, economic, cultural, and environmental setting". An interrelated formulation that we have developed is the expression of our intent to build an institution "committed to the topmost echelons of academic excellence, inclusiveness to a broad demographic, and maximum societal impact", with the associated tagline "Excellence, Access, Impact."

Guided by a number of working drafts of comprehensive strategic plans to guide the development of the institution, we deem ourselves in the midst of a decade of unprecedented reorganization and decisive maturation (2002-2012), expanding and intensifying the capacity of the university for teaching and discovery in all disciplines while addressing the challenges of burgeoning enrolment with a distributed model. The evolving strategic plan centers on four basic university goals, all of which are interdependent but critical to achieving a set of eight "design aspirations", considered in the following section. The goal of "access and quality for all" recognizes our responsibility to provide opportunities in higher education to all qualified citizens of the State of Arizona without impacting the highest levels of quality. A second goal is the establishment of "national standing for colleges and schools in every field". "Becoming a national comprehensive university by 2012" will build regional competitiveness and national and global distinction to the state and region. The fourth goal recognizes the university's responsibility towards the region it serves, and focuses on "enhancing our local impact and social embeddedness".

'Design aspirations' for a New American University

There are many ways to parse the concept of the New American University, but, in brief, its objectives are inherent in the following "design aspirations" that, reduced to their essential terms, enjoin academic communities to: (1) embrace the cultural, socioeconomic and physical setting of their institutions; (2) become a force for societal transformation; (3) pursue a culture of academic enterprise and knowledge entrepreneurship; (4) conduct use-inspired research; (5) focus on the individual in a milieu of intellectual and cultural diversity; (6) transcend disciplinary limitations in pursuit of intellectual fusion; (7) socially embed the university, thereby advancing social enterprise development through direct engagement; and (8) advance global engagement. Taken together, these tenets comprise a new paradigm for academic institutions, both public and private, that I advocate without reservation (Crow, 2002).

The design aspirations should be considered guiding principles rather than hard-and-fast imperatives — the complex academic operations of a research university do not correspond neatly to a single design aspiration but generally embrace many. And not all design aspirations could possibly be relevant to any given student or scholar or team of researchers. For example, the unique challenges associated with the location of the university and the demographics of metropolitan Phoenix and the American Southwest engage a majority of the design aspirations, especially the recommendations that we leverage our place; transform society; enable student success; and advance social embeddedness. Similarly, the design aspiration to value entrepreneurship refers to academic enterprise as the creative expression of intellectual capital and knowledge-centric change. Perhaps the most obvious dimension of academic enterprise is the process of innovation from the research laboratory to the marketplace, but our conception transcends the commercialization of university research (Slate & Crow, 2007). At ASU we consider entrepreneurship the process of innovation and spirit of creative risk-taking through which the knowledge and ideas within the university are brought to scale to spur social development and economic competitiveness. ASU is committed to embedding the paradigm of entrepreneurship into the fabric of our institutional culture through a supportive infrastructure of resources to inspire students, faculty and staff, and provide them with the necessary skills to turn their ideas into reality (Crow, 2008c).

A federation of schools (the 'school-centric' model)

In its present form Arizona State University is the youngest of the roughly 100 major research institutions in the United States, both public and private, and, with an enrolment approaching 70,000 undergraduate, graduate and professional students, the largest American university governed by a single administration. To promote access to excellence despite the challenges of burgeoning enrolment we have adopted a distributed model, operating from four differentiated campuses of equally high aspiration, with each campus representing a planned clustering of related but academically distinct colleges and schools. We term this empowerment of colleges and schools "school-centrism". Predicated on devolving intellectual and entrepreneurial responsibility to the level of the college or school, the model calls for each school to compete for status, not with other schools within the university, but with peer schools around the country and around the world. Schools are encouraged to grow and prosper to the extent of their individual intellectual and market limits ("One University in Many Places," 2004).

The reconceptualized "school-centric" organization has produced a federation of unique interdisciplinary colleges and schools that, together with departments and research institutes and centers, comprise close-knit but diverse academic communities that are international in scope. Consistent with this school-centric model we have conceptualized and launched 22 new interdisciplinary schools, including the School of Human Evolution and Social Change, and the School of Earth and Space Exploration. Although we are first and foremost committed to educating the students of Arizona, we are equally a cutting-edge discovery organization, dedicated to contributing to regional economic development through enhanced research and academic programs, including major interdisciplinary research initiatives such as the Biodesign Institute, focused on innovation in healthcare, energy and the environment, and national security; the Global Institute of Sustainability (GIOS), incorporating the world's first School of Sustainability; and the Center for the Study of Religion and Conflict. In the process we have eliminated a number of traditional academic departments, including biology, sociology, anthropology and geology (Capaldi, 2009). We consider such academic entities arbitrary constructs that may once have served certain social or administrative purposes but are no longer useful as we prepare to tackle global challenges (Committee on Facilitating Interdisciplinary Research [U.S.], 2005).

Unprecedented demographic challenges to higher education in Arizona

Situated in the heart of an emerging megapolitan area that stretches from the Prescott region southward to the border with Mexico, ASU is the sole comprehensive university in a metropolitan region of four million projected to increase to eight million — a metropolitan region the size of Chicago. Demographic projections suggest that this emerging megapolitan — the so-called Sun Corridor — will become one of perhaps 20 significant economic, technological and cultural agglomerations in the United States (Crow, 2008d; Gammage et al., 2008; Lang, Muro & Sarzynski, 2008). Yet the higher education infrastructure of Arizona remains under-built and undifferentiated. In other metropolitan regions, responsibility for higher education is shared by a number of institutions. Major research universities in the metropolitan Los Angeles region, for example, include UCLA, USC, and Caltech, with UC Santa Barbara, UC Irvine, UC Riverside, and UC San Diego within close proximity. A host of other institutions — public (several California State University campuses) and private (Occidental College and the prestigious Claremont Colleges and Claremont Graduate University) — complement these research universities.

Because we wish to move beyond the conventional model of the research university as preoccupied with the discovery of new knowledge to the exclusion of concern with the social outcomes of its research, we actively seek to imbue metropolitan Phoenix with the quality-of-life and quality-of-place characteristics that attract the intellectual capital and competitive advantage that accompanies the influx of "knowledge workers" (Kotkin & DeVol, 2001) and the "creative class" (Florida, 2002). If the university does not envision and guide such outcomes, we face the prospect of the sort of decline witnessed in such cities as Cleveland and Detroit, both of which have not been able to adapt to changing economic circumstances rapidly enough. The university models of the past are similarly as stagnant and irrelevant as the most dated and discarded concepts of urban planning. If our universities remain hidebound and regard change and evolution as recourses of last resort, then we can dismiss the adaptive capability of this important mechanism of capital creation and societal advancement.

Access to excellence: Towards egalitarian admissions practices

While the direct correlation between educational attainment and standard-of-living and quality-of-life indicators has been widely documented (Mortenson, 1999), leading institutions of higher education have almost without exception during the course of the past half-century become increasingly *exclusive* — that is to say, they have chosen to define their excellence through admissions practices of exclusion. It is generally taken for granted that there are two types of universities: the small cadre of elite institutions that focus on academic excellence and discovery, and the majority of less selective schools that offer access yet often provide no more than a rudimentary level of higher education. Institutions that focus on academic excellence generally admit only a fraction of applicants, many of whom come from privileged socioeconomic backgrounds and have enjoyed undeniable advantages. All other students are expected to attend less competitive schools. In terms of societal outcomes, this implicit calculation is not only shortsighted, but may in the long run prove to be a fatal error. There is growing social and economic stratification between those with access to a quality higher education and those denied the opportunity. More and more students who would most benefit from access to this most obvious avenue of upward mobility — those whom we might categorize as "disadvantaged" or "underrepresented" — are denied access for lack of means or choose not to pursue for lack of understanding a high-quality university education (Bowen, Kurzweil & Tobin, 2006; Douglass, 2007; Haskins, 2008; Haskins, Holzer & Lerman, 2009).

If we continue to exclude a high proportion of the population from reaching their potential by excessive and sometimes arbitrary "culling", we deprive countless individuals of opportunities to attain prosperity. We need to make more of an effort to understand how to educate greater numbers of individuals successfully, but we must also educate students to be successful. This economic dimension is intrinsic to the societal mission of colleges and universities. Individuals deprived of higher education through lack of funds represent not only personal opportunity lost, but also the loss of societal economic prosperity. Individuals deprived of college educations will likely earn lower wages and generate fewer jobs than they would have as graduates (Hill, Hoffman & Rex, 2005). A recent report on high school graduation rates in the 50 largest U.S. cities underscores the urgency of the problem: according to the study, 17 of the nation's 50 largest cities had graduation rates lower than 50% (Swanson, 2009).

We believe that many public universities in the United States, particularly research-grade institutions, have abandoned core elements of their public mission and in some sense morphed into hybrid or semi-privatized institutions that operate on a narrow bandwidth of engagement. We reject the notion that excellence and access cannot be integrated within a single institution, and alone among American research universities have sought to redefine the notion of egalitarian admissions standards by offering access to as many students as are qualified to attend. Our approach has been to expand the capacity of the institution to meet enrolment demand and provide expanded educational opportunities to the many gifted and creative students who do not conform to a standard academic profile, as well as offering access to students who demonstrate every potential to succeed but lack the financial means to pursue a quality four-year undergraduate education.

When President Barack Obama spoke at our 2009 commencement exercises, he was especially excited about our newly established program to ensure that resident undergraduates from families with annual incomes below $60,000 admitted as incoming freshmen would be able to graduate with baccalaureate degrees debt free. We estimate that for fall semester 2009, the President Barack Obama Scholars program will allow approximately 1,600 freshmen an opportunity to attain their educational objectives. The program epitomizes our pledge to Arizona that no qualified student will face a financial barrier to attend ASU and underscores the success of the longstanding efforts that have led to record levels of diversity in our student body. While the freshman class has increased in size by 42% since 2002, for example, enrolment of students of colour has increased by 100%, and the number of students enrolled from families below the poverty line has risen by roughly 500%. Our success in offering access regardless of financial need is easily one of the most significant achievements in the history of the institution.

Indicators of success in the reconceptualization process

An overview of the indicators of success in our experiment in institutional innovation may be justified. As evidence of our new stature and prominence, we note that during the past six years our research enterprise more than doubled its expenditures, surpassing the $300 million level for the first time in FY 2009. ASU is one of only a handful of institutions without both an agricultural and medical school to have surpassed the $200 million level in funding, with institutional peers in this category including Caltech, MIT and Princeton. According to the National Science Foundation, ASU now ranks among the top 20 leading research universities in the nation without a medical school, and for the third year ASU has been ranked as one of the top 100 universities globally in the international assessment of the Institute of Higher Education, Shanghai Jiao Tong University, placing 93rd in their 2008 "Academic Ranking of World Universities". To provide some perspective on the momentum of the trajectory, ASU conducted no funded research whatsoever in 1980.

A short list of accomplishments during the past six years would also include the following: We have increased enrolment by more than 9,000 net new students and added 500 new faculty members. We have attained record graduation and retention rates and all academic indicators similarly track record quality. We now enrol more freshman National Merit Scholars than almost any public university in the nation. More members of the National Academies have joined our faculty during the past six years than have served on the faculty during the past five decades. More than 50 new interdisciplinary research centers and institutes have been established. Seven million square feet of new academic space has been added, including one million square feet of world-class research infrastructure. We have developed a master plan to guide the build-out of our campuses and restructured the institution by clustering our colleges and schools by their academic focus on four campuses distributed across the Valley.

For ASU self-determination as the foundational model for the New American University has meant embracing fundamental change: we have confronted the complexities associated with advancing robust institutional innovation at scale. We took the bold step of asking ourselves how we might best combine excellence with access while through a focus on regional challenges seeking solutions to the problems that confront global society. While all public research universities must be inherently committed to teaching and discovery, there is no reason why each cannot advance unique and differentiated research and learning environments that address the needs of their particular region. In our case this reconceptualized vision calls for inclusivity rather than exclusivity, an emphasis on outcomes rather than inputs, and an attempt to recover the egalitarian tenets of the true public university once envisioned in our society.

TOWARD MORE DIFFERENTIATED
AND RESPONSIBLE INSTITUTIONS

In the rapidly changing and highly competitive global knowledge economy, the importance of higher education both to the individual and the collective has never been greater. Education is the means by which a skilled workforce is produced and the source of new knowledge capital and thus economic growth and advances in society, for the benefit of both the individual and the collective. Even as the wage gap between those with education and skills and those without continues to widen, more and more knowledge inputs are increasingly required to perform almost any job. The economic success of individuals contributes to the success of a society — in fact, it is the main driver (Hill, Hoffman & Rex, 2005). Without it, the United States and nations of Western Europe may face a reduction in our quality of life in the next generation, something unheard of in the past. In order for any nation to remain competitive, it is imperative that its universities prepare students to learn rapidly, and make them capable of integrating a broad range of disciplines in a rapidly changing world. But we must recognize that the institutional models we inherited from the 19th century will not instil in our graduates the drive and innovation required to meet the challenges of tomorrow. Nor do these institutions necessarily have the capacity to mount responses commensurate with the scale and complexity of the challenges that confront us as well as those yet to come in ensuing decades.

To anyone who has looked at the role of innovation as a driver of economic development during the past half-century, the most obvious mechanism to enhance the long-term economic competitiveness of any nation is through investment in research universities. Research universities educate students in a milieu that advances discovery and innovation while contributing to the development of a highly skilled workforce and the diversification of the economy. Yet across the globe our educational infrastructure remains dangerously under-built and undifferentiated. In the United States as elsewhere, we need new institutions, new designs and new models for higher education. Our colleges and universities remain little changed from the mid-20th century and are unable to accommodate projected enrolment demands at scale. America's colleges and universities require greater and not less diversification. While our nation urgently needs more research-intensive and research-active institutions, both public and private, it also needs more liberal arts colleges, four-year regional colleges, community colleges and technical institutes. The challenge, as I have argued, is about institutional design, about designing knowledge-producing enterprises that understand and respond to their constituents as well as the needs of global humanity.

REFERENCES

Atkinson, Richard C., & Blanpied, William A. (2008). "Research Universities: Core of the U.S. Science and Technology System." *Technology in Society* 30, pp. 30-38.

Atkinson, Robert D. (2007). "Deep Competitiveness." *Issues in Science and Technology* 23, no. 2, pp. 69-75.

Blakemore, Arthur, & Herrendorf, Berthold. (2009). "Economic Growth: The Importance of Education and Technological Development." Tempe: W. P. Carey School of Business, Arizona State University.

Bok, Derek. (1982). Beyond the Ivory Tower: Social Responsibilities of the Modern University. Cambridge, MA: Harvard University Press.

Bowen, William G., Kurzweil, M. A. & Tobin, E. M. (2006). *Equity and Excellence in American Higher Education.* Charlottesville: University of Virginia Press.

Capaldi, Elizabeth (2009). "Intellectual Transformation and Budgetary Savings Through Academic Reorganization." *Change* (July/August 2009): pp. 19-27.

Committee on Facilitating Interdisciplinary Research (U.S.); Committee on Science, Engineering, and Public Policy (U.S.). (2005). *Facilitating Interdisciplinary Research.* Washington, D.C.: National Academies Press.

Committee on Prospering in the Global Economy of the Twenty-First Century (U.S.) (2007). *Rising Above the Gathering Storm: Energizing and Employing American for a Brighter Economic Future.* Washington, DC: National Academies Press.

Crow, Michael M. (2002). "A New American University: The New Gold Standard." Tempe: Arizona State University. http://www.asu.edu/president/inauguration/address/

Crow, Michael M. (2007a). "Perpetual Innovation: Universities and Regional Economic Development." Keynote address, International Economic Development Council (IEDC), Scottsdale, Arizona, 17 September 2007. http://president.asu.edu/files/2007_0917PerpInnovation.pdf

Crow, Michael M. (2007b). "Enterprise: The Path to Transformation for Emerging Public Universities." *The Presidency* (American Council on Education) 10, no. 2 (Spring 2007): pp. 24-30.

Crow, Michael M. (2008a). "Building an Entrepreneurial University." In *The Future of the Research University: Meeting the Global Challenges of the 21st Century.* Proceedings of the 2008 Kauffman-Max Planck Institute Summit on Entrepreneurship Research and Policy, Bavaria, Germany, 8-11 June 2008. Kansas City, MO: Ewing Marion Kauffman Foundation.

Crow, Michael M. (2008b). "Sustainability as an Interface Problem." Remarks to Annual Science Board, Santa Fe Institute, Santa Fe, New Mexico, 12 April 2008.

Crow, Michael M. (2008c). "The University at a Crossroads: How Higher Education Can Meet the Demands of the Entrepreneurial Community." Based on remarks made during a panel discussion at Milken Institute Global Conference, Santa Monica, CA, 28 April 2008.

Crow, Michael M. (2008d). "Fulfilling the Sun Corridor's Promise: Creating an Economic, Technological, and Cultural Center." Foreword to Grady Gammage Jr. et al., "Megapolitan: Arizona's Sun Corridor." Phoenix: Morrison Institute for Public Policy.

Douglass, John Aubrey. (2006). "The Waning of America's Higher Education Advantage: International Competitors Are No Longer Number Two and Have Big Plans in the Global Economy." Research and Occasional Paper Series: CSHE: 9-06. Berkeley: Center for Studies in Higher Education, University of California, Berkeley.

Douglass, John Aubrey. (2007). The Conditions for Admission: Access, Equity, and the Social Contract of Public Universities. Stanford: Stanford University Press.

Duderstadt, James. (2000). A University for the Twenty-First Century. Ann Arbor: University of Michigan Press.

Duderstadt, James. (2005). "The Future of the University: A Perspective from the Oort Cloud." Remarks presented at Emory University Futures Forum, Atlanta, Georgia, 8 March 2005.

Florida, Richard (2002). The Rise of the Creative Class: And How It's Transforming Work, Leisure, Community, and Everyday Life. New York: Basic Books.

Gammage, Grady Jr. et al. (2008). "Megapolitan: Arizona's Sun Corridor." Phoenix: Morrison Institute for Public Policy.

Geiger, Roger L. (2004). Knowledge and Money: Research Universities and the Paradox of the Marketplace. Stanford: Stanford University Press.

Haskins, Ron. (2008). "Education and Economic Mobility." In Julia Isaacs, Isabel Sawhill & Ron Haskins. Getting Ahead or Losing Ground: Economic Mobility in America, pp. 91-104. Washington, DC: Economic Mobility Project, Pew Charitable Trusts.

Haskins, Ron, Holzer, H. & Lerman, R. (2009). Promoting Economic Mobility by Increasing Postsecondary Education. Washington, DC: Economic Mobility Project, Pew Charitable Trusts.

Hill, Kent, Hoffman, D. & Rex, T. R. (2005). "The Value of Higher Education: Individual and Societal Benefits." Tempe: L. William Seidman Research Institute, W. P. Carey School of Business, Arizona State University.

Kash, Don E. (1989). Perpetual Innovation: The New World of Competition. New York: Basic Books.

Kerr, Clark. (2001). The Uses of the University. Fifth edition. Cambridge: Harvard University Press.

Kitcher, Philip. (2001). Science, Truth, and Democracy. Oxford: Oxford University Press.

Kotkin, Joel, & DeVol, Ross. (2001). Knowledge-Value Cities in the Digital Age. Santa Monica: Milken Institute.

Lang, Robert E., Muro, M. & Sarzynski, A. (2008). "Mountain Megas: America's Newest Metropolitan Places and a Federal Partnership to Help Them Prosper." Washington, D.C.: Metropolitan Policy Program, Brookings Institution.

McPherson, Peter, Shulenberger, D., Gobstein, H. & Keller, C. (2009). "Competitiveness of Public Research Universities and Consequences for the Country: Recommendations for Change." NASULGC Discussion Paper working draft.

Mortenson, Thomas G. et al. (1999). "Why College? Private Correlates of Educational Attainment." Postsecondary Education Opportunity: The Mortenson Research Seminar on Public Policy Analysis of Opportunity for Postsecondary Education 81 (March 1999).

"A New American University". (2008). Tempe: Office of University Initiatives, Arizona State University. http://ui.asu.edu/docs/newamu/New_American_University.pdf

"One University in Many Places: Transitional Design to Twenty-First Century Excellence". (2004). Tempe: Office of the President, Arizona State University.

Rhodes, Frank H. T. (2001). The Creation of the Future: The Role of the American University. Ithaca: Cornell University Press.

Sarewitz, Daniel. (1996). Frontiers of Illusion: Science, Technology, and the Politics of Progress. Philadelphia: Temple University Press.

Sarewitz, Daniel & Pielke, R. A., Jr. (2007). "The Neglected Heart of Science Policy: Reconciling Supply of and Demand For Science." *Environmental Science and Policy* 10: 5-16.

Schramm, Carl J. (2006). The Entrepreneurial Imperative: How America's Economic Miracle Will Reshape the World. New York: Harper Collins.

Simon, Herbert A. (1996). *The Sciences of the Artificial*. Third edition. Cambridge: MIT Press.

Slate, Peter J. & Crow, Michael M. (2007). "The New American University and the Role of "Technology Translation": The Approach of Arizona State University." In *Intellectual Property Management in Health and Agricultural Innovation: A Handbook of Best Practices*. Edited by Anatole Krattiger, Richard T. Mahoney *et al.*, 1661-1672. Oxford: Centre for Management of Intellectual Property in Health Research and Development.

Stokes, Donald E. (1997). *Pasteur's Quadrant: Basic Science and Technological Innovation*. Washington, D.C.: Brookings Institution Press.

Swanson, Christopher B. (2009). "Closing the Graduation Gap: Educational and Economic Conditions in America's Largest Cities." Bethesda, MD: Editorial Projects in Education.

Theil, Stefan. (2008). "The Campus of the Future." *Newsweek* (9 August).

Veysey, Laurence R. (1965). *The Emergence of the American University*. Chicago: University of Chicago Press.

CHAPTER 15

The German Excellence Initiative: Changes, Challenges and Chances for German Research Universities

Bernd Huber

INTRODUCTION

For more than 200 years, the German university system has followed the ideas of Wilhelm von Humboldt — the unity of research and teaching, the freedom of teaching being the most important of Humboldt's principles. These ideas have been followed until today, even though the external conditions that universities have to cope with have changed dramatically. On the one hand, the rising number of students asking for an academic education has led to the modern mass university; on the other hand, universities have to deal with numerous economic constraints. Above all, the public expects universities, as a motor of innovation and wealth, to provide answers for the most urgent questions and problems facing mankind (Hinderer, 2007; Boulton & Lucas, 2008). In spite of these different demands, the egalitarian tradition of the German university system has been continued until today, based on the conviction that all universities are basically similar and that a student or professor finds equal opportunities and conditions, no matter at which university he or she studies or works. This assumption has been put to a test in recent years with the so-called Excellence Initiative of the German Federal Government. Now, only three years after this program was launched, huge changes can be observed in the scientific landscape.

In this paper, I would like to highlight how the German university system is being challenged and changed through the Excellence Initiative. Furthermore, I will outline the general role of research at universities, and how it is affected by the Excellence Initiative. I will raise various issues that I think are important and could serve as a basis for further discussion.

THE EXCELLENCE INITIATIVE IN GERMANY

In 2006, an immense innovation movement began in Germany's university landscape. Initiated by the Federal Government and supported by the state governments, a program was set up providing 1.9 billion Euros to support top-level research at German universities. The program consists of three funding lines: Graduate Schools to promote young researchers and train outstanding doctoral students; Clusters of Excellence to establish internationally visible, competitive research and training facilities; and Institutional Strategies to develop top-level university research in Germany and to increase its competitiveness on an international level (Deutsche Forschungsgemeinschaft, 2009). With the Excellence Initiative, universities were asked to form outstanding research clusters and to develop institutional strategies preparing universities for global competition among research institutions. For the first time in German scientific history, a competition had been initiated not only on research contents, but also on the strategies of universities for building the proper framework and surroundings to facilitate and foster excellent research and attract the best researchers in the world. As this caused considerable movement within the German university landscape and received great attention abroad, the German government recently decided to continue the program for another five years until 2017, with increased funding of 2.7 billion Euros (Verwaltungsvereinbarung zwischen Bund und Ländern, 2009).

Motives behind the Excellence Initiative

Various reasons led to the launch of this new program. The initial idea was developed under the former federal minister for research, Edelgard Bulmahn, who developed the idea of boosting selected universities in Germany to enable them to compete with world-class universities like Harvard, Oxford or Stanford. At that point, this idea was rather new and was welcomed by the scientific community that had demanded long before a substantial increase in research funding and a commitment to promoting top-level research in some excellent universities in Germany (Bundesministerium für Bildung und Forschung, 2005; Schultz, 2007).

Under-investment in research in Germany

The first reason for developing this program was and still is the severe under-investment in research in Germany and Europe in general. The following figures show clearly that in terms of percentage of the GDP dedicated to research, Europe is far behind the U.S. and, even more so, Japan. The 27 E.U. countries spend an average of 1.8% of their GDP (Germany: 2.5%) on research and development, while the U.S. invests 2.7% and Japan 3.2% (Eurostat, 2008). This under-investment in R&D concerns both the private and the public sector. To some extent, the situation in the private sector is even more serious. In Europe, roughly just half (50%) of the total R&D spending occurs in the private sector, while the respective figure for the U.S. is 61%, and for Japan as high as 75% (Eurostat, 2008).

What is particularly worrying is the fact that the gap between the U.S. and Europe may widen over the years to come. In the recent stimulus package of the new U.S. government, almost US$78 billion will be spent on education, training and research (http://www.recovery.gov, 2009). In comparison, the German government decided to invest the sum of 18 billion Euros in the next ten years for universities and research institutions, 2.7 billion Euros thereof for the continuation of the Excellence Initiative (Verwaltungsvereinbarung zwischen Bund und Ländern, 2009). Although this is the biggest sum ever invested in R&D in Germany since World War II, the important conclusion is that we still need more money for research both in Germany and in Europe. This is a key message, and European universities should state it as clearly as possible at every single occasion. It must be clear that we have to spend more on research — not repeating the mistake of subsidizing ailing industries — if we want to stay competitive relative to other countries, and emerge from the current crisis as innovation leaders of the future.

Strengthening research at universities

With the Excellence Initiative, research at universities was significantly strengthened and moved to the centre of public attention. What is important in political and strategic terms is that the Excellence Initiative explicitly focuses on research at universities. This is notable because Germany has a strong tradition of non-university research institutions like the Max Planck institutes or the Helmholtz and Leibniz association. With the decision to promote research at universities, the government gave a clear statement of support to universities and their role in research.

One could easily imagine a situation where a large part of research is conducted and concentrated outside universities. Similarly, the original idea behind the foundation of a European Institute of Innovation and Technology (EIT) was to build a completely new research unit outside universities, at the European level (Communication from the Commission to the European Council, 2006; LERU, 2005, 2006).

So the question is: is there a comparative advantage of universities relative to other research institutions? In my opinion, the answer is a strong yes. And I will underline this with two main reasons. Firstly, universities are the only institutions that are able to cover the trans-disciplinary nature of many themes in research. For example, life expectancy in European countries dramatically varies in different groups of the population. In some major European or American cities, you will move from areas with a life expectancy as low as 55 years to areas where life expectancy is close to 80 years (Fogarty International Center, 2008). This fact raises many medical, sociological and economic issues which can be dealt with by the interaction of various researchers at universities. But how to tackle this kind of interdisciplinary research outside universities is a difficult question. Looking at the outcome of the first round of the Excellence Initiative, we can undoubtedly state that most of the successful Excellence Clusters in Research are of a clearly trans-disciplinary nature. They involve different faculties of one university, and also integrate neighbouring research institutions and research departments of private companies, thus providing an ideal environment for innovative research.

The second reason why research should be undertaken at universities lies in the education and training of new researchers. Each new generation of researchers learns analytical rigour and the ability to study complex issues by doing research. In this sense, research at universities is a necessary condition, a prerequisite for any society active in research, even if a larger part of it might be concentrated outside universities.

This gives universities a unique role in the process of research, and I think that we as universities too often forget to explain and promote the particular strength of our institutions and the benefits we provide to society (Boulton & Lucas, 2008).

Competition

A brand-new component of the Excellence Initiative was the fact that funds were granted on a competitive base. This was an entirely new element since it introduced the idea of competition between universities to the German university system; the German system and the majority of the university systems in other European countries have a strong egalitarian tradition with the basic idea that, at least in theory, each university offers the same level of quality in research and teaching. According to this tradition, it should not matter to a student to which university he or she is admitted. Similarly, professors would find equal conditions for their work, no matter which university they conduct their research at. The Excellence Initiative showed that this scenario was not a realistic one. What had been common knowledge for all stake-holders, though never admitted in public, had now been openly revealed: There are better and worse universities; there are universities that conduct top research in some areas, but are only average in others; and there are universities that do not play a crucial role in research at all, but have an important part in regional development and teaching. By taking up the challenge of competition, it became obvious that the different roles of universities had to be acknowledged and taken into account (Hinderer, 2007).

Changes originated by the Excellence Initiative

By explaining the main motives behind this competition, I have already hinted at some major changes that were brought about by the Excellence Initiative. Nevertheless, I want to stress three major fields where huge changes in recent years can be illustrated.

Reputation

Although the total funds granted in the Excellence Initiative are not particularly high, the whole program has had a considerable echo abroad. Before the Excellence Initiative, the German science system had to some extent fallen off the map. With the start of the program, Germany's visibility on the science landscape has been considerably strengthened. What is more, not only the German system as a whole, but particularly successful universities have noticed a huge gain in reputation. The German program and its outcomes have been widely debated in the national and international, general and special-interest press, giving it good credit and praising it as an example of innovative science policy. The results of this international attention can be seen in the many requests for information and cooperation which — above all — the nine so-called "Excellence Universities" could register. On the other hand, these universities had far fewer problems in gaining access to and starting new forms of cooperation with the world's most renowned universities, success in the Excellence Initiative serving as a door-opener for them.

Strengthening of the research base

As I stated above, the total amount of funding was relatively modest in international terms, but it brought about nevertheless a significant strengthening of the research base, as the sum was divided up between a few winning universities. With this concentration of funds, these institutions experienced a considerable increase of their individual budgets, allowing them to set up new internal programs for research funding and for the promotion of young researchers. But it also allowed them to dedicate a certain share of the money as seed funds for high-risk research endeavours that — under normal circumstances — would have had no chance of being funded, but that nevertheless sometimes turn out to open up whole new fields of research. It is quite a new experience for German universities to be provided with the possibility of opening up new fields of research rather than cutting some of them back or struggling to maintain them.

Competition and Differentiation

The Excellence Initiative introduced a competitive element into the German research funding system: Universities had to decide whether or not to take part in the competition, and if they decided to do so, they had to prepare for it. Therefore, the Excellence Initiative kicked off a previously unknown movement in the university system. Universities started to sharpen their profiles, strategic plans were set up and huge efforts made to increase research performance. For the first time in years, extra money was invested in the system — and not to be cut off at another end, but to be invested in research excellence, new structures and new positions. It added considerable dynamics to the German university landscape. Certainly, there are winners and universities that benefited only marginally or not at all from the Excellence Initiative. But it is by far more important that there was at last movement in one or other direction. Universities had to rethink their own role and where they wanted to stand in the future. These simple questions alone have led to a repositioning and to immense changes nobody would have previously thought possible in Germany.

Looking at the issue of differentiation from a European perspective, one just has to bear in mind that there are roughly 1,000 universities in Europe which define themselves as research-oriented institutions. Thus, Europe has a broad base in terms of research capacities. But, despite this broad research base, one key weakness of the European university system is that the number of truly world-class research institutions is not sufficient. We all know the limitations of rankings. But, if one considers the well-known (though debatable) "Academic Ranking of World Universities" conducted by the Jiao Tong University Shanghai, it turns out that only ten European universities are among the top 50 universities. From these ten universities, five are from the U.K. where things are slightly different from on the continent (Shanghai Jiao Tong University, 2008). Thus, despite its huge economic and scientific potential, the European continent possesses only a very small number of world-class universities.

This is not a particularly popular conclusion, but Europe has to improve in this respect. What we need is a careful differentiation of the European university system through increasing competition between universities by, for example, competitive research funding. In the longer run, we will then probably move to a system where a limited number of universities are truly internationally competitive, a large group of universities have a couple of departments with high performance, and a certain group of universities have a strong emphasis on teaching — comparable to the development that has been initiated by the Excellence Initiative in Germany. Nevertheless, many stakeholders in research and politics in Germany, after becoming aware of the possibly increasing differentiation of the university system due to the Excellence Initiative, have begun a discussion on whether this is the right path to follow. This proves that the Excellence Initiative represents a true philosophical shift, a reorientation in policy by introducing competition and, as a consequence, differentiation into the German university system.

Knowing that this process of differentiation is a difficult one, I think that we have to move into this direction if Europe really wants to make full use of its scientific potential.

CHALLENGES FOR THE FUTURE

Before pointing out some of the challenges German "excellence universities" have to face resulting directly from the Excellence Initiative, I would like to turn the issue more generally towards the overall design of research policy.

Research policy and open innovation

Universities depend on public funding and public support, and thus have to respond to the demands of the public. As an economist, I would say that universities have to serve the political market. Over recent years, governments, the general public and the business community have increasingly taken what you may positively call a utilitarian view of universities. In terms of research at universities, this means that universities are seen as institutions which should deliver innovation that can be used to develop new products or improve existing ones. This view is not wrong, but it contains several shortcuts. First, it entirely ignores the role of the arts and humanities and the social sciences. Innovation and new ideas generated from these fields need not necessarily result in new products, but can nevertheless have a direct impact on society.

The second flaw is that this view entirely ignores the nature of research processes at universities: The primary motive behind most research projects is not to find an idea for a new product, but to analyse a scientific issue, to understand certain phenomena and to find answers to scientific questions (Boulton & Lucas, 2008). The great challenges the world community is facing, like poverty and climate change, will only be resolved if scientists from every field do research on these issues. Only together, the sciences, the arts and humanities and social sciences can contribute to the cause. It is the universities' legitimacy to take care of these issues — and they need proper funding for it.

In other words, thinking in terms of the direct economic impact leads to a distorted view of the process of research at universities and the motives of researchers. It would be extremely helpful if a broader perspective could be established in the political and public debate. Therefore, I am strongly in favour of the idea of "open innovation" which is currently under discussion in European research policy. Originally, this means that no university and no company can claim or be sure to have contracted all experts in one research field. Therefore, it is important to combine internal and external ideas, as well as internal and external experts, to advance the development of new technologies or, in the case of universities, of new research findings. The structure of the innovation processes is changing from a "closed" innovation model, in which research and development are tackled completely within organizations, to an "open model" in which ideas are generated and sought from different sources (Chesbrough, 2003). European universities have a common interest that this concept becomes a key part in the overall formulation of the European research policy.

But to establish the right atmosphere for this idea of "open innovation", universities need to set the right frame with incentives and challenges directed to the researchers. The Excellence Initiative is one key element in this framework of incentives and challenges, rewarding new and daring ideas and approaches in research that have been set up by a team of researchers inside and outside universities.

'Arms race' and political interference

Nevertheless, German universities also have to cope with some problems arising out of this new scenario of competition. One of them that has developed, especially after having digested the first results of the Excellence Initiative, is the "arms race" that some of the German federal states are now putting into practice. Not having been among the winners in the first place, some state governments have started to put great efforts into preparing some chosen universities for the second program in order for them to come out successfully. With a maximum of 12 universities probably being admitted as Excellence Universities and with nine existing ones, a fierce competition until 2012 will begin in order to remain with or gain the status of an Excellence University and receive the additional funds.

Tensions between and within universities

Another problem caused by moving away from the egalitarian system is the rising tension across and within universities. The institutions that will not be rewarded with the label "Excellence University" — and that will be the majority — need to develop perspectives and strategies in regard to their self-conception. As described above, each university has to find its place in a differentiated science landscape and this will not happen without severe friction and tension. Similarly, universities that have gained a share of the funds in one of the three funding lines have to cope with severe tensions between the fields of research within the universities. There are some departments that have gained considerable extra funding, enabling them to attract excellent researchers, bringing about new excellence, whereas there are others that have to cope with severe budget constraints and struggle to maintain a certain level of quality. These disparities being all against the egalitarian scenario described above, universities need to develop strategies to foster excellent research without creating tensions that will harm the institution as a whole.

The role of teaching and education at universities

Another important question that has to be handled is the role of teaching and education at universities, having to deal with the political and public demands to considerably increase the number of students at universities. The Excellence Initiative has been developed to promote excellent research and, actually, there is little benefit for students. This creates an issue in terms of legitimacy and perception. The label "Excellence Universities" has attracted a great number of students, especially in the fields that have been rewarded Clusters of Excellence and Graduate Schools, without providing special treatment for them. Apart from being taught by renowned scholars who often only have to give reduced hours of lectures, there are, in principle, very few advantages for students. Therefore, it is very important for universities to emphasize their educational role in the future. If the above mentioned reasons why research should be conducted in universities are taken seriously, then we have to make sure that talented students who will be the researchers of the future find excellent conditions at our universities.

CONCLUSION

In the past five years, the German universities have seen three major changes that have shaped their future prospects significantly. With the so-called Bologna process, Germany and the other member countries of the European Union introduced Bachelor and Master degrees, with the goal to enhance transparency and mobility in the science system, even if it will take some time to reach this goal. Furthermore, the critically discussed initiation of a tuition fee changes not only the budget of universities, but also the way students plan their studies.

But the major change is the Excellence Initiative, bringing about a much needed reform process that leads to differentiation and thus an innovative university landscape. This process, which started three years ago, has not yet ended. Even universities that did not participate in the first round are now realizing that — in order to secure their future — they should at least take a stand and decide in which league they want to play. The Excellence Initiative has moved the role of universities and their quality to the centre of discussion.

Therefore, all stakeholders and key players of research should promote that increasing research and university budgets is one of the key elements to initiate and carry forward innovations. It is now that funds have to be invested if the European countries want to take a leading role in innovation and progress at the outcome of the global economic crisis, with a well-trained workforce being allocated to future industries and markets, and with the best scientists conducting research in their universities.

For the continuation of the Excellence Initiative, it is crucial that the budget will be raised — as announced — from 1.9 billion Euros to 2.7 billion Euros, as the funding of new projects and strategies, as well as the continuation of already existing ones, will have to be decided in 2012 (Verwaltungsvereinbarung zwischen Bund und Ländern, 2009). In order to give excellent projects a fair chance to be financed, universities need a considerable increase in funding.

Chances are good that at least a few German universities enter the league of the world's top universities if the ideas behind the Excellence Initiative are continued and if the German science system will admit and finally be able to break with the egalitarian tradition.

REFERENCES AND FURTHER READING:

Boulton, Geoffrey & Lucas, Colin. (2008). *What are Universities for?* Leuven: LERU.
Bundesministerium für Bildung und Forschung. (2005). *Exzellenzinitiative und Pakt für Forschung und Innovation starten.* (Online). Berlin: Pressemitteilung 147/2005. Available at: http://www.bmbf.de/press/1505.php. (Accessed 9 September 2009).
Chesbrough, Henry W. (2003). Open Innovation: The New Imperative for Creating and Profiting from Technology. Boston: Harvard Business School Press.
Communication from the Commission to the European Council. (2006). *Implementing the renewed partnership for growth and jobs. Developing a knowledge flagship: the European Institute of Technology.* (COM [2006] 77 final). Brussels: Commission of the European Communities. Available at: http://eur-lex.europa.eu/LexUriServ/Lex-UriServ.do?uri=COM:2006:0077:FIN:EN:PDF. (Accessed 9 September 2009).
Deutsche Forschungsgemeinschaft DFG. (2009). Available at: http://www.dfg.de. (Accessed 9 September 2009).
Eurostat. (2008). *Key Figures on Europe 2007/2008.* Available at: http://epp.eurostat.ec.europa.eu/portal/page/portal/eurostat/home/. (Accessed 10 August 2009).
Fogarty International Center. (2008). Marmot assails health disparities. *Global Health Matters,* (Online). 7 (6), p. 7. Available at: http://www.fic.nih.gov/news/publications/global_health_matters/ghmnov-dec2008.pdf. (Accessed 9 September 2009).
Hinderer, Walter. (2007). Die deutsche Exzellenzinitiative und die amerikanische Eliteuniversität. liberal Verlag Berlin.
LERU. (2005). Competitiveness, research and the concept of a European Institute of Technology. Opinion. Leuven: LERU.
LERU. (2006). Purpose, structures and function of a European Institute of Technology. Commentary. Leuven: LERU.
Schultz, Tanjev. (2007). Der lange Weg zur Förderung. *Süddeutsche Zeitung,* 16 October 2007. Available at: http://www.sueddeutsche.de/jobkarriere/817/421579/text/. (Accessed 9 September 2009).
Shanghai Jiao Tong University. (2008). *Academic Ranking of World Universities.* (Online). Available at: http://www.arwu.org/rank2008/EN2008.htm (Accessed 9 September 2009).
Verwaltungsvereinbarung zwischen Bund und Ländern — Exzellenzvereinbarung II — 24. (June 2009). (Online). Available at: http://www.gwk-bonn.de. (Accessed 10 August 2009).

CHAPTER 16

New University Paradigms for Technological Innovation

James J. Duderstadt

I n today's global, knowledge-driven economy, leadership in innovation is
essential to a nation's prosperity and security. In particular, technological
innovation — the transformation of new knowledge into products, processes and services of value to society — is critical to economic competitiveness, national security and an improved quality of life. The United States has
long benefited from a fertile environment for innovation, such as a diverse
population continually renewed through immigration, democratic values that
encourage individual initiative, and free market practices that drive the ongoing process of creative destruction (à la Schumpeter). But history has shown
that public investment is necessary to produce the key ingredients for technological innovation including: new knowledge (research and development),
human capital (education, particularly at the advanced level), infrastructure
(physical and now cyber) and supportive policies (tax, intellectual property)
(Augustine, 2005).

Although the flow of knowledge from scientific discovery through development and technological innovation, commercialization and deployment was
once thought of as a linear, vertical process, it is now viewed as far more complex, both vertical and horizontal, and involving many interacting disciplines
and participants. As Nam Suh has suggested in his paper for this Glion Colloquium (Suh, Chapter 19), for innovation to occur, there cannot be any
missing steps or elements in the continuum of necessary activities.

Traditionally, one thinks of the appropriate activities for each of the key
factors in the innovation continuum — namely, government, industry and
universities — in terms such as basic research, applied research, development,
commercialization and deployment. For example, basic research activities,

usually speculative, long term and driven by scientific curiosity, are usually viewed as the proper role of research universities, while use-driven basic research, applied research and development are more commonly roles for government or industrial laboratories. Commercialization and deployment are similarly viewed most appropriate for industry (both established and entrepreneurial).

Yet, there are other types of research important to the innovation continuum. In his theory of scientific revolution, Thomas Kuhn suggested that major progress was achieved not through gradual evolution of conventional disciplinary research, but rather through revolutionary, unpredictable transformations after the intellectual content of a field reaches saturation (Kuhn, 1963). The U.S. National Science Foundation refers to such activities as *transformative research*, "research driven by ideas that stand a reasonable success of radically changing our understanding of an important existing concept or leading to the creation of a new paradigm or field of science. Such research is also characterized by its challenge to current understanding or its pathway to new frontiers" (National Science Board, 2007). While it might be assumed that such transformative research would most commonly occur in research universities, ironically the peer pressure of merit review in both grant competition and faculty promotion can discourage such high-risk intellectual activities. In fact, transformative research occurs just as frequently in some industrial research laboratories (e.g., Bell Laboratories in the past and Google Research today) where unusually creative investigators are freed from the burdens of grant seeking or commercial deadlines. It also occurs in a small number of unique government agencies such as the Defense Advanced Research Project Agency (and hopefully in its spinoffs of ARPA-E and IARPA), where pathbreaking research is shielded from the pressures of grant competition and application deadlines.

At the other end of the innovation continuum is translational research, aimed at building the knowledge base necessary to link fundamental scientific discoveries with the technological innovation necessary for the development of new products, processes and services. While translational research is both basic and applied in nature, it is driven by intended application and commercial (or social) priorities rather than scientific curiosity. Such translational research is a common feature of the biomedical industry, moving "from bench to bedside" or from laboratory experiments through clinical trials to actual point-of-care patient applications. While it is also a necessary component of the innovation continuum in other areas, particularly in corporate and federal R&D (with Bell Laboratories and the U.S. Department of Energy Laboratories as prominent examples), it has generally not been identified as a specific activity of research universities.

DISCOVERY-INNOVATION INSTITUTES

Over the past several years, there has been an increasing recognition that U.S. leadership in innovation will require commitments and investments of resources by the private sector, federal and state governments, and colleges and universities. In 2005, the U.S. National Academies issued a series of reports suggesting that a bold, transformative initiative, similar in character and scope to initiatives undertaken in response to other difficult challenges (e.g., the Land Grant Acts, the G.I. Bill, and the post-WWII government-university research partnerships) will be necessary for the United States to maintain its leadership in technological innovation (Augustine, 2005). The United States will have to reshape its research, education and practices to respond to challenges in global markets, national security, energy sustainability and public health. The changes envisioned were not only technological, but also cultural; they would affect the structure of organizations and relationships between institutional sectors of the country.

To this end, it was the recommendation of the U.S. National Academy of Engineering that a major federal initiative be launched to create translational research centers aimed at building the knowledge base necessary for technological innovation in areas of major national priority (Duderstadt, 2005). These centers, referred to as *discovery-innovation institutes*, would be established on the campuses of research universities to link fundamental scientific discoveries with technological innovations to create products, processes and services to meet the needs of society. With the participation of many scientific disciplines and professions, as well as various economic sectors (industry, government, states and institutions of higher education), discovery-innovation institutes would be similar in character and scale to academic medical centers and agricultural experiment stations that combine research, education and professional practice, and drive transformative change. As experience with academic medical centers and other large research initiatives has shown, discovery-innovation institutes would have the potential to stimulate significant regional economic activity, such as the location nearby of clusters of start-up firms, private research organizations, suppliers and other complementary groups and businesses.

More specifically, discovery-innovation institutes would be characterized by partnership, interdisciplinary research, education and outreach:

Partnership: The federal government would provide core support for the discovery-innovation institutes on a long-term basis (perhaps a decade or more, with possible renewal). States would be required to contribute to the institutes (perhaps by providing capital facilities). Industry would provide challenging research problems, systems knowledge and real-life market knowledge, as well as staff who would work with university faculty and students in the institutes.

Industry would also fund student internships and provide direct financial support for facilities and equipment (or share its facilities and equipment). Universities would commit to providing a policy framework (e.g., transparent and efficient intellectual property policies, flexible faculty appointments, responsible financial management, etc.), educational opportunities (e.g., integrated curricula, multifaceted student interaction), knowledge and technology transfer (e.g., publications, industrial outreach), and additional investments (e.g., in physical facilities and cyberinfrastructure). Finally, the venture capital and investment community would contribute expertise in licensing, spin-off companies and other avenues of commercialization.

Interdisciplinary Research: Although most discovery-innovation institutes would involve engineering schools (just as the agricultural experiment stations involve schools of agriculture), they would require strong links with other academic programs that generate fundamental new knowledge through basic research (e.g., physical sciences, life sciences, and social sciences), as well as other disciplines critical to the innovation process (e.g., business, medicine and other professional disciplines). These campus-based institutes would also attract the participation (and possibly financial support) of established innovators and entrepreneurs.

Education: Universities hosting discovery-innovation institutes would be stimulated to restructure their organizations, research activities and educational programs. Changes would reflect the interdisciplinary team approaches for research that can convert new knowledge into innovative products, processes, services and systems and, at the same time, provide graduates with the skills necessary for innovation. Discovery-innovation institutes would provide a mechanism for developing and implementing innovative curricula and teaching methods.

Outreach: Just as the success of the agricultural experiment stations established by the U.S. Land Grant Acts depended on their ability to disseminate new technologies and methodologies to the farming community through the cooperative extension service, a key factor in the success of discovery-innovation institutes would be their ability to facilitate implementation of their discoveries in the user community. Extensive outreach efforts based on existing industry and manufacturing extension programs at universities would be an essential complement to the research and educational activities of the institutes. Outreach should also include programs for K-12 students and teachers that would build enthusiasm for the innovation process and generate interest in math and science.

Research Priorities: The National Academy report envisioned a very wide range of discovery-innovation institutes, depending on the capacity and regional characteristics of a university or consortium and on national priorities. Some institutes would enter into partnerships directly with particular federal agencies or national laboratories to address fairly specific technical challenges, but most would address broad national priorities that would require relationships with several federal agencies. Awards would be made based on (1) programs that favour fundamental research driven by innovation in a focused area; (2) strong industry commitment; (3) multidisciplinary participation; and (4) national need. Periodic reviews would ensure that the institutes remain productive and continue to progress on both short- and long-term deliverables.

Funding: To ensure that the discovery-innovation institutes lead to transformative change, they would be funded at a level commensurate with past federal initiatives and current investments in other areas of research, such as biomedicine and manned spaceflight. Federal funding would ultimately increase to several billion dollars per year distributed throughout the university research and education enterprise, with states, industry, foundations and universities investing comparable amounts in these research centers. To transform the technological innovation capacity of the United States, the discovery-innovation institutes would be implemented on a national scale and backed by a strong commitment to excellence by all participants. Most of all, they would become engines of innovation that would transform institutions, policies and cultures, and enable our nation to solve critical problems and maintain its leadership in the global, knowledge-driven society of the 21st century.

A CASE STUDY: ENERGY RESEARCH

Sustainability and security challenges plague the world's energy production and delivery system. The global economy currently relies on fossil fuels for nearly 85% of its energy. By 2030, global energy use is projected to grow by 50% over 2010 levels. At the same time, recent analyses of world petroleum production, known reserves, and the impact of rapidly developing economies suggest that an increasing imbalance between supply and demand will drive up global oil and gas prices, placing a nation's economy and security at risk. While the world has substantial reserves of other fossil-fuel resources, such as coal, tar sands and oil shale, the mining, processing and burning of these fossil fuels with current technologies are expensive and characterized by increasingly unacceptable environmental impact in light of climate change concerns and intensive land and water utilization (IPCC, 2008; Friedman, 2008).

Today's energy challenges stem from an unsustainable energy infrastructure, largely dependent on fossil fuels characterized by unacceptable environmental impact and supply constraints, with clear implications for a nation's economic, public health and national security. Addressing these challenges will require substantial investments in clean and efficient energy technology, much of which has yet to be developed, making innovation the centerpiece of successful energy policy (Lewis, 2007).

Transformative innovation will be required to address fundamental energy challenges. As Presidential Science Advisor John Holdren warns, the multiplicity of challenges at the intersection of energy with the economy, the environment and national security — led by excessive dependence on petroleum and the dangerous consequences of energy's environmental impact, particularly global climate change — requires a major acceleration of energy-technology innovation that, over time, can reduce the limitations of existing energy options, bring new options to fruition and reduce the tensions among energy-policy objectives and enable faster progress on the most critical ones (Holdren, 2006).

Near term impact can be achieved from adopting existing technologies and practices that improve the efficiency of energy utilization, bringing fuel savings and creating new jobs. Yet, large and sustained efficiency investments in existing technologies will not be enough to achieve global sustainability goals. New technologies and practices are needed to mitigate the harmful impact and resource constraints of existing energy sources. Of longer term importance is the deployment of affordable, carbon-free renewable energy technologies, which will require energy storage technologies and an expanded electricity grid. With today's renewable technologies, a substantial gap remains in achieving the scale and cost structures necessary for major impact.

Here, innovation is needed not only through greatly increasing R&D in energy technologies but to demonstrate these on a commercial scale and deploy them rapidly into the marketplace. Yet, over the past two decades, energy research in the United States has actually been sharply curtailed by the federal government (75% decrease), the electrical utility industry (50% decrease), and the domestic automobile industry (50% decrease). The energy industry has the lowest level of R&D investment (relative to revenues) of any industrial sector. In 2009, federal investment in energy R&D amounted to less than $3 billion, compared to the federal R&D effort characterizing other national priorities such as health care ($30 B/y) and defense ($80 B/y) (Kammen, 2005; Friedman, 2008).

Furthermore, today's United States energy research program does not have the mission, capacity or the organizational structure to equip the nation to meet the full span of its challenges. It continues to be primarily conducted by national labs that are not only fragmented and insulated from the marketplace, but fail to tap the considerable resources of the nation's industry and research universities (Vest, 2003). Major innovation in research paradigms, policy and management will be necessary to bring about the needed pace of energy-technology innovation (Holdren, 2006):

- To provide the scale, continuity and coordination of effort in energy R&D and demonstration needed to bring an appropriate portfolio of improved options to be commercialized in a timely way.

- To tap the nation's top scientific and engineering talent and facilities, which are currently distributed throughout the nation's research universities, corporate R&D centers and federal laboratories.
- To address adequately the unusually broad spectrum of issues involved in building a sustainable energy infrastructure, including, in addition to science and technology, attention to complex social, economic, legal, political, behavioral, consumer and market issues.
- To build strong partnerships among multiple players — federal agencies, research universities, established industry, entrepreneurs and investors, and federal, state and local government.
- And to launch robust efforts capable of producing the human capital and public understanding required by the emerging energy sector at all education levels.

In view of these market and governance challenges, it is clear that the search for breakthrough technologies and practices should be placed at the center of energy research efforts. This will require a far more comprehensive and interactive engagement of the entire national research enterprise: research universities, corporate R&D laboratories and federal laboratories.

To address these challenges, a recent report by the Brookings Institution made two important recommendations (Duderstadt, 2009):

The United States should first commit itself to increasing federal investments in energy R&D to a level appropriate to address the dangerous and complex economic, environmental and national security challenges presented by the nation's currently unsustainable energy infrastructure. Comparisons with federal R&D investments addressing other national priorities such as public health, national defense and space exploration suggest an investment in federal energy R&D, an order of magnitude greater than current levels, growing to perhaps $20 to $30 billion per year, with most of this flowing to existing research players and programs (e.g., national laboratories and industry).

A significant fraction of this increase should be directed toward a new research paradigm consisting of a national network of regionally-based *energy discovery-innovation institutes* (e-DIIs) that serve as hubs in a distributed research network linked through spokes to concentrations of the nation's best scientists, engineers and facilities.

Recall that the discovery-innovation institute concept is characterized by institutional partnerships, interdisciplinary research, technology commercialization, education and outreach. In this sense, the e-DII paradigm would place a very high priority on connection and collaboration rather than competition to achieve deeper engagement of the nation's scientific, technology, business and policy resources in an effort to achieve a sustainable energy infrastructure for America.

As envisioned here, therefore, the proposed e-DIIs would do the following:

Organize around a theme, such as renewable energy technologies, advanced petroleum extraction, carbon sequestration, biofuels, transportation energy, carbon-free electrical power generation and distribution, or energy efficiency. Each e-DII would be charged with addressing the economic, policy, business, and social challenges required to diffuse innovative energy technologies of their theme area into society successfully. This mission would require each e-DII to take a systems-approach to technology development and help to transcend the current "siloed" approach common at DOE and its national labs.

Foster partnerships to pursue cutting-edge, applications-oriented research among multiple participants, including government agencies (federal, state and local), research universities, industry, entrepreneurs and investors. The e-DIIs would encourage a new research culture based on the nonlinear flow of knowledge and activity among scientific discovery, technological innovation, entrepreneurial business development and economic, legal, social, and political imperatives. In a sense, e-DIIs would create an "R&D commons" where strong, symbiotic partnerships could be created and sustained among partners with different missions and cultures. Building a sustainable energy infrastructure depends as much on socioeconomic, political and policy issues as upon science and technology. The e-DIIs would encompass disciplines such as the social and behavioral sciences, business administration, law and environmental and public policy, in addition to science and engineering.

Act as the hubs of a distributed network, linking together as spokes, the basic research programs of campus-based, industry-based and federal laboratory-based scientists and engineers, research centers and facilities, to exploit the fundamental character of discovery-innovation institutes to couple fundamental scientific research and discovery with translational research, technology development and commercial deployment. But the hub-and-spoke network architecture would go further by enabling the basic research group spokes to interact and collaborate among themselves (through exchanges of participants, regularly scheduled meetings and cyberinfrastructure). Just as the rim of a bicycle wheel greatly strengthens its hub-and-spoke structure, the direct interaction of the basic research groups (the spokes) would greatly facilitate collaboration and research progress, creating a basic energy research community greater than the sum of its individual parts and with sufficient flexibility, synergy and robustness to enable the participation of leading scientists and engineers to address the unusual complexity of the nation's energy challenges.

Develop an effective strategy for energy technology development, commercialization and deployment, working closely with industry, entrepreneurs and the investment community. For example, this might draw on the experience of major medical centers (the commercialization of translational research through business startups), agricultural and industrial extension programs, federal initiatives for regional economic development or entirely new paradigms for technology transfer.

Build the knowledge base, human capital, and public awareness necessary to address the nation's energy challenges. The e-DIIs are envisioned as the foci for long-term, applications-driven research aimed at building the knowledge base necessary to address the nation's highest priorities. Working together with industry and government, the e-DIIs would also lead to the development of educational programs and distributed educational networks that could produce new knowledge for innovation and educate not only the scientists, engineers, innovators and entrepreneurs of the future, but learners of all ages, about the challenge and excitement of changing the U.S. energy paradigm. Thus, the e-DIIs would have a fundamental educational mission of public education through the involvement of their scientists and engineers in sharing best educational practices and developing new educational programs in collaboration with K-12 schools, community colleges, regional universities and workplace training that lead to significantly increased public engagement.

Develop and rapidly transfer highly innovative technologies into the marketplace. The treatment of intellectual property is critical to the rapid and efficient transfer of energy technologies to the marketplace. The e-DIIs should provide a safe zone where intellectual property issues could be worked out in advance. Technology transfer within e-DIIs should be structured to maximize the introduction and positive societal impact of e-DII technologies, learning from successful industry-university partnerships (e.g., BP and the Universities of California and Illinois).

Encourage regional economic development. With the participation of many scientific disciplines and professions as well as various economic sectors, e-DIIs are similar in character and scale to academic medical centers and agricultural experiment stations that combine research, education and professional practice and drive transformative change. This organizational form has been successful at generating jobs and stimulating regional economic activity, by the nearby location of clusters of start-up firms, private research organizations, suppliers and other complementary groups and businesses. The e-DIIs should have an explicit mission to focus, at least in part, on the unique energy needs and opportunities characterizing their home regions, to ensure that new technologies would respond to local challenges and thus could be rapidly deployed.

Expand the scope of possible energy activities. The partnership character of the e-DII, involving a consortium of universities, national laboratories, industry, investors, state and federal government, coupled with its regional focus, would give it the capacity to launch projects that are beyond the capability of a national laboratory or industry consortium alone.

To achieve a critical mass of activities, our report recommended the creation over the next several years of a national network of several dozen energy discovery-innovation institutes distributed competitively among the nation's research universities and federal laboratories:

- *University-based e-DIIs:* Those e-DIIs located adjacent to research university campuses would be managed by either individual universities or university consortia, with strong involvement of partnering institutions such as industry, entrepreneurs and investors, state and local government, and participating federal agencies. While most university-based e-DIIs would focus both on research addressing national energy priorities and regional economic development from new energy-based industries, there would also be the possibility of distributed or virtual e-DIIs (so-called "collaboratives") that would link together institutions on regional or national bases. As mentioned earlier, each e-DII would also act as a hub linking together investigators engaged in basic or applied energy research in other organizations.

- *Federal laboratory-based e-DIIs:* There should be a parallel network of e-DIIs associated with federal laboratories. To enable the paradigm shifts represented by the discovery-innovation institute concept, these e-DIIs would be stood up "outside the fence" to minimize laboratory constraints of security, administration and overhead and driven by the bottom-up interests of laboratory scientists. Like university-based e-DIIs, their objectives would be the conduct of application-driven translational research necessary to couple the extraordinary resources represented by the scientific capability of the national laboratories with the technology innovation, development and entrepreneurial efforts necessary for the commercial deployment of innovative energy technologies in the commercial marketplace. A given national laboratory might create several e-DIIs of varying size and focus that reflect both capability and opportunities. There might also be the possibility of e-DIIs jointed, created and managed by national laboratories and research universities.

- *Satellite energy research centers:* The large e-DIIs managed by research university consortia or national laboratories would anchor "hub-and-spoke" sub-networks linking satellite energy research centers comparable in scale to DOE's Energy Frontier Research Centers or NSF's Engineering Research Centers, thereby enabling faculty in less centrally-located regions or at institutions with limited capacity to manage the large e-DII hubs to contribute to the nation's energy R&D as an element of the national e-DII network.

A merit-based competitive process would award core federal support ranging from $5 M/y to $10 M/y for modest centers in single institutions to as much as $100 M/y to $200 M/y for large e-DIIs managed by consortia of universities and national laboratories. Federal funding would be augmented with strong additional support and participation from industry, investors, universities and state governments, for a total federal commitment growing to roughly $6 billion/y (or 25% of the recommended total federal energy R&D goal of $20 to $30 billion/y estimated to be necessary to address adequately the nation's energy challenge.)

In May 2009, the U.S. Department of Energy announced the first step of building just such a significant energy research program by launching a new *transformational* research program patterned after the U.S. Department of Defense's Advanced Research Projects Agency (DARPA) known as ARPA-E and funded at an initial level of $400 M/y; funding 46 new Energy Frontier Research Centers on university campuses and national laboratories for small research teams; and creating an initial set of eight "energy innovation hubs", similar in concept to the energy discovery innovation institutes, for *translational* research funded at $280 M for the first year. President Obama has also committed to increasing federal energy research by at least $15 B/y, hence beginning to approach the target set by our Brookings report (Chu, 2009).

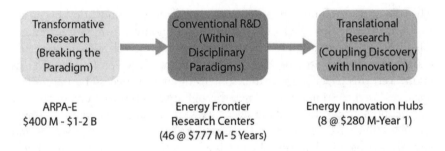

Transformative Research (Breaking the Paradigm)	Conventional R&D (Within Disciplinary Paradigms)	Translational Research (Coupling Discovery with Innovation)
ARPA-E $400 M - $1-2 B	Energy Frontier Research Centers (46 @ $777 M- 5 Years)	Energy Innovation Hubs (8 @ $280 M-Year 1)

Interestingly enough, this strategy has important antecedents in American history. In earlier times during periods of great challenge or opportunity, the United States responded to the changing needs of the nation with massive investments in the nation's research capacity. The Land Grant Acts of the 19th century created, through the great land-grant universities, the capacity to assist the nation's transition from an agricultural to an industrial economy. The Manhattan Project developed the nuclear technology to protect the nation during a period of great international peril. The post-WWII research partnership between the federal government and the nation's universities was not only critical to national security during the Cold War, but drove much of America's economic growth during the latter half of the 20th century. The Apollo Program fulfilled mankind's dream to conquer space by sending men to the moon.

Most analogous to the present situation was the visionary action taken by Congress to respond to the challenge of modernizing American agriculture and industry with the Hatch Act of 1887. This act created a network of agricultural and engineering experiment stations through a partnership involving higher education, business and state and federal government that developed and deployed the technologies necessary to build a modern industrial nation for the 20th century while stimulating local economic growth. The proposed network of regional "energy innovation hubs" is remarkably similar both in spirit and structure, since it will bring together a partnership among research universities, business and industry, entrepreneurs and investors, and federal, state and local government working together across a broad spectrum of scientific, engineering, economic, behavioural, and policy disciplines to build a sustainable national energy infrastructure for the 21st century while stimulating strong regional economic growth. It will represent an important element of a broader national effort to achieve a sustainable energy future for both our nation and the world.

CONCLUDING REMARKS

The role of research universities in contributing to the innovation necessary to compete in a knowledge-driven global economy is widely recognized. Clearly, the traditional approaches to fundamental research and education are essential for creating the new knowledge and knowledge professional to this effort. Yet, this paper suggests that something more is necessary: *transformational* research to stimulate the breakthrough discoveries that create entirely new economic activities and *translational* research and development to transfer new knowledge generated on the campuses into products, processes and systems capable of addressing the needs of society. These, in turn, will likely require new paradigms for university research similar to those suggested in recent U.S. National Academy and National Science Foundation studies and currently being applied to address the urgent need for sustainable energy technologies.

REFERENCES

Augustine, N. (chair). (2005). National Academies Committee on Prospering in the Global Economy of the 21st Century, *Rising Above the Gathering Storm: Energizing and Employing America for a Brighter Economic Future*. Washington, D.C.: National Academies Press.

Chu, Stephen. (2009). Presentation on Department of Energy 2010 Budget. United States Department of Energy. http://www.energy.gov/media/Secretary_Chu_2010_Budget_rollout_presentation.pdf

Duderstadt, J. J. (chair). (2005). Committee to Assess the Capacity of the United States Research Enterprise. *Engineering Research and America's Future: Meeting the Challenges of a Global Economy*. Washington, D.C.: National Academies Press.

Duderstadt, J. J. (chair). (2009). *Energy Discovery-Innovation Institutes: A Step Toward America's Energy Sustainability*, Brookings Institution Blueprint for American Prosperity. Washington, D.C.: Metropolitan Policy Program, Brookings Institution.

Friedman, T. (2005). *The World Is Flat: A Brief History of the 21st Century*. New York, New York: Farrar, Strauss, and Giroux.

Friedman, T. (2008). *Hot, Flat, and Crowded: Why We Need a Green Revolution — and How It Can Renew America*. New York: Farrar, Strauss, and Giroux.

Holdren, J. (2006). The Energy Innovation Imperative: Addressing Oil Dependence, Climate Change, and Other 21st Century Energy Challenges, *Innovations*, 1 (2), p. 3.

IPCC. (2007). Intergovernmental Panel on Climate Change. *Climate Change 2007*. Cambridge, England: Cambridge University Press.

Kammen, D. M. & Nemet, G. F. (2005). Reversing the Incredible Shrinking Energy R&D Budget, *Issues in Science and Technology*, Fall 2005, pp. 84-88.

Kuhn, T. S. (1963). *The Structure of Scientific Revolutions*. Chicago, Illinois: University of Chicago Press.

Lewis, N. S. (2007). Powering the Planet. Caltech: *Engineering & Science*, No. 2, p. 13.

National Academies. (2007). America's Energy Future: Technology Opportunities, Risks and Tradeoffs, study under way.

National Science Board. (2007). *Transformational Research*. Washington, D.C.: National Science Foundation.

Suh, Nam. (this book) *"On Innovation Strategies: An Asian Perspective"*. In Luc E. Weber & James J. Duderstadt (Eds.), University Research For Innovation, London, Paris, Geneva: Economica.

Vest, C. M. (chair). (2003). Final Report of the Secretary of Energy's Advisory Board Task Force on the Future of Science Programs at the Department of Energy, Critical Choices: Science, Energy, and Security. Washington, D.C.: U. S. Department of Energy.

CHAPTER 17

Hi-Tech Industry and Universities: A Perspective on Dating for Joint Innovation

INTRODUCTION

As recorded since the very beginning of our written history, knowledge has been progressing by accumulating the experience of past and present generations (Van Doren, 1991). The creation of new knowledge has been performed by various actors: priests, hunters, philosophers, farmers, artists, craftsmen, soldiers, faculties, business people, scientists, managers, etc. Relationships between these various knowledge creators have occurred either formally (in schools, or corporations, or public forums) or informally (in all possible venues, including individual visits, migrations and dramatic events). One can say that innovation has been able to happen in almost all possible circumstances, including and even better under adversity.

More recently, a critical mass of knowledge has been created and accumulated in academia, public research institutions and industry. With the world becoming more global and innovation more important for the development of countries, there has been a growing need for these different institutions to

1 This paper was written with the collaboration and help of several colleagues of the HP Open Innovation Office team whom I would like to thank: Vinnie Jauhari (based in India), Martina Trucco (based in Puerto Rico), Lueny Morell (based in Puerto Rico), Sheri Brodeur (based in Boston, U.S.), Igor Belousov (based in Russia), Xiang-yi Yao (based in China), Shinya Nakagawa (based in Japan), Jason Tan (based in Singapore), Arnaud Pierson (based in Switzerland) and Rich Friedrich (based in Palo Alto, U.S.). Also I would like to give special thanks to Luc Weber for reviewing this paper.

251

collaborate more and better (Weber, 2006). For sure such collaborations had already happened many times in the past, but recent economic trends have created a specific increased need for academia, public research institutes and industry to perform joint innovation.

This paper is about the special relationship between academia, public research institutes and industry when it comes to jointly innovate. In section 2 the paper first explores the new motivation for the Hi-Tech industry to increase its external relationships to better innovate. Then in section 3 the planning, dating and execution for joint innovation are described in detail. Section 4 then addresses the new global context in which such joint innovations are performed. Examples are taken from the corporate experience of the author and his colleagues of the Open Innovation Office at HP Laboratories. The conclusion looks at some future trends for joint innovation.

HI-TECH INDUSTRY RESEARCH AND INNOVATION

R&D Spending Trends

In September 2005, Technology Review published the Corporate R&D Scorecard (Fig 1.a). R&D spending of 150 Hi-Tech companies was analysed in terms of absolute spending in US$, R&D as a percentage of sales, and R&D per employee. First significant differences in average R&D investment could be seen between sectors: about 23% of sales for biotechnology, 7% for computer hardware, 14% for computer software, 2% for consumer products, 16% for semi-conductors and 4% for transportation. Also within a given sector like computer hardware, one could notice different levels of R&D spending ranging from 4% to 17% of sales. Different business models could explain such differences within the same sector. Some companies would mainly compete on the technology innovation level (like Sun or EMC), while other companies would rather compete on the business model and spend less on R&D (like Dell). Such differences in R&D spending were also noticeable in other sectors like computer software and telecommunications. This study shows that the needs for acquiring external knowledge and R&D from universities are not similar between companies, even within a different sector.

Need for Innovation

Companies spend most of their R&D budget doing D (Development) rather than R (Research). The development time for a new product is closely linked to the life-cycle of the product. Some products, such as printers, have a life-cycle of a couple of years and their development time can be as short as three months. Other products, such as computing servers or software releases, have a much longer life-cycle (up to a few years) and their development time can scale up to several years. Usually time-to-market is a key parameter for the success of the product and little or no time can be spent to accommodate external partners with a different agenda and timetable to develop product components. In addition cost constraints are intense in Hi-Tech product development and constant tradeoffs have to be made by the development team between functionality, time-to-develop and cost. In some cases, razor-thin margins in the lower one-digit numbers gave cost constraints a lead in the absence of breakthrough innovation, such as for personal computers before 2005. In other cases the innovation factor was so overwhelming that cost constraints became secondary, such as for the iPod ®. In this complex environment, most external product development partnerships are usually between industrial companies used to operate within similar constraints, and rarely with universities. For developers in a Hi-Tech company, universities can perform targeted tasks unrelated with critical product development, such as tests in specific scientific environment, or sanity checks about some new technological assumptions, or search for alternative technologies. The university faculties and students can provide interesting and provocative, out-of-the-box concepts which can be of great interest for development teams when planning next product releases or checking the market acceptance of new products. One interesting case can be read about the Illinois Institute of Technology and HP in digital photography in the late 90s (Frascara, 2002, pp. 208-218.)

Relationships with Universities — Dating for Joint R&D

While the most attractive target for industry-university partnerships is product development, it is also the most difficult to succeed into. A common fallacy is to believe that a university will act like an industrial partner when dealing with product development, and this unfortunately leads to severe misunderstandings, to unmet commitments and deliverables, and ultimately to a deterioration of the relationship between the two partners.

Some companies have kept within their R&D budget a significant component for R (Research). Usually the R component is a one-digit percentage of the total R&D budget. However for large companies like HP, IBM or Intel, this R budget is still significant in terms of absolute dollars. Research Labs in private industries are special entities where research is conducted in selected areas of interest with the expectation to develop future products within 5-10 years, sometimes even later. In this respect, industry research Labs share some similar goals with universities and public research entities, and have a natural need and interest to collaborate with them (see Fig. 1b). This collaboration can start with public domain presentations and publications at conferences and journals, and expand into joint research projects and participation to public research programs, such as those organized by the National Science Foundation in the U.S. or the Framework Programs in the E.U.

However this initially attractive-looking match has to be balanced with several constraints and the organization of partnerships between private industry labs and universities or public research entities has to take these constraints into account. The first constraint is still related to life-cycle considerations. Usually the turnover of named strategic research topics in private research labs is faster than those within public institutions or those of public research programs. This can lead to discrepancies in terms of the actual length of the planned joint collaboration and its desired outcomes. It also potentially limits the company lab in its ability to change research directions according to new business interests. The second constraint to handle is still related to cost. Large research investments from private companies are usually not rewarded by Wall Street, and are seen more as a cost than an investment, or even than an asset. This tendency has taken more importance in recent years with the pressure on companies to reward their stockholders sooner rather than later and therefore to cut all perceived unnecessary costs accordingly. As a consequence, the current size of most research projects undertaken by private companies is relatively limited and has a hard time to be scaled up in the absence of external funding. Government-sponsored public research organizations have well understood these two constraints and provide more attractive frameworks and conditions for private companies to undertake research in collaboration with local universities or public research labs. This happens especially in many emerging economies; however more mature geographies have been ramping up their attractiveness for company research programs as well.

The environment for joint research projects between private company labs and universities and public research institutes is therefore more favourable than the environment for joint product development projects, even if the size of the projects is smaller. For the private company lab, the deliverables of such projects can in some cases be expressed in research results otherwise hard or impossible to get alone, along with important direct or indirect talent recruitment.

Open Innovation Model

Recent frameworks such as Open Innovation in opposition to traditional Closed Innovation (Fig 1.c) have been developed in the literature to explain the growing importance of external research partnerships and their attractiveness for all parties involved.

The Open Innovation Model (Chesbrough, 2003) calls for partnerships between a company R&D entity and researchers from the following institutions:

- Universities.
- Public Research Laboratories.

- Government Research Programs (such as NSF, EU FP, MEXT, etc.).
- Non-for-Profit organizations.
- Other companies.

The initial assumption is that for a given research theme expertise and talent are not concentrated only inside the company, but rather disseminated among the institutions mentioned above. The next step is to find these external talents and to collaborate with them in order to join forces and obtain potentially better research results. The gain in time, resources and effort often offsets the exposure taken by collaborating openly with external organizations.

At HP we have been implementing Open Innovation since several years and have practised several different instances:

- A global Call for Proposals to Universities (http://www.hpl.hp.com/open_innovation/irp/).
- Collaborations with companies in global joint projects (www.opencirrus.org).
- Several participations to DARPA, EU FP7 and other government programs.
- Organization of Open Source Federations (www.gelato.org, www.dspace.org).
- Joint Programs with UNESCO and Joint Research and Education Programs in specific countries (http://portal.unesco.org/fr/ev.php-URL_ID=27009&URL_DO=DO_TOPIC&URL_SECTION=201.html).

PLANNING, DATING FOR AND EXECUTING EXTERNAL R&D WITH UNIVERSITIES

Planning

Setting up an Agenda

The first task to be performed in the planning of External R&D is the establishment of a comprehensive agenda. As mentioned in the previous section, corporate R&D can be conducted to discover new technologies for future products, or to produce new business models, or to perform a combination of both. Usually the list of R&D topics that have to be investigated by the company R&D organization is a long list, addressing multiple problems. It is frequently the case that the resources available are outnumbered by the needs expressed in the list. In addition the company R&D organization sometimes does not have all the right skills and people to address a particular problem,

Figure 1a: Corporate R&D Scorecard

*BASED ON DATA FOR MOST RECENT FISCAL YEAR, ENDING MAY 31, 2005. SOURCES: STANDARD AND POOR'S; COMPANY WEBSITES; *TECHNOLOGY REVIEW*

56 FEATURE STORY   TECHNOLOGY REVIEW SEPTEMBER 2005

Company name (country)	Rank by Innovation Index	R&D spending 2004* (in millions)	R&D percent change	Absolute change over 2003 (in millions)	R&D as a percentage of sales	R&D per employee	Research focus
Computer hardware							
IBM (U.S.)	23	$5,167	2%	$99	5%	$15,705	Deep computing, displays, e-commerce, semiconductors, storage
SUN MICROSYSTEMS (U.S.)	38	$1,926	5%	$89	17%	$59,080	Business PDA applications, device networks, speech technology, Java
TOSHIBA (Japan)	55	$3,149	2%	$49	6%	$19,523	Film, optics, wireless communication, transistors
HEWLETT-PACKARD (U.S.)	59	$3,506	-4%	-$146	4%	$23,219	Internet systems, wireless communication, security, privacy, printing
EMC (U.S.)	72	$848	18%	$129	10%	$37,352	Storage
FUJITSU (Japan)	90	$2,346	-12%	-$326	5%	$15,025	Internet services, ubiquitous computing, computational science, security
NEC (Japan)	91	$2,400	-13%	-$370	5%	$16,739	Banking systems, e-government systems, optical, IP and device networks
SEIKO EPSON (Japan)	114	$833	-2%	-$13	6%	$9,808	Printers, projection, electronic components, optics
Average	**68**	**$2,522**	**-1%**	**-$61**	**7%**	**$24,556**	
Computer software							
MICROSOFT (U.S.)	2	$7,779	67%	$3,120	21%	$136,474	Multimedia, search, knowledge management, security, machine learning
ELECTRONIC ARTS (U.S.)	41	$633	24%	$122	20%	$103,398	Enterprise software, extensible systems, open-source software
SAP (Germany)	62	$1,298	3%	$33	14%	$40,290	Business process applications, e-business
AUTOMATIC DATA PROCESSING (U.S.)	96	$581	16%	$82	7%	$13,837	Data processing and outsourced services
ORACLE (U.S.)	118	$1,278	8%	$98	1%	$30,678	Grid computing, Web services, Java, Linux, open-source software
COMPUTER ASSOCIATES (U.S.)	122	$690	4%	$28	20%	$45,098	Mobile gaming, motion capture, 3-D face and body rendering
Average	**74**	**$2,043**	**20%**	**$581**	**14%**	**$61,629**	

Source: Data from Technology Review 2005 http://www.technologyreview.com/articlefiles/2005_rd_scorecard.pdf

Figure 1b: Timeline of university research, company research and product development (from HP)

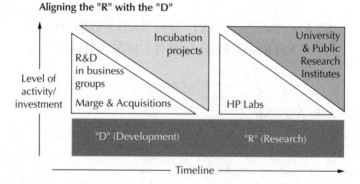

Aligning the "R" with the "D"

and building such capacities takes a long time. Finally some problems are perceived as temporary and requiring a short-term effort rather than a long-term organizational involvement.

All these reasons call for an in-depth look at the opportunity to outsource R&D, especially to universities or public research organizations. This is a

Figure 1c: Closed Innovation vs. Open Innovation models

The Closed Innovation Model
The classic research lab

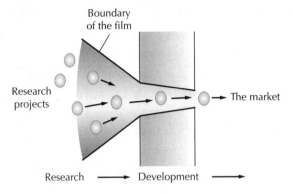

The Open Innovation Model
Successful companies require partnerships

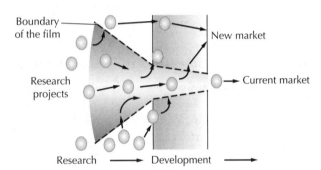

make vs. buy decision, which has to be prepared carefully. In particular, the following points have to be clarified before selecting a particular topic in the list for external R&D candidate topics:

- Is this topic considered strategic? Does the company want to own the knowledge about it?
- Is the research affordable? How long would it take to get results? At which cost?
- Where is the expertise located for this topic? Who would be best positioned to help?

Answering these key questions is a pre-requisite before entering into the investigation for potential external R&D partners. Once these questions are answered for each topic targeted for external R&D, an agenda can be constructed. Sometimes this agenda can be shown as a "technology map" where the different R&D topics and their main components are shown and their source (internal or external) is mentioned. Such a map (as shown in Fig 2) can help to make trade-off decisions between topics and refine the external R&D strategy.

Figure 2: Example of technology map used for building an external R&D agenda

	Topic 1	Topic 2	Topic 3	Topic 4
Relevance for the company R&D	Not strategic	Strategic	Not strategic	Public Domain
R&D effort estimated	1 Man/Year	2 Men/Year	3 Men/Year	10 Men/Year
Potential external R&D partners	Universities A, B, C and D	Competitor X University C	Company Y	NSF or EU project
Proposed decision	Outsource using Call for Proposal	Do internally	Negotiate partnership	Participate to the project
Cost	Low	High	Low/Medium	Low
Time to market	Not critical	Critical	Medium	Not critical

Dating, selecting potential partners and thinking out-of-the-box

Once the external R&D agenda is built, the next step is to identify among the potential external partners those likely to provide the R&D as required. This is a match-making process which can be run in very different ways with potential external partners:

- Individual meetings and conversations at exhibitions or conferences.
- Call for Proposals sent to universities globally or in a given geography.
- Regular relationships with particular campuses or research institutes.
- Web 1.0 and 2.0 interactions with targeted external researchers and faculties.

Each of these dating approaches has its own pros and cons, and the authors have been practising most of them at different stages for different purposes. Conferences and exhibitions are grouping specialists of a given topic in a location to make presentations, publish papers or posters and exchange ideas during coffee breaks and dinners. Such events are very powerful for identifying potential external R&D partners and exploring their interest and availability to build a R&D partnership.

A broader or next approach is to publish a Call for Proposal on a given set of topics to universities. Universities are asked for project proposals with a submission deadline. Once the proposals are received, they are reviewed and a few of them are selected. This approach has the advantage of identifying new unknown partners and offering potential positive surprises to the company R&D organization. An example is the Call for Proposal performed by HP Labs in 2008 and 2009 (http://www.hpl.hp.com/open_innovation/irp/).

The practice of a regular and strategic relationship with selected research partners (companies, universities and public research institutes) provides a rich networking environment where ideas can be explored and R&D partnership established when there is a match in areas of interest. This approach however requires dedicated local company representatives to cover selected major campuses, public research institutes and private partners.

Finally today websites provide a rich database of papers, public research results repositories and descriptions of research activities which can be consulted for identifying and calling potential external partners. It is also possible to scale-up this investigation with Web 2.0 technologies (blogs, forums, twikis etc.) which provide a more dynamic exchange and sometimes even instant results for the investigation (Tapscott, 2007).

One important opportunity which is frequently overlooked or not taken into account is the investigation of external R&D partnerships outside the traditional research areas of the company R&D organization. Sometimes problems identified by a company R&D organization were already solved, at least partially, by another organization. For example, in HP Labs one very efficient data centre energy optimization technology was recently bought from the aerospace industry, where air flow optimization has been one key expertise since the very beginning of plane construction. In identifying and assessing potential external R&D partnerships it is therefore important to keep an open approach to allow out-of-the-box opportunities, or "black swans", to be investigated and considered (Taleb, 2007).

To summarize, the investigation and selection of potential external research partners are one of the most intriguing and interesting steps of the planning of external R&D. This is also a challenging task since it provokes make-or-buy considerations and out-of-the-box thinking.

Competitive Analysis

The world of R&D partnerships is a busy world where competition is intense to team with the best and brightest in a given technology topic. When considering a potential R&D partnership, several questions have to be addressed about the potential partner:

- How qualified is the potential partner? What is his/her research reputation?
- Is the potential partner available? Or already booked? What would the turnover cost?

- What is the price of the collaboration? What would the terms and conditions be?
- What is the overall relationship between the company and the potential partner?

The question of the qualification and research reputation of the potential partner is an important one. Beyond the expected quality of the research, there are also time to market and marketing considerations to consider carefully. Partnering with recognized world experts on a given subject derives fame or even hype, but also exposure and a strong expectation to succeed.

Even the best research partner can fail to deliver if his/her agenda is already full. Project turnover is a key parameter to investigate when considering a new R&D collaboration.

The price of the collaboration depends on geographic, political and economic factors. Besides the price of external researchers and their infrastructure, overhead costs have to be considered as well. One sticky point can be the price of the intellectual property (IP) generated by the project and the ease of doing business with the Technology Transfer Organization of the partner.

Finally a very important factor to watch carefully is the overall relationship between the company and the potential partner, including the commercial relationship when applicable. R&D partnerships can be plagued by poor commercial relationships or unsustainable competitive pressure.

All these points are trade-offs at the source of intense debates within R&D organizations. It is interesting to watch how different companies answer some of these questions by either teaming with big dollars with only a couple of top campuses, or by spreading their money thinner with multiple but less famous partners.

Execution

Investment Strategies

When there are many topics retained for potential external R&D and significant investments to be decided, a portfolio analysis may be needed. The goal of the portfolio analysis is to position the different potential external R&D activities in a risk/reward diagram, and to look at the overall risk that the company is planning to take. Senior management can then decide which risk strategy is acceptable and guide the overall investment accordingly. The investment strategy consists in the following steps:

- Evaluation of expected return and risks.
- Evaluation and choice of a portfolio strategy.

Return: The total planned external research investment includes cash, personnel and expense costs. This total amount has to be compared to the investment which would be needed internally to execute the same research. Thus a conservative expectation for the return of external R&D should be the equivalent return if the project were done internally. Having considered this, one might want to consider more aggressive investments, i.e. focused investments expected to return much more than the standard investment described above. This may happen in the following scenarios:

- Leverage of a significant external funding opportunity (in specific emerging economies etc.), or seeding of a relationship that develops into a collaborative partnership with significant external funding (in E.U. with FP7, in the U.S. with NSF, etc.).
- Focus on a campus powerhouse expected to deliver much higher returns.
- Focus on a transformation topic in an out-of-the-box approach.

Risk: The risk on any individual investment includes a factual risk and a perceived risk. The factual risk includes the dollar amount of the investment plus the internal people cost which will be involved in the external project. The perceived risk derives from the importance the company R&D organization assigns to the hype of a subject, the reputation of a campus, the history of a relationship and the ultimate belief that everything will be fine or not. This latter risk can play in two directions: increased confidence or increased defiance.

The goal of the company R&D organization will therefore be to maximize the expected Return while minimizing the Risk (especially the perceived risk) of the portfolio of investments.

A *Conservative Portfolio* allocates the investment in a uniform way, and may or may not allow a couple of more focused aggressive investments. It can then be difficult to raise the expected average return beyond the return of the same projects internally. The risk can be perceived as low. Companies that are new in the business of external R&D partnerships usually adopt a conservative portfolio by teaming with well-recognized faculties from top campuses. In a similar way that an IT manager in the 80s would not be fired by choosing IBM (a common stand at that time), an External Research manager is unlikely to be blamed for choosing to work with a few top faculties from major campuses in the company areas of interest.

A *Balanced Portfolio* makes a few bigger bets in focused areas, decrement more conservative projects accordingly, but still invest in those that are most promising. Compared to the conservative portfolio, the balanced portfolio can raise the expected average return by a factor of two or three. The factual risk certainly increases as well. The balanced portfolio encourages the company R&D organization to increase reasonably its risk tolerance with academic projects. Companies like pharmaceuticals usually cultivate a balanced portfolio with a set of major campus partnerships and a few major investments.

An Aggressive Portfolio increases significantly the number of focused invest-ments and leads to factual and much higher perceived risks. However the potential return can scale up to about five times the expected one with a conservative portfolio. Some Hi-Tech companies cultivate an aggressive port-folio approach, by placing significant investments behind a few well-targeted directions.

Negotiation

Once the investment strategy has been chosen and the potential partners defined, negotiations can start with the potential partners. This is a combina-tion of science and art. Science is based on partnership contract templates, different IP terms and other contractual parameters that the company can pre-pare as negotiable or non-negotiable items. The practice of the negotiation itself shows that even if this contractual science was prepared carefully, Art often applies in getting a win-win outcome. The literature and experience relate some successes, but also some significant failures. In any case, the length and the cost of negotiation should usually not be higher than the length and the cost of the joint project.

However in today's world IP is often perceived by all parties (industry, uni-versity, government) as a key strategic asset around which the whole partner-ship negotiation has to be articulated. This assumption is popular because IP can be measured with some well recognized parameters: number of patents, licensing revenues and other trade statistics. The assumption that IP should rule the negotiation is better suited for some industries than other, the difference being often time to market. For example, in the IT industry it is frequent to see hot new technologies becoming common or even public domain after a couple of years (Raymond, 1999). Therefore the window of opportunity can be very short for major IP revenue goals. The situation is of course completely opposite in other industries, such as the pharmaceutical industry. For this reason in many cases IP negotiations should be taken with an open mind and with the desire to find mutually reasonable terms, rather than to maximize IP revenues.

Partnership negotiations also have to take into account other factors, such as the other on-going relationships between the company and the university. These relationships can include a vendor-customer relationship, transfer of people between the two parties (visits, sabbaticals or even hiring) and other contacts (VIP visits, joint participation to events, joint PR and communica-tions). Therefore a positive and friendly business relationship climate has to be maintained during the negotiation, regardless of the financial goals of some of the negotiators. Major account management techniques have to be prac-tised to ensure that no dispute will disrupt the company-university relation-ship, or affect other company business in the geography.

Finally the practice of negotiations in different geographies requires the accommodation of different cultures and practices. This can be cultivated at the company headquarters level in close partnership with local employees and company partners. In the global world of R&D partnerships, local policies, economic conditions and business practices do play a major role.

Project Management

Once the joint R&D project is signed, and after the reception and cocktails, the joint R&D work can start. Traditional project management techniques (Bauer, 1992) can of course apply to ensure that the project will deliver the desired results. However a few very specific and important considerations have to be taken into account.

The project will be co-run by two teams with complete different cultures. R&D corporate culture is very different from academic culture. Initial meetings should concentrate on building mutual understanding and trust before rushing to the deliverables. It is a good practice to organize in the beginning of the project frequent visits, discovery meetings and social events to build the joint team. What will be spent for this purpose will be saved manifold for the project in the future.

A university will unlikely develop a commercial product. The joint R&D team has to rather concentrate on goals like exploring new concepts, doing sanity checks and building proofs of concept or prototypes. The company R&D team should rather leverage the fresh innovative approach of university faculties rather than try to force them to apply product development techniques.

R&D engineers and project managers are measured by their management by comparing the results of their projects to clear articulated project goals. Academics are evaluated by their peers according to the review and success of their publications. Therefore it will be important to accommodate these two different sets of values in the evaluation of the joint project results. Initially this looks like mixing fire with water, but in practice it can turn out to be easier. For example the peer review of academic publications is a very thorough process requiring the faculty to submit well documented research results with proofs and examples. Such results and their presentation can often be of great interest for the industry partner.

The ability to accommodate different geographies in the joint research project portfolio can be a tremendous opportunity and competitive advantage for a company external R&D agenda. However it requires a careful understanding of the local education system, policies and working practices. This applies in the practice of the joint R&D project as well. Having two teams from two continents collaborating requires special care and techniques to make communications successful and projects completed.

Measuring Success

The measurement of success in external partnerships or open innovation is a science and an art. The science includes multiple well- or not-so-well-engineered operational parameters which can be measured along the lifetime of the external partnership: number of publications, financials, number of people, etc. The art includes serendipity, intuition and luck.

For sure the marital life between both science and art is a delicate experience, which requires a lot of openness and patience from the stakeholders. Here are a few of the tradeoffs.

Process vs. Content

Process and content are closely linked to each other, and the success of external partnerships requires a good balance between both. A pure process-driven approach may miss lifetime opportunities and the ultimate power of intuition. A pure content-driven approach may often lead to the exhilarating cultivation of joint dreams with the external partners, with little or no likelihood for any tangible result.

Human Capital vs. Finance

Financial measurements such as Return on Investment, External Funding and Licensing Business Forecasts are important to put the project in perspective, especially for large multi-year collaborations. However Human Capital is also in the essence of success in R&D, beside investment. Access to talent has to be a key objective of open innovation.

Publications and Technology Transfers

As mentioned before, the reward systems of academia and industry are completely different. The success of the partnerships will therefore have to be measured using publications (rewarding for academia) and technology transfers (rewarding for industries). Some campuses however, such as Stanford University, have cultivated a very strong track record of managing a pipeline of successful start-ups out of the innovation projects.

THE GLOBAL CHALLENGE

In today's flat world (Friedman, 2006) the competition between universities is intense on a global basis to perform the best research and the best curriculum. Between governments there is also an intense competition to develop the most attractive education and research economic strategy (Vietor, 2007). Many countries, at the national or regional level, offer comprehensive programs to attract external R&D investments from the private sector. Government matching funds, or tax returns, or other facilities (real estate opportunities in technology parks, student programs, etc.) are offered to attract corporate R&D investment. This plays a very important role in the selection of external R&D partners.

While financial and logistical conditions can make or break a deal, it is important to keep a cold focus on the initial external R&D objective. The trade-off is then to find the right balance between R&D and business (sometimes even company trade balance) objectives. For companies which are growing on a global scale, initial beachheads can be made in new geographies using external R&D partnerships within an attractive local economic environment favourable to such new ventures. On the other hand, geographies which make it difficult to establish R&D collaborations or do not provide any economic incentives can plague the development of company external R&D despite the availability of local talent. Recent experience has shown that easy-to-do-business-with IP policies are also played by several geographies as a competitive factor in order to attract companies R&D investments.

The 'undisputable' Attraction of Emerging Geographies

The numbers are all pointing in the same direction: emerging geographies (Brazil, China, India, Korea, Middle-East, Russia, Singapore, etc.) are dramatically scaling up their innovation capabilities in technology and science. This starts with the number of students in the higher education system, the ranking of universities and ultimately the number of graduates (Fig. 3).

Figure 3: Global Trends in Higher Education: New Engineers in 2008 in the World

The world produces about one million engineers every year:

USA & Canada	≈100,000
China	≈400,000
India	≈300,000
Europe	≈100,000
Australia	≈8,000
Korea & Japan	≈150,000
L & S America	≈200,000
Middle-East and Africa	≈50,000

Source: Data from Professors Seeram Ramakrishna (National University Singapore) and Venky Narayanamurti (Harvard) IFEES conference in Paris, May 2008.

In addition to the ramp-up of their talent pool, emerging geographies have been cultivating since several years a set of other competitive advantages:

- Cost, skill and motivation of workforce.
- Ease-to-do-business with attractive public policies.
- Motivation to grow, perform and develop national capabilities.

The combination of these factors is today building a true economic comparative advantage to emerging geographies universities when it comes to attract, perform and deliver external R&D for global or local companies. One of the important facts confirming this trend is the reverse brain drain from mature economies of the western world towards emerging geographies: talented faculties and knowledge workers are leaving mature economies to join new innovation structures in emerging geographies. This applies not only to people who were born in these emerging geographies and went to the mature countries to study or get initial work experience, but also to mature geographies-born citizens who are attracted by new opportunities in emerging geographies.

This gives emerging geographies a clear undisputable attraction to companies to perform innovation related work.

The 'still-matters' Attraction of Traditional Geographies

The fascinating TED video shows a novel new human-machine interface for cell phones/computers developed by MIT: (http://www.ted.com/talks/pattie_maes_demos_the_sixth_sense.html). The content of this video speaks by itself: the cocktail of talent, motivation and insight is impressive and shows the power of campuses like MIT when it comes to innovation. Companies are still investing a large fraction of their external R&D dollars to get access to such breakthrough innovation in the major campuses of mature geographies (U.S., Europe, Canada, etc.).

In addition several major campuses have developed over the years a unique and powerful strategy to incubate start-ups and make them successful. For example, the track record of Stanford University is impressive: HP, Sun, Cisco, Yahoo, Google and many other hi-tech companies started from the Stanford campus. Also the venture capital ecosystem is an impressive innovation and growth engine for several geographic locations in mature geographies: Silicon Valley, Oxbridge, Munich, etc. Finally, large public research programs (NSF, DARPA, EU FP7, MEXT Japan, etc.) are also very welcome for companies looking for public domain research with academic and industrial partners.

This makes mature geographies still matter to companies to succeed in innovation related work (Kaufman Foundation Report, 2009).

Some examples

Here are some examples from the HP Laboratories vintage:

HP Russian Institute of Technology (HP RIT):

A joint curriculum between a company and several major universities in Russia.

In February 2009 HP and the community of 12 leading Russian universities announced first results of HP Russian Institute of Technology (HP RIT) program's work. Since it was launched in January 2008, the following results have been achieved:

- HP RIT Community has grown to 12 distinguished universities from all over Russia, such as Moscow State University, St. Petersburg State University, Moscow University of Printing Arts and many others. HP RIT research and education centres have been established or are planned to be established in all universities of the community.
- 22 education courses and 8 laboratory works have been developed and already made available to students at the universities of the RIT community. New courses and lab works are to be launched and shared within the community in the nearest future.
- More than 40 university professors are involved in the program and over 1,500 students have already studied at RIT centres.

The main goal of RIT program is to provide students and university professors with access to the information on the latest technologies. HP provides latest hardware, software and financial support for creation of RIT research and education centres at participating universities. For example, a special Digital Printing Center based on Indigo 5500 has been created at Moscow State University of Printing Arts.

HP experts and professors at universities then work together to develop educational courses and bring IT training programs to the new levels in order to turn their students into highly qualified IT professionals with knowledge of most recent technologies. New courses and laboratory works that cover "Parallel Programming", "Network Technologies" and many others have already been successfully added to the curricula of Moscow State University of Printing Arts, Bonch-Bruevich Saint-Petersburg State University of Telecommunications, Moscow Institute of Physics and Technology, Stavropol State University and Samara State Aerospace University. Additional courses, such as "Nanotechnology", "Bio-informatics", "Virtualization" and several others are currently being developed and will soon be available to all students at universities taking part in the program. Later on the courses will be translated into English so that European universities could add them to their training programs as well. It is also in the plans to make all courses available to the majority of Russian universities upon request.

HP and MIT Alliance:

HP and MIT have had a very long relationship that was formalized into The HP-MIT Alliance in June of 2000, by Carly Fiorina and Chuck Vest, the then President of MIT. This was a $25M/5yr program in "Digital Information Systems" with the goal of launching larger, multi-year programs that would hopefully have more of an impact than a collection of smaller projects.

Under this Alliance five new major programs were launched, one was a consortium with other companies (Oxygen), but the other four were HP-MIT programs, and all yielded good results for both HP and MIT.

The four HP-MIT projects launched under the Alliance were DSpace, an open source digital archiving system, an Imaging research program in printed electronics, a Quantum Information program and the Wireless Networking Center.

HP Innovate Program in India:

This initiative was started by HP Labs Open Innovation Office in India to create a platform to showcase the potential of young engineering undergraduates in India. The program was initiated in the year 2007 and the first round was concluded in the year 2008. Technical submissions and prototypes were invited from more than 200 engineering colleges in the first phase. The themes under which the submissions were invited range from cryptography, embedded technology, image processing, nanotechnology, virtualization, data mining and so on. There were about 17 technology themes which were included for the first round of submissions.

Outcomes of the first round: There were 382 students which participated across 124 teams from 51 institutions. These teams participated from all regions across India and had a maximum of four members per team. Each team had a faculty mentor as well.

The submissions for HP Innovate were all double blind reviewed and had more than 35 reviewers who assessed the submissions. Based on initial assessment, the top ten themes were invited to present their work. The top three teams won HP hardware such as tablet PCs and iPAQs. The winning team was taken to Palo Alto for interaction with HP Labs researchers. The Indo-US Science and Technology Forum in India supported the visit of the HP Innovate winning team's trip to the U.S.

The winning teams were also provided an opportunity to showcase their work in the "Labs to Market" session of EmTech, a prestigious event of Technology Review which was hosted in 2009. The teams had an opportunity to share their work with venture capitalists and other technology firms and institutions.

CONCLUSION: FROM SPEED-DATING
TO LASTING RELATIONSHIPS

Is innovation manageable? This candid question is asked in (Haour, 2004). At the conclusion of this paper it would seem that the answer should be positive rather than negative. A massive and impressive global innovation system is at work today to train the technology professionals, to launch and cultivate ambitious public research programs, and to build more relationships between industry and academia. The recent history of technology progress has shown that managed innovation can score and is likely to score impressive successes. On the other hand it will remain important to keep enough flexibility in the system to encourage and benefit from more chaotic innovation, such as those that happened in the past.

This paper has described several aspects of the organized innovation when it comes to the collaboration between hi tech industry and academia, including in the context of public research programs. Methods and processes are today available and well practised to make this dating process happen. Certainly, this does not always predict the outcome and success of the relationship, and whether this relationship will be closer to speed-dating than to a more lasting one. But at least the steps described may help to organize the intention of the industry-academia relationship and create a positive environment for it.

An interesting next step could be to explore how joint innovation could be further used to work on today's grand challenges and problems. This approach has been pioneered by a few universities which have established specific dedicated centres, such as CITRIS at UC Berkeley (http://www.citris-uc.org/). It might be also interesting to explore how such approaches would facilitate the analysis of future technology trends in a similar way that this has been done for business (Schwarz, 1991).

REFERENCES

Books:

Bauer R., Collar, E. & Tang, V. (1992). *The Silverlake Project*. Oxford University Press.

Berkun, S. (2007). *The Myths of Innovation*. Sebastopol, CA: O'Reilly.

Chesbrough, H. (2003). *Open Innovation*. Harvard Business School Press.

Frascara, Jorge (Ed.) (2002). *Design and the Social Sciences: Making Connections*. London/New York: Taylor & Francis.

Friedman, T. (2006). *The World is Flat*. New York: Farrar, Strauss and Giroux.

Haour, G. (2004). *Resolving the Innovation Paradox*. New York: Palgrave Macmillan

Kaufman Foundation Report. (2009). America's Loss is the World's Gain, America's New Immigrant Entrepreneurs (Part IV). Authors: Vivek Wadhwa, AnnaLee Saxenian, Richard Freeman, Gary Gereffi & Alex Salkever.

Raymond, E. (1999). *The Cathedral & the Bazaar*. Sebastopol, CA: O'Reilly.

Robinson, A. & Stern, S. (1997). *Corporate Creativity*. San Francisco: Berrett-Koehler Publishers Inc.

Schwartz, P. (1991). *The Art of the Long View*. Doubleday (USA).

Taleb, N. N. (2007). *The Black Swan*. Penguin Group (USA).

Tapscott, D. & Williams, A. (2006). *Wikinomics, Portfolio*. Penguin Group (USA).

Van Doren, C. (1991). *A History of Knowledge*. Ballantines Books (USA).

Vietor, R. (2007). *How Countries Compete*. Harvard Business School Press.
Weber, L. E. & Duderstadt, J. J. (2006). *Universities and Business: Partnering for the Knowledge Society*. London, Paris, Geneva: Economica
Weber, L. E. & Duderstadt, J. J. (2008). *The Globalization of Higher Education*. London, Paris, Geneva: Economica.

Websites:

MIT demo: http://www.ted.com/talks/pattie_maes_demos_the_sixth_sense.html
Dspace Federation: www.dspace.org
CITRIS http://www.citris-uc.org/

CHAPTER 18

The Challenge of Establishing World-Class Research Universities in Developing Countries

Jamil Salmi [1]

INTRODUCTION

Preoccupations about university rankings reflect the general recognition that economic growth and global competitiveness are increasingly driven by knowledge and that universities play a key role in that context. Indeed, rapid advances in science and technology across a wide range of areas — from information and communication technologies (ICTs) to biotechnology to new materials — provide great potential for developing countries to accelerate and strengthen their economic development. The application of knowledge results in more efficient ways of producing goods and services and delivering them more effectively and at lower costs to a greater number of people.

Tertiary education plays a critical role in that context. It helps countries build globally competitive economies by developing a skilled, productive and flexible labour force and by creating, applying and spreading new ideas and technologies. A recent global study of patent generation has shown, for example, that universities and research institutes, rather than firms, drive scientific advances in biotechnology (Cookson, 2007). Tertiary education institutions

---

1 This article is derived from a book published in February 2009 under the title *The Challenge of Establishing World-Class Universities*, Washington D.C., The World Bank.

can also play a vital role in their local and regional economies (Yusuf & Nabeshima, 2007).

According to *Constructing Knowledge Societies*, the World Bank's latest policy report on the contribution of tertiary education to sustainable economic development (World Bank, 2002), high-performing tertiary education systems encompass a wide range of institutional models — not only research universities but also polytechnics, liberal arts colleges, short-duration technical institutes, community colleges, open universities and so forth — that together produce the variety of skilled workers and employees sought by the labour market. Each type of institution has an important role to play, and achieving a balanced development among the various components of the system is a major preoccupation of many governments.

Within the tertiary education system, research universities play a critical role in training the professionals, high-level specialists, scientists and researchers needed by the economy and in generating new knowledge in support of the national innovation system (World Bank, 2002). An increasingly pressing priority of many developing countries is therefore to ensure that their top universities are actually operating at the cutting edge of intellectual and scientific development.

The main objective of this chapter is to explore the challenges involved in setting up globally competitive research universities in developing countries that will be expected to compete effectively with the best of the best. Is there a pattern or template that might be followed to allow more rapid advancement to world-class status? To answer this question, the chapter starts by constructing an operational definition of a world-class university. It then outlines and analyses possible strategies and pathways for establishing such universities and identifies the multiple challenges, costs and risks associated with these approaches. It concludes by examining some lessons from recent and ongoing experiences to set up new research universities in developing countries.

WHAT DOES IT MEAN TO BE A WORLD-CLASS UNIVERSITY?

In the past decade, the term "world-class university" has become a catch-phrase, not simply for improving the quality of learning and research in tertiary education, but also, more importantly, for developing the capacity to compete in the global tertiary education marketplace through the acquisition, adaptation and creation of advanced knowledge. With governments keen on maximizing the returns on their investments in research universities, global standing is becoming an increasingly important concern for institutions around the world (Williams & Van Dyke, 2007).

Becoming a member of the exclusive group of world-class universities is not achieved by self-declaration; rather, elite status is conferred by the outside world on the basis of international recognition. Until recently, the process involved a subjective qualification, mostly that of reputation. For example, Ivy League universities in the United States (U.S.), such as Harvard, Yale, or Columbia; the Universities of Oxford and Cambridge in the United Kingdom (U.K.); and the University of Tokyo have traditionally been counted among the exclusive group of elite universities, but no direct and rigorous measure was available to substantiate their superior status in terms of outstanding results such as training of graduates, research output and technology transfer.

With the proliferation of league tables in the past few years, however, more systematic ways of identifying and classifying world-class universities have appeared (IHEP, 2007). Although most of the 45 best-known rankings purport to categorize universities within a given country, there have also been attempts to establish international rankings. The two most comprehensive international rankings, allowing for broad benchmark comparisons of institutions across national borders, are those prepared by the THES and Shanghai Jiao Tong University (SJTU). Table 1 shows the results of the 2008 THES and SJTU world rankings.

Table 1: Top 20 Universities in *THES* and SJTU World Rankings, 2008

Rank	THES (2008)	Rank	SJTU (2008)
1	Harvard University	1	Harvard University
2	Yale University	2	Stanford University
3	University of Cambridge	3	University of California, Berkeley
4	University of Oxford	4	University of Cambridge
5	California Institute of Technology	5	Massachusetts Institute of Technology (MIT)
6	Imperial College London	6	California Institute of Technology
7	University College London	7	Columbia University
8	University of Chicago	8	Princeton University
9	Massachusetts Institute of Technology (MIT)	9	University of Chicago
10	Columbia University	10	University of Oxford
11	University of Pennsylvania	11	Yale University
12	Princeton University	12	Cornell University
13	Duke University	13	University of California, Los Angeles
13	Johns Hopkins University	14	University of California, San Diego
15	Cornell University	15	University of Pennsylvania

Table 1 cont'd: Top 20 Universities in *THES* and SJTU World Rankings, 2008

Rank	THES (2008)	Rank	SJTU (2008)
16	Australian National University	16	University of Washington, Seattle
17	Stanford University	17	University of Wisconsin, Madison
18	University of Michigan	18	University of California, San Francisco
19	University of Tokyo	19	University of Tokyo
20	McGill University	20	Johns Hopkins University

Sources: THES 2008; SJTU 2008.

Notwithstanding the serious methodological limitations of any ranking exercise (Salmi & Saroyan, 2007), world-class universities are recognized in part for their superior outputs. They produce well-qualified graduates who are in high demand on the labour market; they conduct leading-edge research published in top scientific journals; and in the case of science-and-technology-oriented institutions, they contribute to technical innovations through patents and licences.

As illustrated by Table 1, most universities recognized as world-class originate from a very small number of countries, mostly Western. In fact, the University of Tokyo is the only non-U.S., non-U.K. university among the top 20 in the SJTU ranking. If one considers that there are only between 30 and 50 world-class universities in total, according to the SJTU ranking they all come from a small group of eight North American and Western European countries, Japan being again the only exception. *THES* has a slightly wider range of countries of origin among the top 50 universities (11 countries), including Hong Kong, China; New Zealand; and Singapore, besides the usual North American and Western European nations (Figure 1).

Figure 1: Geographical Distribution of World-Class Universities (Top 50 in 2008)

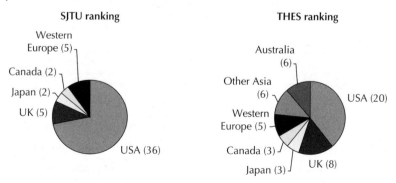

The few scholars who have attempted to define what world-class universities have that regular universities do not possess have identified a number of basic features, such as highly qualified faculty; excellence in research; quality teaching; high levels of government and nongovernment sources of funding; international and highly talented students; academic freedom; well-defined autonomous governance structures; and well-equipped facilities for teaching, research, administration and (often) student life (Altbach 2004; Khoon *et al.*, 2005; Niland, 2000, 2007).

In an attempt to propose a more manageable definition of world-class universities, this chapter makes the case that the superior results of these institutions — highly sought graduates, leading-edge research and dynamic technology transfer — can essentially be attributed to three complementary sets of factors: (a) a **high concentration of talent** (faculty and students), (b) **abundant resources** to offer a rich learning environment and to conduct advanced research, and (c) **favourable governance** features that encourage strategic vision, innovation and flexibility and that enable institutions to make decisions and to manage resources without being encumbered by bureaucracy.

Concentration of Talent

The first and perhaps foremost determinant of excellence is the presence of a critical mass of top students and outstanding faculty. World-class universities are able to select the best students and attract the most qualified professors and researchers.

In the sciences, being at the right university — the one where the most state-of-the-art research is being done in the best-equipped labs by the most visible scientists — is extremely important. George Stigler describes this as a snowballing process, where an outstanding scientist gets funded to do exciting research, attracts other faculty, then the best students — until a critical mass is formed that has an irresistible appeal to any young person entering the field.
Mihaly Csikszentmihalyi (1997).

This has always been the hallmark of the Ivy League universities in the United States or the Universities of Oxford and Cambridge in the United Kingdom. And it is also a feature of the newer world-class universities, such as the National University of Singapore (NUS) or Tsinghua University in China.

Beijing's Tsinghua University said last month it would increase the number of awards this year. Students with high scores, such as champions of each province and winners of international student academic competitions, will be entitled to scholarships of up to 40,000 yuan ($5,700), more than double that of last year.
University World News (UWN) (2008a).

One corollary of this observation is that tertiary education institutions in countries where there is little internal mobility of students and faculty are at risk of academic inbreeding. Indeed, universities that rely principally on their own undergraduates to continue into graduate programs or that hire principally their own graduates to join the teaching staff are not likely to be at the leading edge of intellectual development. A 2007 survey of European universities found an inverse correlation between endogamy in faculty hiring and research performance: the universities with the highest degree of endogamy had the lowest research results (Aghion et al., 2008).

It is also difficult to maintain high selectivity in institutions with rapidly growing student enrolment and fairly open admission policies. The huge size of the leading universities of Latin American countries such as México or Argentina — the Universidad Nacional Autónoma de México (Autonomous University of México, or UNAM) has 190,418 students, and the University of Buenos Aires (UAB) has 279,306 — is certainly a major factor in explaining why these universities have failed to enter the top league, despite having a few excellent departments and research centers that are undoubtedly world-class. At the other extreme, Beijing University maintained its overall enrollment at less than 20,000 until the early 2000s and even today has no more than 30,000 students.

World-class universities also tend to have a high proportion of carefully selected graduate students, reflecting their strength in research and the fact that graduate students are closely involved in the research activities of these institutions.

The international dimension is becoming increasingly important in determining the configuration of these elite institutions. This enables them to attract the most talented people, no matter where they come from, and open themselves to new ideas and approaches. At the University of Cambridge, 18% of the students are from outside the U.K. or European Union (E.U.) countries. The U.S. universities ranked at the top of the global surveys also show sizable proportions of foreign academic staff. For instance, the proportion of international faculty at Harvard University, including medical academic staff, is approximately 30%. By contrast, only 7% of all researchers in France are foreign academics. Unquestionably, the world's best universities enrol and employ large numbers of foreign students and faculty in their search for the most talented.

Abundant Resources

Abundance of resources is the second element that characterizes most world-class universities, in response to the huge costs involved in running a complex, research-intensive university. These universities have four main sources of financing: government budget funding for operational expenditures and research, contract research from public organizations and private firms, the financial returns generated by endowments and gifts, and tuition fees.

In Western Europe, public funding is by far the principal source of finance for teaching and research, although the top U.K. universities have some endowment funds, and "top-up fees" have been introduced in recent years. In Asia, the National University of Singapore, which became a private corporation in 2006, has been the most successful institution in terms of substantial endowment funding. It has managed to build up a sizable portfolio of US$774 million through effective fund-raising, making it richer than any British university after Cambridge and Oxford. The United States and, to a lesser extent, Japan, have thriving private research universities.

A comparative analysis of the SJTU rankings of U.S. and Western European universities confirms that level of expenditures is one of the key determinants of performance. Globally, total spending on tertiary education (public and private) represents 3.3% of gross domestic product (GDP) in the United States versus only 1.3% in the EU25 countries. Per student spending is about US$54,000 in the United States, compared with US$13,500 in the European Union (Aghion *et al.*, 2008). Similarly, there are large spending variations among European universities that are correlated with the rankings results of the respective countries. The United Kingdom and Switzerland have relatively well-funded universities and achieve the highest country scores in terms of rankings, while universities from the Southern European countries, including France and Germany, have lower ranking scores associated with low levels of funding (Aghion *et al.*, 2007). The availability of abundant resources creates a virtuous circle that allows the concerned institutions to attract even more top professors and researchers.

Favourable Governance

The third dimension concerns the overall regulatory framework, the competitive environment, and the degree of academic and managerial autonomy that universities enjoy. The *Economist* (2005) referred to the tertiary education system in the United States as "the best in the world" and attributed this success not only to its wealth but also to its relative independence from the state, the competitive spirit that encompasses every aspect of it, and its ability to make academic work and production relevant and useful to society. The report observed that the environment in which universities operate fosters competitiveness, unrestrained scientific inquiry, critical thinking, innovation and creativity. Moreover, institutions that have complete autonomy are also more flexible because they are not bound by cumbersome bureaucracies and externally imposed standards, even in light of the legitimate accountability mechanisms that do bind them.

The comparative study of European and U.S. universities mentioned earlier also found that governance was, along with funding, the other main determinant of rankings. "European universities suffer from poor governance, insufficient autonomy and often perverse incentives" (Aghion et al., 2007). A subsequent paper reporting on a survey of European universities found that research performance was positively linked to the degree of autonomy of the universities in the sample, especially with regard to budget management, the ability to hire faculty and staff, and the freedom to set salaries (Aghion et al., 2008). With respect to the composition of university boards, the report concludes that "having significant outside representation on the board may be a necessary condition to ensure that dynamic reforms taking into account long-term institutional interests can be decided upon without undue delay."

The autonomy elements outlined above are necessary, though not sufficient, to establish and maintain world-class universities. Other crucial governance features are needed, such as inspiring and persistent leaders; a strong strategic vision of where the institution is going; a philosophy of success and excellence; and a culture of constant reflection, organizational learning and change.

Alignment of Factors

Finally, it is important to stress that it is the combination of these three sets of features — concentration of talent, abundant funding and appropriate governance — that makes the difference. The dynamic interaction among these three groups of factors is the distinguishing characteristic of high-ranking universities (as illustrated by Figure 2). The results of the recent survey of European universities mentioned above confirm that funding and governance influence performance together. They indicate clearly that the higher-ranked universities tend to enjoy increased management autonomy, which, in turn, increases the efficiency of spending and results in higher research productivity (Aghion et al., 2008). A study of the influence of governance arrangements on the research output of public universities in the U.S. arrives at the same conclusion. When competitive research funding is available, the more autonomous universities tend to be more successful in producing patents (Aghion et al., 2009).

Having an appropriate governance framework without sufficient resources or the ability to attract top talent does not work either. Similarly, just investing money in an institution or making it very selective in terms of student admission is not sufficient to build a world-class university, as illustrated by the case of Brazil's top university, the University of São Paulo (USP). Brazil is the 5th-most-populated nation and the 10th-largest economy on the planet, it is among the six largest producers of cars in the world, it has world-class companies such as Embraer and Aracruz Celulose, but there is no Brazilian university among the 100 top-ranked universities in the world.

Figure 2: Characteristics of a World-Class University (WCU): Alignment of Key Factors

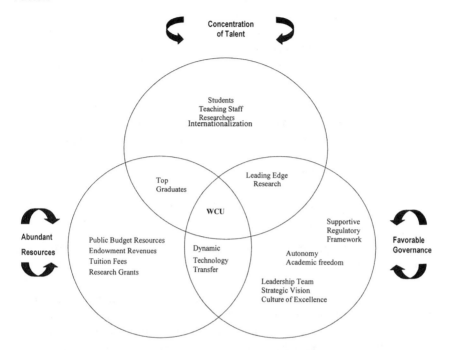

Source: Elaborated by Jamil Salmi

PATHS TO TRANSFORMATION

Two complementary perspectives need to be considered in examining how to establish world-class research universities. The first dimension, of an external nature, concerns the role of government and the resources that can be made available to enhance the stature of institutions. The second dimension is internal. It has to do with the individual institutions themselves and the necessary evolution and steps that they need to take to transform themselves into world-class research universities.

The Role of Government

In the past, the role of government in nurturing the growth of world-class universities was not a critical factor. The history of the Ivy League universities in the United States reveals that, by and large, they grew to prominence as a result of incremental progress, rather than by deliberate government intervention. Similarly, the Universities of Oxford and Cambridge evolved over the centuries of their own volition, with variable levels of public funding, but with considerable autonomy in terms of governance, definition of mission, and direction. Today, however, it is unlikely that a world-class university can be rapidly created without a favourable policy environment and direct public initiative and support, if only because of the high costs involved in setting up advanced research facilities and capacities.

International experience shows that three basic strategies can be followed to establish world-class research universities:

- Governments could consider upgrading a small number of existing universities that have the potential of excelling (picking winners).
- Governments could encourage a number of existing institutions to merge and transform into a new university that would achieve the type of synergies corresponding to a world-class research institution (hybrid formula).
- Governments could create new world-class universities from scratch (clean-slate approach).

Upgrading Existing Institutions. One of the main benefits of this first approach is that the costs can be significantly less than those of building new institutions from scratch. This is the strategy followed by China since the early 1980s, with a sequence of carefully targeted reforms and investment programs. Indeed, Beijing University and Tsinghua University, China's top two universities, have been granted special privileges by the national authorities, allowing them to select the best students from every province before any other university, much to the consternation of the other leading universities around the country.

But this approach is unlikely to succeed in countries where the governance structure and arrangements that have historically prevented the emergence of world-class universities are not drastically revised. A comparison of the experiences of Malaysia and Singapore can serve to illustrate this point. Because Singapore was initially one of the provinces of the Malaysian Kingdom during the first few years following independence from the British, the contrasting stories of the University of Malaya and of the National University of Singapore (NUS) can be quite instructive, given their common cultural and colonial origins.

At independence, the University of Malaya operated as a two-campus university, one in Kuala Lumpur and the other in Singapore. The former evolved into the flagship University of Malaya from the very beginning, and the other became the University of Singapore, which merged with Nanyang University in 1980 to create NUS. By all global ranking measures, NUS today functions as a true world-class university (ranked 19th by the 2006 *THES*), while the University of Malaya struggles as a second-tier research university (ranked 192nd). In examining the different evolutionary paths of these two institutions, several factors appear to be constraining the University of Malaya's capacity to improve and innovate as effectively as NUS: affirmative action and restrictive admission policies, lower levels of financial support, and tightly controlled immigration regulations regarding foreign faculty.

The affirmative action policy implemented by the Malaysian government in favour of the children of the Malay majority population (*Bumiputras*) has significantly opened up opportunities for that segment of the population (Tierney & Sirat, 2008).

But the downside of these equity policies was that they prevented the university from being very selective in its student admissions to target the best and brightest in the country. Large numbers of academically qualified Chinese and Indian students, in particular, were unable to attend Malaysia's best universities and had to seek tertiary education abroad, thereby removing important talent from Malaysia. By contrast, the proportion of foreign students at NUS is 20% at the undergraduate level and 43% at the graduate level.

NUS is also able to mobilize nearly twice as many financial resources as the University of Malaya (US$205 million annual budget versus US$118 million, respectively) through a combination of cost sharing, investment revenue, fund-raising and government resources. The success of NUS's fund-raising efforts is largely the result of the generous matching-grant program set up by the government in the late 1990s as part of the Thinking Schools, Learning Nation Initiative, which provided a three-to-one matching at the beginning and is now down to one-to-one. As a result, the annual per student expenditures at NUS and the University of Malaya were US$6,300 and US$4,053, respectively, in 2006.

Finally, in Malaysia, on one hand, civil service regulations and a rigid financial framework make it difficult, if not impossible, to provide competitive compensation packages to attract the most competent professors and researchers, particularly foreign faculty. NUS, on the other hand, is not bound by similar legal constraints. It is therefore able to bring in top researchers and professors from all over the world, pay a global market rate for them, and provide performance incentives to stimulate competition and to retain the best and the brightest. Indeed, a good number of Malaysia's top researchers have been recruited by NUS.

Merging Existing Institutions. The second possible approach to building up a world-class research university consists of promoting mergers among existing institutions. In China, for example, a number of mergers have taken place to consolidate existing institutions. Beijing Medical University merged with Beijing University in 2000; similarly, in Shanghai, Fudan University merged with a medical university, and Zhejiang University was created out of the merger of five universities.

In 2004, in the United Kingdom, the Victoria University of Manchester (VUM) and the University of Manchester Institute of Science and Technology (UMIST) merged, creating the largest university in the United Kingdom, with the purposefully stated goal of being "top 25 by 2015" (http://www.manchester.ac.uk/research/about/strategy/).

The government of the Russian Federation is also relying on amalgamation as a key policy within its overall strategy of developing elite research universities. In 2007, two pilot federal universities were set up by merging existing institutions in Rostov-on-Don in southern Russia and in the Siberian city of Krasnoyarsk. The two new institutions will also receive additional funding to support efforts to allow them to recruit highly qualified researchers and equip state-of-the-art laboratories (Holdsworth, 2008).

The great advantage of mergers is that they can result in stronger institutions able to capitalize on the new synergies that their combined human and financial resources may generate. But mergers can also be risky, potentially aggravating problems instead of resolving them.

The newly consolidated institution could suffer because of clashing institutional cultures. It has become clear, for example, that the previously mentioned merger between VUM and UMIST has not been as successful as expected or originally perceived. Currently acknowledging a £30 million budget deficit and the likelihood of up to 400 jobs lost on the campus, the University of Manchester has had immediate experience with the complexities of merging (Qureshi, 2007). Among the main problems encountered are duplication of staff and curricular offerings, the political challenges of engendering support for the merger by making promises that have proven detrimental to keep, and the short-term absorption of labour contracts and institutional debt.

Creating New Universities. In countries where institutional habits, cumbersome governance structures and bureaucratic management practices prevent traditional universities from being innovative, creating new universities may be the best approach, provided that it is possible to staff them with people not influenced by the culture of traditional universities and provided that financial resources are not a constraint. New institutions can emerge from the private sector, or governments can allow new public institutions to operate under a more favourable regulatory framework. One of the earlier success stories in that respect was the establishment of the Indian Institutes of Technology, which, in past decades, have gradually risen to world-class status.

Kazakhstan is a country intent on following this path as it seeks to make its economy less dependent on oil and more competitive overall. The government has decided to set up a new international university in Astana. The plan is that this university will follow a highly innovative multidisciplinary curriculum designed in cooperation with leading foreign universities. In the same vein, the government of Saudi Arabia announced in late 2007 its plans for a US$3 billion graduate research university, King Abdullah University of Science and Technology, which would operate outside the purview of the Ministry of Higher Education to allow for greater management autonomy and aca-demic freedom than the regular universities of the kingdom enjoy.

Time is an important dimension that also needs to be factored into the stra-tegic plan of any aspiring world-class university. However, governments are often under pressure to show immediate results, running the risk of taking pre-cipitous decisions and overseeing the fact that the establishment of a strong research university is a long-term process. Building ultra-modern facilities before adequately defining programs, curricula and pedagogical practices that are fully aligned or hiring star researchers from overseas without matching them with a critical mass of national faculty are common mistakes. Develop-ing a culture of excellence in research and teaching does not happen from one day to the next, it requires proper sequencing of interventions, careful balance among the various quantitative and qualitative objectives of the project, and a long-term view.

The creation of new institutions may have the side benefit of stimulating existing ones into becoming more responsive to the global competitive envi-ronment. In several countries, the emergence of high-quality private institu-tions has provoked the existing public universities into becoming more stra-tegically focused. In Russia, for example, the creation of the Higher School of Economics and of the Moscow School of Social and Economic Sciences in the 1990s pressured the Department of Economics at the State University of Mos-cow to revamp its curriculum and get more actively involved in international exchanges.

Strategies at the Institutional Level

The establishment of a world-class research university requires, above all, strong leadership, a bold vision of the institution's mission and goals, and a clearly articulated strategic plan to translate the vision into concrete targets and programs. Universities that aspire to better results engage in an objective assessment of their strengths and areas for improvement, set new stretch goals, and design and implement a renewal plan that can lead to improved perfor-mance. By contrast, many institutions are complacent in their outlook, lack an ambitious vision of a better future, and continue to operate as they have in the past, ending up with a growing performance gap compared with that of their national or international competitors.

Recent research on university leadership suggests that in the case of top research universities, the best-performing institutions have leaders who com-bine good managerial skills and a successful research career (Goodall, 2006). To be able to develop an appropriate vision for the future of the university and to implement this vision in an effective manner, the university leader needs to fully understand the core agenda of the institution and be able to apply the vision with the necessary operational skills.

A crucial element of the vision is the selection of niche domains of research toward which the institution will seek to build and maximize its comparative advantage. In that respect, it is important to underline that a research university — even a world-class university — most likely cannot excel in all areas. Harvard University, widely recognized as the number one institution of higher learning in the world, is not the best-ranked university in all disciplines. Its strengths are especially noted in economics, medical sciences, education, political science, law, business studies, English and history.

CONCLUSION

The highest-ranked universities are the ones that make significant contributions to the advancement of knowledge through research, teach with the most innovative curricula and pedagogical methods under the most conducive circumstances, make research an integral component of undergraduate teaching and produce graduates who stand out because of their success in intensely competitive arenas during their education and (more important) after graduation.

There is no universal recipe or magic formula for "making" a world-class research university. National contexts and institutional models vary widely. Therefore, each country must choose, from among the various possible pathways, a strategy that plays to its strengths and resources. International experience provides a few lessons regarding the key features of such universities — high concentrations of talent, abundance of resources, and flexible governance arrangements — and successful approaches to move in that direction, from upgrading or merging existing institutions to creating new universities altogether.

Furthermore, the transformation of the university system cannot take place in isolation. A long-term vision for creating world-class universities — and its implementation — should be closely articulated with (a) the country's overall economic and social development strategy, (b) ongoing changes and planned reforms at the lower levels of the education system, and (c) plans for the development of other types of tertiary education institutions to build an integrated system of teaching, research and technology-oriented institutions.

Finally, the building pressures and momentum behind the push for world-class research universities must be examined within the proper context to avoid over-dramatization of the value and importance of world-class institutions and distortions in resource allocation patterns within national tertiary education systems. Even in a global knowledge economy, where every nation, both industrial and developing, is seeking to increase its share of the economic pie, the hype surrounding world-class institutions far exceeds the need and capacity for many systems to benefit from such advanced education and research opportunities, at least in the short term.

REFERENCES

Aghion, P., Dewatripont, M., Hoxby, C., Mas-Colell, A. & Sapir, A. (2009). "The Governance and Performance of Research Universities: Evidence from Europe and the U.S." National Bureau of Economic Research. Working Paper No. 14851, April 2009.

Aghion, P., Dewatripont, M., Hoxby, C., Mas-Colell, A. & Sapir, A. (2008). "Higher aspirations: An agenda for reforming European universities". Bruegel Blueprint Series. Number 5.

Aghion, P., Dewatripont, M., Hoxby, C., Mas-Colell, A. & Sapir, A. (2007). "Why reform Europe's Universities?" Bruegel Policy Brief. Issue 2007/04. September 2007.

Altbach, Philip G. (January-February 2004). The Costs and Benefits of World-Class Universities. *Academe*. Retrieved 10 April 2006 from www.aaup.org.

Cookson, C. (2007). Universities drive biotech advancement. *The Financial Times*, 6 May 2007.

Csikszentmihalyi, M. (1997). *Creativity: Flow and the Psychology of Discovery and Invention*. New York: Harper Collins.

Donoghue, S. & Kennerley, M. (2008). "Our Journey Towards World Class Leading Transformational Strategic Change". *Higher Education Management and Policy*. Paris: OECD. Forthcoming.

Economist, The. (2005). "Secrets of success". London: 10 September 2005, Vol. 376, Issue 8443, p. 6.

Goodall, A. (2006). The Leaders of the World's Top 100 Universities, *International Higher Education*. Center for International Higher Education. Number 42, Winter 2006, pp. 3-4.

Harman, G. & Harman, K. (2008). Strategic mergers of strong institutions to enhance competitive advantage. *Higher Education Policy*, 21, pp. 99-121.

Holdsworth, N. (2008). "Russia: Super League of 'Federal' Universities". *University World News*. 26 October 2008.

Institute for Higher Education Policy — IHEP (2007). College and University Ranking Systems: Global Perspectives and American Challenges. Washington D.C.

Khoon, K. A. (2005). Hallmark of a World-Class University. College Student Journal. Retrieved 10 April 2007, from http://findarticles.com/p/articles/mi_m0FCR/is_4_39/ai_n16123684.

Levin, M. H., Jeong, D. W. & Ou, D. (2006). What is a World Class University? Paper prepared for the 2006 Conference of the Comparative & International Education Society. Retrieved 12 April 2007 from www.tc.columbia.edu/centers/coce/pdf_files/c12.pdf.

Niland, J. (3 February 2000). The challenge of building world-class universities in the Asian region. Retrieved 10 April 2006 from http://www.onlineopinion.com.au/view.asp?article=997.

Niland, J. (2007). The Challenge of Building World-Class Universities. In J. Sadlak & N. C. Liu (eds.), *The World Class University and Ranking: Aiming Beyond Status*. Bucharest: UNESCO-CEPES.

Qureshi, Yakub. (9 March 2007). 400 university jobs could go. *Manchester Evening News*. Retrieved 20 May 2007 from http://www.manchestereveningnews.co.uk/news/education/s/1001/1001469_400_university_jobs_could_go.html.

Salmi, J. & Saroyan, A. (2007). League Tables as Policy Instruments: Uses and Misuses. *Higher Education Management and Policy*. OECD, Paris. 19 (2).

Salmi, J. (2009). The Challenge of Establishing World-Class Universities. Washington D.C.: The World Bank.

Shanghai Jiao Tong University. (2007). Academic Ranking of World Universities 2007. Retrieved 30 March 2008 from http://ed.sjtu.edu.cn/ranking2006.htm.

The World Bank. (2002). *Constructing Knowledge Societies: New Challenges for Tertiary Education*. Washington, D.C.: The World Bank.

THES. (2007). The Times Higher Education World University Rankings 2007. Retrieved 30 March 2008 from http://www.thes.co.uk/worldrankings/.

Tierney, W. & Sirat, M. (2008). "Challenges Facing Malaysian Higher Education". *International Higher Education*. Boston: Number 53, Fall 2008, pp. 23-24.

University World News (2008). China: Growing competition for top students. Retrieved 14 June 2008 from http://www.universityworldnews.com

Williams, R. & Van Dyke, N. (2007). Measuring the international standing of universities with an application to Australian Universities. *Higher Education*. 53, pp. 819-841.

Yusuf, S. & Nabeshima, K. (2007). *How Universities Promote Economic Growth*. Washington D.C.: The World Bank.

PART V

•••••••••••••

Paradigm Shifts

CHAPTER 19

On Innovation Strategies: an Asian Perspective

Nam P. Suh

INTRODUCTION

Innovation has become the buzzword of the 21st century and even more so now after the current economic meltdown, as nations around the world have the enormous task of rebuilding their economies. It is generally agreed that innovation refers to the process of converting an idea, invention or scientific discovery into commercially or publicly successful products, processes, services or systems that improve the way we do things.

Societal needs often spark innovation. Today, job creation, economic growth and solutions to urgent problems related to energy, environment, water and sustainability (EEWS) require innovative solutions. Some of the needs for innovation are common to all nations, but specific issues entailed in these problems can be regional in scope.

Innovation is particularly imperative to the future economic and social health of the industrialized nations of Asia. Except for China, these nations have limited natural resources. Their economies have depended on the export of manufactured goods, including ships, cars, steel, semiconductors, computers and television sets. Their trade surplus over the past decade is a testimony to their global dominance in manufacturing. Yet, these countries did not invent or innovate many of the products for which they are known. Rather their competitive strengths are derived from the quality of their products and manufacturing technologies.

This paper reviews the current status of innovation and innovation-related activities in China, Japan and Korea, with a greater emphasis on Korea. This paper will dissect the innovation strategies, identify important issues that affect innovation and discuss possible means of strengthening the innovation process.

There are many questions related to innovation we should answer. In order to provide a common metric for understanding innovation strategies and processes, innovation strategies will be discussed based on a theory of innovation in order to provide a generalized conceptual framework (Suh, 2009).

NATURE OF INNOVATION

The literature on innovation is rich with historical examples, case studies, ad hoc claims, and generalizations (OTA, 1984; Drucker, 1985; Utterback, 1996; Branscomb et al., 2001; Gray, 2004; Nelsen, 2005, Scotchmer, 2006; Welfens et al., 2008).

To understand the nature of innovation, we need to answer some basic questions, such as:

- Why aren't there innovation hubs in Kansas City, Missouri, USA?
- Why are there only a few innovation hubs in the world?
- Why aren't there major innovation hubs — similar to those in the Silicon Valley or Boston, U.S. — in Europe and Asia?
- What do we have to do create an innovation hub?
- What should educational institutions do to generate people who can innovate?

The ability to innovate depends on many specific factors, such as GDP, GDP per capita, expenditure for R&D, the state of industrial development, the quality of education, cultural tolerance for risk taking and politics. However, innovation is not a result of a random process, although sometimes they follow an unpredictable path. Depending on how it is done, the effectiveness and efficacy of R&D investment in creating disruptive innovations can vary between different nations and even between different regions of a country. This paper will attempt to answer the questions posed above and generalize the requisite conditions for innovation based on the three laws of innovation (Suh, 2009).

THREE LAWS OF INNOVATION

The theory of innovation (Suh, 2009) states that there are three laws that govern the innovation process. These laws are based on the three requisites that are essential in innovation processes: innovation continuum, nucleation of innovation hubs (or equivalent entity) and the dominance of the nucleation rate over the diffusion rate.

The three laws of innovation are stated as follows:

The First Law: For innovation to occur, there cannot be any missing steps or elements in the innovation continuum.

The Second Law: Innovation occurs more readily around an innovation hub, which nucleates when sufficient innovation activities are present to create a nucleate that is larger than the critical size needed for stability and to overcome the activation energy barrier for innovation.

The third law: For innovation hubs to nucleate, the nucleation rate of innovation in a region must be greater than the rate at which innovative ideas, people and financial resource can diffuse or move away from the region.

BASIS OF THE INNOVATION LAWS

Definition of Innovation Continuum?

An innovation is a result of undertaking many steps or activities. Initially there may be many ideas for research or many inventions, one of which ultimately becomes a successful innovation (in the form of product, process, systems and service). The essential steps are different depending on the nature of innovation, but some of the common steps may be listed as follows (Suh, 2009):

1. Identification of the need.
2. Basic research.
3. Creation of ideas.
4. Demonstration of the feasibility.
5. Testing of commercial viability.
6. Finding an "angel" who will be willing to fund #4 and #5.
7. Raising venture capital or finding a large company that is willing to develop the idea.
8. Creation or identification of a venture company that can manufacture and sell the product.
9. Hiring talented people for all functions the company must perform.
10. Raising capital for the new venture firm through initial public offering.
11. Selling of the venture company.

These (or equivalent) steps form an innovation continuum from the inception of an idea to its transformation to commercial products. Some of these steps may not be required when it is done in a large company. When one or more of the essential steps of the innovation continuum are missing, the probability of success for innovation decreases significantly.

When the first law of innovation regarding the innovation continuum is not satisfied, innovation cannot proceed. Even after the first law is satisfied, the second law of innovation, which deals with nucleation of an innovation hub, must also be satisfied.

Nucleation of Innovation Hubs

The fact that all the steps of the innovation continuum are in place does not guarantee the nucleation of an innovation. The existence of an innovation continuum is necessary, but it is not sufficient. Innovation occurs more readily if there is an existing innovation hub or a large industrial complex that is willing to develop new ideas. For example, Boston is an innovation hub for biotech. It is easier to start a biotech company in Boston than elsewhere. The large shipbuilding industry of Korea can also be an innovation hub for marine-related products.

One way of enabling innovation is to nucleate an innovation hub. Another way is to induce a heterogeneous nucleation around an existing innovation hub. Heterogeneous nucleation of innovation around an existing hub, à la Silicon Valley, is much easier than homogenous nucleation of a new hub.

In the absence of a pre-existing innovation hub, an innovation hub must be established first through homogenous nucleation. Once an innovation hub exists, heterogeneous nucleation of new innovations can occur around the existing hub. When there is a large industrial base, it can act as a hub and heterogeneous nucleation of innovation can occur around the industry.

The nucleation of innovation hubs is analogous to the nucleation of rain droplets in the atmosphere. When rain droplets form by condensation of water vapour in the absence of any existing particle, it is called homogeneous nucleation. When there are particles, such as previously nucleated water particles or impurity particles in air, the condensation forms around the existing particle by heterogeneous nucleation. Heterogeneous nucleation on an existing particle is energetically more favoured. Therefore, heterogeneous nucleation occurs at a higher rate than homogeneous nucleation.

For homogeneous nucleation to occur, the nucleated entity (e.g., a water droplet formed from the vapour phase) must be larger than a critical size to be stable. If it is smaller than the critical size, the nucleate will go back to its original state, i.e., a water droplet smaller than a critical size evaporates back to vapour. It is difficult to nucleate an innovation hub with only a limited number of innovations. It is much easier if there are tens or hundreds of ideas and activities available for innovation.

When a nucleate formed is larger than the critical size, it grows because the vapour condenses by heterogeneous nucleation on existing droplets rather than nucleating a new droplet. This process makes the nucleate that formed first grow faster than the one formed later. This is the reason why it is easier to nucleate an innovative idea around an existing hub rather than homogeneously nucleate a new one.

This discussion on homogeneous versus heterogeneous nucleation implies that once China, Japan and Korea form innovation hubs, the subsequent innovation processes in these countries will accelerate. In other words, it is difficult to get the innovation hub started, but once it is established, it is fairly easy to sustain the generation of innovations by heterogeneous nucleation. Then the number of innovations may explode exponentially, increasing new innovations.

To better understand the innovation process, the nucleation rate of innovations may be modeled as a rate equation:

$$\frac{dI}{dt} = I_o f_I \exp\left(\frac{-\Delta G}{bH}\right)$$

where I is occurrence of innovation, t is time, the product $I_o f$ is a constant with a dimension of "innovation per unit time", ΔG is the activation energy that needs to be overcome to innovate, and the product bH is a constant that represents the overall energy of innovation activities. The exponential function represents the probability of creating an innovation. ΔG of homogeneous nucleation is larger than that of heterogeneous nucleation, indicating that the creation of new innovation hubs is inherently more difficult than a heterogeneous nucleation on an existing site. Based on this rate model and an energy argument, we can show that there is a critical size of a nucleate below which the innovation hub cannot form.

The second law of innovation may be stated as follows:

The rate of innovation is greater when there are more innovative activities that can overcome the activation energy barrier for innovation. (Corollary: Innovation occurs more readily around an innovation hub, which nucleates when the initial nucleate size exceeds the critical size needed for stability and if the innovative activities can overcome the activation energy barrier.)

Diffusion of Innovative Ideas vs Nucleation of Innovation

Once an innovation hub exists, it tends to grow as new innovative ideas from other regions, as well as from the near-by regions, diffuse to the site and nucleate by heterogeneous nucleation. Ideas and people with innovative ideas can move to an existing hub rather than nucleating a new innovation hub. Therefore, there is a competition between homogeneous nucleation of an innovation hub and the diffusion of ideas and people away from a region with no hub to an existing innovation hub. That is the reason why it is difficult to create new innovation hubs like Boston. About 50% of the revenue of Silicon Valley companies is from Stanford spin-off companies, but, of more than 1,000 companies that were spun-out from Stanford University, only one out of 20 companies used the technologies that came out of Stanford. Many ideas came to Silicon Valley from other regions (Byer, 2006).

In Asia, there are no innovation hubs that are equivalent to Boston or Silicon Valley. Unless nations in Asia can create innovation hubs or provide an equivalent site for heterogeneous nucleation, people with innovative ideas will emigrate to California or Boston.

In countries where large companies dominate the industry and control a large fraction of GDP, it is sometimes much more difficult for entrepreneurs to establish innovative companies. In these countries, creative people work for a large company that provides job security rather than start their own business or work for new venture firms.

The third law of innovation may be stated as follows:

To nucleate an innovation hub in a given region, the nucleation rate of innovation in the region must be greater than the rate at which innovative ideas, creative people and financial resources can diffuse away from the region to an existing hub.

MANUFACTURING, ECONOMY AND INNOVATIONS IN ASIA

During the past several decades, four Asian nations — Japan, Korea, Taiwan and China —have successfully developed their national economies by manufacturing well-established products competitively in large volumes for the worldwide market. To become major manufacturing nations, they have adopted and improved existing technological paradigms and methods rather than innovating new products or systems that are uniquely of their own.

In 2009, people in countries across the world are living in uncertain times because of the unprecedented and largely unanticipated global economic turmoil. Asia is no exception. The current economic crisis poses opportunities as well as risks for China, Japan and Korea. Their ability to innovate will affect the future development and competitiveness of these countries, which will augment their traditional strength in manufacturing.

The overall impact of the current economic downturn appears to be milder in Asia than in the United States. Nevertheless, it has had major impact on economies of the Asian countries. China has lost 20 million jobs and its unemployment rate in 2008 reached 9.0%. In January 2009, its export decreased by 17.5% year-on-year to US$90.45 billion and its imports by 43.1% to US$51.34 billion. Korea has lost jobs as well, although to a less extent than many other countries; its unemployment rate in February 2009 was 3.5%. The Korean currency had lost as much as 60% of its value relative to the U.S. dollar within a few months upon the collapse of the stock market. Since then, it has recovered; as of June 2009, it is down about 25%. The depreciation of the Korean currency has improved the global competitiveness of Korean products. In December 2008, exports from Korea fell 17.4% to US$27.29 billion, while imports dropped 21.5% to US$26.62 billion. On the other hand, the Japanese currency appreciated in value, which has devastated their export industry. Its industrial production decreased by 30.1% from

January 2008 to January 2009. The unemployment rate in Japan stood at 4.1% in January 2009. All three countries are trying to revive their economy by injecting liquidity into their banking systems, increasing domestic consumption and the export of goods, creating jobs and stabilizing the real estate market.

Innovation has been a hot topic in Korea. In 2008, the Korean government created a planning commission (chaired by the author) to identify technologies and industries that could become "new economic growth engines". Some 360 experts participated in the planning exercise and identified 21 technologies. In September 2008, the government adopted 17 of these fields as the priority areas for R&D investment by the public and the private sector.

Two of these projects — On-Line Electric Vehicle (OLEV) and Mobile Harbor (MH) — are being led by KAIST. These products may become paradigm-shifting major innovations, if successful.

STATUS OF INNOVATION IN KOREA, JAPAN AND CHINA

China, Japan and Korea are similar in that they do not have innovation hubs. However, there are significant differences amongst them in terms of GDP per capita, R&D investment, technological levels and political structure (OECD, 2008).

Korea

Korea is a leading nation in many industrial sectors: shipbuilding, DRAM, cell phones, LCD displays, automobiles, desalination, nuclear power plants and steel. Its IT infrastructure is one of the most advanced among all nations. Yet Korea cannot claim to be one of the most innovative countries in the world.

The relative lack of innovation in Korea cannot be attributed to its R&D spending. In 2007, Korea invested 3.47% of its GDP in R&D, the public sector expenditure being 26.1% of the R&D investment. In 2008, about 5% of the government budget was for R&D. As a percentage of its GDP, its R&D spending is about the same as Japan, and its educational spending per capita is comparable as well, although its GDP per capita is substantially less than that of Japan and much larger than that of China. Korea is increasing its R&D budget at a higher rate than many other countries. What Korea has to do is to increase the rate of innovation for the R&D investment made.

The Korean government has invested a significant amount of R&D funds in national laboratories and universities, and has created Science Park in Daejeon City, which is home to some 30 national laboratories, about an equal number of industrial research laboratories and KAIST. The Daedeok Science Park and its adjacent area have several thousand Ph.D.s. The question is why this area has not become an innovation hub.

The government has invested US$3 to US$4 billion per annum in the national laboratories in the Daejeon Science Park. This investment is comparable to the R&D investment made in the greater Boston area of the U.S. by the U.S. National Institute of Health (NIH), which was about US$ 2 billion in 2005 (Nelsen, 2005). This annual NIH investment has created about 350 biotech firms and 150 medical device companies in the Boston area. They employ about 30,000 people. The market cap of the top ten biotech companies was about US$85 billion in 2005. However, the comparable investment made in the Daejeon area has not yielded a comparable degree of innovations and financial returns. Why is there the difference between Boston and Daejeon?

The difference between Boston and Daejeon may be attributed to the fact that Boston satisfies the three laws of innovation, whereas Daejeon does not. Unlike Boston, Daejeon has many missing elements in its *innovation continuum* such as venture capital firms, easy access to the global market and global visibility. It has a limited number of venture capitalists and risk-takers who are willing to convert research results into innovations. Also the research institutes in the Daedeok Science Park might have chosen research projects to increase the number of publications rather than choosing challenging topics that address real societal needs. Also the R&D funding is too fragmented among different research institutes, supporting many small and diverse projects rather than developing systems solutions to satisfy real societal needs. Therefore, for Daejeon to become an innovation hub, it must fill in the missing steps of the innovation continuum and create innovative activities that can overcome the activation energy barrier for nucleation.

In education, which provides the basic foundation for innovation, Korea has been investing heavily and has done well (for example, Korean high school students rank near the top in math and science in the world.) In 2008, the Korean government spent 20% of its budget on education — 11% of which was for tertiary education and 88% for K-12 education. More than 84% of high school graduates go on to colleges and universities in Korea, which is just the inverse of the situation in Switzerland (Eichler, Chapter 8). Korea's K-12 educational system has been criticized for focusing too heavily on preparing students for college entrance examinations. Nearly 50% of Korea's investment in education is for private tutoring and cram schools.

In 1972, the Korean government created the Korea Advanced Institute of Science and Technology (KAIST) to educate scientists and engineers with advanced degrees to augment its investment in heavy industries. KAIST is now the leading university in Korea and is ascending in the ranking of world's best universities. Its engineering program was ranked to be the 34th in the world by the *London Times* supplement in 2008. KAIST has outstanding professors and excellent students. About 70% of KAIST students come from the 20 "Science High Schools" of Korea, which collectively produce about

2,000 graduates a year — academically the top 0.1% of all high school graduates. It also accepts nearly all of the graduates (about 140 a year) of the Korea Science Academy, known as the high school for genius. KAIST's Ph.D.s populate leading industrial firms and universities. KAIST is the home for many innovations such as humanoid robots, new materials, IT products, and others. To innovate major products and advance science and technology, KAIST has established internal research funds entitled "HRHR" (high risk, high return) to enable faculty members and graduate students to conduct preliminary research on innovative ideas and secure intellectual property rights (IPR) before they seek outside support. KAIST also funds innovative research in the fields of EEWS (energy, environment, water and sustainability). KAIST is developing electrical cars — OLEV — that receive electric power from an underground cable. It is also developing a mobile harbor — MH — that will eliminate the need for major harbors, reduce the ground transport systems, and decrease the environmental damage caused by trucks.

Korean educational institutions may become more competitive in the future because of the recent reforms made at KAIST. KAIST has instituted major changes, including the strict tenure system for faculty, tuition for students with low grade point average, and evaluation of faculty performance by experts from both inside and outside Korea. KAIST measures the performance of its faculty based on the impact made by research rather than the number of publications. KAIST promotes "bi-modal thinking" — the ability to think both in the domain of synthesis and analysis. To achieve this goal, a design course is required of all freshmen. KAIST has also launched the Renaissance Ph.D. Program that consists of two years of design of complex systems, followed by three years of analysis of the systems they designed. KAIST will become all English-instruction campus in 2010. Some of the universities in Korea are following KAIST's lead, instituting similar reforms.

Japan

Japan is the most technologically advanced nation among the four Far East Asian nations. Its economy is the second-largest in the world and has dominated many areas of manufacturing technologies. Japan supplies many key components to industrial firms in Korea, China and other countries.

Rather than being the first to innovate, Japan's forte has been improvements on major innovations first introduced in other countries. Japan has made many studies on Japan's innovation and innovation strategies (e.g., National Research Council, 1999). Like Korea, Japan has also invested heavily in national laboratories, with mixed results. To improve the performance of national laboratories, Japan merged 26 of the laboratories and established the Advanced Institute of Science and Technology (AIST). Their goal is to innovate new technologies that are far more advanced than current industrial technologies.

The Japanese higher education system consists of public and private universities, similar to the situation in the U.S. and Korea. National universities have been controlled by the government ministries and are highly regulated. Professors in these national universities are civil servants. To make universities more competitive and innovative, Japan is in the process of privatizing its national universities. However, to make Japanese universities more competitive, they may have to change their R&D funding system to concentrate their major R&D investment in a limited number of carefully selected universities on a long-term basis. They may also have to change the system of university governance to make it more flexible and adaptable.

A committee on Japan's Innovation Strategy states the following (Doyukai, 2006): "One main factor that is impeding Japan's ability to innovate is its rigid social structure which deters change, a side effect of Japan's successful postwar economic revival. Another factor is Japan's homogeneous society, which resents those who stand out and is at the root of an often closed and jealous mind-set." The committee recommended the following three strategies for building a society that encourages innovations:

1. The first strategy is to build an open society.
2. The second strategy is to build a diverse society.
3. The third strategy is to build an attractive society that people can be proud of.

In terms of the three laws of innovation, Japan may have all the elements that constitute the innovation continuum. However, at a local level, the innovation continuum may have missing steps. Also the activation energy for nucleation of innovation hubs may be too large.

China

China is one of the most rapidly developing nations in the world — with a huge market and large human resources. It is the third largest economy and the leading manufacturer of a variety of products in the world. Its lower-cost manufacturing operations modulate the price of many manufactured goods throughout the world, which has deterred many countries from investing in manufacturing. Its large trade surplus vis-à-vis the United States attests to the fact that China has become the factory of the world for many manufactured products.

China is different from Japan and Korea in that its political system is totalitarian, albeit with a healthy tolerance for capitalistic business practices. Its political system will enable it to make major investments in capital-intensive businesses that may not yield short-term returns, but enhance its long-term competitiveness. However, its power may be too centralized with limited flexibility. The R&D expenditure is less than those of Japan and Korea, but its rate of increase is about six times that of Japan and three times that of Korea, indicating that China's R&D expenditure will eventually reach parity with Japan and Korea.

Many foreign companies have set up their R&D laboratories (e.g., Microsoft) in China to make use of the well-educated human resources available at still-reasonable costs. Expanding R&D activities in China makes sense not only because of the labour pool, but also because many potential customers for these products are in China.

Despite this rapid advancement, innovation in China seems to be years away (comparable to that of Korea 15 years ago) since it is mainly interested in manufacturing products that have well-established markets. However, the situation could suddenly change if China takes advantage of its large foreign exchange to make massive investments in select areas of technology.

FUTURE PROSPECTS: INNOVATION POLICY IN KOREA

Korea needs to strengthen the innovation process at both the institutional and the individual level. Korea's ability to innovate is impeded by political, organizational and financial factors. Modifying incentives for innovation and strengthening the reward system to allow risk-taking can remove or counteract these impediments. Korea needs to modify its onerous auditing system, which was instituted to make all organizations supported by taxpayers more transparent, but now discourages risk-taking and hampers innovation.

The policies that should be reviewed are as follows:

1. The Korean government should devise fiscal and monetary policies so as to provide financial incentives for risk-taking and innovation.
2. National laboratories should be made more productive by encouraging them to create large systems solutions that satisfy societal and industrial needs.
3. Korea should establish an "Innovation Policy", in addition to its R&D policy.
4. The public sector's R&D resources should be used to solve major problems that can have significant societal and economic impact in the 21st century.
5. The Korean government should entice foreign venture capitalists to Korea for the purpose of promoting innovation and opening up the global market for innovative products.

CONCLUSIONS

1. The three laws of innovation are useful in assessing what each country must do to increase its rates of innovation. Each country should re-examine their innovation policies to be sure that they satisfy these laws.

2. Major industrialized nations of Asia, i.e., China, Japan, Korea and Taiwan, have done well in well-established industries, but they are lacking in producing major innovations, perhaps because they do not have major innovation hubs.

3. To spur economic growth in the 21st century, Korea must foster major innovations through reforms of its education systems, more investment in new ventures, and changes in R&D culture to encourage independent and creative thinking.

4. Asian countries should analyse their *innovation continuum* to identify missing elements. The current economic turmoil should be viewed as an opportunity to take more calculated risks, conduct creative research and reward innovations.

5. All four Asian nations should have policies of providing a home for innovative ideas and people in their country and encouraging immigration of creative people from other nations. At the same time, these nations should deploy policies that will discourage innovators from leaving their country. It must provide a living environment for high quality of life, including strong educational infrastructure and health care.

REFERENCES

Branscomb, L. M. & Auerswald, P. E. (2001) Taking Technical Risks: How Innovators, Managers, and Investors Manage Risk in High-Tech Innovations, Cambridge, MA: MIT Press.

Byer, R. L. (2006). "The Generality of Silicon Valley Model and Role of University and the Region", Talk presented at Tohoku University and the Federation of Tohoku Economic Organizations, 16 January 2006.

Colton, J.S. & Suh, N.P. (1984). "Nucleation of Microcellular Foam: Theory and Practice," *Polymer Engineering and Science*, Vol. 27, No. 7, pp. 500-503.

Doyukai, K. (2006). *Japan's Innovation Strategy*, Committee on Japan's Innovation.

Drucker, P. F. (1985). *Innovation and Entrepreneurship*, New York: Harper and Row.

Eichler, R. (this book). "Do our students learn right skills?" In Luc E. Weber & James J. Duderstadt (Eds.), *University Research For Innovation*, London, Paris, Geneva: Economica.

Gray, D. O. (2004). "Plenary Session I: I/UCRC Program - 30 Years of Partnerships: Past Successes: An overview of the history, core principles and accomplishments of the NSF I/UCRC Program", Presentation at NSF I/UCRC 2004 Annual Meeting and 30th Anniversary Celebration, 7-9 January 2004.

National Research Council and the Japan Society for the Promotion of Science. (1999). Report on "New Strategies for New Challenges: Corporate Innovation in the United States and Japan".

Nelsen, L. (2005). "The Lesson of the Massachusetts Biotech Cluster 2005", M.I.T., Cambridge, MA.

OECD. (2008). Main Science and Technology Indicators, 2008-2.

Office of Technology Assessment, U.S. Congress. (1984). Technology, Innovation, and Regional Economic Development: Encouraging High Technology Development, Paper #2, OTA-BP-STI-25, February 1984.

Scotchmer, S. (2006). *Innovation and Incentives*, Cambridge, MA: MIT Press.

Suh, N. P. (1990) *The Principles of Design*, New York: Oxford University Press.

Suh, N. P. (2001). *Axiomatic Design: Advances and Applications*, New York: Oxford University Press.

Suh, N. P (2006). *Complexity: Theory and Applications*, New York: Oxford University Press.

Suh, N. P. (2009). "A Theory of Innovation and Case Studies", Submitted for publication.

Utterback, J. (1996). *Mastering the dynamics of innovation*, Cambridge, MA: Harvard Business School Press.

Welfens, P. J. J., Addison, J. T., Audretsch, D. B., Gries T. & Grupp, H. (2008). *Globalization, Economic Growth, Innovation Dynamics*, Berlin: Springer-Verlag.

CHAPTER 20

BILDUNG and Innovation — a *contradictio in adjecto* for today's university education in a globalized world?

Dieter Lenzen

TWO PERSPECTIVES ON THE THEME

I do think that the terms *Bildung* and innovation can be contradictory, at least they express the inner conflict felt by a person, who is responsible for change in an institution — the university — and therefore for innovation and, at the same time, knows how frequently and in what manner this task has been deliberated in the history of the philosophy of education.

To begin with, we must be clear about the three terms that were given to me and which are mentioned in the title of my talk: Globalization, Innovation and *Bildung*.

CLARIFICATION OF TERMS

Globalization

Globalization refers to the interaction of four macrostructural developments, the effects of which have increased exponentially since the 1980s [1].

---

1 These notes on globalization are closely based on our presentation in the 2008 year book of the Action Committee for Education (Aktionsrat Bildung): vbw — Vereinigung der Bayerischen Wirtschafts e.V. (Ed.): Blossfeld, H.-P., Bos, W., Lenzen, D. (Chair), Müller-Böling, D., Prenzel, M., Wößmann, L.: Bildungsrisiken und -chancen im Globalisierungsprozess. (Wiesbaden 2008.)

- The increasing internationalization of the financial, product and labour markets. This development leads to new forms of division of labour across country boundaries with related employee requirements.
- The internationalization of markets implies stronger competition between countries, all competing to be the most favoured locations. This competitive development leads to extended forms of liberalization, privatization and deregulation, the educational sectors included. For an individual, this development implies above all stronger competitive pressures. Competitors in the labour market are no longer people with the same qualification in the same country, but all equally qualified citizens in all countries of the world.
- The globalization of markets is facilitated and indeed in some cases made possible by the erratic progress in new information and communication technology. The resulting opportunities imply, at the same time, the requirement that individuals are able to cope with and exploit these new technologies.
- The globalization of markets also implies a higher economic instability and vulnerability for the countries where businesses are located. The most extreme expression of this can be found in the current financial crisis, the worldwide effects of which are not yet predictable. Nevertheless, in terms of structure, the likely results are an increase in aggression and social adversity and an accelerated loss of values.

These four developments have had empirically observable consequences in the international comparison of educational systems. This phenomenon is referred to as "mass education" (cf. Meyer, Ramirez & Soysal 1992). The rapidly emerging commonalities between educational systems are remarkable, for instance: state educational administration, professional training of teaching staff and quality control procedures. High cost educational programs in the university sector, such as "Erasmus" for the international exchange of students and teaching staff, "Leonardo da Vinci" for connecting universities and businesses, or "Tempus" for supporting and peripheral measures in the European higher education systems, have led to an accelerated standardization, at least inside Europe, which has culminated in the Bologna Process.

In the light of globalization, the challenges for the development of individuals are to be found in the requirement for certain qualifications and behaviours, for which the university sector is not currently prepared, especially not after the Bologna reforms. These requirements are, inter alia, that:

- Young people must learn to replace their heuristic behaviour, that is acting spontaneously according to whatever pops into their head, with rational, strategic action.

- Young people must learn to deal with ambiguities, i.e. both to develop a kind of perceptive filter for apparent uncertainty and to be able to deal with incertitude.
- Young people must learn to think about the future, even when it seems unpredictable.
- Young people must learn to cope with the feeling of not having sufficient information themselves, which results from the plethora of information around them.
- Young people must learn that blind trust in opinions expressed in public spaces, such as experts' opinions, Wikipedia and political promises, should be called into question.
- Young people must find a reasonable balance between keeping options open in the face of growing uncertainties and making sustainable personal decisions, both in the private space of social relationships and in relation to training and occupation.

Universities, therefore, have the task of transforming the tendency to volatility of individual behaviour, and thus the tendency to generate further individual uncertainties, into an ability to exploit uncertainty within the globalization process, as an opportunity to develop an individual biography (or career). This depends on young people learning:

- To act rationally despite uncertainties, i.e. to calculate uncertainty, to weigh up personal actions, to rely on intuition only when it is based on experience, to develop an ability to make personal judgments and to be prepared to make individual decisions.
- Young people need a "stable awareness of instability". Young people must be aware of all these uncertainties and still attempt to make judgments, to check information themselves, to collate new information and to be prepared to make conscious decisions and to correct them latterly, where necessary.
- The pre-condition for all this is — more than ever before — that young people in the university learn to act and to judge from a firm knowledge base. They need a solid knowledge of circumstances, knowledge of serious sources of information and of advisory institutions, knowledge of how decisions are made in other cultures and knowledge of appropriate strategies for taking decisions.
- Besides knowledge, young people in a university need training to avoid thinking linearly, but instead to act according to objectives and training in how to structure these objectives. They need to be able to analyse their own situation, should be prepared to evaluate their own behaviour continually and to step over their own shame-threshold, which prevents them from discussing their uncertainties and insecurities.

Innovation

I belong to the advisory board of an organization, the German Innovation Indicator, which is run by the Deutsche Telekom Trust and the Federation of German Industries (BDI). (See: www.innovationsindikator.de and www.telekom-stiftung.de/innovationsindikator) The German Institute for Economic Research (DIW Berlin) uses a basis of 180 indicators to calculate annually for us the innovation performance of Germany in comparison with other countries. These are weighted and integrated to produce a complex model. A look at the individual indicators shows that different sub-systems of society must be considered in order to describe the innovative performance of each country: besides the economic system (with components such as funding, market demand, transformation of ideas into products, networks etc.), there is the political system (with components such as regulation and competition), the communication sub-system (with the main components of societal innovation climate, including for instance the innovation-friendly demands of consumers), and above all the education system (with the components research, development and training).

Do we now know what innovation is? When I look at the colourful brochures of innovation propagandists, I see pictures of Google, wind farms and digital cameras. Certainly, these are gigantic drivers of consumption, but what is innovative about them? Windmills existed in antiquity, the search for information can be answered through good old library catalogues and classic cameras such as Hasselblad still cannot be beaten by digital cameras.

No, I see innovation as something quite different, as something often referred to as "thinking outside the box". Thus the Pythagoras Theorem was an innovation, the concept of Zero, the number Pi, the Theory of Relativity and the discovery of DNA. In the area of the social sciences, the "contrat social" of Rousseau, Adam Smith's *The Wealth of Nations*, the invention of paper money, the introduction of double entry bookkeeping by Luca Pacioli or the concept of shares developed by the "Oostindische Companie". Not all, but some of these innovations were developed in universities and there could possibly have been more, if more freedom of thought had been allowed for from the start.

The people who can achieve such things are talented; they discover something before others, conceive of new combinations of old concepts and develop patterns, through which and in which others see nothing, people who are obsessed by their search, according to the formula: 95% perspiration, 5% inspiration.

It is noticeable that when we talk about innovation, we are speaking about only one section of the up and coming university generation, whose requirements we have described in the context of the clarification of the term globalization. The young people, who really will develop these innovations, i.e. scientific breakthroughs, are people with unique intelligence, curiosity and interest, broad knowledge, optimism and perseverance and the luck to be in a social environment where innovation is appreciated and promoted. It is not easy to describe how such talents can be promoted and supported, as most determinants remain unknown. As well as knowledge, intelligence and perseverance, something else is required, which our universities after Bologna can barely offer, that is: the time to play, the time for day-dreaming and fantasy, the possibility of searching for solutions, the preparedness of the university to respect unusual ideas and not to ridicule them, the determination not to accept authority without question (and a number of further "dos and don'ts").

Bildung

The tasks of the university as set out in the context of the clarification of the terms "globalization" and "innovation" did not sound as though they could be implemented by a "teaching engineer". However, that is exactly the misunderstanding of university teaching and learning, which lies at the heart of the Bologna Process and many other tertiary education reforms across the world. It is assumed that the demands of innovation and globalization are categorically new and that they therefore require totally new forms of teaching and learning. We have arrived at the clarification of the term *Bildung*.

The assumption that reality today is fundamentally different from the time when universities were first conceived is false. That is not to say that the same framework of conditions exists now and that everything can carry on as it did at the time of Humboldt.

In 1963 the German sociologist Helmut Schelsky argued, in his famous book *Einsamkeit und Freiheit* ("Solitude and Freedom"), that the obligation of the university was to educate for world citizenship, which was not commonly accepted 45 years ago. He wrote:

Real cosmopolitan citizenship means that an individual in our contemporary situation must connect his personal, spiritual and cultural striving for perfection with the economic, technical, social, political and cultural development of those societies and cultures, which will come together in a unified civilization on the world's horizon. The eradication of cultures, which is connected with this, will not spare our own culture, and to preserve it would mean to stifle future development. Only when we take the word "world" seriously in a totally realistic sense, can we express our educational assignment with the words of Wilhelm von Humboldt, who wrote to his wife on 9th October 1804: Whoever, when he dies, can say: I grasped as much of the world as I could and transformed it into my humanity, has fulfilled his task... In the higher sense of the word, he has lived — and it would be folly to undermine life with a an ulterior purpose. (Loose translation from Schelsky, 1963, p. 294.)

With this reference to the classic ideal of the German university, Schelsky reminds his readers — that was already taking place — that the university offers a chance to deal with the challenge of — what we now call — globalization, even for those who plan to follow a non-scientific career. This is connected to an attitude, to scientific scholarship, which is close to the concept mentioned above, "thinking outside the box". It is more than the education of talented people, who have innovative abilities — they must also have the attitude of scientific scholarship, dedication and devotion to the object of analysis, cool-headed analysis, the quest for alternative solutions, self-criticism and much more, which leads to the development of key qualifications for coping with life under the conditions of globalization and the expectations of innovation.

Is this expectation at all justified? Has the concept of scientific, university education been proven to be the best form of general education? Was it not scientists, who were trained in top universities — as we would say today — who carried out human experiments on concentration camps victims? Was it not this type of scientist, who invented the atom bomb and mustard gas? And was it not scientists, who, just as today's economists and business leaders have done, developed optimizing formulae for capital maximization without reflecting losses — this, by the way, as early as in the second half of the 19th century.

These doubts are justified. They are, however, directed not towards the ideal of the classic university, but rather towards how it is implemented. A more careful look at the misuse of scientific knowledge, which occurs daily, shows that it is nothing more than the use of knowledge not *for* a better life, but *against* it. What made this possible was the fact that science was already conceived of as being free from values and judgments in the fundamental texts on the idea of the German university, such as those by Schelling on the absolute definition of science (Schelling, 1956, p. 9). In this definition, which comes from one of the founding texts for the Berlin University from 1803, Schelling attempts to separate knowledge from action, when he criticizes knowledge — and the generation of knowledge in the university — as a medium for action, and action as the unique purpose of knowledge and learning. This attitude played a significant role in the history of the German university. Non-judgmental science opened the way to the use of science for the battles in Verdun and the gas chambers in Auschwitz. However, that did not necessarily have to be the case. One of the most important fathers of the German university, who often stood in the shadows of the name Humboldt, was Fichte, and he saw it quite differently:

One does not study in order to eternally express what has been learnt to the examiner, but to apply it to similar cases in real life in order to transform it into actions. It is not simply to repeat, but to create something other from and with it; thus the final purpose is not knowledge, but rather the art of utilizing knowledge. This act of utilizing scientific knowledge in life requires another component, which is foreign to academia, namely an insight into life and the exercising of judgment in the application of science to life... (Loose translation from Fichte, 1910, p. 6f.)

In 1807, no lesser person than Fichte himself argued — as would educational-psychologists later — that only that which is learnt through doing and with a "clear and free conscience" is well learnt. He required the university to train a competency, which at the end of the 20th and start of the 21st century has often been prized as a new discovery: attention should be drawn not primarily to discrete knowledge, but to the development of the capacity to learn (*ibid*, p. 7), i.e. learning how to learn. Fichte called this competency "understanding" and derived from that the purpose of a university; that is as "a school for the art of the scientific use of understanding" (*ibid*, p. 8). Scientific learning, therefore, had a significant role in the university, because Fichte trusted the university to develop understanding.

But that is not sufficient. Wilhelm von Humboldt goes one step further when he relies on science not only to educate for understanding, but also for humanity, in other words not to use understanding in just any way, but in one that will achieve the higher development of the whole of humankind. It is not just any science that can achieve that, according to Humboldt, but only one that is connected with studies in classical philology. Humboldt was influenced by the concept that the idea of a humanitarian society, as propagated by Greek philosophy, was inseparably linked to the study of the Greek language. Thus on the basis of his specific linguistic theory, he saw the relationship in language between *ergon* and *energia* as influencing both mentality and behaviour. If young people, therefore, were to learn Greek in the Gymnasium, then they would also be learning humanity. In this sense, the university is not only an organization for the development of understanding, but also one in which, in the humanitarian sense of the term, reason is developed and represented.

These complicated idealistic constructions are based on a theological source. This is the concept that, by God's creative act, all men and women are intrinsically good and it is the task of education to bring out and develop this intrinsic goodness of humanity. The process is referred to in the educational, philosophical and daily German language as *Bildung*. The term contains the idea that the image of God, the "*imago dei*", is reflected in mankind in such a way that it is possible for him or her to act according to God's example. To educate someone through *Bildung* is, therefore, to orientate him or her towards God's image and example. (The German term *Bildung* stems from the German word for image, which is *Bild*.)

Two further elements belong to this educational philosophy. Firstly, the idea that the education of an individual leads to a positive development of humanity in general, i.e. that this type of "higher" education is possible. This means that the possibility of the development of humanity is dependent on the university. The second element consists of the understanding that *Bildung* is not a process that can be implemented by teachers; in other words it is not possible to impose education in the sense of *Bildung* on someone. Rather

Bildung is self-reflective. This agrees with an idea that has also been proven empirically, which says that the "learning consciousness" — as we would formulate it in neurological and constructivist terms — constructs its own reality. The understanding, which is developed according to God's image, is therefore able to educate people towards their self-development and in this way leads to the development of humanity.

For the university, this means, briefly summarized, that the student develops an understanding through inquisitive learning (thus the necessary unity research and teaching), which provides him or her with knowledge that can be applied, on one hand and on the other, a humanitarian competency for judgment, which in turn means that the individual becomes humanitarian in the emphatic sense of the word. The university has, therefore, the greatest possible task: it is responsible for the further development of a humanitarian world through the acquisition of knowledge and humanitarian behaviour through inquisitive, research-driven learning.

The fathers of the classic German university, who found so many followers across the whole world, were not above describing universities in all their detail, including the behaviour expected of professors, in order for a university to fulfil all its tasks. Those who read it today are surprised at the high level of observation and the breadth of knowledge and thoughts of the great philosophers of 200 years ago, whose ideas are only just beginning to be empirically verified. On the basis of this description, a methodological arsenal and a curriculum were developed for the university, which should be considered under the term "research-driven learning", which often sounds hollow these days, but continues to be required of the university and rightly so. This inquisitive learning should be carried out in "solitude and freedom", two further conditions for a functioning university. Freedom means freedom from the state, which the Prussian government actually granted to the newly founded universities, and "solitude", which, for Humboldt, did not refer to the situation of the student or the teacher, who researches, in fact, without communicating with others. For him, by contrast it referred to a learned society of students and teachers, for whom solitude lies in the individual encounter with the truth. The solitude therefore describes something of a superior nature. The individual stands before truth in its totality, in the immense unknown, and in this situation he or she develops his or her individuality.

THE LIMITS OF THE CLASSICAL UNIVERSITY IDEAL

After this interim conclusion, which followed a clarification of the terms globalization, innovation and *Bildung*, we now have a brief idea of the classic university, which, since it was implemented in enlightened Prussia, made science so great in Germany and elsewhere. When we reflect on these deliberations, we should remember that an ignorant shaking of heads over such complex and demanding ideas was more frequent than the cry of "Eureka" followed by the statement: "That is exactly what we must do."

We must ask ourselves why this idea of the university is no longer considered relevant after 200 years, and how, as a result, an E.U.-bureaucratic reform such as the Bologna Process could be put in place and be deemed necessary. There are a number of causes that led to this outcome, which I hesitate to call a disaster:

- The freedom granted to academics and students alike was so exhaustive that it was misused as a reason for doing nothing, for plagiarism, fraud and indeed for corruption.
- The solitude has often been generously misunderstood to mean that the academic and his or her students do not have to deal with reality and that science is often practised like the glass-bead game from Hesse. The effects of this are seen not only in Auschwitz.
- The number of people with an intellectual capacity large enough for real self-development through scientific Bildung was always small.
- Both academics and students have a tendency towards social isolation by "holding the stirrups" for a new social class, which has taken the place of the aristocracy and now looks down on the rest of society in disgust, which — however — earns the money that is spent in the universities.
- The methodological development of science tends towards the emergence of a particular logic whereby the next scientific step is orientated not towards societal needs, but towards the next interesting scientific question, even when this question is quite absurd.
- At the end of the 19th century a new direction emerged within German philosophy, called Geisteswissenschaften — Humanities — which was very powerful and defined its relationship to reality in such a way that it is the task of science, not to explain reality or to change it, but only to understand it. This so-called hermeneutic relationship to reality can be seen as the main reason for the failure of the German university in the face of epochal crimes against humanity.

The postulation of an empirical non-judgmental research was not an appropriate means of confronting this development, since value-free insights can always be seen as meaning that no account has to be taken of the consequences of one's own ideas. It was not until the 1960s and 70s that this empirical-analytical understanding of science began to be heavily criticized and it is only in the last two decades that science has recovered without returning to the previous errors. One can already predict that following the current financial crisis, rational choice theories will find it hard to survive without normative criteria.

Nevertheless, no one is interested in substituting this rationality with a mix of animosity towards religion, technology and innovation and a misunderstood conception of *Bildung*; a concept that satisfies itself with demanding that universities make people into good citizens, Muslims, CO_2-avoiders or Greenpeace-donors. This should be rejected not because it is reprehensible, but because it does not work. We know empirically that it is impossible to educate someone in such a way that they take on certain values and act accordingly. Thank God, we should say, thoughts are free, as is the will to follow them. These thoughts do not realize the ideas of the ruling class, when they are impressed against the will of the learners.

Bologna and the future of *Bildung*

One has the impression that the biggest reform initiative for the tertiary sector in wider Europe, the so-called Bologna Process, is making exactly this mistake. I will not bother to analyse the content of all the declarations from Lisbon to Leuven. The result would be too awful. There are few texts in the history of universities worldwide that are as sketchy and empty as that which the politicians have agreed upon for the future of European universities.

They did, however, start out from a correct analysis. The observation that European universities stretching between the Arctic Circle and Gibraltar differ massively in the quality of their provision was correct. The observation that national higher education systems with different study forms and final qualifications make a consolidation of Europe's tertiary sector difficult was correct. The analysis that many universities no longer seem to be interested in carrying out research and teaching for the current needs of an up and coming generation was also correct. And the assumption that the university would not have been able to create a European compatibility all on its own was yet again correct.

If the patient — the European University — was seriously ill, then it needed decisive action. However, every village doctor knows that you can only treat a patient against his will as long as he is unconscious. When he awakes, even the best therapy will not work without his cooperation. The patient must consult the doctor and not the other way around. It would have been correct (and sufficient) — to remain with this metaphor — to have revived the European University from being unconscious. Instead of this, the European politicians have caged the universities in a barred hospital. On the entrance it reads "BA-MA-Ph.D". I don't want to be misunderstood: there is nothing against harmonizing academic processes worldwide and there is nothing wrong with basing these reforms on American qualifications, based on which 20 of the 4,800 American universities are internationally respected as successful. The problem, rather, is the detailed regulation of university processes. Simply to use the word "workload" in connection with learning and the reduction of the weekly learning "burden" to 40 hours, in order to then allocate the successful completion of these "working hours" as a monthly wage in the form of credits, is such a perversion of the idea of the university that it is no surprise when professors and students act like miners, who — in their world justifiably — fight and strike against every hour of extra work and for every extra cent of higher wages.

The idea that it is possible to determine in Brussels the relationship between occupations and university study programs is both stupid and ignorant. When one sees what individual universities have done using this prescription, one applauds the slyness of reasoning, which allows such codswallop to be undermined.

In many universities special curricula, which teach teamwork, presentation techniques, equality for women and Mandarin for beginners, have been developed alongside subject-focused courses. With the exception of the language courses, such initiatives are completely nonsensical if they are separated from the subject studies and are orientated towards a reality about which neither professors nor students have any clue. Presentation techniques are learnt, in fact, through making presentations, teamwork, through working together on scientific problems — Humboldt knew that better — and whoever treats women badly deserves a clip around the ear and not a curriculum.

If we can assume that both those who act in the political sphere and bureaucrats are not entirely stupid and wicked, but do honestly want to reduce study duration, minimize the costs of tertiary education and teach a solid, school-like curriculum, then without a doubt they have achieved what they set out to do. *Causa finita.*

In fact, they have led to the emergence of a new type of university, at least in Central Europe, which has little to do with the classic university. In this type of university, one can train chemists, lawyers, doctors and translators. These people will do their job and be well-behaved and — to return to our three terms — will find their place in the globalized world. They will take part in the competitive labour market and will find a job between the North Cape and Cape Town. They will invent new windmills and energy-saving lights and make colourful boxes for pills and they will prohibit investment banking. They will do what is expected of them and have no crazy ideas. They will not create new worlds or paradigms, will not make quantum leaps and will not contribute to the enlightenment of humanity. In brief: they will not be *learned.*

And where will that other place be, where research is learnt in solitude and freedom? In the university, where else? To make this possible, we will have to take institutional decisions. We have the following alternatives:

We can create a new type of university, worthy of its name, and leave the current "universities" to become vocational schools.

We can differentiate the institution using the name "university" internally, so that academic-vocational training is offered in a separate department to the one for higher academic *Bildung*.

We can argue — because we know better — that courses in a university, including those for vets and nursery nurses, should always contain a minimum of academic scholarship, a space to search and be inquisitive with at least the appearance of solitude and freedom, even when we know that only very seldom does a precious orchid grow in this tropical forest. However: we know that these orchids require shade, which is provided by the forest, so that they do not get burnt in the sun of the practical demands of daily life.

If we so desire — and I think we should — the real Bologna Reform is still before us. It will be a reform in the attitude of students, but particularly of teachers, who are driven by the insight that being a scientist is not just any job, but usually a badly paid but privileged job, in which one is able to decide what to research and to teach and where one can be independent of the political steering of research contracts. If this is what we want, we must expect bitter battles, in which scientific revolutionaries are set against politicians who claim to represent the will of the people, those they normally ignore until the next election and for whom the details of science are irrelevant. But only until science is finally recognized as being dedicated to mankind and the idea of a better life, only when evaluations are orientated towards the interests of those who continue to provide the university with the privileges which it has enjoyed, in different forms, for over 1,000 years.

REFERENCES

BDI/Deutsche Telekom-Stiftung: *Innovationsindikator Deutschland* (2008). www.tele-kom-stiftung.de/innovationsindikator, www.innovationsindikator.de.

Fichte, J. G. (1910). "Deducirter Plan einer zu Berlin zu errichtenden höhern Lehran-stalt", In: E. Spranger, (ed.): *Fichte, Schleiermacher, Steffens — über das Wesen der Universität*, Leipzig, pp. 1-104.

Meyer, J. W., Ramirez, F. O. & Soysal, Y. N. (1992). "World Expansion of Mass Edu-cation, 1870-1980", In: *Sociology of Education*, Vol. 65, pp. 128-149.

Schelling, F. W. J. (1956). "Vorlesungen über die Methode des akademischen Studi-ums", In: *Die Idee der deutschen Universität*, Darmstadt, pp. 1-124.

Schelsky, H. (1963). *Einsamkeit und Freiheit*, Reinbek bei Hamburg 1963.

vbw — Vereinigung der Bayerischen Wirtschaft e.V., Blossfeld, H.-P., Bos, W., Len-zen, D. (Chair), Müller-Böling, D., Prenzel, M. & Wößmann, L. (eds.). (2008). *Bildungsrisiken und -chancen im Globalisierungsprozess: Jahresgutachten 2008*, Wies-baden 2008.

CHAPTER 21

Injecting Relevance to make Innovation more Impactful at Universities

Gururaj 'Desh' Deshpande

Afret a short tenure in teaching at universities, I have pursued an entrepreneurial career since 1980. Nine years ago, when I joined the MIT Corporation in Cambridge, Massachusetts, I got reconnected back to the academic world. Together with other like-minded individuals at MIT, I have been experimenting with ways in which to make the innovation at MIT have a bigger economic and societal impact. After the initial success of the approach at MIT, my wife and I started a similar effort in India targeted at fostering innovation in Indian universities to make a difference in social entrepreneurship. The effort in India is now five years old. This paper summarizes the results of these two efforts to encourage discussion on how such approaches can be used to further the innovation in the 21st century.

THE EFFORT AT MIT

MIT with its culture of *"Mens et Manus"* (mind and hand) already excels in making the technological innovation useful to the world. However, there is an opportunity to make it better. The "Deshpande Center for Technological Innovation" was set up at MIT in 2002 with funding of $20 million. The Kauffman Foundation did an extensive study of this center and the von Liebig Center at the University of California San Diego. They found the models to be successful in promoting academic innovation to directly address real world problems. Lesa Mitchell, Vice President of Advancing Innovation at Kauffman Foundation, is facilitating similar centers at other universities. The following are some of the lessons I have learned from this effort.

315

Insight

Researchers who work on applied research always think about how their ideas can impact the world, both economically and socially. There is no lack of desire on the part of the researcher to see the impact. The idea has to be directed towards solving a burning problem in the world to have an impact. You cannot mandate innovation. However, bringing the knowledge of what the world needs to the innovator will help the innovator make choices that increase the probability of impact.

Research at universities now is where the engineering practice was in industry a few decades ago; an engineer designed the product and the salesman then went looking to sell the product. Today in industry, an engineer only starts designing the product after fully understanding what the customer needs. However, in the current practice of research, the researcher innovates, patents the idea and then the technology licensing offices try to find applications for the patents. The Center at MIT has found that bringing the practitioners and the researchers together early on changes the culture of innovation. There is a lot of give and take between what is possible and what is worth solving to come up with an innovation that can have impact. Injecting relevance early in the process of innovation increases the probability of that innovation having a bigger impact on the world. The faculty members fully embrace this idea. In fact, MIT has created a new course called I-TEAM which brings engineering and MBA students together to explore how to target ideas at appropriate markets. This has been a very popular course.

Researchers, in the campus environment, are idea generators. When a new idea comes along, the researcher is not only excited by the elegance and novelty of the idea, but is also excited about where it can be useful. A few months down the road, the researcher will have ten more ideas that have sprung up from the original idea. Left to himself or herself, a researcher will choose to pursue one of those ideas that makes sense to his or her own environment. However, if the researcher is connected with practitioners, he would have the benefit of relevance to pick an idea that has a better chance of creating a bigger impact.

Process

The Center achieves its mission through several approaches: Grant Program, Catalyst Program, Innovation Teams (I-Teams) and Events.

Faculty members apply for grants to the Center twice a year. The funding from the Center enables the faculty and their students to pursue exciting new avenues of research on novel technologies that could have a significant impact. These grants are selected by a panel of faculty and business leaders, and are selected based on potential for impact, technical merit, team considerations and timeframe. Ignition Grants of $50,000 are awarded to fund proof of concept explorations, and Innovation Program Grants are awarded in the range of $50,000-250,000 to build on existing innovations at MIT and bring them closer to commercial viability. The objective of the funding is to nurture ideas with market potential and reduce the uncertainty around them so that an external party would invest in the technology. This could occur through various means, such as a VC-funded start-up or licensing by a company. In addition to the funding, the grants bring with them publicity, mentoring and connections with the business community.

Volunteers from the business community are central to achieving the Center's mission of helping MIT innovators achieve market impact. Catalysts are a highly vetted group of individuals with experience relevant to innovation, technology commercialization and entrepreneurship. Catalysts provide individual contribution to the Center and do not represent any company interests in their role as Catalysts. Catalysts are chosen based on the following qualifications:

- Experience in commercializing early stage technologies and/or mentoring researchers and entrepreneurs, and industry expertise.
- Willingness to proactively provide assistance to MIT research teams.
- Willingness to abide by the time commitment, confidentiality and conflict of interest guidelines.
- Commitment to the interests of MIT researchers and the Center.

The I-Teams (Innovation Teams) program provides an action-based learning experience for graduate students where students evaluate the market potential for research projects being conducted at MIT and develop "go-to-market" strategies.

The Center hosts a variety of events to bring together minds from the MIT and business communities.

The IdeaStream Symposium, held each spring, is our largest event. The Symposium is intended to showcase new MIT technology, educate the business community about leading-edge new technologies and facilitate connections between VCs, entrepreneurs, industry and MIT innovators. These symposia are by invitation only. The Center also collaborates with other programs on and off campus to promote a variety of events to enhance innovation within the community.

Results

So far the Center has reviewed 450 proposals submitted by the faculty. The Center has supported over 70 projects with about $10 million in grants. The grants have resulted in 18 startups that have raised over $140 million in capital. Over 60 faculty and 500 students have participated in the program and a new course has been designed to capture the process of taking the innovation to the market. The process can be summarized by three actions: Select, Connect and Direct. Active participation of the business community in all three activities is essential for success: Selecting appropriate research to fund, Connecting the innovator to the marketplace and Directing them when they need help.

To further stimulate the economy and take advantage of the innovation across all the universities in Massachusetts, two other initiatives have been launched recently: MassChallenge and Venture Café. MassChallenge is a business plan competition supported by the Massachusetts government and local entrepreneurs to pick the top 25 plans and provide the seed capital. The goal of this program is to kick start 25 companies a year for the next three years to stimulate the Massachusetts economy. Venture Café is a coffeehouse, about 12,000 square feet, with WiFi connections and hookups for projectors and other devices to hone projects and ideas. The expectation is that such a place will energize the entrepreneurs and accelerate the ideas to the marketplace.

THE EFFORT IN INDIA

India is a vast country and several educational institutions have come up over the last 60 years. There are institutions like the Indian Institutes of Technology, All India Medical School, National Law schools, Indian Institutes of Management and Indian Institutes of Public Health which have international recognition. They get their strength from being able to select a few thousand from millions and holding smart students together in a campus environment. The faculty members at these institutions are dedicated, but lack the research infrastructure. This is improving, but has a long way to go.

India has to deal with two issues; millions of people and low affordability. If innovation is to have an impact, Indian universities have to bring new solutions at very affordable prices to millions. Indian scientists have shown promise; the Indian space program has shown results with modest investments. Indian industry understands the opportunity; for example, Telecom companies add 10 million cell phones a month that can be recharged incrementally 2 cents at a time and Tata Motors recently started selling a $2,000 Nano car.

India graduates approximately 400,000 engineering undergraduates from approximately 3,000 colleges. We picked BVB Engineering College, a college in a small town called Hubli, to see how we can bring innovation to this institution. The college has 4,000 engineering students and runs on a budget of $4 million a year. The students are bright and the teachers are dedicated. However, the students are taught to study and do well in exams. Students spend their time preparing themselves to provide canned answers to questions posed at the exams at the end of the academic year. There is a total lack of innovation in that education system. Students walk around with hundreds of problems all around them, but they do not know that they have the ability to solve them.

In order to connect the students and the faculty to the problems in the surrounding area, we built a center for social entrepreneurship in the campus. For the last five years we have been funding approximately 70 programs by NGOs (non-governmental Organizations) in the areas of Education, Agriculture, Livelihood and Health. The enthusiastic participation by the students to get involved in these programs has been overwhelming. The participation started from the engineering campus and now has spread to all the surrounding colleges. Last year 1,000 students conducted 250 projects. This year we have 10,000 students involved with 2,000 projects. The enthusiasm of the students has now spread to the young faculty. They are bringing technological as well as other innovations to projects.

Problems exist in this world because people do not see a solution. Therefore, you need innovation to solve even the simple problems. The innovation always comes from a fresh perspective. The Social Entrepreneurship Center provides that fresh perspective to the students and young faculty by bringing their bright minds and the problems together. We also have 10 young men and women from the United States who spend a year on fellowship. There are approximately 30 students who spend the summer at this center from University of Southern California, Berkeley and North Carolina University. These visitors are the change agents in the social ecosystem.

The results of this effort have been excellent. For example, a kitchen was built in the city that serves midday meals to 185,000 school children every day. The kitchen uses good management tools and technology to maintain very high quality standards and has managed to serve nutritious meals that the kids love for 12 cents a meal. After the program was optimized in this city, it is now duplicated in other parts of India. This program currently serves 1 million meals to school children every day. By using a similar model as the Center at MIT, difficult social problems are being solved in India by connecting the academic innovation of universities to the needs of the real world.

CONCLUSIONS

The 21st century poses several grand challenges; clean water, clean air, climate change, energy, biodiversity and sustainability. The Universities can play a central role in coming up with solutions to these problems. The solutions will need "Eminent Technological Innovations" and thousands of innovative ways to localize the Eminent Innovations. The universities of the 21st century have to create educational programs and an echo system that injects a lot more innovation and entrepreneurship into their institutions to remain relevant to the world.

Institutions like MIT, with their depth in technology can come up with "Eminent Innovations". This paper shows that the probability of Eminent Innovation having a big impact on the world goes up substantially by connecting the innovator to the relevance.

An eminent Innovation will not impact all the six billion people in the world unless innovation is spread out to everyone in the world. The second example of the program being experimented in India shows that students can be energized to participate in solving local problems during their University education. In the process, students learn how to adapt big ideas to local problems to come up with affordable solutions.

In both cases, if the universities want to remain relevant, they need to reach beyond their campuses to connect young innovative minds to the world's problems.

CHAPTER 22

Learning in/for a World of Constant Flux: *Homo Sapiens, Homo Faber & Homo Ludens* revisited

John Seely Brown and Douglas Thomas

The educational needs of the 21st century pose a number of serious problems for current educational practices. First and foremost, we see the 21st century as a time that is characterized by constant change. Educational practices that focus on the transfer of static knowledge simply cannot keep up with the rapid rate of change. Practices that focus on adaptation or reaction to change fare better, but are still finding themselves outpaced by an environment that requires content to be updated almost as fast as it can be taught. What is required to succeed in education is a theory that is responsive to the context of constant flux, while at the same time is grounded in a theory of learning. Accordingly, understanding the processes of learning which underwrite the practices emerging from participation in digital networks may enable us to design learning environments that harness the power of digital participation for education in the 21st century.

For much of the 20th century, learning had focused on the acquisition of skills or transmission of information or what we define as "learning about". Then, near the end of the 20th century, learning theorists started to recognize the value of "learning to be", of putting learning into a situated context that deals with systems and identity as well as the transmission of knowledge. We want to suggest that now even that is not enough. Although learning about and learning to be worked well in a relatively stable world, in a world of constant flux we need to embrace a theory of *learning to become*.

In order to understand both what that means and how it might be achieved, we need to examine some of the recent transitions in learning which have emerged in the 21st century. In particular we need to consider several dimensions of learning (knowing, making and playing) that have taken on new, more distributed forms in the networked age.

THE DEATH OF THE READER

The second half of the 20th century witnessed a radical transformation in the nature of authorship. From Barthes' and Foucault's discussions of the death of the author to reader response theory, there has been a radical reformulation of the ways in which we conceive of the process of reading. Indeed, in many ways the movement away from the sole authority of an author's text to a publicly interpreted version of that text marked by Roland Barthes' work in the 1970s has introduced the idea of reading as a social practice, rather than individual practices, and opened up the idea of interpretation as something done by communities rather than individuals.

When Barthes and others declared the author dead, they were describing a paradigm shift that moved from the transmission of meaning toward active interpretation. What we are witnessing now, with new media, is a second transformation, marked by a shift from interpretation to participation (Jenkins, 2006). In just the past ten years, we have seen that change happen throughout the world of journalism, with news itself first being seen as factual, later being seen as interpretive, and with the emergence of the blogosphere, finally being seen as participatory.

In a remarkable reflection on new media, Andrew Sullivan discusses how it is that blogs are beginning to remake the landscape of journalism: "The blogger can get away with less and afford fewer pretensions of authority. He is — more than any writer of the past — a node among other nodes, connected but unfinished without the links and the comments and the track-backs that make the blogosphere, at its best, a conversation, rather than a production." (Sullivan, 2008)

The transformation that Sullivan is reflecting upon is not simply a change in readership, access or feedback. It is a structural transformation in the way that communication happens and in that transformation is as dependent on the experiences of the audience as it is on the text the writer produces. In blogging, authorship is transformed in a way that recognizes the participation of others as fundamentally constitutive of the text. It is not an author writing to an audience, but, instead, a blogger facilitating the construction of an interpretive community. But, beyond that, Sullivan draws two parallels to music, which begin to reveal a sense of what new media may be about. The notion of the author has been transformed not only in relationship to the reader, but also in function. He writes: "There are times, in fact, when a blogger feels less like a writer than an online disc jockey, mixing samples of tunes and generating new melodies through mashups while also making his own music. He is both artist and producer — and the beat always goes on." It is that first comparison we want to discuss as the framework for a new form of interactivity that new media invites, possessing an inherent malleability that is directed toward social ends.

As important, however, is the second comparison Sullivan makes between new media and music: "To use an obvious analogy, jazz entered our civilization much later than composed, formal music. But it hasn't replaced it; and no jazz musician would ever claim that it could. Jazz merely demands a different way of playing and listening, just as blogging requires a different mode of writing and reading. Jazz and blogging are intimate, improvisational and individual — but also inherently collective. And the audience talks over both." In contrast to Sullivan (who is writing as a blogger), our goal is to explore that aspect which is inherently collective and to understand the structure of that participation.

The act of participating in new media provides a set of experiences that is fundamentally different from the experience one gets from engaging with tradition forms of media (particularly broadcast). We believe that the ways learning happens in the context of new media is also fundamentally different. Where broadcast media, as a one to many system, presumed that learning was a function of absorbing (or interpreting) a transmitted message, new media presumes learning to be a process of engaging with information and using it *in a broader social context* as a crucial part of what we describe as "productive inquiry".

The notion of productive inquiry dates back to John Dewey's pragmatism and certainly applies to notions of older, broadcast media as well. But the social framework of new media begins to open up an aspect of productive inquiry unimaginable and unavailable in Dewey's time. As we read Dewey, perhaps the single most important aspect of productive inquiry is the ability to engage the imagination. The infrastructure of new media has enabled the fusion of network technology, communities of interest and a shared sense of co-presence, resulting in emergence of what we have deemed a "networked imagination".

If the paradigm for learning in old media is a notion of direct transfer, the question that interests us most is "what does a theory of learning look like for collective, social and participatory media?"

To get at that question, we believe it is necessary to understand the epistemological foundations of social and collective participation, to understand how people are learning in the social context of new media. In doing so, we examine learning in the context of three frames: knowing, making and playing.

The goal of this paper is to advance three central theses. First that the world of the 21st century is characterized by a sense of constant change and that such a landscape requires us to further rethink our notions of interaction with new media toward a deeper understanding of participation (knowing) as in the Andrew Sullivan story. Second, how the notion of experience (and participation) within new media contexts has shifted from a traditional sense of experiencing content to using content as context to construct a social world with others (making). Third, understanding how networked media supports a kind of play (playing) that allows people to navigate the complexities of a constantly changing world. What may be most important to understand is that each of these dimensions of learning is in the process of evolving in response to the demands of the 21st century. In a world of flux, knowing, making and playing emerge as critical components of *becoming*.

THREE PERSPECTIVES ON LEARNING

In the opening pages of *Homo Ludens*, Johan Huizinga suggests that the relationship between play and culture may be more complicated than we have suspected. It was a concept that was prescient in 1933 when the work was written and has only begun to find full expression in the digital world. In fact, the premise of Huizinga's book is that culture emerges from play and that all of our most vital cultural elements, indeed the very notion of the sacred itself, emerge from the basic human instinct for play. We contend that Huizinga offered a fundamental insight which is now more relevant than ever to learning. Our effort is an attempt to reconcile the theoretical notions of knowing, making and playing through an understanding of the affordances that new media provides. In doing so, we contend that there is something special in networked media that illuminates not only how important each of these three concepts is for knowledge construction, but that the interactions of these ideas shows us just how powerful these tools are for establishing a theory of learning.

Much of the recent thinking about learning and new media has focused on the concept of transfer, with the primary question being "does information from the digital world transfer to the real world?" Games in particular have been subject to this test and much of the literature on games and learning has been directed at either answering that question (arguing for transfer) or reframing it (arguing that different things may transfer than what is supposed). Our position is different. We believe the basic assumption of knowledge transfer is wrong. It is, quite simply, not how learning works.

In particular, we draw upon the work of Michael Polanyi who suggests that knowledge itself is always composed of both an explicit dimension and a tacit dimension. In that sense, to view knowledge as an object, divorced from experience and embodiment (the central elements of the tacit dimension) is to fundamentally misunderstand the nature of knowledge. One of the primary consequences of Polanyi's insight is that if knowledge is not objectifiable, it is not capable of being transferred as suggested by most traditional education paradigms. If we cannot divorce the explicit dimension of knowledge from the tacit, then knowledge transfer begins to lose its conceptual coherence. *This is especially true as we think about knowledge in a rapidly changing world.* In a stable world the part of the tacit that could be made explicit was made explicit (through the social processes of science, etc) and that part of the tacit that was truly tacit became a part of the shared practices of the (epistemic) community. These slow maturation and absorption processes don't work as well in a world of rapid change and are being transformed (often unwittingly) with new media with fluid genres, new practices and networked infrastructures.

Perhaps as important is the shift that occurs when we begin to take the idea of the tacit seriously. The tacit begins to honour the social dimension of knowledge that the explicit does not. When we look to new media, we can begin to see social contexts in which knowing, constructing and playing all start to emerge as central elements of learning and that the structure of learning within these new contexts are related to the interaction of these terms. These three elements of learning also correspond to three broader frames which we can begin to understand as *Homo Sapiens* (human as knower), *Homo Faber* (human as maker) and *Homo Ludens* (human as player).

While Huizinga focuses on the notion of playing (*Homo Ludens*), rather than knowing (*Homo Sapiens*) or making (*Homo Faber*), it is our contention that it is the combination of all three and their interaction within a social and participatory context that deserves critical attention. In what follows, we map out the affordances of these three fundamental positions and then provide a model for how we might understand their interactions in the networked world.

Homo Sapiens

As the term itself suggests, *Homo Sapiens* or "knowing (hu)man" or "(hu)man as knower" is a fundamental statement about what it means to be human. It is also an ontological statement about learning. The past decade has ushered in substantial changes in how we think about what it means to learn, based primarily in the context of rapid change in our networked world. There are three senses in which learning happens in relation to change. The most basic sense is "learning about", which corresponds to contexts in which information is stable. We learn about things which are stable and consistent and not likely to change over time. The second sense is "learning to be", which requires engagement with an epistemic community and provides as sense of enculturation in practices which allow one to participate and learn how to learn and even shape practices within that community. The third sense, which emerges out of a context of rapid and continual change, is a sense of *becoming*. This sense of learning is itself always in a state of flux, characterized by a sense of acting, participating and knowing. Like the changes we describe in the structure of knowledge above, becoming (unlike learning about and learning to be) is responsive to context, rather than content. As the context changes, so does one's sense of becoming.

There are two elements of new media which are worth pointing out, both of which depend on realizing the ways that, as Henry Jenkins discusses, new media is at base a participatory culture. The first requires us to think more directly about what we mean by "knowing", particularly in the context of the 21st century. New media provides a sense of agency in the most basic sense. In an Internet based world, how we know things and what sources of information we give authority are become increasingly complicated. In a context where knowledge is ever shifting and in a process of continuous flow, how we know things (and how we know what we know) has become more important to us than the factual status of information itself. In most areas of human activity, knowledge is both contingent and in flux. We expect "facts" to change on a continuing basis, because they are facts about a changing world and because we have a technological infrastructure that can support rapid updating of information without high material costs. This shift demonstrates an increasing importance to the context of information. Much of the 20th century information infrastructure focused on accuracy, the *what* of information. New media technologies, while not losing sight of the *what*, force us to consider both the *where* (what is the authority behind the information) and the *when* (is the information current and relevant to my particular problem). This warranting of information signals, again, the importance of the tacit dimension of knowledge, the things which cannot be rendered explicit, but which form a large part of the basis of what it is that we know. Equally important, these factors depend almost entirely on the social context of the information, which is also the driving force for shaping one's sense of becoming.

As a result, we would argue that there has been a shift in the practices around these new forms of learning. While the traditional model of learning has been grounded in the concept of "learning about", the idea that knowledge is something to be studied and accumulated, new theories of learning have begun to understand the affordances in the networked world that privileges notions of "learning to be", the ability to put the things we learn into action, often within the context of an epistemic community or community of practice. But neither of these has yet embraced the concept of "becoming" as an epistemic foundation for knowing. Futhermore, although the tightly bounded social context of communities of practice and communities of interest facilitate a sense of perceived permanence or continuity over time (established by and communicated through shared practices), the relatively unbounded space of the networked world unmoors learning from a particular trajectory. Where a participant in a culture who is learning to be a doctor may not know exactly what that entails, they have a sense of being enculturated into a set of practices that are generally shared among group over a period of time. In the case of today's world, with the continual sense of becoming, there is no telos directing that sense of learning. The learning itself is the practice of participating and that participation is constitutive of the social context in which the learning takes place. The telos is defined by the context, which is continually changing with each act of participation. These communities of becoming themselves are rich constructs that fuse notions of interest, technological infrastructure and co-presence (often in the form of joint work) into the idea of a "networked imagination". Thus this sense of becoming is both afforded by and amplified by *participation in the networked imagination*.

Participating in a networked imagination throws the distinction between learning to be and becoming into relief. Learning to be involves enculturation into a set of practices rather than stockpiling knowledge. Becoming involves a rich and deeply intuitive understanding of the tacit. The end result is not knowledge per se, but a new set of tools for looking at the world and engaging in inquiry, hopefully productive inquiry. Becoming, then, becomes a powerful subject position from which to manage and embrace the flux and constant change which is beginning to shape and define the world of the 21st century.

Homo Faber

In contrast to *Homo Sapiens*, *Homo Faber* is "(Hu)man as maker", stressing our ability to create. This is perhaps the one of the most important and transformational elements of the networked world and provides a unique set of affordances for understanding the relationship between new media and learning. As new media has evolved, it has increasingly tended toward providing agency to users, allowing them to creatively express themselves, often within a context that allows for commentary, feedback and criticism. *Homo Faber* is more than simply making; it is making within a social context that values participation. It is akin to what Michael Polanyi has described as "indwelling", the process by which we begin to comprehend and understand something by connecting to it and, literally, living and dwelling in it. In that way, making also taps into the richness of becoming. We learn through making, building and shaping not to produce something static, but to engage in the process of participation. In fact, we may go so far as to say there can be no sense of becoming, particularly as it relates to learning, without the dimension of *Homo Faber* as indwelling.

The richness of Polanyi's concept marks a fundamental transformation in what we think learning is. Rather than thinking of learning as an accumulation of knowledge as an object or endpoint, Polanyi's framework invites us to think about the process of learning as *knowing*, exploring both the explicit and tacit dimensions of knowledge. As he writes: "We may identify, therefore, our knowing of something by attending to something else with the kind of knowledge we have of our own body by dwelling in it" (Polanyi, 1974, p. 142). Polanyi posits that we come to understand and to comprehend the particulars of an object only when we dwell in the "coherent entity" that they, the particulars, jointly constitute. Or put differently, *Homo Faber* constitutes *knowing* as an embodied set of experiences that we create through our practices of being in the world and attending to things in the world through our experiences with them. To know something *deeply* is to understand the explicit dimension though our embodied engagement with its tacit dimension.

New media opens up the possibility of this kind of deep knowing by providing the agency to participate, create and build, with the recognition that building is always being done within a social context. Most critically, within the context of a networked imagination, making is a creative process which shapes the social context in which the creation itself has meaning.

In doing so, we can begin to see *Homo Faber* as creating an epistemology which is centred on *knowing and becoming*, rather than knowledge and being and which takes practices of fabrication, creation and participation as the cornerstones of learning. Accordingly, *Homo Faber* no longer divorces knowledge from knowing, or explicit from tacit understanding. Instead, *Homo Faber* invites us to think about the ways in which the two are inherently connected and supplemental to one another. Through creating we come to understand and comprehend the world, not merely as a set of object, artifacts or creations, but as coherent entities which we come to dwell in and which we make sense of the "jointness" and interconnection of the parts that constitute the whole, both at the explicit level of the object itself and at the tacit level in terms of its social context and relations. It is this level of tacit knowledge, that which is known, embodied and most importantly *felt* that begins to constitute a new way of learning.

Homo Ludens

The third element, *Homo Ludens*, "(hu)man as player", is perhaps the most important, yet overlooked, element of understanding our relationship to new media. Huizinga's thesis is that play is not merely central to the human experience; it is constitutive of all that is meaningful in human culture. Culture, he argues, does not create play; play creates culture. In almost every example of what he describes as the sacred, play is the central and defining feature of our most valued cultural rites and rituals. As such, for Huizinga, play is not something we do; it is who we are.

To truly understand the connection between play and learning, we need to fully grasp how play puts us in a different mindset. Play is a complex and complicated idea, which is usually held in opposition to most of what have been considered the most stable pillars of learning in the 20th century. Play is thought of as the opposite of work. It is fun, rather than serious. Its connection to learning is often seen as secondary or incidental.

Play, we want to argue, pace Huizinga, is probably the most overlooked aspect in understanding how learning functions in culture. It is easy to identify spaces in which networked culture provides opportunities for play, video games being a clear example. But thinking about play as a cultural disposition, rather than as merely engaging with a game, reveals something more fundamental at work. Much of what makes play powerful as a learning environment is our ability to engage in processes of experimentation. All systems of play are, at base, learning systems. They are ways of engaging in complicated negotiations of meaning, interaction and competition, not only for entertainment, but also for the making of meaning. Most critically, play reveals a structure of learning that is radically different from what most schools or structured learning environments create, one which is almost ideally suited to the notions of flux and becoming that we have outlined throughout.

In play we are presented with yet a third perspective on learning in a world of constant flux. In the case of play, the process is no longer smooth and progressive, but is constituted by a gap between the facts or knowledge we are given and the end result or outcome we wish to achieve. This dynamic accelerates in the context of flux and rapid change, where stable paths and linear progression are no longer viable. As Espen Aarseth describes the dynamic, it is one of *aporia* and *epiphany*. As Huizinga lays out the framework, it follows the structure of a riddle. In both cases, the information provided is insufficient to reach a conclusion about meaning or knowledge. What play provides is the opportunity to leap, to experiment, to fail, to fail and continue to play with different outcomes or to "riddle" one's way though a mystery. That leap that you take is more than simply a means to cross the chasm between what you know and what you want to achieve. It is, as both Aarseth and Huizinga suggest, an *organizing principle*. Figuring out a riddle is more than simply getting the right answer. It is an answer which organizes and makes sense of the riddle. In that sense, our understanding comes not from a linear progression, but, instead, by thinking about the problem from all angles, but ultimately seeing its logic only at the end. Riddles make sense only retroactively. That is the nature of an epiphany.

Likewise, for Aaresth, an *epiphany* is more than an answer. It is a moment which throws all that has come before it into sharp relief, by making sense of a progression which may have seemed disorganized, dishevelled or even nonsensical up until the moment when some greater understanding is reached and its meaning is revealed *by* the player. And which couldn't happen without the playfulness of mind.

Perhaps most critical in this sense of play is the way in which the sense of agency emerges. Where traditional notions of learning position the learner as a passive agent of reception, the *aporia/epiphany* structure of play makes the agency of the player central to the learning process. How one arrives at the epiphany is always a matter of the tacit. The ability to organize and make sense of things is a kind of "attending to" characteristic of the tacit dimension.

The value of play is never found in a static endpoint, but instead in the sense that the player is always in a state of becoming. Whatever it is that one accomplishes in play, it is never about achieving a particular goal (even if a game may have an endpoint of end state). It is always about finding the next challenge or becoming more fully immersed in a state of play. What we do in play may best express the sense of becoming.

This sense of play then provides us with a third, and very different, sense of learning. One which is neither about the process of learning to be, or an embodied sense of indwelling (though it may be consonant with either or both), but which is structurally different in how it organizes our understanding and comprehension of the world. In play, learning is not driven by a logical calculus but, instead, by a more lateral, imaginative thinking and feeling. In sum, playing, like making and knowing, derives its power from the tacit dimension.

THREE PERSPECTIVES AS A FRAMEWORK FOR LEARNING

If we examine each of these three perspectives independently, we can see how each might produce a framework for learning. *Homo Sapiens*, for example, is well suited to thinking about learning as reflection, while *Homo Faber* can be understood as a constructivist approach à la Seymour Papert, which values putting the learner in contact with the tools they use to build. Likewise, *Homo Ludens* may fit into paradigms of situated learning, as has been suggested by Jean Lave and others.

Our goal is neither to reinvent these theories nor critique them directly. Instead, we see this world of constant flux as an opportunity to problematize the very notion of what it means to learn, as well as to better understand what these kinds of practices tell us about learning more generally. Put differently, each of these perspectives tells us something valuable about the process of learning, but there has been a tendency to view these almost exclusively from the perspective of how each contributes to the transmission of explicit forms of knowledge. While each of these perspectives may identify and be identified with certain practices, none of them has fully considered the implications of tacit learning.

The potential revolution for learning that the networked world provides is the ability to create scalable environments for learning that engage the tacit as well as the explicit dimensions of knowledge. The term we have been using for this, borrowed from Polanyi, is *indwelling*. Understanding this notion requires us to think about the connection between *experience, embodiment* and *learning*.

While we have known that these elements are connected on a deep level from the early works on experience and learning from Piaget, Levi-Strauss and Vygotsky, placing them at the centre of a learning paradigm has proven elusive. We believe there have been two reasons for this. First, until now we have lacked any infrastructure that has been capable of placing experience and embodiment at the centre of a theory of learning. They have always been understood as secondary mechanisms to enhance learning, but never been thought of as the core of it.

Second, taking the tacit dimension seriously conflicts with our fundamental urge to abstract and de-contextualize what is happening in the process of learning. Tacit understanding begins from the premise that every learning experience is different and bound to both the learner and the immediate context in which the learning takes place. The process and results are not replicable.

The lessons from the networked world allow us to tackle both of these problems at the same time. Large scale network structures now provide environments which not only allow for tacit knowing and understanding, they presume it. Engaging with digital media is almost always experiential. In most cases, we learn with digital tools by doing. More and more, we also learn by feeling and acting in an embodied way. It is that sense of engaging with the tools at hand which gives us access and insight not only into their immediate use, but also a set of possibilities for future action that may be revealed only by confronting new problems or situations.

The indwelling that we see happening in these spaces is a fusion of all three frameworks: knowing, making and playing. The affordances of the digital worlds with which we engage determine the degree to which we engage in each element, but we are seeing with increasing frequency that digital worlds and virtual spaces are beginning to understand the importance of all three to creating a successful and sustainable sense of community.

This calls up the second problem, which is abstraction and replication. A theory of learning that is only able to describe what learning took place retroactively cannot serve as a paradigm for new learning. Focusing on the tacit, then, seems to relegate such a theory to a purely descriptive mechanism. But that is only true if your concern is what kind of *explicit* knowledge is transferred.

When we move to the tacit dimension our concern shifts. If we are concerned now with *indwelling* rather than explicit knowledge, then the proper area of inquiry is not on outcome or replication, but an *environment*. From this perspective, we can begin to ask, not *what* are they learning, but *where* are they dwelling or in what are they dwelling. Of concern then is the question of what is afforded by the spaces of digital and networked worlds. While results and processes are not replicable, learning environments are.

At the nexus of knowing, making and playing is the idea that the tacit dimension of learning is grounded in understanding how we use the ideas of experience and embodiment to make small changes in our understanding, practices and experimentation, to adapt what we know to a changing environment.

MAPPING LEARNING TO PARTICIPATION: WHAT NETPUBLICS TEACH US ABOUT HOW WE *LEARN*

Tangentially, but in order to provide a glimpse of today's and tomorrow's students and how they are learning, we include here an overview of a critical ethnographic study of social media participation. Mimi Ito, now at the University of California, Irvine, and her cohorts in a large scale MacArthur Foundation DML project construct a typology of practices describing participation as: "hanging out", "messing around" and "geeking out". We believe that these three practices frame a (potential) progression of learning that is endemic to digital networks. When we tie these notions of participation to the frames of reference we have outlined above, we can begin to see not only how each level of participation produces a richer sense of learning, but also how the affordances of digital media environments start to come into play in the construction of various knowledge communities.

Knowing: Hanging Out

At the most basic level, participation in digital environments requires a sense of *knowing*, of "learning to be". As Ito argues, "participation in social network sites like MySpace, Facebook and Bebo (among others) as well as instant and text messaging, young people are constructing new social norms and forms of media literacy in networked public culture that reflect the enhanced role of media in young people's lives." Digital networked environments provide not only an extension of real-world interaction; they provide an enhanced environment for sharing information and engaging in meaningful social interaction.

This notion of hanging out is what we see as the beginning of and essential to the process of indwelling. But the notion of indwelling, as Polanyi makes clear, is much richer than simply having a feeling of presence or belonging. It goes beyond the process of enculturation and understanding of social norms, roles and mores. The beginnings of indwelling in the digital world are rooted in the notion of "being with". What Ito's work reveals is that hanging out is more than simply gaining familiarity with the tools, spaces and affordances of the digital. In fact, it is probably not an exaggeration to say it is not about the digital at all. Hanging out, in Ito's terms, is about learning how to be with others in spaces which are mediated by digital technology. Again, in this notion we find learning that applies to the digital world, but which is also building and foundation for learning that transcends the bounds of the virtual.

Hanging out, we contend, begins to develop the first aspect of indwelling: experience. That experience is governed by a central question: what is my relationship to others?

Playing/Knowing: Messing Around

The second notion of participation that Ito explores is messing around, which she defines accordingly: "When messing around, young people begin to take an interest in and focus on the workings and content of the technology and media itself, tinkering, exploring and extending their understanding." Within this framework, we begin to see a second dimension emerge, one which not only engages a second frame of reference, playing, but which begins to bring the two frames of reference into contact with one another.

The function of play, above all else, is to problematize the familiar. We can see this in nearly every meaning of the word itself, but perhaps most directly on the sense of space opened up by use. For example, when we say a steering wheel in a car "has a little play in it", we mean there is some flexibility, a difference between how it should be and how it is. Those gaps become known through experience, through the process we discuss above as hanging out. For some users in digital environments, hanging out leads to the next stage which is characterized by Ito as "open ended", "self-taught" and "loosely goal directed". That moment causes a shift in perspective, where the process of knowing is no longer about our relationship to others, but instead becomes about understanding our relationship to the environment.

What we see as critical in this second stage is the shift in agency that occurs. Where hanging out is about acquiring a sense of social agency, figuring out how to use technology to maintain or enhance social relationships, messing around is about the user's relationship with the technology or environment itself.

In hanging out, that relationship is easy to assess. Digital media are tools to facilitate social interaction. Their function is purely instrumental. The transition to messing around, as Ito describes it, is typically personal and involves the development of a sense of personal agency: "what is characteristic of these initial forays into messing around is that youth are pursuing topics of personal interest. In our interviews with young people who were active digital media creators or deeply involved in other interest-driven groups, they generally described a moment when they took a personal interest in a topic and pursued it in a self-directed way."

This process, we would describe as moving from experience to embodiment, where the personal investment in digital media changes the focus from social agency to personal agency. Technology and digital media begin to be viewed as an extension of the self. Not surprisingly, most of the introductions to messing around that Ito describes involve things that are heavily connected to personal identity, such as personal videos and pictures, MySpace profiles and gaming activity that is about player modification.

What messing around reveals most fundamentally is that the relationship between us and our environment is rich, complex and changing. Our process of knowing is no longer instrumental; it is instead structured by a sense of play. As a result, understanding our relationship to our environment requires experimentation, play and riddling. That subtle shift transforms our experience into a set of tools for understanding the environment. Playing serves as a frame of reference to problematize the familiar, and the "play" we have in our own experience invites us to think through the possibilities of altering, shifting and experimenting with the things we know as ready-at-hand.

The kind of tinkering that characterizes messing around is not instrumental, it is not intended to find solutions or make things work better. It is, instead, focused on helping us understand who we are in relationship to our environment.

Messing around constitutes the next step of indwelling: embodiment. In doing so, it asks the question: what is my relationship to the environment?

Playing/Knowing/Making: Geeking Out

The final stage of participation, "geeking out", is the most complicated. Within our framework, there are two aspects of "geeking out" that merit particular attention. First, the conditions under which geeking out occurs, the technological infrastructure that makes it possible: "For many young people, the ability to engage with media and technology in an intense, autonomous and interest-driven way is a unique feature of the media environment of our current historical moment. Particularly for kids with newer technology and high-speed Internet access at home, the Internet can provide access to an immense amount of information related to their particular interests, and can support various forms of geeking out."

Second, and, for our purposes, the most critical aspect of geeking out is the manner in which it extends both the social agency of hanging out and the personal agency of messing around: "Geeking out involves learning to navigate esoteric domains of knowledge and practice, and participating in communities that traffic in these forms of expertise."

It is the richness of experience and social agency produced by hanging out, the sense of embodiment and personal agency created by messing around, combined with the third frame of reference, *making*, that produces what we think is the ultimate goal of indwelling: learning. Geeking out provides an experiential, embodied sense of learning within a rich social context of peer interaction, feedback and knowledge construction enabled by a technological infrastructure that promotes "intense, autonomous, interest driven" learning.

It is the third frame of reference, the making, which values understanding joint work, including the ways in which the community functions of hanging out and the personal functions of messing around can be harnessed and compounded to produce the "specialized knowledge networks" and "Internet-base communities and organizations".

The learning taking place at the nexus of knowing, playing and making is radically different from any learning environment we have seen before. It is an environment that emerges from a sense of indwelling, embodiment and agency. As a result, it is a learning environment that gains almost all of its power and benefits from the tacit dimension.

CONCLUSIONS

As each of these aspects come together to produce what we can think of as a new set of epistemological frames for understanding a world in flux, we can begin to see that we need a new, broader framework for understanding the processes of what learning and knowing look like. Where traditional models of learning have moved from models of direct knowledge transfer to broader notions of skills, we believe that neither of these is sufficient to explain and account for the fundamental epistemic shifts and new affordances that 21st century presents.

Accordingly, we believe that the best way to understand how learning, and indeed knowing, can be understood and harnessed for educational practices and institutions is by understanding these epistemological frames, why each matters, and, ultimately, how they can all come together to create a new understanding of learning environments.

As the educational landscape changes in the 21st century, our paradigms for learning, knowing and education also need to shift. The tools of the digital world are just now beginning to open up new affordances, new possibilities and new tools that make inquiry and process based learning not only possible, but what is likely to become the standard for learning. In a world where knowing, making and playing are growing at an incredible pace, we need to develop the tools, practices and theoretical frameworks to understand that new world, and models to harness its power, build upon those ideas and be responsive to them.

We face a world today of almost infinite complexity, endless possibility, and near constant change. If our educational institutions and our informal learning environments are going to take advantage of these changes, our approach to education and learning needs to be as rich and complex as the challenges and opportunities we face.

REFERENCES

Aarseth, E. (1997). *Cybertext: Perspectives on Ergodic Literature*, Baltimore: The Johns Hopkins University Press.

Huizinga, J. (1950). Homo Ludens A Study of the Play-Element in Culture. New York: Beacon Press.

Ito, M. (2009). *Hanging Out, Messing Around, and Geeking Out: Kids Living and Learning with New Media*. Cambridge: MIT Press.

Jenkins, H. (2006). Convergence *culture: where old and new media collide*. NYU Press.

Pendelton-Jullian, A. (2009). *Design Education and Innovation Ecotones*. Available: http://president.asu.edu/files/ Design%20Innovation%20and%20Innovation%20Ecotones.pdf. Last retrieved 11 September 2009.

Polanyi, M. (1967). *The Tacit Dimension*. New York: Anchor/Doubleday.

Polanyi, M. (1974). *Scientific Thoughts and Social Reality: Essays*. Madison, CT: International University Press.

Sullivan, A. (2008). "Why I Blog," *Atlantic Monthly*, November 2008.

PART VI

•••••••••••••

Summary and
Second Glion Declaration

CHAPTER 23

Summary of the Colloquium

James J. Duderstadt, Mary O' Mahony and Luc E. Weber

SESSION 1: GENERAL DISCUSSION OF INNOVATION

Chair: Georg Winkler
Luc Weber: The Next Decade, a Challenge for Technological and Societal Innovations
Charles Vest: Technological Innovation in the 21st Century
Ellen Hazelkorn: Community Engagement as Social Innovation

The first session began with the observation that it was precisely a century ago, in 1908, that Schumpeter introduced the terms "innovation" and "entrepreneurism" into economics at both the University of Vienna and Harvard, which, together with Lausanne (near Glion), comprised the centres of economic theory at the time. Over the past several months, his theory of creative destruction has been in evidence once again as our world has been shaken by the current global financial and economic crises, in which over $3 trillion of wealth has been destroyed by flawed financial, economic and regulatory policies. It was suggested that what has really happened is that the "real" economy, based on wealth generated by goods and services, rather than financial gymnastics and "quants" — e.g., credit default derivative swaps — has returned with a crash. We have learned once again that while technological innovation can drive economic growth, social innovation is necessary to sustain development in the face of human frailty and misadventures.

The motto of many of today's companies has become "innovate or abdicate", as the explosion of knowledge, coupled with the evolution of a truly global economy driven by rapidly evolving information, communication and transportation technologies, has enabled innovation to flourish wherever bright, motivated and entrepreneurial people can gather. Yet, as the speed of innovation has accelerated, so too has its complexity, becoming both competitive and collaborative, spanning the disciplines and extending far beyond technology. In fact, today the greatest wealth comes not from technological but rather organizational innovation, as evidenced by new paradigms such as "open innovation" and "global sourcing" in which companies discard old-fashioned, "not-invented-here" constraints to tap ideas and talent wherever it exists, "open source — open content" knowledge that is available to anyone with Internet connectivity, and human capital both distributed and accessible about the globe.

In this rapidly changing environment, all social institutions and communities are challenged to adapt to new challenges with innovative new forms. In particular, universities face the challenge not only to adapt to a world driven by innovation, but in turn, to produce the new knowledge and creative graduates capable of producing that innovation. Yet, concern was expressed about those forces constraining the ability of the university to respond to the challenge of change: governments (and perhaps policies such as the Bologna process) that restrict both autonomy and diversity, students and faculty who fear the "contamination" of academic purity by university engagement with the economy, and the disciplines themselves rigidly moored to their intellectual canon. The issue of autonomy was of particular concern to the leaders of European universities as organizational innovation becomes increasingly important. Yet, while greater university autonomy is certainly necessary if institutions are to achieve the flexibility demanded by an innovation-driven world, this can only happen if institutions are also willing to be held more accountable for their contributions to society and their adherence to fundamental academic values.

In summary, the discussions occurring during this session revealed the following themes: First, technological innovation is not enough to address today's challenges. Social or societal innovation is equally important, with organizational or institutional innovation increasingly emerging as a critical goal. The interaction among these different types of innovation is key, and universities are well-placed to play a role in stimulating that interaction. For that they will need to stress greater interdisciplinarity in academic programs, more leadership roles for younger faculty, and more autonomy to enable innovative approaches to society's needs.

This session also was characterized by an important theme that propagated through the entire colloquium: the role of young people in shaping innovation. While it is evident that the new world of innovation will be determined by the next generation, it is encouraging that today's students seem to understand the growing importance of innovation and their role in creating new knowledge. Even while enrolled in our institutions, our students are contributing to innovation in curricular development driven by their changing modes of learning (e.g., social networking, immersive technology). Hence it is important not only to engage them in learning activities beyond the classroom, such as research and public service, but to also allow them the time and flexibility to develop their creative skills.

SESSION 2: AGENTS OF INNOVATION

Chair: Frank Rhodes

Jean-Lou Chameau: Curiosity and the Transformative Impact of Fundamental Scientific Research

Wayne Johnson: Industry as a Catalyst of Innovation

Frans van Vught: National Innovation Policies: Governments as Innovation Agents of Higher Education and Research

While many universities have sought to enhance their contributions to technological innovation and entrepreneurial activities through organization such as incubators, technology transfer offices and research parks, in the end their impact almost always depends primarily upon the efforts of individual faculty. A study of successful faculty entrepreneurs such as Carver Mead at Caltech or George Whitesides at MIT reveals the importance of scholarly reputation and institution quality. Furthermore, the most important players in the transfer of the scientific knowledge from campus research activities into the commercial marketplace are usually the students they educate, particularly at the graduate and postdoctoral level. This strong dependence of innovation on the exceptional abilities of a few highly creative people should be kept in mind by those seeking to stimulate entrepreneurial activities. The important factor — and hence investment — was the building of relationships, which takes time and requires substance. Here a question was raised as to whether the close relationships characterizing smaller institutions (e.g., Caltech) gave them advantages, although this was countered by the greater intellectual breadth and diversity characterizing larger universities. There was agreement that in today's world, human talent is not only institutionally but globally distributed and accessible through modern information and communication technologies.

In the United States, it has been estimated that perhaps as much as 50% of economic growth during the latter half of the 20th century was driven by technological innovation, much of which was produced in a small number of world-class research universities (e.g., MIT, Stanford, Caltech), large corporate research laboratories (e.g., Bell Laboratories, IBM Research Laboratories, the Lockheed Skunkworks), and federal laboratories (e.g., Los Alamos, Oak Ridge, Jet Propulsion Lab). Yet, as the monopolies enabling generously supported corporate research laboratories disappeared, world-class research universities proliferated around the globe, and rapidly evolving ICT allowed unrestricted access to talent and ideas anywhere, anytime, the new paradigms of open innovation were embraced that distributed R&D, innovation and entrepreneurial activities on a global scale. New forms of collaboration appeared, in which the triple helix of industry, government and higher education joined together to generate the knowledge and human talent to drive innovation and economic value. Organizations that once demanded secrecy and exclusivity of intellectual property began to share and collaborate to address fundamental technological challenges, even as they continued compete aggressively in the marketplace of products and services. University faculty formed consortia with colleagues both at home and abroad. National governments not only joined in international scientific efforts (e.g., the LHC, ITER, and International Space Station) but began to outsource both scientific research and technology development in areas where others had greater capabilities.

As nations seek to promote innovation as an engine of economic growth, higher education and other research organizations have become crucial objects of national policy. Yet, such policies usually fall into one of two approaches: i) to set themes and priorities for the allocation and concentration of resources, and ii) to emphasize competition among key players such as universities through competitive grants programs or market incentives. It was noted that in large systems, competition appears the best strategy, while in smaller countries a concentration strategy seems better. Yet, the environment for innovation is continuing to evolve (e.g., the shift to open innovation and global sourcing), while the information concerning institutional performance and hence policy effectiveness remains scant. It was suggested that nations should adopt a *policy learning strategy* based upon valid, publicly accessible information on both institutional performance and economic impact as a key supplement to policy strategies such as prioritization and competition.

Here a concern was raised that perhaps regional strategies such as the Lisbon Agenda might prove more effective in the long run than national innovation strategies, which actually could conflict with regional efforts. It was also suggested that the strong emphasis that governments were placing on the role of universities in stimulating the innovation key to economic prosperity might overwhelm the other critical missions of the university.

In summary, the key themes of this discussion session were: The role of students is particularly important in successful university-driven innovation activities. Here the strong involvement of U.S. undergraduates in significant research was particularly beneficial. There was discussion concerning the appropriate role of university leadership in promoting interaction across faculties within the context of an innovation strategy. Successful innovation strategies for industry-university interactions required a careful strategy in the selection of partners to enable the focus sufficient time and resources to design and sustain the interaction. The current trend of government funding to focus on funding individuals needed to be broadened to support the innovation that occurred in partnerships or larger systems. The nature of government innovation strategies, e.g., competitive vs. concentrated, depends on the scale of the enterprise.

SESSION 3: NATIONAL AND REGIONAL INNOVATION STRATEGIES

Chair: James Duderstadt

Georg Winckler: Innovation Strategies of European Universities in the triangle of Education, Research and Innovation

Ralph Eichler: Team Players to shape our Future; Do Our Students Learn the Right Skills?

Heather Munroe-Blum: The Innovation Society: Canada's Next Chapter

Bertil Andersson: Singapore: Successful in Research; Struggling for Innovation

Fawwaz Ulaby: KAUST, An International, Independent, Graduate Research University

Arif S. Al Hammadi: Transforming an Economy through Research and Innovation

Juan Ramon de la Fuente: Research and Innovation in Latin America

This session focused on the experience of various nations in creating research universities capable of contributing to innovation-driven economies in various regions including Europe, North America, Asia, the Middle East and Latin America. European higher education evolved from the medieval humanist themes of 17th and 18th universities into institutions primarily focused on graduate education and scholarship in 19th century Germany and Austria, a theme that soon propagated across Europe and then throughout the world. While recent efforts to better unify European higher education through the Bologna Process, the European Research Area and the Lisbon Agenda have clearly enhanced collaboration and facilitated the mobility of students and faculty, innovation strategies continue to exist primarily at the national rather than the E.U. level, without the cross-border innovation pressure and demands that one finds in the United States. There is a growing recognition that demands of innovation-driven economies require that the process to achieve European integration in higher education be balanced with efforts to achieve greater autonomy, agility and mission differentiation among European research universities.

Since research and innovation are quite different activities, the former transforming money into knowledge and the latter transforming knowledge back into money, fundamental changes in pedagogy will also likely be necessary. Creativity, innovation and entrepreneurship are most effective acquired through deep student engagement in knowledge-generating projects rather than traditional content-based learning. There is a need to better integrate scientific research in Europe with educational programs, much as it is in North America, rather than keeping it at arms length in separate research institutions, as it tends to be in much of Europe. Yet this will be difficult in some nations where universities tend to be supported at the regional level while research institutes are supported by the national government.

In the United States and Canada, universities have evolved that blend the missions of broad undergraduate studies, research-focused graduate programs and deeper engagement with society through service activities. While the United States benefited from both a philosophy and scale that enabled a sufficient degree of diversity and autonomy of universities with respect to mission, resource base, quality and character to serve a rapidly changing nation, Canada has faced more of a challenge in coupling high quality academic programs to the nation's needs for innovation and entrepreneurial engagement, particularly at the graduate level. The absence, until recently, of strong tax incentives to encourage philanthropic support of higher education similar to those in the United States, has also been a challenge. To this end, a national Canadian Foundation has been created and capitalized to stimulate through large institutional grants major new initiatives aimed at better coupling graduate education and research to market-driven innovation.

In both Asia and the Middle East, there are bold efforts to create world-class research universities. Although Singapore is expanding its universities to serve an increasing population, of particular importance is an effort to work with major international universities (e.g., MIT, Imperial College, Technion, Duke) to build major graduate-research programs in key strategic areas. Although Singapore's investment in such research efforts has now grown to 3% of GDP, there remains a concern about whether creativity and innovation may be hindered by its rigid social structure, e.g., "Can you win a Nobel Prize in a country that does not tolerate graffiti?" It was stressed that deep innovation required a tolerance for failure, a trait currently missing in risk-adverse cultures such as Singapore.

A contrasting approach was Saudi Arabia and Abu Dhabi. There was recognition that these two nations have mounted major efforts to build world-class institutions, working with established universities faculty from around the world to create an innovative culture. Saudi Arabia has launched a major graduate university, King Abdullah's University of Science and Technology, recruiting leading scholars from around the world and building an extraordinary campus on the Red Sea. Abu Dhabi has taken a somewhat different approach with the Khalifa University of Science, Technology and Research, focusing first on high quality undergraduate education in partnership with several international universities. In both cases, the commitment of extraordinary resources and establishment of strong partnerships to build initially several small, highly focused institutions may allow these nations to leapfrog to world-class status quite rapidly. However this global connectivity could create tensions with the strongly rooted local cultures in these nations.

While such small institutions are nimble and capable of significant impact in highly focused intellectual areas, rapidly growing populations of Latin America, characterized by great social diversity and income inequality, demand a very different approach. Even very large institutions such as the National Autonomous University of Mexico (300,000 students) are unable to keep pace with the educational needs of a growing young population, now estimated at over 100 million between the ages of 15 and 25 in Latin America. Innovative approaches in higher education, such as the use of open educational resources and distance learning, will be necessary to meet these needs while allowing sufficient investment in the advanced education and research required by increasingly technologically sophisticated economies. This would require as well greater political continuity and stability of government programs and support.

This session concluded with a broader discussion about the balance between elitism and scale in determining innovation and entrepreneurism. In a sense, the world is both flat (in the sense of Thomas Friedman) and spiky (in the sense of Michael Porter). This discussion raised several important questions. What attracts creative people to regions? World-class universities or world-class educational systems? Are we trying to approach intensely human characteristics such as creativity and entrepreneurism with a systems approach? How do we nurture stubborn individuals? Perhaps in our efforts to define world-class status through simplistic surveys such as league tables, we are losing the diversity in people, institutions and programs that may be key to generating new ideas and wealth. Since institutional diversity is important in stimulating innovation, there was a call for broadening reputational mechanisms such as league tables beyond simply measuring research performance.

Key themes in the session included: the importance to recognize that drivers of innovations come from many different actors, not just universities. The key attraction to company investments in university partnerships are excellent graduates. As the competition for talent and global reputation intensifies, research output has become an even more important index. Finally, as open innovation becomes more common, at the regional level innovation involving a diverse range of partners may be more important than that driven by a specialized centre of excellence.

SESSION 4: INNOVATION STRATEGIES
AT THE INSTITUTIONAL LEVEL

Chair: Michel Bénard

Michael Crow: The Research University as Comprehensive Knowledge Enterprise: A Prototype for a New American University

Bernd Huber: The German Excellence Initiative: Changes, Challenges and Chances for German Research Universities

James Duderstadt: New University Paradigms for Technological Innovation
Michel Bénard: Hi-Tech Industry and Universities: A Perspective on Dating for Joint Innovation
Jamil Salmi: The Challenges of Establishing World-Class Research Universities in Developing Countries

The discussion turned to several examples of how institutions — universities, industry, nations — were exploring new approaches to better position educational and research programs to respond to the needs of innovation-driven societies. The lead off discussion concerned the efforts to transform one of the United States' youngest major universities, Arizona State, into a "new American university" paradigm. Taking advantage of its location in Phoenix, one of the most diverse and rapidly growing regions in the nation, the university has not only taken steps to restructure its organization, but even more important, its culture. Included in its objectives were the characteristics of: leveraging its place, transforming society, valuing entrepreneurship, conducting use-inspired research, enabling student success, fusing intellectual discipline, becoming socially embedded and engaging globally.

On a different level and scale, the German Excellence Initiative to achieve focused excellence at world-class levels in a select number of institutions was described. Here, the concerns were the low level of Germany's R&D, currently at only 0.8% of GDP, the need to stimulate a greater commitment to research conducted by German universities, and the desire to introduce competitiveness into the university system in an effort to improve performance. Although Germany has a federal structure similar to the United States and Canada in which universities are primarily dependent upon regional (state, provincial) resources, the federal government has committed a five-year program of $2 B per year to fund grants for graduate education and research to encourage key universities to develop strategies to achieve excellence. Already there are early signs of increasing quality and competitiveness. The German Excellence Initiative was also praised for its effectiveness at relatively low cost, perhaps because it relied upon academics rather than politicians to make the final decisions on centres of research excellence.

Yet, there remain challenges to the program, since it creates tensions within the selected universities among those academic programs and missions benefiting from federal funding and other units. There is also tension at the national level among "haves" and "have-nots" that will likely be exacerbated as excellence funds are removed from some institutions and reallocated to others in the next round. There remain other challenges, such as the large amount of basic research (50%) conducted by independent research institutions (such as Max Planck or Fraunhofer Institutes) compared to that performed in universities, in contrast to the leading role played by research universities in nations such as the U.S., U.K., Switzerland and Scandinavia.

The discussion then moved to the evolving innovation strategies of industry as companies attempted to cope with the rapid acceleration and globalization of innovation-driven competitiveness. Most high-tech companies have already shifted from concentrating R&D efforts in central corporate laboratories to highly distributed efforts where R&D activities are located in key markets and developing strong relationships with external players including companies (even sometimes competitors) and particularly research universities. However, they face a "Mars vs. Venus" challenge since the research cultures and incentives of universities are quite different from industry. Furthermore, since open innovation strategies frequently involve other players, such as venture capital and investment communities, economic and social innovation can become as important as technological innovation (a theme that was stressed in the first session).

Universities, governments and industry are joining together in efforts to stimulate greater innovation and entrepreneurship in key priority areas such as biomedical research and energy sustainability. Although the flow of knowledge from scientific discovery through development and technological innovation, commercialization and deployment was once thought of as a linear, vertical process, it is now viewed as far more complex, both vertical and horizontal, and involving many interacting disciplines and participants. Traditionally, one thinks of the appropriate activities for each of the key actors in the innovation continuum — namely, government, industry and universities — in terms such as basic research, applied research, development, commercialization and deployment. For example, basic research activities, usually speculative, long term and driven by scientific curiosity, are usually viewed as the proper role of research universities, while use-driven basic research, applied research and development are more commonly roles for government or industrial laboratories. Commercialization and deployment are similarly viewed most appropriate for industry (both established and entrepreneurial).

Yet, there are other types of research important to the innovation continuum. At the earliest stage is *transformative research*, research driven by ideas that stand a reasonable success of radically changing our understanding of an important existing concept or leading to the creation of a new paradigm or field of science. Such research is also characterized by its challenge to the current understanding or its pathway to new frontiers. While it might be assumed that such transformative research would most commonly occur in research universities, ironically the peer pressure of merit review in both grant competition and faculty promotion can discourage such high risk intellectual activities. In fact, transformative research occurs just as frequently in some industrial research laboratories (e.g., Bell Laboratories in the past and Google

Research today) where unusually creative investigators are freed from the burdens of grant seeking or commercial deadlines. At the other end of the innovation continuum is *translational research*, aimed at building the knowledge base necessary to link fundamental scientific discoveries with the technological innovation necessary for the development of new products, processes and services. Recently, the United States has launched a major new research structure for energy research involving new *transformational* research program patterned after the U.S. Department of Defense's Advanced Research Projects Agency (DARPA) known as ARPA-E and funded at an initial level of $400 M/y; funding 46 new Energy Frontier Research Centers on university campuses and national laboratories for small research teams; and creating an initial set of eight "energy innovation hubs" for *translational* research funded at $280 M for the first year.

Yet, all of these efforts are dependent to some degree on the presence of world-class universities and faculty and students of exceptional quality and creativity. Yet, how does one define a world-class university? Apparently every nation wants one. But what is it? How does one create such an institution? By upgrading or merging existing institutions or creating *de novo*? And how does one know when world-class status is achieved? Through popular league tables? Through global competition, à la FC Barcelona? Nations make many common mistakes in attempting to build such institutions, e.g., placing too much focus on building physical campuses, depending too heavily on foreign partners, paying insufficient attention to operational costs and financial sustainability, and perhaps most important, not recognizing that this takes time, regardless of the capacity to commit massive resources.

Additional themes of the discussion included the importance of making major investments in global challenges. Since rankings (league tables) of universities are likely to continue to be used in determining investment strategies, it might be best if universities joined together to better define how they are willing to be measured than simply attempting to reject such rankings altogether.

SESSION 5: PARADIGM SHIFTS

Chair: Charles Vest
Nam Suh: On Innovation Strategies: An Asian Perspective
Dieter Lenzen: BILDUNG and Innovation — a contradictio in adjecto for Today's University Education in a Globalized World.
Gururaj "Desh" Deshpande: Injecting Relevance to Make Innovation More Impactful at Universities
Stuart Feldman: Industry-University Innovation Collaboration
John Seely Brown: Learning in/for a World of Constant Flux: Homo Sapiens, Homo Faber and Homo Ludens Revisited

The session began with the application of a theoretical analysis of innovation to Korea's efforts to build in its Korean Advanced Institute of Science and Technology (KAIST) an Asian counterpart to MIT. It was suggested that the innovation process follows a well-defined continuum of activities, i.e., identifying a need, building a knowledge base through research, creating an idea, demonstrating feasibility, testing commercial viability, finding "angel" investors and then venture capital, hiring talented people, and raising adequate capital. The absence of any step in the process dooms the innovation. Furthermore, the growth of a regional hub of innovation activity involves a balance between the conduct of sufficient activities to nucleate in stable innovation hubs and the rate at which innovative ideas, people and financial resources can move away from a region. A critical feature of successful innovation hubs is the ability to rapidly learn from failure. Examples were provided as to how KAIST was focusing on key themes such as ship building, electric transportation, DRAMS and nuclear power where there was potential for the formation of innovation hubs.

This discussion of a more abstract foundation of innovation was extended to a consideration of the early characteristics of the 19th classical German research university, associated with the Prussian philosopher and minister Wilhelm von Humboldt, who stressed science not only for knowledge's sake but also to serve humanity. Hence, broader forms of pedagogy are necessary beyond the disciplinary canons necessary for creativity and innovation. Thinking outside the box may require other experiences such as greater student involvement in research and/or public service. Yet today, the Bologna process threatens to impose a uniform standard and regulation to all of higher education rather than valuing institutional diversity. While the Bologna process has reduced fragmentation and enabled a general framework that stresses communication and collaboration, some believe it has pushed the goal of a liberal education out of universities because of the disciplinary overload demanded by a three-year baccalaureate program. Perhaps students need more time to explore, experiment and contemplate to develop the capacity for creativity and innovation.

The contrasts and similarities between "eminent innovation" and "universal innovation" were illustrated by contrasting a highly focused innovation program for students and faculty at MIT with the creation of an entrepreneurship ecosystem in India. Both attempted to connect innovation to compelling problems to stimulate the excitement and commitment of young people who in turn are changing the content of teaching and developing their own course materials. New occupations are emerging, particularly in the services economy, for which different graduate schools are needed such as the ability to work both within and across teams and driving social innovation and value.

Yet, the very nature of innovation is changing, in part driven by emerging technologies such as ICT substrates or "clouds", the support of both hardware and software services through massive cyberinfrastructure installations (e.g., Google, Microsoft, Amazon, Unisys) that not only significantly extend access to state of the art capacity but significantly accelerate the rate of experiment and change. This shifts the "iron" triangle of interaction among universities, industry and governing from "I" shaped (knowing only one area in depth) to "T" shaped (knowing one area in depth along with broad shallow areas) to "pi" shaped (knowing many areas in depth).

In the final presentation, it was suggested that there was a more fundamental epistemological shift occurring from:

- individual → collective
- skills → dispositions and imagination
- explicit → tacit
- stocks → flows
- learning to do → learning to be.

In a rapidly changing world, innovation no longer depends only upon the explicit dimension characterizing conventional content-focused pedagogy focused on "learning to do". Rather, one needs to enable an integration of tacit knowledge with explicit knowledge. Emerging ICT technologies that enable social networking to form learning communities and immersive virtual environments for simulation and play facilitate the "deep tinkering" that provides the tacit knowledge necessary to "learn to be", tools already embraced by the young if not yet the academy. In a sense, learning has become a "culture", in the sense of the Petri dish that is in a state of constant evolution. And just as innovation itself has become more open, accessing ideas and talent on a global basis, the new paradigms of open educational resources (open courseware, library digitization, social networking) have extended both learning and scholarship to a highly interactive global ecosystem of institutions and communities.

A FINAL SESSION: THE GLION DECLARATION — TEN YEARS LATER

This final discussion session began by posing three questions:

1. What are the principal differences in the world of the research university from 1998 to today?
2. What is the audience for a new Declaration similar to that drafted a decade earlier at the first Glion Colloquium?
3. What would be the major themes of such a Declaration?

During the past decade, trends such as increasing populations, environmental impact, global health, poverty and resource depletion have intensified concerns about global sustainability, even as we have transitioned to a knowledge economy increasingly dependent upon educated people and their ideas. The needs for the contributions of universities have intensified. Yet today, there is an increasing tendency to view the university in local economic terms, through utilitarian, reductionist and highly local lenses. We need to look more broadly to identify the themes our institutions should address to serve a global society — or perhaps even better, a civil society. Our institutions need to be challenged to address the grand challenges of the 21st century, with the most urgent among these being global sustainability: sustainable development; resource issues such as energy and food; global poverty and health, policies to sustain stable economic growth; social issues such as urbanization, poverty, health and migration; reducing conflict and terrorism; and the role of government at the nation-state and supra-national level. Our audience should be not only university and government leaders, but also our various constituencies both on campus (faculty, students, staff) and off (industry, NGOs, media, public) and the newly emerging universities throughout the world.

Yet, much of higher education seems deaf to these challenges, as they are to calls for accountability and greater engagement in society. Many nations have succumbed to government efforts to apply uniform policies to all institutions at the expense of diversity, even as the aspirations of most institutions continue be focused on becoming world-class research universities. This combination of eroding autonomy and uniformity is disturbing since more diversity in both the nature of institutions and how they serve society will be needed to address the challenges of the next several decades. Both universities and their patrons seem at times to be deaf to calls for accountability and unresponsive to the need for deeper engagement with society.

There are major challenges facing today's universities, some familiar, such as the issue of the cost, price and value of a college education, the need for a better balance between institutional autonomy and accountability, and the importance of institutional diversity. But there are also new challenges: the implications for both students and institutions of the need for lifelong learning, the globalization of higher education, and the appearance of new learning paradigms enabled by powerful technologies enabling social networking (Facebook, Twitter), immersive environments (Second Life), and "open" learning (OpenCourseware, Google's Book Scan). In fact, it was suggested in discussions that it was time to move beyond the language of a decade ago when one talked of higher education as a "system" and instead view our institutions as just one species in a continually evolving "ecosystem" or "ecology" of learning, from cradle to grave, both in learning institutions and beyond, through life experiences.

During a time when universities tend to be viewed through utilitarian, reductionist and economic lenses, we need to be challenged to look more broadly at our institutions and their roles. We need especially to examine learning environments in a new way. Learning is no longer confined to school. In fact, to paraphrase a well-known statement: "It takes a village to educate a child." One of the most important themes emerging from the past decade of Glion conferences has been the importance of innovation in the rapidly evolving ecosystem of higher education.

CHAPTER 24

Universities
and the Innovative Spirit
GLION DECLARATION II (June 2009)

In the spirit of the first Glion Declaration I, published in 1998 following the first Glion Colloquium, this second Glion Declaration has been drafted by Frank H. T. Rhodes on behalf of the participants in the VII Glion Colloquium and has been endorsed by them by way of circulation. It is also being distributed more broadly as a separate document and available online on the website of the Glion Colloquium www.glion.org.

THE FIRST DECADE OF THE NEW MILLENNIUM: A RETROSPECTIVE

As we approach the end of the first decade of the new millennium, it is useful to review the road that our global community has travelled. The dawn of the new millennium was a time not only of celebration, but also of optimism and hope. Contemplating the remarkable transformation of the past millennium, and especially the extraordinary achievements of its last century, commentators throughout the world reflected a sense of satisfaction in the progress of the past, and high expectations for the prospects for the future.

A decade later, the mood is less euphoric, in part because of developments of the past decade. The statistics provide part, but only part, of the explanation:

- In 1999 the world population was 6 billion; in 2009 it is 6.7 billion.
- In 1999 per capita grain production was 312 kilograms; in 2009 it is 303 kilograms.
- In 1999 the estimated total of hungry people was 842 million; in 2009 it is 963 million.
- In 1999 the number of refugees and displaced persons was 14 million; in 2009 it is 16 million.

Beyond these sobering statistics lie other troubling realities and additional concerns. From the growing prosperity at the dawn of the millennium, we have moved into a period of severe economic dislocation and financial crisis. The spread of HIV/AIDS has assumed alarming proportions, especially in parts of the African continent, and though, overall, the rate of population growth has declined, it continues unabated in some of the world's poorest regions, imposing major stresses on Earth's limited resources, including top soil and water. Climate change has become a growing concern. Terrorism has become a daily event in several areas.

In contrast to these discouraging trends, there are, however, other developments that are positive and offer encouragement. Thus the effects of the 2008 financial crisis were limited by prompt, co-operative government intervention. An experimental HIV vaccine — RV144 — is proving safe and effective in clinical trials. Economic development is improving the lot of those in a number of impoverished countries. Thanks to the European Union, Europeans have enjoyed over 60 years of stability and prosperity. Rapid improvements in information technology are providing a far more connected world, with all its benefits. Longevity is increasing in most countries. Mandated improvements in energy efficiency and conservation are having a growing impact.

THE SECOND DECADE: THE BATTLE FOR THE FUTURE

If we are to confront successfully the challenges of sustainable development, we shall require not only all of our collective scientific and technical expertise in the environmental sphere, but also economic, social and political policies that nurture sustainable communities within the endlessly varied settings and ways in which we live. And, complex as these issues of physical and biological sustainability are, they are dwarfed by those of social sustainability. No challenge is more urgent or more difficult than developing, harmonizing and implementing these technological and social innovations.

Every generation has had its challenges, but those of the early 21st century are unique in the extent to which they will determine the future well-being of our species. Given the sum of the trends we have described, it becomes clear that we are about to conduct a whole Earth experiment in real time as we sharply escalate the already heavy demands that we are placing on our planet for food, energy, materials and water. It is also clear that "business as usual", a casual continuation of our present patterns and current practices, is not sustainable in the longer term, at least, not without growing hunger, disruption and social dislocation.

Navigating our collective way towards some new equilibrium will instead require new approaches, new thinking, new partnerships and new technology. And this, in turn, will require a change in outlook and a degree of innovation whose very boldness will be disruptive of much conventional thinking and many established practices.

A CALL TO THE UNIVERSITIES

The creative thinking behind such innovation will require the contributions and cooperation of every segment of society, including not only those in government, but also those in business, industry, the professions, public life, foundations, civic bodies, learned academies and NGOs. But, most of all, it will require the active participation of the universities, for it is in these institutions that the leaders of each new generation are nurtured; it is there that boundaries to our existing knowledge are explored and crossed; it is there that unfettered thinking can thrive and unconstrained intellectual partnerships can be created. It is there, within each new class, within each new generation, that the future is forged.

A sustainable future will require the world's leading universities to continue to supply a growing stream of well-grounded and ethically responsible professional practitioners and leaders in every field of public life and endeavour, from medicine to engineering, from urban design to earth science, and from agriculture to economics. But it also will require that the sustained scholarship, basic research, imaginative thinking and creative technology that the universities have long provided should be nurtured, encouraged and supported.

It is especially to the universities, then, that we must look for the development of the innovations and the innovative spirit that will allow us to create a sustainable future. But that, in turn, means that within the universities, too, "business as usual" will no longer suffice. Disciplinary constraints, departmental structure and long-standing practices must not be allowed to stifle the development of the bold and creative thinking that will be required.

We address these recommendations, then, to our colleagues in the universities, in the belief that they need to play an increasing role if our societies are to overcome the serious challenges that now confront us.

The social compact

Universities must reaffirm and continue to fulfil their role in the unwritten social compact by providing new knowledge, educated leaders, informed citizens, expert professional practitioners, services and training, as well as individual certification and accreditation in these fields. In exchange for the responsible and effective provision of these services, society supports higher education, contributes to its finance, accepts its professional judgment and scholarly certification, and grants it a unique degree of institutional autonomy and scholarly freedom. Within this compact, higher education has a reciprocal obligation for impartial scholarship, professional integrity, sensitivity to the various needs of society and an appropriate degree of public accountability.

The great web of learning

Research universities are only a small part of the greater web of learning represented by schools, colleges, technological institutes and countless other agents of instruction, investigation and discovery, ranging from family and social groups to learned societies. Vital though research universities are, their effectiveness in serving society depends upon the health of other members of this great web. We need far better understanding of the broad ecology and culture of learning, both within and among these other institutions. Universities need to play a leading role in developing this understanding.

New knowledge networks

There is a particular need for universities to develop an open interface between their own work and that of their clients, including government at all levels, civil society, industry, business, the professions and NGOs of all kinds. New knowledge networks, including especially electronic networks, need to be developed among these multiple users, interests, and groups. The university's role as both convener and catalyst of such networks could support a sustained dialogue and partnership among the various stakeholders in addressing society's greatest needs.

The integration of discovery and learning

It is vital that research universities, in every aspect of their institutional practice, emphasize and demonstrate the intimate linkage between discovery and learning, and between enquiry and instruction. Too often, these are still regarded as discrete fields of activity. Universities need to explore and develop new and effective ways of bringing together discovery and learning, for example, by expanding the use of studio-type courses or public service projects where group enquiry and action can provide a powerful means of learning.

The nurture of leaders

Decisions made by the current and the following generation of leaders are likely to have a decisive impact on humanity's future efforts to achieve a just, sustainable, dynamic social equilibrium. This will require the cultivation and nurture of responsible leaders, whose technical and professional competence is matched by their critical thinking, intellectual breadth, moral awareness and social responsibility. This places an obligation on educational leaders to support and promote those liberal studies that have long provided a foundation for civic virtue.

Because many of the challenges that face humanity are of global extent and international proportions, and thus cannot be solved in isolation, it is essential that the university community itself should remain international in its membership and open to multiple cultural traditions, aspirations and needs.

The power of partnership

The world's grand challenges — such as water supply, food production, health care, energy and climate change — are not likely to yield to narrow disciplinary analysis and resolution. Universities need constantly to cultivate and support interdisciplinary approaches and team projects, and develop ways of encouraging such partnerships in goal-oriented research. Such research will not succeed, however, without a reservoir of fundamental scientific knowledge, created through research in the basic sciences. Our commitment to basic research must not only be maintained, but also increased, even as we seek to apply its findings to societal needs.

The social dimension

The grand challenges to our future well-being also involve issues of daunting social and economic complexity. The humanities, social and behavioural sciences are an integral part of the analysis and solution of these various societal challenges. Every problem today is systemic in nature, so it needs to be investigated through a socio-technical lens.

Creative coalitions

Individual schools and colleges within the university have opportunities to create new alliances to address these challenges. Thus schools of business and management can provide a ready forum for considering these issues, and can also form creative coalitions with business, industrial and other leaders to develop workable strategies for addressing them. New problems require new approaches, especially within the university. New coalitions and new partnerships with external partners, so that ideas filter into the university as much as they filter out, can contribute much to the creation of such new approaches.

The necessity for innovation

The need for innovation is not confined to business, industry and government. Every area of modern life and professional practice, from architecture to urban design, from agriculture to social services, must embrace innovation, including especially universities themselves. Only innovative universities can expect to make meaningful contributions to the solution of the world's problems. Within those institutions, the arts, humanities and social sciences, as much as science and technology, can be sources of innovation.

The less privileged

Throughout the world the underprivileged and the most needy are largely unrepresented in higher education, as in many other aspects of modern life. Improved access to higher education for the less privileged must remain a priority and will require continuing attention and support.

The foundation of freedom

None of the roles and responsibilities we advocate can be discharged effectively within institutions unless freedom of enquiry and freedom of speech are honoured and defended. It is only in the context of such freedom that there can be hope for the creation of a sustainable future, and it is only in the enjoyment of such freedom that a sustainable future offers grounds for hope. Universities must remain at once both the champions of such larger freedom and the agents of hope through the contributions they make to the societies that nurture them.

The priority of hope

The daunting complexity of the challenges that confront us would be overwhelming if we were to depend only on existing knowledge, traditional resources and conventional approaches. But universities have the capacity to remove that dependence by the innovations they create. Universities exist to liberate the unlimited creativity of the human species and to celebrate the unbounded resilience of the human spirit. In a world of foreboding problems and looming threats, it is the high privilege of universities to nurture that creativity, to rekindle that resilience and so provide hope for all Earth's peoples.

Glion above Montreux, Switzerland, June 23, 2009

Réalisé en P.A.O. par STDI - Z. A. Route de Couterne - 53110 Lassay-les-Châteaux
Imprimé en France. - JOUVE, 1, rue du Docteur Sauvé, 53100 MAYENNE
N° 501019H. - Dépôt légal : Janvier 2010